A Hidden Impact

D0887573

A Hidden Impact

◆

The Czechs and Slovaks of Louisiana from the 1720s to today.

James Hlavac

Mary Ann DeVille,
Enjoy this exploration of
our Czech heritage — Jim Hlavac

iUniverse, Inc.
New York Lincoln Shanghai

A Hidden Impact
The Czechs and Slovaks of Louisiana from the 1720s to today.

iUniverse books may be ordered through booksellers or by contacting:

iUniverse
2021 Pine Lake Road, Suite 100
Lincoln, NE 68512
www.iuniverse.com
1-800-Authors (1-800-288-4677)

ISBN-13: 978-0-595-40372-1 (pbk)
ISBN-13: 978-0-595-84747-1 (ebk)
ISBN-10: 0-595-40372-7 (pbk)
ISBN-10: 0-595-84747-1 (ebk)

Printed in the United States of America

"The tragedy of modern man is not that he knows less and less about the meaning of his own life, but that it bothers him less and less."

Vaclav Havel
author, playwright, dissident and former president of the Czech Republic.

Contents

Foreward

The United States of America has always been a popular destiantion for waves of immigrants brining thousands of Czechs and Slovaks to the "new world." Louisiana definitely belongs among the territories with prominent Czech and Slovaks communties whose members cherish the heritage of their forefathers. The book reminds us that the history of Czech Louisiana beings in the middle of the 18th century when two brothers, Hans-Jacob and Jean-Jacques Tutzek, both born in Prague, arrive and settle down with their families. They were the first one followed by many others from Bohemia, Moravia, Silesia and Slovakia.

The importance of the port of New Orleans can be compared to that of Ellis Island in New York, Galveston in Texas or Baltimore in Maryland. Hundreds of the Czechs and Slovaks came to America through this port of entry. Many of them continued to Nebraska, Iowa, Illinois, Wisconsin, Texas, Oklahoma, Minnesota and elswhere to find their new homes and start their new lives. The reasons for leaving their homeland in the center of Europe have always been numerous—social, political, religion, philosophical. The port was their gateway to the new world.

Through his book, Jim Hlavac presents exciting stories of Czech and Slovak individuals and families that settled in all parts of Louisiana—for example, New Orleans, Baton Rouge, the Florida Parishes and the German Coast—often mingling with other nationalities, such as French, German and others. Compelling passages describe the past and present days of the two communities in the central part of this state, in Rapides Parish—Libuse and Kolin. It is always very pleasing to the heart to know that these two names, so closely tied with the Czech Republic, have their place in a land so far away from Central Europe. Furthermore, the family names of Beranek, Cervenka, Holoubek, Konvicka, Laska, Noha, Prochaska, Zelenka, to name only a few examples representing many Louisiania residents, unequivocally prove the "Czechness" of their bearers. Delving into Hlavac's writing, we proudly learn about the work, activities and destinies of these Czech descendants.

We are thrilled to discover that non-Czech inhabitants have also joined in the efforts of protecting Czech culture and traditions in this part of the United States by starting a Czech dancing group. We are gratified to read that the non-Czechs together with the Czechs in Louisiana were eager to sponsor the Kolin and Libuse historical markers. These instances of collaboration and mutual understanding make us optimistic in regards to the future of Czech causes in this corner of America.

The book is a tremendous achievement. Jim Hlavac managed to compile a publication describing the history, contemporary life and activities of the Louisiana Czechs and Slovaks. The author laudably mentions Leo Baca from Texas, giving him credit for his research which resulted in assembling long lists of Czech immigrants coming to the United States in the second half of the 19th century. There is no doubt that Hlavac's work will serve, like Baca's endeavors, as a precious source of knowledge for those searching for detailed information related to Czech-American issues, in Louisiana and elsewhere. A lot of hard work and meticulous research can be felt on each and every page.

It is also highly significant and symbolic that the author was able to persuade officials in various repositories, courthouses, libraries and archives that there really are Czechs and Slovaks in Louisiana, and not only a few. They might be surprised to learn that it was from the Czech lands that the beads so popular during the Mardi Gras festivities were imported to the United States soon after the Reconstruction period. It is even more important that in many cases Jim Hlavac, a New Yorker himself, managed to help various local groups and individuals of Czech and Slovak origin get to know each other and realize how big and strong their presence in the state is. For them, the book offers valuable information and guidance related to Czech and Slovak history, languages, cultures, folklore, cuisine and more, as well as for future generations.

In reading the final pages of the book, we learn that its primary motive was to help establish a Czech and Slovak museum in Louisiana. The significance of the Czech and Slovak communities in this region is enormous, and they absolutely deserve an official museum. We are certain that through cooperation of all those involved the goal can be achieved. This publication has contributed immensely.

Martin Palous
Ambassador of the Czech Republic to the United States of America

Introduction

Louisiana, like most American states, has attracted immigrants from all over the world. Two groups that have been here since near the beginning of European settlement yet have been overlooked are the Czechs and Slovaks. The first Czechs in Louisiana were recorded in the 1720s. The first Slovaks well before the Civil War. Starting with the earliest and continuing through 1950, this book, encyclopedic in scope, presents the history of just about 575 families and individuals from these ancient lands in Central Europe who came to settle in Louisiana. This makes them two of Louisiana's smallest ethnic groups. They have, however, been making an impact on Louisiana for nearly 300 years. Even today just some 5,000 people in the state claim Czech or Slovak heritage out of a population of nearly 4½ million people. But given the numbers of children these immigrants had, Americanizations of their surnames and marriages of their daughters into other ethnic groups there is every likelihood that there are far more Louisiana citizens with some Czech or Slovak heritage than are currently identified.

This book includes both Czechs and Slovaks for two simple reasons. The first is that while Czechs and Slovaks now reside in two separate countries, the Czech Republic and the Republic of Slovakia, to the average Louisianian these two nations are known by their former name as one country: Czechoslovakia. In both languages the name literally means "the Czechs and the Slovaks." The second is that Czechs and Slovaks share a connected ancient history, a common culture and similar languages. That is one of the major reasons why they were joined together in one nation. I will not endeavor here to explain how this came to be for the history of this region of Europe is long, complex and confusing. There is ample information on this subject in many a Louisiana (and for that matter any other,) library. I will, though, broadly and briefly in this introduction layout who is included in this book and why for those who are unfamiliar with this region of Europe.

Czechoslovakia was a political construct created from the break up of the Austro-Hungarian Empire at the end of the First World War. It did not exist prior to 1918. The Republic of Czechoslovakia existed until the Germans invaded in 1938–39. Hitler divided the country into three Protectorates, or "sub-nations" of the German Reich: Bohemia, Moravia and Slovakia. He was merely using the ancient names of these places. In 1945 Czechoslovakia reconstituted itself as one nation. From 1949 to 1989 it was essentially a colony of the Soviet Union. In 1989, with the fall of the Berlin Wall and the USSR, Czechoslovakia became a free nation once again. Thus, for nearly 70 years Czechs and Slovaks once again were subjected to oppression by more powerful neighbors.

In 1992 Slovaks asked the Czechs for a "divorce." This is the actual word Czechs and Slovaks use to describe the division of the country into two independent republics. The Czechs agreed. In what is probably the world's only peaceful division of a country the two sides effected the "Velvet Divorce" on January 1st, 1993. They fairly, equitably and in complete agreement divided the land, the assets, the military and every other aspect of Czechoslovakia. The only "shots" fired were toasts made with the local fiery plum brandy called Slivovice to congratulate each other on a job well done. Both countries cooperate closely with each other in virtually every area of human endeavor. They think of themselves as cousins; closely related but from different families.

An oddity of the Czechs is that there is no geographical place called "Czech." Their lands have been called Bohemia and Moravia since Roman times. Bohemians comprise a little more than one half of the Czech people and live in Bohemia. Moravians comprise a little less than one half of the Czech people and live in Moravia. Both together or individually have been called Czechs, Bohemians or Moravians for more than 1,500 years; the terms are virtually mutually inclusive. Czech is thus the name of the people who live in Bohemia and Moravia and the name of their language. This is why uniquely among European nations the country must be called the "Czech Republic"—and cannot be called the "Republic of Czech" or just plain "Czech" as compared to, say, Spain.

Slovakia, on the other hand, is the name of a distinct land, a geographical place—much as Spain and France are distinct lands. Likewise, as the French live in France and the Spanish in Spain, Slovaks live in and on a land called Slovakia. For its entire history Slovakia was a province of the many nations that surround it. It was never independent until 1993. Slovakian is a distinct language from Czech. It is not considered a dialect of Czech, nor vice versa. But it is very similar to Czech and they can speak to each other with relative ease. The best comparison is the way Americans and British people can speak to each other in English. Both languages have one letter in their alphabets that represents a sound that the other does not have: ř for the Czechs and l' for the Slovaks. Both languages are written in the Latin alphabet, as this book is, plus a few extra letters that look like they have a little "v" on top of the regular letters.

The Czech and Slovak people had lived on these lands for more than 1,500 years by the time of the creation of Czechoslovakia. First among their ancient nations was the Margravate of Moravia. This was formed in the late 600s AD. It survived as an independent principality until the mid 1300s. Moravians were the basic ethnic group which lived here, along with what are now considered Poles, Silesians, Germans and others. Its ancient capital is the city of Brno. The second entity was the Dukedom of Bohemia. This country's creation was authorized by a series of popes in the second half of the 900s AD; later it evolved into the Kingdom of Bohemia. Its demise can be pin-pointed to the Battle of the White Mountain in 1620 when the Austrians overran the Czech people and began nearly 250 years of subjugation. Prague was its first and only capital city. Bohemians were the predominate ethnic group in this nation.

In the 1300s Bohemia and Moravia were joined through royal marriages. Over the centuries Bohemia either conquered or joined together through royal marriages with substantial parts of southern Poland, southeastern Germany, Slovakia, Hungary and northern Austria (all of which were small and independent principalities and kingdoms and not the nation-states we know today.) Its borders shifted frequently as wars were fought, won and lost. There was no great nation building in this region of Europe as occurred in France or England. On the other hand, Prague was the capital of the Holy Roman Empire (a supposed successor to the Roman Empire) for nearly 600 years. During these centuries it was a far bigger and more important city than London, Paris, Rome, Vienna or Berlin.

The Holy Roman Empire was a loose confederation of more than a hundred mini-states. It dominated a vast portion of continental Europe from the fall of the Roman Empire in 500 AD until Napoleon removed it from the political scene in 1806. Its politics were very convoluted, complicated and confusing. But the reason that Prague was its capital was that ½ of all the silver and gold mined in Europe during the Middle Ages was from the area right around Prague. Because the Holy Roman Emperors wanted to be near the source of their wealth they chose Prague as their capital. Because Prague was so cosmopolitan the word "bohemian" with a little 'b' entered the English language meaning just that—a cosmopolitan person.

Some immigrants from these lands to American and Louisiana self-indentified themselves. That is, they called themselves "Bohemians" or "Moravians" and not Czechs at all. Though others did call themselves Czechs. Slovaks almost always refered to themselves as Slovaks. It was always a very personal decision. It was American authorities who had conflicts with this self-identification. Confusing the issue is the bewildering array of cultural and national labels that were used by American and Louisiana census takers, historians and other record keepers to define the Czechs and Slovaks. Among there were such terms as Czechoslovakians, Czechs, Bohemians, Moravians, Slovaks, Slovakland, Austro-Bohemia, Germano-Bohemia, Austro-Moravia, Hungary-Slovak, Austro-Hungary, Austria and Hungary and many more. I've identified at least 50 different terms that were used at one point or another. There is no consistency from census to census, or within censuses, or in any other records that were maintained by the various levels of government in Louisiana. Neither the French, Spanish or American governments which ruled Louisiana across her history were consistent at any point in time or with any family. A family's ethnic and cultural designation could change from document to document, year to year.

Unlike other European nations, the Czechs and Slovaks come from a large variety of religious traditions and ethnic mixes. This mix stems directly from Bohemia's place in the forefront of the Holy Roman Empire. The Czech lands, and to a lesser degree Slovakia, were among the world's first melting pots. Just as all ethnic groups to America become American, ethnic groups that moved to the Czech lands and Slovakia became Czech and Slovak. Thus to be Czech or Slovak can be either an ethnic reality of blood or a mental or philosopical, even metaphysical, reality of thought. To sort them out is impossible. The vast majority of people of any ethnicity or religion who came to the Czech and Slovak lands soon began to consider themselves Czechs or Slovaks and adopted the Czech and Slovak view of religion—and thus they are all included in this book.

Among the Christian believers were Roman Catholics, Eastern Rite Catholics, Presbytarians, Lutherans, Methodists and many other denominations and sects. Who adhered to what religion varied from town to town and from time to time—it all depended on to which religion the local ruler wanted his subjects to adhere. Changes in religious adherence were frequent as the fortunes of war and ruling families ebbed and flowed. Czechs today are considered the most non-religious people in Europe. In fact, they are frequently religious in belief but adhere to no formal religion whatsoever. It is suggested by some that Czechs simply gave up trying to belong to one religion or the other and simply became believers without a formal religion.

There has always been a large number of Czech Jews. Jews have been part of the Czech religious traditions since the dawn of recorded Czech history. Ethnically they consider themselves Czech. Indeed, the oldest surviving operating synagogue in Europe is the oddly named "Old New Synagogue" in Prague. For nearly 1,000 years this house of worship has functioned without interruption.

Even the Nazis did not interfere with this ancient house of worship. There are, even more oddly, an "old old" synagogue even more ancient than the "old new" one and a "new new" synagogue from the 1600s. Such is the history of Jews in the Czech lands that Czechs almost never had a problem with Jews. Rather it was the Germanic neighbors who were forever invading and trying to subjugate the Czech lands who had issues with Jews.

There were also many adherents to the four native religions of the Czechs: Hussites, the Moravian Brethren, the Bohemian Brotherhood and Freethinkers. All four are known as anti-clerical and non-liturgical religions. All four are pacifist by design. These four were unique to Czechs, though have many non-Czech adherents today. These four religions are all practiced today within the Czech Republic, as well as in neighboring countries and in many places around the world. Pennsylvania and North Carolina in particular are centers of the Moravian Brethren today, as is Nicaragua in Central America. The Bohemian Brotherhood has much in common with the Moravian Brethren as is obvious by their names.

Hussism was Protestantism about 130 years before most people think Protestantism started with Martin Luther. Jan Hus wanted to reform the Catholic Church as early as the 1370s. Alas, the Catholic authorities burned him at the stake in 1415. This act started the Husite Wars which raged for more than 100 years. Basically this was a series of wars pitting the Czechs against invading Catholic and Lutheran armies. Americans are aware of Hus peripherally in the phrase "his goose was cooked." "Husa" is the Czech word for a goose and Jan's last name is related to this word—after he was burned at the stake the phrase entered the Czech language and eventually made its way into English. Freethinkers just avoided anything to do with established religion whatsoever but are essentially Christian in outlook and belief. All these religious beliefs are represented among the Czech and Slovaks of Louisiana.

Because Austria had ruled the Czech lands for centuries there were Czechs with German names, and Germans with Czech names. The many millions of neighboring Germans and Austrians have always either trickled or poured (it depended on which century one looks at,) across the border over the centuries into the less populated Czech lands. However, many did slowly become Czech in their minds despite their heritage and names. It is not uncommon at all to find Czech speaking people with names that look completely German. These families have been so long in the Czech lands that they became Czech and lost all traces of their German heritage.

The Slovaks of Slovakia are very similar in culture and language to the Czechs but they are different in significant ways. They are mostly Roman Catholic.

There are fewer Jews among them. The Slovak lands were ruled primarily by the Hungarians for nearly 10 centuries, though by others also. Many Slovak names have Hungarian phonetic spelling but they are recognizably Slovak. Hungarians are not a Slavic people like the Czechs and Slovaks. Indeed, they are unrelated enthically and linguistically to any other Europeans.

Besides these three main regions of the Czech and Slovak republics there are two smaller areas of unique cultural heritage. Silesia was only once an independent principality, a long time ago. Its people are variously refered to as Wends, Sorbians or Silesians. It has been nearly 1,000 years since these people were any more than a subdivision of Germany, Poland and the Czech and Slovak Republics. Ruthenians are also a somewhat distinct, though nearly extinct, group of people at the eastern end of Slovakia. Ruthenian is a dying dialect of Slovak. They mostly adhere to Eastern Rite Catholocism. Modern Silesians and Ruthenians consider themselves Slovak. The pop artist Andy Warhol is perhaps the most famous of all Ruthenians in the United States; he considered himself to be Slovak, however.

All these groups and subgroups are included in this book because they considered themselves first and foremost as Czech and Slovaks and only secondarily as their former ethnic identity. I identify them mostly as they wanted to be identified. Though I also use the terms Czech and Slovak to refer to them generally. Where necessary I use the more descriptive Bohemian or Moravian or Slovak. I never use the term "Czechoslovakian" for such people do not exist. Nor is there any such language as "Czechoslovakian." Again, this name is a just a political construct of nation building by the United States after World War I.

So why a book on this small and obscure group of immigrants in Louisiana? Because despite their minuscule number most Louisianians encounter the legacy of some of these Czechs or Slovaks every day. From the emblematic St. Charles Avenue street car line and St. Louis Cathedral to the water control system that protected them in New Orleans, to a theater in Shreveport, to historic structures in the downtowns of Houma and Covington, to the state's largest wholesale food company, to one of the hippest restaurants in Lake Charles for decades, to many of the major government and civic buildings in Baton Rouge, to knowing one of the many hundreds of descendants of one of Louisiana's earliest Czech families now scattered across Acadiana, to the many Bohemians involved in the life of Rapides Parish, Czechs and Slovaks have a proud place in the history and current events of Louisiana. Despite the many ethnicities, religions and self-identifying names they fall under, they all considered themselves, loosely, Czechs and Slovaks. They had what can only be called a hidden impact on Louisiana.

In a twist on the usual American immigrant story just half of these immigrants wanted to assimilate and become Americans. The other half very much wanted to preserve their Czech culture. Thus, there are two parts to the story of Czech and Slovak immigration to Louisiana. This book is thus divided into two halves to reflect these differing aspirations. I call the two parts, quite naturally, Assimilation and Preservation.

Like other immigrants to Louisiana these families and individuals chronicled in the first part of this book worked at becoming Americans as soon as they could. They Americanized their names as necessary, learned English and French when necessary and did their best at fitting into the broader social and economic currents that swirled around the state during and after their time of arrival. There was, however, no great wave of Czech and Slovak immigrants as there were with the Cajuns, French, Scots-Irish, Italians and Germans—the major groups of immigrants to the state—who came by the tens of thousands in the 18th and 19th centuries. Nor did they come to Louisiana nearly as a whole like the small number of Yugoslavs, Hungarians, Poles, Lebanese, Belgians, Russians and others during that distinct period between 1890 and 1917 when America and Louisiana saw the greatest influx of immigrants. Instead, Czechs and Slovaks came as a trickle, one here, one there, never more than three dozen in any year, over nearly three centuries of Louisiana's history. No one family seemed to ever know or be aware that there were other families of the same heritage, except for the Slovaks in Cameron Parish. They simply came as individuals.

Because they were so few, spread far and thin, we find no ethnic organizations, or grand buildings holding ethnic societies, or Louisiana published old-language newspapers, or churches filled with immigrants and their progeny. There are many examples of these among the Cajuns, Irish, Germans and Italians. Neighborhoods were not teaming with Czechs and Slovaks as we find with the major ethnic groups. Only a handful were well-known in their own time and place. Now they are mostly mere footnotes in history. You will find no Czechs or Slovaks among the well known people of Louisiana's nearly three centuries of political and civic life. Of their known legacy virtually nothing has been written of their Czech or Slovak connection.

Because there were so few we are able to look at every single family and individual who came from the Czech and Slovak lands. In all there are only about 250 families and individuals chronicled in the first part of this book. The story begins, however, at the dawn of the settlement of Louisiana, when it was still a French colony in the wilderness in the early 1700s. They did, though, settle in every corner of the state. Only a few of them stayed for a long time or even left descendants around the state; though one of the earliest families now comprises nearly 2,000 descendants. For many we have only a single record of their brief appearance on the scene. What became of those who were fleetingly in the record can only be guessed at. Perhaps these succeeded so successfully at assimilation that we lose all track of them in Louisiana; many obviously moved on after just a brief sojourn in the state. All of these are presented here in four chapters in the first half of this book: The First Czechs, who came at the founding of Louisiana; the Movers and Shakers who had a lasting if little recognized impact on New Orleans; the nearly anonymous Big City Immigrants who lived throughout New Orleans; and finally, the families and individuals who settled in many other parishes of the state as Farmers and Tradesmen. Though, among this last group are several who had a larger-than-life impact on Louisiana. They are presented in a roughly alphabetical order within each of the well recognized regions in the state, such as Acadiana or the Florida Parishes.

I also give two other chapters in the first part of the book. One is on the commerical relations that have long existed between the Czech lands, and to a lesser degree Slovakia, and Louisiana. Though these commercial relations are little known, among them are Czechoslovakian-made beads thrown from Mardi Gras parades for decades. Strands of these colorful glass trinkets are now a highly sought after collectible. There has also been an on-going relationship between Charles University in Prague and the University of New Orleans. Oddly, the clean-up crews at Wal-Marts statewide during the 1990s and first few years of the new millennium were comprised entirely of Czech immigrants. With Hurricanes Katrina and Rita many new connections were made. Concluding Part One is a small chapter that looks at the idea of name changes that Czechs and Slovaks had to face as they entered American life.

The second part of this book is a story of preservation. Beginning in 1908 a group of Bohemians, never numbering more than 350 families total and just about 100 families at any given time, endeavored to create a Bohemian colony in Rapides Parish. There were never more than about 450 individuals at a time. They are, however, unique in Louisiana's history. Their goal was to keep their Bohemian heritage alive—and to keep separate from the surrounding American and French culture. They wanted no part of assimilation, though they were not entirely successful in their goal. They did not even want to include Moravians or Slovaks. They founded two Bohemian towns, Libuse and Kolin, in the raw wilderness. Part Two of this book chronicles the founding and nearly 100 year history of these communities and their attempt to create a slice of Bohemia in the New World. This history is presented in six chapters organized in a chronological fashion. Of some families in these two towns we know a lot. We know other families only from a single property record in the Rapides Parish Courthouse.

In both parts of this book I present every tidbit of information I could find: their names, birth and death years, number of years married, dates of arrival and sometimes the name of the ship they traveled on, from which towns in the Czech and Slovak Republics they hailed from, their ports of embarkation and arrival, their occupations and economic conditions, as well as their addresses or locations in Louisiana. This information was found among more than 3,000 sources including census records, obituaries, property records, newspaper articles, books, the Internet, magazines, professional journals and personal or business papers. I traveled to or contacted people in nearly every parish of the state looking for this information. If I was able to locate descendants I learned more anecdotes about these families; I stop these stories about the 1950s because of a respect for the privacy of living people. For some I found only a single reference from the distant past. In a broad bibliography I detail where and how I was able to find this information.

The reason I present all this information is that I hope to uncover more about these immigrants. Because they were mostly ignored or somehow mislabled or misfiled not one history book or journal or article about Louisiana has a word about them. This book is simply the first time this information has been compiled and presented to the public. I am fairly sure that there is a lot more information about these families that I could not find. My purpose here is to provide a baseline for future research. The extensive bibliography is from Louisiana and America-wide sources but I could never hope to list all 3,000 sources I looked at. Oddly, it was all surprisingly easy to locate, especially since so many Czech and Slovak names just jumped off the page at me as I scoured the records.

This book, with its encyclopedic scope, is the first time that all these stories are brought together. Perhaps some readers will feel that there are too many facts and dates and other information. But since no one has ever written about these people before I felt compelled to provide as much detail as possible just to prove the point that these immigrants had a remarkable impact on Louisiana. Some professional historians will perhaps say the plethora of information is unnecessary. Some readers of the manuscript prior to publication wondered at the rich details. Some keep looking for some overarching theme or narrative. There is not one story. There are 575 individual stories.

This is a book about individuals who simply all showed up in the same place after having come from the same place in Europe. There is not even one reason they left the Czech and Slovak lands. The Irish mostly came because of the famine in that country. Germans came because of political instability. Italians left because of the grinding poverty in that nation. Jews left Europe to avoid the pogroms against them. Czechs and Slovaks each came for their own reason. There are as many reasons as there are individuals. Some did come because of religious or political oppression, some to obtain their own lands, some to avoid conscription into the Austrian army and some because of poeverty. But there were also those who simply wanted to try something new. There is, though, simply no one or two reasons that Czechs or Slovaks left Europe for America and wound up in Louisiana. Without more concrete information on each of these families and individuals it is impossible to determine why they left for America and came to Louisiana. However, this encyclopedic scope is also precisely because it will likely be the only book on this subject for a while.

Then there is also perhaps the question of why I felt competent to write this book. After all, if not one professional historian had bothered it is fair to ask why me. First off, I am not a professional or trained historian. I am not a trained sociologist or some person involved in ethnographic studies. I am not sure that one must be to write a history book. I do have a fine college education from New York University which doubtless was training enough to research and compile the facts. I will leave for those "professionals" in the various fields I mentioned to make any interpretations or suppositions about the facts. But at least I have provided these facts to future writers. They are available in no other place.

I am, however, completely of Czech heritage. While I am not of Slovak heritage I am well acquainted with Slovakia. After all, for the vast majority of my life I had to say my family was from "Czechoslovakia" for a lack of a better description. Three of my grandparents were born in what is now the Czech Republic. One of my grandmothers was born just a few years after my greatgrandparents arrived in New York. Each, however, was the only member of their family to set out for the New World. They left many brothers and sisters behind. My father's family is from Moravia, my mother's from Bohemia. My forefathers have lived where they live today for time immemorial. These four branches have also practiced the various different religious traditions of the Czech lands. We have no one religion in my family, though perhaps we mostly adhere to the Hussite and Freethinking traditions.

When I was a child my greatgrandparents and grandparents spoke to me in Czech and I answered in English. I attended a Czech summer camp for 10 years. I belonged to the Czechoslovak Society of America for many years. There were nearly 100 words in Czech that I did not know the English equivalents to until I was in high school or older, so common at home were they. I even have a reasonable command of the Czech language. In my childhood we ate Czech traditional cooking regularly, and to this day I can cook these Czech national foods. Traditional Czech music was played often in my house. Basically, it was a bilingual household with a very strong Czech cultural heritage. Indeed, like many Czech families in America, we were very slow at assimilating into the wider American culture. I am thoroughly immersed in this culture. Plus, with a name like Hlavac I have been compelled almost daily throughout my life to explain to others what Czechs and Slovaks are; during my twenty years in Louisiana even more so. I am, after all, the only person with this surname out of more than four and a half million residents in the state.

Furthermore, unlike many immigrants to America the American side of my family never lost contact with our European side. We have stayed in constant contact (except during World War II) since the moment my forefathers so recently set foot on these shores. Mine is not the case of wondering about long lost relatives in unknown villages in a strange land. Mine is the situation of knowing exactly to whom and where I have been writing in the Czech Republic for decades. I entertain my Czech born relatives when they travel to America and I stay with them when I travel to the Czech Republic. It is not much different than a family in Louisiana visiting its relatives in Texas. To me, its just right over there, so to speak. Czech culture and my Czech roots are not some alien past—it is the immediate current for me.

Since the moment I became aware of the two Czech towns in Central Louisiana I have been intrigued with what other Czechs and Slovaks came to Louisiana. Even though as I looked through Louisiana history books and journals and found nothing substantial I knew there had to be more for there were many odd references and footnotes and paranthetical remarks to these "unknown" people. So I set a course to see what could be found. I scoured every source and locale in Louisiana to find this information. As I said above, it was so easily found. Even when nearly every Louisiana archivist, librarian, recordkeeper and historian I encountered in my research said there were no Czech and Slovaks in Louisiana I persisted in looking. There was significant information in each repository. What I found in total should astound many of them. It will at least, I hope, educate them about a part of Louisiana history that has not been presented until this book.

I also set the course for the creation of the Louisiana Czech and Slovak Museum. I served as the first president of this fledgling organizaton. What will comprise the exhibits and archives of this museum is in this book. Indeed, without this book we would not know what to put in this museum. I believe I have spoken to nearly every one of Czech and Slovak heritage in the state. My compe-

xxii   A Hidden Impact

tence comes simply from my Czech heritage combined with dogged research, the refusal to quit, the faith that there was more than what was previously reported or was apparent and a persistance that any professional historian should well appreciate.

Whether of Czech and Slovak heritage or not all readers of this book will surely be equally amazed at what I found. Surely, the contribution of Czechs and Slovaks to Louisiana can no longer be ignored. A Hidden Impact is the culmination of seven years of research. I sincerely hope that it opens the eyes of many and spurs much greater research. In all, I hope that this book shows how a small group of immigrants from a little known place in Central Europe has had a long and continuing impact on Louisiana. Czechs and Slovaks, you will see, have a special place in the history of our state.

Jim Hlavac
Baton Rouge, Louisiana.

PART I
Assimilation

1

The First Czechs

Until this book the Czech families presented in this chapter had been ignored by every historian of early Louisiana. Those historians concentrated on the French, Spanish and Germans. The families I present here are listed in literally dozens of footnotes, asides, paranthetical comments, indices or as just some confusing data that no one wanted to look at further. Often they were refered to as "other" or "unknown." The constant changes in spellings to the names, first and last, were glossed over as too confusing to bother with. In no one place were all the facts available presented. It was as if these historians simply could not believe that Czechs (if they even knew who Czechs were) were among Louisiana's earliest settlers. That they are Czech cannot be doubted. That Czechs arrived before the first Cajuns also cannot be doubted as we shall see.

I gathered several hundred references to these families from dozens of books and archival materials and present all of this here for the first time. My purpose is not to rewrite Louisiana history as such—it is only to add another layer to the rich history of the early years of the Louisiana colony. I deal first with the largest of these families. It also happens to be the only one of them that have had a continuing presence in the state. The others died out long ago. The items in italics are translations from the French by various historians in abstract books and other sources.

The Touchet Family

It is perhaps understandable that the oldest continuing Czech family in Louisiana should be so thoroughly assimilated that most of the large clan of Touchets across Louisiana today have no idea they descend from Wenceslaus Tutzek of Prague. They have been thoroughly Cajunized. Yet, among the first Czechs documented in Louisiana were his sons Hans-Jakob and Jean-Jacques. They arrived sometime prior to 1742. This year is when the two sons first appear in any known records.

Their mother was named Dorothe. Her maiden name is not known. Wenceslaus was born in 1701. Dorothe was born in 1707. They were married in 1722 in Prague, "Boheme." This is the French word for the land of Bohemia, which is part of the Czech lands. This information is from the marriage records of the sons in Louisiana. Perhaps not surprisingly this first Bohemian family grew to have the largest number of descendants of any Czech family in Louisiana. There are more than 2,000 descendants of Wenceslaus and Dorothe Tuček in Louisiana today.

We don't know the exact names these sons were born with. While Hans-Jakob is a Germanization of a Czech name, which may have been the Czech "Jan Jakob," the original Czech name of his brother Jean-Jacques cannot be discerned. Only the French version of his name is in the records. The similarities of the two names does lead to some confusion. Yet, there were definitely two brothers as we shall see. There is no evidence that the Tutzek sons ever communicated with their parents again. There was a primitive mail system that usually took months using an irregular system of transfers. Perhaps they sent a letter or two to tell their parents of their fortunes in the New World but that is not known. Only if Jean-Jacques followed his older brother a few years later can we assume there was some communication.

The surname Tutzek is actually already a German spelling of the Czech Tuček. This is pronounced "Too-check." It is a fairly common surname in the Czech Republic. The name underwent many other spelling changes over the years, including Touchex, Touchette, Toutcheque, Tuchique and others; more than a dozen overall. The name changed from document to document in the notarial records we rely on for the early history of this family. As do the names of their neighbors. The names changed repeatedly even within documents.

When refering to any particular document I use the spelling as found in it. I put in parantheses the alternate spellings of people's names. The reason I do this is to enable future researchers to perhaps find more documentation of the early years of this family in Louisiana. By the early 1800s most everyone seems to have settled on the French spelling "Touchet" as the family name. Though there are still some Toutcheques, and other spellings, in Louisiana phone books today. Any one with this name, however spelled, is descended from Wenceslaus. Touchet, or its variants, is simply not a French name at all.

The notary had a unique place in early Louisiana history. He was responsible for writing and then keeping public records of significant commercial dealings. He was an agent of the government but operated independently. There was no central repository for these records. Each notary kept his own records. To look up any given record, however, you have to know the name of the notary who made the document. Not every transaction was subject to a notarial act. Not all notarial records survived the ravages of time. There are still many more that have not been translated or assessed so more information about the early Touchets may yet surface. It is, though, from these early notarial records that survived that we know anything of the Touchet family.

Though their native language was Czech, the two brothers must have had a command of German, not only to learn of the new colony, but also to talk to their new neighbors. They probably learned this language in Prague as was common at the time. The Austrain Empire was the ruling power at the time and they required all people to learn German. They also spelled Czech names in German to avoid the hAček and čarka—the little marks over Czech letters that Germans could not comprehend. Like most early settlers the Touchet brothers quickly learned French. Indeed, all their children were given French names. All the early documents are in French. It is probable that the brothers were proficient enough in the language to understand what they were signing.

The first German Coast was settled mostly by Germans beginning in the 1720s. It was a scheme by John Law and the French Government to bring settlers to the new colony of Louisiana. The second was settled beginning in the 1730s. Several hundred Germans, and obviously a few Czechs, settled 10 to 20 miles up river from New Orleans. They created four small villages named Marienthal, Augsbourg, Hoffen and Carlstein. Carlstein happens to be the name of one of the most famous castles in Bohemia. None of these settlements survived by name and the whole area came to be called the Cote Des Allemands, French for "German Coast."

It was strictly a farming community. Farms were laid out as usually 5 arpents along the river front and 40 arpents deep from the river. This is roughly 3/4s of a mile. An arpent is an old French units of land measurement common in Louisiana. It is the equivalent of roughly 96 feet. These farms were thus roughly rectangular plots of about 5 acres each. In documents the 40 arpents is repeatedly referred to only as "the customary depth." Larger farms may have had their own landing on the river. Many farmers, however, used public landings, paying a fee for each time they used it. Abutting the rear of the fields that any farmer was able to clear were cypress swamps and raw wilderness.

Even this early in Louisiana's settlement levees were being built to protect hard won agricultural gains from the river and its frequent floodings. Life was fairly brutal. People lived at first in mere huts. Weather of all extremes was a constant threat that rose up without much warning. Hurricanes, or just the garden variety summer rain storm, could wreck havoc on crops. There was much pestilence in the swamps; mosquitos and snakes being two major scourges. There was much early death and disease, hunger and filth, along with endless hard work eking out subsistence in a wilderness.

How the Tutzek brothers came to settle in these difficult circumstances is not known. There are a few possibilities. John Law printed up thousands of flyers that he had distributed around Alsace-Lorraine along the modern French-German border. He also ran newspaper advertisements in the German speaking areas of Switzerland. One possibility is that one or both of the brothers were in an area where this information was available. The other possibility is that this information made its way to Prague in the hands of some traveler. It cannot be determined from the known record if the two brothers traveled together. But given the probable birth year of Jean-Jacques either he was just a teenager when he arrived or he came over on a later voyage to join his brother. In any event, they settled near to each other.

Hans-Jakub Tutzek

His first marriage record clearly states that Hans-Jakub was born in Prague in 1723. He was married in 1742 on the German Coast. This date is the earliest confirmed appearance of one of the brothers. This most likely places him in Louisiana some time in the late 1730s. This is actually the "Second German Coast." The First German Coast was settled closer to New Orleans less than two decades earlier. This gives the Touchet brothers enough time, however, to meet the women who would become their wives. Later, the two brothers shared the wedding date of July 2nd, 1748. It is only from these two marriage records that we can be sure that there were two Touchets in Louisiana. This double marriage could be because priests came to the German Coast on an itinerant basis. They simply got married at the opportune moment. In any event, it must have been a joyous occasion for the two new Tutzek families.

Hans-Jakob died in the early 1760s in St. Charles Parish. He was no more than 40 years old and had three or four children. He stayed on the German Coast once he was in Louisiana. We have eleven notarial records giving some detail to his family's and his own life. None are clear about the births and deaths of this branch of the family. He first married Barbe Ackerman on January 9th, 1742 in Louisiana; they apparently had no children. She died within a few years. He then married Anne Barbe Foltz on July 2nd, 1748.

The first property record we have occurs in mid-1760. It states that Jacop Touchex (sic) sold a farm 5 arpents wide to Lionanar La Segne (Leonard

Lasseigne.) The exact date is not legible on the surviving document. The price was 600 livres. That was a considerable sum. It also means that the farm was well developed. Perhaps the entire plot was cleared and planted. It may well have had a few stock animals such as cows and mules since similar farms with this price did have them. No inventory of his farm survived. The price is more than ten times what was paid for other less developed farms. It is also possible that a slave was included in the sale but not mentioned in the sales document. Reflecting the continuing changes in his name, Touchex signed himself "Jakob Tutzek." He did so in a firm and clearly well practiced signature. Obviously he had some education. Many of his neighbors were illiterate. However, in just this one document there are two spellings of the surname.

From other more complete records it is obvious that farms of the era were a mix of crops. This typically included vegatables, cotton and sugar, as well as dairy products from a few cows. Poultry was free range underfoot around the farmstead. The houses were primitive and often just a step or two above being a barn with one or two rooms. The roads were often muddy and always rutted. The work day was from sun up to sundown. The labor was hard and the watery environment often dealt setbacks to even the most diligent farmer. Deaths were frequent. Step-children were common as men and woman remarried; they were unable to live without each other in a time of strict division of labor. New arrivals filled the depleted ranks of settlers. Yet, by this time the German Coast was providing foodstuffs to New Orleans. The German colonies were considered prosperous, and the term "hardworking" was frequently applied to the colonists by travelers to the region and later historians.

On December 15, 1764, a petition was notarized by Louis Champagne and his wife, Marie (Anne) Fols (Folse) asking that *"the few effects that she brings to their marriage be considered community property."* The record states that there was no inventory taken of the estate that she shared with Jacob Toutchek. This document also states: *"She claims to have very few effects owing to the fact that most were sold during the long illness of her late husband."*

With his union with Anne Barbe he had sons named George and Pierre. They also had a daughter named Marie-Charlotte. Nothing more is known about George and Marie-Charlotte. They appear in the records just once. Perhaps they died in one of the frequent epidemics which swept across the young Louisiana colony. Of his youngest son Pierre we know quite a bit, including the fact that he had a son named Pierre, too. It is these two that appear most in the notarial records for this branch of the family.

res, father and son, bought a considerable amount of property ... On October 24, 1768 a man named Pierre Audin sold a farm 4 arpents wide by the customary depth to the elder Pierre Touchet. It was located between the farms of Dupard and the widow of Jean Hypolite. In early Louisiana notarial records property descriptions were often set down as a piece of land between this person and that person. With so few people, and the linear progression of farms along the river, it was fairly easy for the authorities, sellers and purchasers to figure out to which piece of property they were referring. This referencing of neighbors was a convention that property records in the state used well into the early 1900s.

The elder Pierre is next found in a record dated June 28, 1774. This is when he bought a piece of land 6 arpents wide by the customary depth from Marie Francoise Berry. This stems from an unfortunate state of affairs in the Berry family. Marie Francoise Panquiere (Pankerne), wife of Antoine Berry, and Alexandre Chenet and Toussaint Tanguier, her brothers-in-law, *"declared that Antoine had been absent for a long time and that Marie Francoise has been left to support their only child, Jean Antoine Berry, just 10 years old."* Marie Francoise petitioned to sell her farm, bounded by the properties of a Maxant and Joseph Barbier. The witnesses were Joseph Quarantin, Louis Barbay and Jacque Echetayre. Often just the last names were used to identify neighboring property owners. It is apparent that Pierre could not write. His name was written by the notary next to his "marque ordinaire," that is, an X, as it appears in all the documents he signed. Different signers of the documents actually made marks, or X's, that were different from other people's.

The date that Pierre got married to Catherine Hoffman is not known. It is known, though, that he died November 17, 1783. There was an inventory of community property of "the late Pierre Touchet and his wife, Catherin Houfman (Hofmann)" that took place on December 12, 1783. Pierre Touchet was recorded as his only surviving child. The inventory of community property was taken by Alexandre Chenette (Chenet) and Morand Wilick (Willing) in the presence of the widow; Jacques and Andre Waguenspack, her sons by her first marriage; and Andre and Urbain Picou. Debts were *"owed by the community to Widow Berry, Maturin Lamoriere, Jean Mayer, Charles Dufresne, Andre Waguenspack and Jacque Waguespack."* On December 18, 1783, there was a succession sale of the movable property that had been inventoried the week before. The inventory notes that there were 12 cows sold. Prices ranged from 12 to 47 piastres for single cows. There were also two bulls sold; both for 24 piastres.

A man named Maurice O'Conor, who was a well known notary in the area, went to their farm to proceed with a public sale. The sale was announced by Gile Wuentin (Cantin.) Proceeds of the sale were placed in the hands of Urbain Picou who was named surrogate tutor of the minor children. Nearly two dozen people bought items from the succession. At the end of the day, Catherine Houfman, declared for the record that there was nothing left to sell. This act was witnessed by Giles Cantin, Robert Lavigne, and Urbain Picou. Total proceeds of the sale was 782 piastres. Pierre's debts amount to 103 piastres. The sum of 41 piastres went to the two minor children, Andre Wagenspak, (Waguenspack) and Veronique Haro. They were from Catherine Hoffman's second marriage according to the inventory taken by the "late" Nicolas Verret, then commander at St. James Parish. This would seem to mean that Pierre Touchet was her third husband. 637 piastres were left to be partitioned between Catherine and her children with Pierre "Toutchec." This was yet another spelling variation. The amount of money, though, shows a somewhat prosperous young man.

Pierre, the son, served as a witness to his half-brother's land sale on January 29, 1783. On this date Jacques Waguenspack sold a farm 3 arpents wide to Francois Torqui for 200 piastres. Torqoi paid cash. In a land of self-sufficiency cash was acquired from sales of foodstuffs to New Orleans. The farm bordered Pierre's and it is probable that they helped each other with farm labors. Neighbors helped neighbors on a regular basis according to many of the records.

It was two years later, in a document dated February 12, 1785, that Andre Waguenspack and Jean Baptiste La Capelle (son and son-in-law of Catherine Hofmann) declared in the presence of Urbain Picou and Achilles Trouard that they received the amount due them from the succession of their father (and father-in-law). This was probably when the minor children reached the age of majority. Since Catherine had a son-in-law it can presumed she had a daughter. There is no other evidence for this child.

On February 12, 1785, Catherine Hougman (Hofman,) petitioned that a "tutor and surrogate tutor be named for her minor child." This minor child is her son Pierre Touchet. The same Maurice O'Conor who ran the auction summoned Jacque and Andre Waguenspack, Jean Battiste La Chapelle, her son-in-law, and Urbain Picou, godfather of the minor child, to a meeting to determine the tutorships. Also present as witnesses were Achilles Trouard and Jean Roy. They named Catherine Hofmann tutor and Urbain Picou surrogate tutor. The elder Pierre died when young enough to leave a minor child and a wife who could get remarried. But if he was born in 1756 or 1758 he was just 25 or 27 when he died.

"Because of her infirmities and the youthfulness of her child, Pierre Touchets, fils, Catherine Houghman, widow of Pierre Touchet, petitions to sell her farm of 6 acres." It was *"bounded on one side by the farm of Jacque Waguenspack and on the other by that of Christian Phellipson (Christian Phillips Zahn,)"* reads yet another record. Partially due to the fact that woman were not wholly free to buy or sell land independently she had to get the permission of her son-in-law, Jean Baptiste LaChapelle. He consented to the sale of the farm. This was another convention that lasted until the early 1900s and that we will see repeated. This is probably the land that the elder Pierre bought in 1774. The petition was granted and the sale was announced by Jean Baptiste La Chapelle. Bids were submitted by (Jean) Martin Verret, Jean Baptiste LaChapelle, Louis Blondeau and Andre Waguenspack. The sale to her son, Andre, was confirmed on February 9th, 1784, for 207 piastres. The receipt for full and complete payment for the farm he purchased is dated February 2, 1784. That is odd, because it comes a week before the supposed sale. Is this an early example of the nepotism for which Louisiana is known?

From a notarial record dated February 10, 1790 it can be determined that Catherine Houghman, "widow of Pierre Toutchet," held on to at least one of the farms that her husband Pierre bought. On this date she sold a piece of land 3 arpents wide by the customary depth, bounded below by the property of Pierre Bossie and above by that of Pierre Cusot (Coussote) to her son Jacques for 500 piastres. The act was witnessed by George Deslonde and Jacques Lamotte. It took Jacques nearly 5 months to pay her. She finally declared the debt paid on June 8th, 1790.

Pierre the son's tutor, Urbain Picou, died September 26th, 1792. The customary inventory of his belongings was taken by Robert Lavigne and Antoine Cambre on October 4, 1792, in the presence of Urbain Picou, son of the deceased, and Jean Treguer (Tregre,) George Shof (Schaf) and Teodore Treguer, sons-in-law of the deceased. The heirs declared that money was still owed to the "Touchet minors," implying at least two children. Yet there is no record of the names of any other child or children.

The first record of a sale by the younger Pierre Touchet was February 16, 1793. This means by this date he was at least 20 years old. That was the earliest age he could enter into his own commercial dealings. Pierre Sanssouci, acting for Marguerite LeGau, who was the widow of Jacques, Touchet's half-brother, sold to Pierre "Toucheque" 1½ arpents of land. It was bounded above by the property of "Widow Wagenspak," his mother, and below by that of Pierre Bouvier. The price was 60 piastres. This was probably undeveloped land and Pierre had to set to work to make it profitable.

On February 1, 1794, Pierre declared in the presence of Verloin DeGruys and Firmain Songy that he received the amount of 420 piastres, drawn on the account of Andre Himelle. This was owed to him from the succession of Urbain Picou. Three months later, on May 15th, 1794, Pierre again acknowledged, in the presence this time of George Delsonde and Jean Duhart, the receipt of 131 piastres from the estate of Urbain Picou. This document clearly states that *"Together with 420 piastres which Touchet has already received this amount constitutes his share of the succession of the Urbain Picou."* This was no small inheritance at the time.

He took the money that he inherited and bought a slave. On May 17, 1794, Antoine Clereaux (Clerot) sold a slave named Baptiste, about 25 years old, of the Macoua nation, to Pierre for 400 piastres. This is apparently the only slave that Pierre bought, at a time when many of his richer neighbors were beginning to buy multiple slaves to ensure the commercial production of cotton and sugar. If he had bought un-tamed land he would have needed a second pair of hands to help clear the brush and palmetto palms and fell the trees. The young Pierre could have seen Baptiste as an ideal workmate.

Either the labor was done, or he had second thoughts about slavery, but just three years later, on February 20, 1797, Pierre declared in the presence of Louis de Grandmont and Firmain Songy, that he sold the same slave, *"Baptiste of the Macoua nation,"* to Jean-Baptiste Olivier. Olivier was a resident of New Orleans. The price was 200 piastres. This time the slave's age is listed as 35; one or both of the ages must be wrong. Pierre did not receive the money directly. In a somewhat complex transaction it is noted that Olivier *"is to pay the following people what Pierre owes them: Louis Blondeau, Etienne Renne, Charles Picou, Philipe, Andry and Tonis Vicner."* The document does not reveal the amounts or reasons for the debts. Maybe Pierre just sold the slave to raise money to pay his debts. In any event, the sale of the slave saw Touchet loosing nearly half of the original value of Baptiste, though no reason is stated why. Perhaps it was because of injuries Baptiste gained while clearing the land or his advanced age.

1799 saw two transactions that Pierre was involved with. First, in November, he sold a piece of land, 1½ arpents wide, to Charles Picou for just 66 piastres. Then in December he bought another farm, also 1½ arpents wide, from Alexandre Chenet for 70 piastres. These land records show that slaves were more valuable than the farms they worked on.

The final notarial record we have of Pierre is dated September 22, 1800. He went before a man named Andry to declare, *"in the presence of Louis de Grandmont and Jacques de Lagroue, that he is ceding to Louis Jolie the property that he bought from Alexandre Chenet."* This appears to be the end of this line of Touchets. The younger Pierre is never recorded as even getting married. Perhaps he too died in one of the epidemics which scoured the colony. When exactly he died is unknown.

All of these records point to a family that was well settled in the area for three generations. They knew and were known by their neighbors. They engaged in the similar pursuit of farming at just a little above subsistence level and selling their excess to New Orleans and beyond. These Touchets were neither richer or poorer than their neighbors but were just about average. Nor did they seem to get hit with any misfortune beyond which their neighbors experienced. They lived the live expectancy for the time. It is also clear, then, that the so-called German Coast had a heady mix of nationalities all struggling to make it in the newly cleared wilderness.

Jean-Jacques Tutzek

Hans-Jakob's brother, Jean-Jacques, was born in Prague about 1730. Exactly when he came to Louisiana is not clear. He did, though, leave a much bigger imprint on Louisiana than his brother. He was obviously a young teenager when he first arrived. On July 2, 1748, when he was just about 18 years old, he married his first wife, Barbe Vaguespach. It was the same day as his brother was married for the second time. It is this double wedding that confirms that there were two brothers from Bohemia in Louisiana at the dawn of her history.

His new wife was from Baden, Germany. Though he married her on the German Coast in Louisiana. She must have died soon after the marriage took place, definitely within two years. Shortly afterward he remarried. His second wife was Marie Barbe Foltz. The wedding date is not known. Marie was probably the sister of Anne Barbe Foltz. Which is the rather interesting situation of Jean-Jacques marrying his brother's wife's sister. This man was also known as Jacob Touchec in some documents, causing some confusion with his brother Hans-Jakob. From this union came two sons, Jacque and Georges. It is these two sons who spread the Touchet family which is now thoroughly Cajunized and living across Acadiana.

We have several notarial records of the father Jean-Jacques, sometimes referred to as Jacob. On the 19th of September, 1776, Francois Cheval declared in the presence of men named Bore and Meullion that Cheval sold a slave to "Jacob Touchec." The slave was a 20 year old woman named Silvie. Jacob didn't finish paying the 360 piastres price until more than two years later, according to the final receipt filed with the original document. From Jacob's sale of Silvie in 1781, we know that she was from Guinea in Africa. Louis Vaguesback (Waguesback,) who was somehow related by marriage to Touchet, bought her for also 360 piastres, and her age was now listed as 35.

A census of the militia for the Attakapas region in 1777, lists "Jacques Toutcheque" as a 40 year old "Creole." He was a fusilier, also known as an infantryman. He served in the 2nd Company with Louis Hulin, a 35 year old Creole, also a fusilier. From this we can see that the people around Jacques considered him a local. Creole is the word used to describe those of mixed heritages in early Louisiana. He obviously knew he was born in Prague, yet, he was quite comfortable being listed as a Creole. His accent had to give him away as non-French. His surname also had yet another spelling.

The few notarial records found for this side of the Touchet family are found in repositories 60 miles apart. One is dated January 12, 1781. This is when "Jacque Toutchec" sold a slave named Etienne, who was 30 years old, to Scrimar Bellile. Bellile was a "lieutenant-colonel of his Majesty's Army." The price was 500 piastres. There were three witnesses to the act: Pierre Bossie, Jean Baptiste Barre and Jean Pierre Bossie. Only it is not clear whether it was the father Jean-Jacque or his son Jacque who owned the slave. Whichever made this document it was done on the German Coast.

The very next day, January 13, 1781, saw two transactions. First, there was a sale by Jacques of a slave named Marguerite, a 30 year old from Senegal, to Charles Olivier. The price was 550 piastres. Pierre Darensbourg and Pierre Trepagnier were the witnesses. Second, Olivier sold a slave of the Mandinga nation also named Jacques, and just 24 years old, to Touchec. The sale price was 583 piastres. The birthplaces of the slaves are written in the original documents. Why this swap was done can only be guessed at.

The Touchet family members collectively owned five slaves, Baptiste, Silvie, Jacques, Marguerite and Etienne. Though they did not seem to own any one slave for a long period of time. It is almost as if they used the labor provided for the necessary task and then sold the slave. Whether any of these slaves went on to launch a living legacy with descendants to this day would be virtually impossible to determine. But if they did it means that there are some African-American families in South Louisiana with a Czech connection.

On the 7th of December, 1783, the elder Jacques is mentioned as a witness in a marriage record. Philippe Verete, *"son of the deceased Nicolas Verete & Marie Cantrelle, a native of New Orleans,"* married Marie Hebert. She was the widow of Anselme Hebert, a native of Acadia. Witnesses for the groom were Jacques Toutcheuqe and a man known only as "Carien." Witnesses for the bride were Mathurin Hebert and Joseph Hebert. Clearly Jacques had some friends among his neighbors.

At some point Jacques moved to the Attakapas County. This is the region which is now known as Acadiana. This is clear from a record from 1788. Clair Dauterive Bubuclet engaged Jacques Touchet to build a house on a *"high ridge overlooking Lake Tasse, now Spanish Lake, in the Attakapas County."* The document was notarized by a Mr. De Clouet. The price was 1,200 dollars. The price paid half in milk cows and half in cash. This was quite a sum in those days. The house must have been quite large. It was on January 13, 1783, that Bubuclet received a Spanish Land grant covering a *"vast expanse of virgin forest from Parque Perdue on the south to the winding of the Teche on the north."* We can assume by the date that this Jacque was the son of Jean-Jacques. It can be determined that sometime between 1781, when he was involved in the slave sales on the German Coast and 1788 when he was listed in the Attakapas country he moved his family. He also apparently was a skilled carpenter and builder if he was able to get the contract from Bubuclet. It is not known exactly when the elder Jean-Jacques Touchet died. The best guess is that it was no earlier than the late 1770s and not later than 1800.

The Spread of the Touchet Family

Jean-Jacques had two sons: Jacques and Georges. They both fathered many children who went on to have many more children of their own. From these two sons began the ever spreading branching that encompasses all those with the surname Touchet and its variants in Louisiana today. Plus, there are many descendants of all the many Touchet daughters. Marriages led them to have different family names but all their progeny have some Czech blood. What follows is a genealogical portrait of the Touchet family. We have this information chiefly from the Sacramental Records of the Catholic Church for Southwest Louisiana. These notices of births, marriages and deaths are brief. Usually just the dates of the events and the name of the parents are given. Rod Touchet and Keith Touchet, distantly related to each other but descendants of Jean-Jacques Touchet, shared the cattle brands with me.

I follow each son for two or three generations before going back to the next child of Jacques and Georges. I only go so far as to show to whom their daughters got married. The genealogy otherwise gets too complex; this family perhaps warrants a book in themselves. Land records have not been found for these people, yet they must exist. There also appears to be no other known documentation other than the Sacramental records; again, there must be more buried in the state archives. Eventually I hope that this other documentation will be found so we can get a truer portrait of one of the earliest and probably the largest Czech family in Louisiana. I present this information well aware that it is not the most exciting reading. I do so in the hope that the extended Touchet family can figure out where in this family tree they fit and to elicit new information as more records are uncovered. Because the Touchets were not Cajun they were often ignored in the histories of the Cajuns in Louisiana that were written in the past 150 years. Yet it is clear that they married into Cajun families.

What can be concluded from the spread of the family is that they were intricately involved in the growth of towns throughout the region. In the early 1800s various memebers of the Touchet family came to settle in several parishes including Vermillion, Acadia, Cameron, Lafayette and St. Martin. Indeed, they were among the easliest settlers in many regions of these parishes. They could only marry into the wider Cajun and German cultures because there were no other Czechs around. This fact led to the Cajunizing of the family. By the third generation it is probable that few if any of the Touchets had any inkling of their Czech roots.

Other than the Sacramental Records there are just three other vague records of Touchets prior to the Civil War. During the War of 1812 a Michel Touchet was a private in Baker's Regiment of the Louisiana Militia and a Pierre Touchet was a private in DeClouet's regiment of the Louisiana militia Exactly how these two fit into the family is unclear. Nothing more is known about them. Given the duplication of names within the family it could be any one of a number of different individuals.

There is also a vague record is the 1785 census of the Attakapas Post that identifies a family only as "Touchec." No first names are given. The records only give age ranges. The household had two adults under 50 and one over 50. There was one "free non-white male" in the household. Exactly who these people are is not clear. Perhaps it is the older Jean-Jacques or his widow and two sons. But they are part of the larger Touchet clan for sure.

One further odd record is found refering to what is probably a second Czech family in the Attakapas Country. In the same 1785 census there was a man named J. Caratek. This surname is almost certainly a Czech name. The suffix "-tek" is often used in Czech names as a suffix related to "being of a profession." A "caratek" may well be an old form of the Czech word, "rag dealer," from "cara," which is the word for rag. What is clear is that this suffix is not used in any French or German names of this period and place. All that is known is that his household had one adult younger than 50, one older than fifty, 1 free non-white resident and one slave. How this man and his family came to be in this time and place and what happened to them afterwards is a complete mystery. This is the only mention of the Carateks in any record found to date.

Jacques Touchet

That first son, Jacques Toutchec, was born February 29, 1752 on the German Coast. When he got married to Marie Gaspard he was listed as "of St. Charles on The Mississippi." In 1772, when he was just twenty, he served as a witness to the land sale of Simon Gaspard to Charles Legau; the date was March 21st of that year. A year later, almost to the day, he served as witness again to a land sale by Simon Gaspard. Simon may have been his father-in-law. In 1793 there is a record dated February 6th, that used Jacques Toucheque's property as a defining term in a title clearance document. The Pujol family farm, about which there had arisen a dispute, was "bounded above by Jean Champagne and below by Jacque Toucheque." The farms were located 15 miles above New Orleans on the "left side," or west side of the Mississippi River. This would seem to suggest that Jacques farmed the land for more than 20 years.

Jacques fathered four sons and a daughter. Things must have been good for the Touchets for all the children survived to raise families of their own. At least there is no mention of any children dying in childhood. Whether he passed on stories of his Czech heritage can only be a matter of supposition but he had to know that his father and uncle were born in Prague and that they were not French as their neighbors were. During the Spanish period he was known in the records as Santiago. He died August 1, 1802, at the age of 50. That was considered fairly old for the times. He had to know his grandchildren. In the Sacramental records there is much basic information on Jacques' family. Only instead of living in St. Charles Parish the family was listed in St. Martinville. This small town is the parish seat of St. Martin Parish. It is nearly 70 miles to the west of where he was born. This was during the same period that the first Cajuns came to settle this area. Jacques had a cattle brand that looked like two crossed barbecue tools, showing two tines each, and handles. He registered this on July 16, 1793 and didn't sell it until December 30th, 1833; Narcisse Dugat was the buyer.

Jacques' first son was also named Jacques (Jacob) Touchet. (Both names are in the records) The surname, though, had begun to obtain its final form. This son was born September 12, 1792 and was baptized three months later in December, 1792. This time the father is listed as "Jacques Touchet, son of Jacques and Marie Gaspard." Jacob was married August 1, 1815 to Scholastique Thibodot. No children are recorded. He was the only child to have a Czech-inspired name.

The second son was Michel, baptized in April, 1795, "at age 2 months and 8 days." He went on to marry Celeste Connor on September 1, 1818. They took the Biblical injunction to "go forth and multiply" to heart and had 11 children, though that was not that unusual for the times. What was unusual was that most grew to adulthood. To support all these children he ran a farm. Hiis cattle brand was registered on the 10th of May, 1822. It was a fork combined with the letter R and somewhat resembles the modern sign for prescriptions.

The first of Michel and Celeste's children was Celestine. She was baptized on October, 1826 at the age of 4½. She went on to marry Theodule Guidry on the 28th of March, 1842. In another example of itinerant priests reaching those in rural areas only occasionally two of their children were baptized the same date, October 21, 1826. One was Edmond, when he was one year old. The other was a sister, Marie Marcelite, at the age of 2 years. Marie Marcelite eventually married at the age of 23 to the 26 year old Francois Frederic. The date was November 12, 1844.

This Touchet family must have lived pretty far out in the countryside and perhaps did not get in to town that often. This can be assumed by the fact that they waited so long to baptize these three children. Another possibility is that the parents just did not believe in baptism, which would not be that unusual for a Czech. In any event, it is unlikely that a priest was not in the area for 4½ years. The children must have been healthy, for parents usually baptized sick children as soon as possible in case the child was to die; they wanted the blessings of the church on the young one.

A fourth child, a son also named Michel, was born June 6, 1820. He eventually married Aurelian Frederic, perhaps the sister of Francois. They had a son, Alexandre, on April 28, 1844. He moved to Vermillion Parish, where he had his own cattle ranch to support his family. His brand was registered on June 31, 1849. It was a backwards S next to a backwards J, with a small cross above them. Vermilion Parish at the time was the edge of the wilderness. Michel and Aurelian were far from family, from old friends, in fact, far from everything. Abbeville, the parish seat, was just a small collection of houses and businesses in the 1840s. Their first house must have been something akin to a log cabin with dirt floors. There are still Touchets in this parish.

The fifth child was Susette, baptized in June, 1830, at age 3 years. Then came a son, Evarice, baptized at the age 4 of months on May 24, 1834. Another daughter followed, Elisee (Elisa?) "Lisa," who was baptized in August, 1833, at age 27 months. Yet another daughter came, whom they named Marie Melaide. She was baptized on March 28, 1838 when she was 1 year old. Still another daughter was Theogene. She was baptized July 11, 1836 at the age of 5 months. Following this were three sons, Valsain, born June 8, 1839; Valerien, born July 25, 1841; and finally Alexander, whose dates we do not know.

Marguerite was born to Jacques and Marie Gaspard on February 17, 1797 and baptized in March the same year. She was their only daughter. Marguerite grew up and married Theophile Abcher on April 2nd, 1815. This family, sometimes spelled Abscher, grew to be another large "Cajun" family in Acadiana but were German in origin. Nearly all the current Abchers in Louisiana are descended from this couple. Thus, nearly all the Abchers have some Czech heritage too.

A son, Frederic, was born to Jacques and Marie Gaspard on the 3rd of July, 1799 and baptized a month later. His parents were now known as "deceased Philippe and Marie Gaspard." Why Philippe was listed as his name and not Jacques cannot be determined. When he was about 19 years old, he was living in the Attakapas country. That's were young Frederic came to marry Euphrosine Schexnayder on the 8th of April, 1822. They had nine children. All of them have French or Cajun names, indicating that the father and mother were completely immersed in the area's culture. Frederic was thoroughly of Louisiana, with no vestige of his Czech heritage at this point. Though it is unimaginable that he did not know about his grandfather's birthplace in Prague. He had also registered a cattle brand on July 15, 1819, that was a combination of a backward S and a forward facing C. He sold it to John Miia (sic) on December 1, 1845.

Their first child, Frederic Jr., was born April 12, 1823 and baptized August 16, 1823. He apparently married a cousin Suzanne when he was in his early 20's. She spelled the family name "Toupcheck," and they had a daughter named Elizabeth who was born 28 October, 1846. Though this would seem to mean that Pierre or George Touchet, from the other side of the family had at least one daughter, though we have no other record of this Suzanne.

The other children of Frederic and Euphrosine, and their birth or baptismal dates, were Jacques, the third in a row, who was baptized June 22, 1826, at the age of 6 months. Euphasine, a daughter, was baptized July 12, 1827, at 5 months and 20 days. Azeline was baptized on August7, 1830, 4 months after her birth. A son, Francois, was baptized at the age 3 months on September 11, 1834. Another daughter, Adelaide, had her baptism on July 12, 1836 at the age 3 months. Her next youngest sister was Marie Eugenie, baptized November 28, 1838, also at the age of 3 months. Their youngest son, Martin, was born July 29, 1840. Finally they had yet another daughter, Maurelle, who was born June 22, 1845. This branch of the family alone accounted for some thirty new descendants in the generation that was to come after the Civil War.

Joseph was Jacque and Marie Gaspard's fourth son, and came to this world on December 12, 1801. He was baptized on January 26, 1802. He married Marie Hahn Schneider or as sometimes spelled in the records, Sixnayder or Schexnayder, on May 23, 1821. 8 children came to their union. He, too, supported his family through farming and ranching. His cattle brand was registered on August 2, 1820. He sold it to Louise Zeline Meres 10 years later, on November 30, 1830.

These eight children, spouses and their own chidren are Joseph, who was born November 16, 1823, and grew up and married Arsene Meaux. They in turn had a son, Joseph, who was born in March, 1846. The second child was a daughter, Marie Virginie, who was baptized September 30, 1825, at age 8 months. Another son, Joachim, was baptized August 2, 1827, at age 1 month 7 days. His father was listed as "Jacques Touchette," which was yet another spelling variant. Uraine was born February 23, 1829, and baptized October 14, 1829. Following her was a son, Charles; born February 27, 1831. Then came a daughter, Caroline, whose baptismal date was August 12, 1833, at age 8 months. Three years later Simon was born. He was baptized June 12, 1836, at age 10 months. Two years following him another son was born, this one named Jean, who was baptized March 28, 1838, at age 8 Months. Once again we can see the complete immersion into the surrounding Cajun culture through the use of French names.

Marie Hahn Schneider died sometime after the birth of her son Simon, and Joseph, the father, had a second wife. Her name was Marguertie Orgeux (Hargrove.) It was with her that he had his last child, Marguerite. She was born October 28, 1847. All these children went on to have many more of their own children, spreading the Touchet family across Acadiana.

Georges Touchet

Georges Touchet, the second son of Jean Jacques and Marie Barbe, was born April 5, 1754. He died in 1815 when he was 61 years old. He, too, was old enough to know his grandchildren. The records list "George Touchek (Touchet) de la Cote des Allemand," marrying on the 3rd of January, 1785, to Marie Magdeleine Fostin (also known as Lise) des Illinois at St. Martin de Tours Church in St. Martinville, Louisiana. She was the major, or eldest, daughter of Jacques Fostin and Francoise Vien. They had four children; three sons and a daughter. His name is given in different records as both the French spelling Georges and the English/German spelling of George. For simplicity I use "George" below.

George was a farmer and cattle rancher. On February 2, 1776, he attended the sale of the late George Rixner and his wife Anne Marie Frederic, where he bought a few things. Anne Marie may have been a relative of his, since a son of George's brother married into the Frederic family. His farm grew big enough to have its own brand. His brand looked like a heart followed by the number 2. He registered it on the 23rd of July 1792. The brand was transferred to his daughter-in-law, Magdeline Menard on the 22nd of September, 1829. He registered a second brand, a barbecue fork lying on its side, on 24th of October, 1798. He reregistered the heart-2 brand on October 21, 1808.

Their first son, Francois, was born the 14th of October, 1789, and baptized February 16, 1790. In 1810, of the 7th of August, when he was just 20 years old, Francois registered his own cattle brand. It was an upright fork and a letter S standing side by side. At the age of 23 he married Marie Menard; the happy date was February 4, 1812. In the record he was known as "Francois Toutcheque, inhabitant at L'ile des Cypress." This couple had a son, also named Francois, who was born September 29, 1812. The record states Francois the father died at the age of 40 on September 2, 1846, but this appears to be the wrong age. If the date is correct he was 56 years old. The succession date was November 19, 1846. Marie Menard died shortly after the birth of her son, Francois, or perhaps in childbirth itself.

Francois, the father, then married again on September 9, 1815 to Francoise Menard, perhaps Marie's younger sister or a cousin. A document dated September 9, 1815, and made by Christine Dore, widow of Pierre Menard, gave permission for her daughter, then 19, to marry Francois, then aged 28, and referred to as the son of *"the late George Toutcheck and Lise Fostin."* A judge named Briant married the couple. They had seven children. Their first son was Ursin, who was born on the 5th of March, 1816 and baptized in April, 1816. A second son was born September 4, 1817; his name was Achilles. He married Marie Leonite Badeaux on August 12, 1844, and they had at least two daughters: Marie Leontine, born June 16, 1845, and Rosalie, born December 26, 1846.

Following Achilles, Francois and Francoise had a daughter they named Estelle, who was born February 12, 1820, and was baptized on April 1, 1820. The little girl died 10 October, 1822 at 3 years and was buried the same day. Perhaps her body was considered contagious. A daughter Elisa was born January 29, 1823 and baptized on March 30, 1823. She survived to adulthood to marry to Manuel Viator on August 28, 1837.

Another daughter died young. Marie Aglaca, born on July 16, 1825, died August, 2nd 1826, at about 1½ years. Soon to follow, though, was a son, Hubert Dolse, born July 15, 1827 and baptized April 13, 1828. Their youngest child was Odile, who was born June 23, 1830 and baptized in October, 1830. In the record for her marriage, Odile was listed as "Adele." She married Antoine Viator, who may have been the brother of Manuel, on the 4th of May, 1846.

There were two other documents related to Francois Toucheuqe. One is dated June 25th, 1816. Francois and his brother George bought items from the joint estate of the couple Joseph Romero and Julie Gusserand, who apparently died within just a few days of each other. In August of 1818, the succession of Louis Lingois, a highly successful farmer, states that Francois was in debt to Lingois, though the amount of the debt is not stated.

Back to the children of George and Marie Magdaleine. They had a daughter, Francoise Belonie, who was born October 2, 1787, and baptized November 4, 1787. On November 13, 1804, Francoise Bellonie married Jean Lopes; she was 25 years old. Her father George is listed in the record as deceased by now, though this might be mistaken. They were married for nearly 25 years given that there was a succession filed for Jean Lopes on the 25th of July, 1829.

George and Marie had a son named George, too. He was born April 20, 1786 and baptized two months later on June 25, 1786. This George Touchet was married September 9, 1806, to Magdeleine Menard, who is perhaps another sister, or cousin, of Marie and Francoise Menard. Perhaps these were the proverbial girls next door. They had six children who lived into adulthood and three that died very young. A copy made of an 1818 map shows that George owned a farm of a few acres with his immediate neighbors being Louis Judice, a successful landowner in the area with several large farms, and Pierre Grolob. Within walking distance lay some 30 neighboring farms and the small town of St. Martinville itself. Though there was no Menard farm visible on the map; it may have been just out of reach of the survey.

His eldest son was named Georges, the third in a row, listed as the son "of Georges of l'ile des Cypress and Magdeleine Menard." He was born on Valentine's Day, 1808. The baptismal took place on March 21, 1808. This Georges was married on July 26, 1830, to Marguerite Phelonise Bouillon. They had eight children over 14 years.

First they had a son, the fourth generation with the name Georges. His middle name was "Belisaire," and he was born June 6, 1831. Following the next year was daughter Marie Arthemise, born August 22, 1832. A second daughter, Louisa, was born August 25, 1834. Their third daughter, Marie Delzen died at the age of 10 on June 29, 1846. She was born July 31, 1836. A child whose name defies determining the gender, Cesiare Ozeme, was born in September of 1838. Yet another daughter, Victorine was born on March 15, 1841, but died July 14, 1846, at the age of five years. She died just two weeks after her older sister, so it seems that some epidemic was sweeping the area. Their son Severin, born May 19, 1843, survived to adulthood. Their final child was a daughter, Cleonise, born September 1, 1845.

George and Magdaleine had a daughter named Louise Clemence on July 22, 1810. She was 19 when she married Francois Garry on August 31, 1829. The descendants of this family are still present in Acadiana today. They are almost certainaly unaware of their Czech connection.

On January 27, 1813 Georges and Magdaleine were blessed with twins. Their baptism was six months later in June. One twin was a daughter whom they named Francoise Aspasie. She, too, was 19 when she got married. Her husband was Jean Baptiste Boillon; the nuptials were performed on July 20, 1832. The other twin was a boy named Lufroy. He married Rosalie Champagne, and they had a daughter Marie Azelie on June 5, 1846. When the twins were born the family was listed living in New Iberia. Perhaps this Lufroy is named after the other Lefroy, who was possibly an uncle.

Their son Paul was born April 5, 1817 and baptized August 31, 1817 and his parents were now listed as back at L'ile De Cypress. Paul married Emerante Boullion, of Iberville, on May 18, 1835. They had four children: three daughters, Emerante, February 13, 1836, Marie Philomene, August 6, 1840, and Marie Celisie, born March 23, 1843. Their one son was named Paul Alfred; he was born September 10, 1845. On March 12th, 1836, at the age of 21 he was living on his own farm in St. Martin Parish. It was this date that Paul registered a cattle brand. This time the 2 was before the heart, a reversal of the earlier brand.

The fourth son of George and Magdaleine was Joseph Eugene, born April 18, 1821, and baptized in October, 1821. Joseph married Caroline Berthile Petit. They had two sons and a daughter: Auguste Eduourd, born December 1, 1841, Euguene Ernest, born September 20, 1843 and Henriette Anne, born October 9, 1845.

Drausin was their fifth son, born on November 17, 1826 and baptized March 25, 1827. He was married to Marguerite Gonzales on September 21, 1846. We don't know if they had any children. While the copy of the records we have says that "Drozin" registered a cattle brand on the 12th of March, 1836, this must be mistaken for he would have been just 10 years old. It is more probable that the date should have read 1846. His brand was the number 3 followed by a heart, and clearly played off the design of other family brands.

Yet another son, Faustin, was born May 22, 1832. Nothing more is known about this sixth son. George and Magdaleine experienced the tragic death of a young boy three times. The first was a nameless boy who died at birth on the 28th of April, 1816. Four years later another nameless boy died "at his parent's home," aged 5 weeks, on March 31, 1820. The third young Touchet to die was Francois. He was born February 12, 1823 and baptized, on April 6, 1824. The little boy died November 10, 1826 at 2 ½ at his parents home at L'ile De Pesuer.

Their fourth son, Ursin, died April 12, 1812, at age 19, apparently never having gotten the chance to get married. There can be no doubt that this extended family lived near each other and helped each other with the tasks at hand. More than a few projects on any farm of the era required extra hands, such as building and repairs. The extended Touchet family formed a work team that was probably put to good use over and over again. As each son and daughter set out on their own they would build their own farmstead and that required a good number of hands.

George Touchet must have moved his family to the Attakapas country fairly early, for on August 11, 1811 he was able to establish a solid claim to his land based on the "order of survey" taken on February 4, 1783. The land in question was in "Township 10, Range 6 East, Section 99," in the new American style property designation system being implemented as Louisiana was going through the process of becoming a territory and then a state. He owned a piece of land roughly 6 by 40 arpents, or about 240 square arpents. As was the custom of the time he cultivated some and let cattle free range on the remaining land. A survey by James C. Johnson submitted on April 2, 1811, found that the tract contained 203.10 acres. There was a dispute over 4.29 acres with his neighbor Joseph LeBlanc settled in Touchet's favor.

One last bit of factual information on George Touchet was that on June 31, 1807 he bought one piece of platille for $20 from the estate of Joseph Melacon. Platille is a sort of fancy white cloth, originating in Silesia in Europe, but having spread throughout the continent and to the New World. It was used in finer garments and perhaps he bought it for his wife or daughters. This must have been a substantial quantity given the price, perhaps a large bolt of cloth.

Two other Touchet sons?

There are hints of two other sons of Jean-Jacques and Marie Barbe. One was named Francois, though we don't know for certain who this is. There is a record of a Francois Touchet, with the dates of July 24rd, 1792, to August 7th, 1811, having a cattle brand. If these are his dates he died young, just 31 years old. The other is Lefroy Touchet, who is said to have had registered a cattle brand on March 16, 1811, and transferred it to Fostin Toutcheque on the 15th of December, 1835. These two men are not recorded anywhere else, nor do they seem to fit the dates of the known people. These are, though, possible alterations in names. It is quite possible that these were sons who grew to adulthood and then died shortly after getting established but never got married. They would not have existed in the record until they reached the age of majority and made their own transactions.

The Civil War Touchets

The lack of property conveyances and other records could indicate that the families, once situated on a piece of land stayed there. Many of the sons went on to father three to five sons of their own, passing down the Touchet name. Over the years these Touchets began to fill the cities of Lafayette, Abbeville and other towns in the vicinity with their descendants. The family tree is preserved in the Sacramental Records of the Attakapas County, and still later the Diocese of Lafayette and other churches throughout the area. The record grows quite complex as each generation saw many sons and daughters, often with the same or similar names. The daughters, too, spread the Touchet legacy as they married into various levels of the social order around them. Indeed, many a Cajun family in the region wound up maried into the Touchet family and thus they have a smidgen of Czech blood in their veins.

We find some evidence that the next generation of Touchets served in the Civil War. One reference is an affidavit made on April 3, 1916, by Vilmo Romero who claims to have been a member of Company I of the Seventh Regiment of the State of Louisiana with Captain Charles Taltria. A man named Touchet is listed as one of the men who served with Romero who can attest to Romero's service. The first name is illegible on the document. From Andrew B.

Booth's *Records of Louisiana Confederate Soldiers & Confederate Commands*, we know from an undated list from St. Martin Parish that there were several Touchets conscripted into the Confederate army. The name was spelled Toucheck, and we find Belezaire, Cesare, Charles, Dolze, Drausin and Pierre listed in the role. There is no evidence that they saw any action.

Three other Touchets did serve in active duty. Alexander, Theosine and Valerian Touchett, sic, all served as privates in Company 1 of the 1st Louisiana Heavy Artillary. They saw action at Vicksburg. The Confederates had them listed as "absent without leave," but Union records show that they were captured on July 4, 1863, in Vicksburg All three were from Vermillion Parish; they were either brothers or cousins. They refused parole and asked to take the oath of Allegiance to the United States and then be released. All were sent to Yankee prison camps, first in St. Louis, then in Illinois and finally in Indiana. They remained prisoners for the remainder of the war. Presumably they returned home after the cessation of hostilities. One Charles Touchet was a private in the 3rd Company of the Governor's Guard and stayed in Louisiana.

One thing that remained in common with all the sons was that they remained small farmers and ranchers. They performed their labors without the assistance of slaves. Perhaps they were just above the subsistence level. None of the Touchets seems to have made a major name for himself in Louisiana history over the centuries. While most were farmers it appears that some moved into towns with their trades and skills over the next hundred years. A look at the extended family after 1840 would require a book in itself. They quietly went about their business and produced enough to take care of their families.

One Touchet did make a somewhat infamous name for himself. There is record of an "Elisee Toutchique," which is just another variant on the spelling of this last name, in the late 1850s. This man was fined 100 piastres, a currency still lightly in use in the hinterlands of Louisiana, for shooting a gun out of his bedroom window at Adrien Nunez. This is not as innocent as it first appears. Elisse was a bandit near l'Ile Perdue (Lost Lake) in Cameron Parish. His brigrandmates were other notorious figures: Jean Lacourture, Aladin Corner and Meance Primo. Apparently Touchique was taking pot shots at his fellows. Exactly who he was fined by is not clear in the record.

By the second generation there was apparently no awareness of the Czech origins of the family. Indeed, in successive generations they were listed as French or Americans. The whole extended family came to consider themselves Cajuns. There is every probability that family members spoke the Cajun French of their neighbors. Their surname looked French and they chose first names of French origin for their children. There is no evidence that any Czech was left in their vocabulary. They conducted commercial relations with their neighbors. They had to have been interacting with their neighbors during festivals and holiday seasons, as well as helping each other with difficult tasks on the farms they had. This was a time when communal efforts to pick up a farm after a disaster such as a fire or hurricane were common. Neighbors immediately helped neighbors in a time of trouble or crises. There can be no doubt that everyone considered this to be just another Cajun family on the prairie.

By the 1830s there were more than 70 living descendants of Jean-Jacques Touchet, immigrant from Prague. This number doubled with every new generation. All the Touchets in Louisiana can trace their roots back to this man. There are many people in the family who probably consider themselves "full blooded" Cajuns. Today there appears to be nearly 2,000 family descendants bearing the Touchet name. There is perhaps a similar number stemming from the Touchet daughters. Any search of Cajun genealogy shows Touchets marrying into this or that family, some more prominent than the others. The vast majority are unaware of their Czech origins.

In yet another new outpost for the family the 1860 census report shows that Achille, Belizare, Dorzy, Draszen and Doile Touchet were all heading their own households in New Iberia. The expanding family was living in at least 5 different parishes by this time.

It was Rod and Keith Touchet who first discovered their Czech roots. They both relayed to me their complete surprise at finding Wenceslaus Tutzek in Prague as their common ancestor. They are the many-great greatgrandsons of Jean-Jacques Touchet who immigrated from Prague nearly 250 years ago. One is descended from the first George Touchet in a direct line of sons, including many Georges, the other from Jacques. Keith Touchet has the odd situation of being descended from both sides of the family, in a long line of sons from the first Jacques Touchet and through the female line of George Touchet. Each discovered Wenceslaus independently as they went backwards generation by generation through their "Cajun" roots only to discover an educated man from the cosmopolitan city of Prague.

This Bohemian family has had a continuing impact on Acadiana, innocently masquerading as a Cajun family. There is even a Cajun band called the "Touchet Brothers" that has been playing since the 1940s. Descendants today run the gamut from Police Jury member to lawyers and dentists, from tradesmen to worker in the modern economy; there are still a few farmers among them. There are even a few petty criminal Touchets in the lot, making their names in newspaper police blotters. There are nearly 150 Touchet families in the Lafayette phone book alone; other phone books for the area all have numerous Touchets. Some family members still use Toutcheque and Toucheque, and a few other spellings are listed here and there in phone books across South Louisiana. With all this we now know that a Bohemian family was making its way in Louisiana before the influx of Cajuns, German, Irish, Italian and Anglo-Scots-Irish immigrants who came in such numbers that they became the dominant cultures.

The Novak Family

Another Bohemian family we find in the early records of Louisiana went by a name that is variously given as Novark, the French phonetic spelling Novaque, and the original Czech Novak. No matter how the name was spelt this family is among the early Czechs in the state. The name means "New Man" or "New Comer," which is apropos considering the early date at which this family is recorded. It is also the most common Czech and Slovak surname, like Smith in America; four other Novaks show up across the next two centuries of Louisiana History.

The family immigrated together, parents and their son. According to the Abstracts of the Civil Records of St. John the Baptist Parish, 1753 to 1803, compiled by noted Louisiana historian Glenn Conrad, Georges Novarck, husband of Catherine Strada, was the father of Jean Georges Novarck. In Jean Georges' marriage papers it is indicated that he was "a native of Bohemia," and thus the parents were married in what is now the Czech Republic. We do not know when the parents died. The Czech for George is "Jiři,' though the French notary would not have known this. The two Georges could have known that Georg was the German for their name, and thus the correct translation was made.

In the Archdiocese of New Orleans Sacramental Records for 1715–1750 it is stated that *"Jean Georges Novarck, the son of Georges and Catherine Utrada (sic), and a native of Lovchartrovis, Bohemia"* married Marie Apolonie Frederich on April 7, 1750. A look at current towns in the Czech Republic does not reveal the actual town; this name here probably being corrupted. The marriage took place on the German Coast. The witnesses were Andre Dreger, Georges Stele, Bernard and Alexandre Portuer. Catherine's last name is written as both Strada and Utrada. "Strada" itself is related to the Czech verb for "he lives in poverty," and given Czech naming conventions this is the likely surname.

The exact year on their arrival is impossilbe to determine but we can assume it was sometime in the 1740s. Though it could certainly have been earlier if Jean

Georges was just a child when they immigrated. That gives Jean Georges at least a year to meet the woman who was to become his wife. If Jean Georges was between 20 and 25 years old when he got married, which was the usual age for men in those times, it means he was born between 1725 and 1730 in Bohemia. We do have a notarized record dated June 16, 1756, stating that Jean George Novaque sold a piece of land 4 arpents wide to Simon Langou, though the document does not state a price. The second page of the short document seems to state that Jean George bought it for 24 piastres on the 29th of January, 1752. He most likely had put a lot of work into the farm, as this was his only means of survival in the harsh wilderness.

They were not married long for he died sometime before 1759. On January 1, 1759, a record was made authorizing Nicolas Gaulois, Marie Appollone's son, (in yet another variant on spellings,) to sell land that she inherited from "the late Novaque." From this it appears she was married twice, first to a man named Gaulois, and then to Jean George, for Nicolas would have to be old enough to complete the transaction. The land was a farm 4 arpents wide by the customary depth of 40 arpents that Jean George had bought from the Wiltz family. Either he bought this farm after the sale of his first farm to Langou or he had two farms at the same time.

The sale to Francois Bossier was approved by a member of the Darensbourg family who probably was the tutor for Nicholas when he was a minor after his own father died. Darensbourg signed many documents with just his last name written large and clear. The reason given for selling the land is "*The widow no longer want to live on this land, indicating that she is going to live with her brother.*" Nicolas had his name affixed to his customary mark, indicating that he was illiterate.

There is no evidence that Jean George and Marie Apolonie had any children together. These few records referred to are the only information we have on this family. Perhaps the ravages of the primitive conditions snuffed out the family at the dawn of its presence in the New World. This might have been the end of this line but it shows that a second Bohemian family came to Lousiana sometime before 1750.

Other Czechs on the German Coast

From the research of Louisiana historian Albert Robichaux we know of a few other people who immigrated from the Czech lands to Louisiana. In the census of 1724 of the German Coast one Balthazar Menthe, 42, was listed as a "native of

Troppau." Troppau is the German name for the city of Opava. Opava is the Czech name for the capital of the region of Silesia. Silesia itself is a slice of northern Moravia. The city is ancient. It first appears in Czech records in 1195. It was at a strategic crossing point between Moravia and Poland and had an important place in the history of Greater Moravia and the Kingdom of Bohemia. There was a population of Germans in the city since the early 1500s but it was predominately Czech.

On the German Coast he worked as "laborer." He had a wife and a daughter who was 18 months old. He also had 2 pigs and a farm that was one arpent and 2 verges (a verge is a subunit of an arpent) wide. He had been living there for three years. The census is quite detailed about him: *"He harvests 13 or 14 barrels of corn in spite of having been ill during most of the summer. He plans to remain in the village having no trees to chop down on his terrain and because he cannot himself clear a comparable one elsewhere on account of the wounds he received in prior Military service. He is well established on his place. A good worker."* The battles were probably with the Indians.

Balthazar died October 22, 1727, at the age of 45. Except for a daughter, Catherine Menthe, no other children are mentioned. Catherine was married February 6, 1741 to Alex Portier at the Parish Church of St. Charles on the German Coast. This is a family name that has lived on in Louisiana. They lived in the *"old German village at a quarter league from the border of the river."* Balthazar left Opava when he was just a young man. He arrived in the second decade of the 1700s at Karlsruhe on the Rhine River which was probably where he heard of Louisiana. He married Anne Marie Berghuberin on the 19th of September, 1719, in Karlsruhe. A German record dated April 17, 1720, notes that "both are Papists" and they "are moving to Mississippi." The fact that he was an adherent of Rome indicates that he definitely Czech; The Germans of his era were Lutherans. He probably, though, spoke both German and Czech. If he arrived in 1721 or 1722 that would make him the first person to arrive in Louisiana from the Czech lands although this is not known for certain.

Another Bohemian from Czech Silesia was Marc Til, native of a town called in German Bergweis. It is a town long gone, but whose Czech name would be Bilyhrad, which is a geographic name found in the area. He was a Lutheran according to the census of 1724. He made his living being a shoemaker. With his wife he harvested 6 barrels of corn, a small amount owing to his "having always been ill." We know nothing more about Til and his wife.

Someone we know even less about is a man named in the records only as Zonek. In just one record we find that he bought a barrel of rice for 40 livres.

This was 30 less livres than the asking price of 70. There is a notation that he took advantage of people's misfortunes. Despite this one reference the one thing we know for sure is that Zonek is a Czech name. These three are perhaps the earliest people from Bohemia who came to Louisiana if the record is to be believed.

Tzinek

Also among the families on the German Coast in 1700s we find two families that are probably Czech though we have no direct evidence for it. We do have references from several early sources to "Bohemians" in the plural, mostly in Glenn Conrad's many histories and books of abstracts, though in other places, too. However, Conrad and other historians basically ignored anyone who was not French and did not bother to delve deeper into their lives. So these could be some of the people of whom they spoke. We have a record that on April 12, 1728, that there was a marriage act between Rudolf Guilan (or Guilal) and Dorothe Tzineck, daughter of *"deceased Jacque Jacob and Marieanne Tzineck (Tzinek) resident of Parish of Les Allemands."* There is also a mention of one Jean Callandre, as Dorothe's brother-in-law. And that means she had a sister.

We don't know for sure but we can surmise that this could very well be one of the first Czechs in Louisiana, for the name seems Czech. By the process of elimination we can rule out French, Spanish or German origins of the name. French would have stayed pretty much the same, German would seem more French as was the custom, and Spanish has nothing like the "Tz" at the beginning of this name. On the other hand, "tz" was the German way of writing the "č" in Czech. Her father's name, Jacques Jacob, could just be a French form of the name doubled up with the Czech Jakob, as was sometimes the case with many German Jakobs. In addition, Dorothe was a common first name for Czech girls in the early 1700s. In any event, the name died out because the deceased left daughters. Who those daughters married, if anyone, is unknown.

The Poleck-Louchetik Family

There is another family of probable Bohemian extraction and that is Francois Louchetik and Marguerite Poleck. Not much is known of their early time on the German Coast, but we do know that Marguerite Poleck (Polsine) died about April 1, 1781. She was married first to Jean Foque (Vogt). And after he died, she remarried to Francois Louchetik, also known as Loustique, and even Lajoie. She was the mother of Francois Louchetik and Baltazard and Nicolas Foque.

On April 4th, 1781, an inventory of the community property of Francois Louchtik (Lajoye) and Marguerite Poleck, his wife, was taken. Marguertie Poleck died a few days before this date. Robin de Logny named Jacque Him Percle, (Joachim Bueckel) and Claude Joseph Gros to take the inventory of community property. The inventory was taken with the son Francois Louchtik and David Vicner being present. The first item inventoried was a farm 4 arpents wide by the customary depth, bounded below by the property of Jacque Him Percle and above by that of Joseph Gros. There were debts owed by the community to Nicolas Aite, Ingleart (also known as Jean Engelhardt,) Pierre Keller, and to Bedeau for the internment of Catherin Poleck (Polsine's) mother. Two smaller debts were due to Madame Bossie and Magdelaine Rome.

Two days later there was a public sale of the farm of Francois Louchetik the father. The announcement of the sale was made by Giles Quentin (Cantin.) Bids were submitted by Giles Quentin, Fancois Louchetik (Lajoye,) the son, Baltazard Vicner, Chrisitan Vollion, and Andre Lipse. In the final disposition of the farm a grant was made to Christian Vollion to enjoy this farm as his property, but it still belonged to Francois Louchetik, the son, because no one offered a reasonable price for the property. Voillion's grant was made in consideration of 250 piastres which can be called the rent.

A receipt was made by Baltazard Vicner (Vicnair) on November 10, 1781, when declaring to Robin de Longy, in the presence of Leonard La Seigne, and Antoine Monce (Montz) that he received from Christian Vollion one-half of the above consideration to be split between Baltazard and Nicolas Fauq (Vogt,) his wards

Two weeks later, on April 22, 1781, there was a final succession sale of the belongings of Francois Louchetik and his late wife, Marguerite Poleck. The community property was inventoried on April 4, 1781. Proceeds of the sale were to be partitioned between young Francois Louchetik and Baltazard and Noclas Fauq (Vogt,) the orphaned children of Jean Fauq (Vogt) and Marquertie Poleck. The sale was announced by Giles Quatin (Cantin.) 18 people from the area bought goods at the sale. The proceeds amounted to 379 piastres. Debts amounted to 71 Piastres. 308 piastres was divided between "Louchetike" and the Fauq children. This must have been a substantial farm with a lot of backbreaking work behind it.

Though there is no direct evidence presented in the Conrad book that these two were Bohemian, their last names can be deciphered as Bohemian. Louchtik in particular is clearly not French or German and the names of these two nationalities are always clear. But Lučik, Lučtik and Luček are names still existing in the

Czech Republic and derived from the Czech word for a "small meadow" are possibilities. We can see that nearly everyone had multiple spellings of their names. Thus, it is quite possible that this was a name change also. Early French censuses and church records did not always record the nationality of the people but throughout the early records of Louisiana both French and German names seem never to end with the letter K. On the other hand K is a common last letter in Czech names as can be seen in Novak, Caratek and Tuček/Tutzek. So for the lack of other possibilities we will also claim Louchetik, Poleck and Tzinek as early Czechs in Louisiana.

All together we have 6 definite and 3 probable Czech families (and several false Bohemians,) in Louisiana in the first decades of her settlement. Because the vast amount of historians looking at the early period on Louisiana history concentrated on the French, Spanish and German immigrants these few Bohemians are almost paranthetical entries in the long lists of settlers. Perhaps this was because most died out; indeed, only one family still survives, the Touchets. These Czechs do not appear together in any one history of Louisiana. Rather they are scattered throughout the various histories and records as mere afterthoughts. In the various ethnographic studies of this period they are often missing or ignored yet clearly Czechs are one of the ethnic groups that came early to Louisiana.

The False "Bohemians"

There have been several undocumented references in articles and history books about a group of "Bohemians" that had settled in Rapides Parish in the 1700s. A casual reader would perhaps conclude these were Czech Bohemians. While the local records of Rapides Parish were burned during the Civil War there are extant Spanish documents in archives in Cuba that show that several "Bohemians" settled in what was then called "Poste du Rapides;" today's Alexandria, Louisiana. This region was a part of Spain at the time we find these families. The first source we have for these families is a book by Louisiana historian Winston Deville, who had the opportunity to examine the original documents in Cuba. What Deville says is that under the heading "Boheme," *"written in large letters"* in the 1773 census of the Post are several families. The Bohemians wre identified separately in the census report, along with just three other categories: "Habitants," who were all French, "Americans," and "Indians."

First we find the 50 year old "Widow Varangue." She was quite successful with 11 horses, 9 cattle and 8 pigs. She had a son, Jean, who was 21. Also in the household was a married Marie Barbe, just 17, She, in turn, had a daughter,

Marie, who was just 1 month old. Marie Barbe may well have been the wife of Jean, though she is listed as daughter of the widow. We also know that a Jean Baptiste Varangue maried Marie L'Assomption Torres on January 12, 1801 This Jean Baptiste could have been the son of Jean, as the year would seem possible.

Also in this 1773 census was the "Bohemian" Louis Laprerie, a 40 year old farmer with 6 cattle and 4 pigs. He was born about 1732 in New Orleans. He was the son of Jean Phillip Laprerie and Jeanne Talon. Louis married Marie Jeane Jauna Castel at New Orleans in April, 1766. In the census she is said to be 30 years old. They had four children at this time. A son, Louis, 3, was born circa 1770. Cicille was 7. Later it is recorded that she spoke French, and was born in New Orleans about 1766. Cecille married Jean Baptiste Jeannot at "St. Jean Baptiste des Natchitoch, Natchitoches Post, France," in March, 1793. They had one son, John Baptiste Johnette, sic, who was born on August 20, 1798, and died on July 3, 1840. Another daughter was Louise, 5, who was born in New Orleans, too, circa 1768. A third daughter was Marie Anne, who was just 1 at the time of the census.

In a census report dated April 14, 1788, and done by a man named Layssard, there are also four categories: "Habitants," that is French, "Unmarried Men," "Americns" and "Bohemians." This time Louis Laprerie is listed as a "Bohemian" farmer who produced "500 carrotts of tobacco, 100 quarts of corn." His family had grown. Marie, his wife, was still living. Their children were listed in broad age groups. In the older group we find Louis, Marie Anne and Michel, who was a militiaman. The younger age group saw Marquerite, Manuel and Marie.

Also in the 1788 census and listed as a Bohemian was the "Widow Roman," who produced 200 carrotts of tobacco and 40 quarts of corn. Her son, Guillame, was a militiaman. The census notes that Louis Roman, her husband, died this very year. We also find one Celestine Bissinte under the category of Bohemians, though this was often an Indian name, according to Deville.

The Lapreire's were in the 1792 census, which does not break down the ethnicity of the people listed. Louis was still married to Marie Jeanne. There were the sons, Louis, Michel, who was still a militiaman, and Manuel. Four daughters are listed: Marie Anne, Marie Jeanne, Marguerite and Marie. These last two were in a younger age category than their sisters. Cecille must have been off in her own household with her own husband. In 1799 Louis Laprarie was now listed as a "white male over 50." The whole family was still listed as living together, though listed vaguely as 3 sons in the 25–49 age group and 3 daughters in the same group. He was a bit more successful, and his farm was listed as being 1 arpent wide, and it was probably the "customary depth," or 40 arpents, though this is not clear from the record. He had 4 horses and 15 head of cattle. The final census listing of a Laprerie was for Michel and Made in 1810.

Now, Laprerie, Varangue and Roman are not Czech names. Deville speculates that these people were actual Bohemians. He mentions the possibility that they could have been Gypsies, and the French used the word "Boheme" as a synonym for Gypsy. But he discounts this as he felt it more likely that actual Bohemians immigrated to this region than Gypsies. Recent research has shown that the LaPrarie family, at least, came from the city of Liege in Belgium and through the frequent wars was a displaced family without any permanent residence. The French authorities periodically rounded these people up and called them "Bohemes" as a synonym for Gypsy. They were sent to the new Louisiana colony simply as a way to clean up the streets of undesirables. This might well be a very early incidence of the word "Bohemian" being used for a rootless transient person in the sense that we use it today. The one certain thing is that the enumerator in at least two censuses felt compelled to list them separately as Bohemians but they most definitely were not really Czech nor from Bohemia. I include them here if only to correct the historical record.

Observations on the First Czechs

One thing for certain with the first Czechs in Louisiana is that those who were not at all Czech were the only ones that any Louisiana historian bothered to list as Czech. This is, of course, a glaring error. For lack of a better term I call them False Bohemains. These other historians merely took the word of long ago French census takers and did not bother to examine the truth. On the other hand, because the real Bohemians were problematic they were simply ignored. What can now be said with certainty is that at least 7 families from the Czech lands were in Louisiana well before the first Cajuns. While this is not a rewriting or revision of history surely it is an important addition to the story of early Louisiana.

2

Movers & Shakers

In New Orleans in the 1800s were several families that were from what are now the Czech Republic and Slovakia. They had a significant and lasting impact on the city. No one can escape their legacy. On the other hand, no historian of Louisiana ever felt compelled to delve into their Czech and Slovak origins. At most these families are sometimes mentioned in passing when recounting the history of New Orleans. For the most part they were ignored. Once again, what was recorded is all paranthetical to the major themes of French, Spanish and American development of New Orleans. This is the first time that their legacy is explored in any great detail.

What can be proven, though, will somewhat surprise people familiar with New Orleans. These movers and shakers are the Kohn, Latrobe, Frankenbush, Pokorny, Pollatsek and Laska families. What I posit here is that two of the most well known emblems of New Orleans, St. Louis Cathedral and the St. Charles Avenue Street Car Line, are the products of Czech men. These families also had a significant economic impact on New Orleans far out of proportion to their number in the larger population. They were among the richest citizens and were involved in multiple business ventures all of which came to shape the city we know today. At one point in time nearly one fourth of all the builidngs in downtown New Orleans had been built and were owned by a Czech or Slovak family. That they were ignored in all tellings New Orleans' history is perhaps unfair however understandable this was given the lack of knowledge about Czechs and Slovaks. Yet, it is undeniable that no future history of the city can ignore them after what I present here is considered.

Samuel, Joachim, Carl and Gustave Kohn in New Orleans

Horany is a small village a short walk from the large town of Karlovy Vary—better known to Americans by its German name, Carlsbad. Long a spa town in Western Bohemia that has had a mix of Germans, Czechs, Jews it also attracted many international visitors. Karlovy Vary attracted the rich and famous of Europe for hundreds of years to the natural mineral springs that are sprinkled among the low mountains. It still does. The economy was good and that brought many people to work there. The town had quite a cosmopolitan aire. The Kohn family was one such family that migrated to the area, arriving in the early 1600s. Samuel Kohn was born here to a poor Czech Jewish family in the Jewish section of the city.

Like many Czech towns Horany had a Germanic name equivalent, Horeth. The town's population was about 1/3 ethnic German, 5% ethnically Jewish and the remainder Czech, about the balance in many towns in the area. From this small beginning began the important New Orleans family by the name of Kohn. This family of Bohemian Jews, Samuel, his brother Joachim, and his nephews Carl and Gustave, all made their own important contributions to New Orleans and Louisiana. While not ethnically Czech there is no doubt that the Kohn family was based in Bohemia for many centuries. They considered themselves Bohemian first and Jewish second.

Samuel Kohn

Samuel Kohn was apparently a sluggard at home, both in school and work. He was given to gambling and drinking. Lucien Wolf, a respected British Jewish Historian, related to Samuel by marriage, relates a story how Samuel was known as a good buddy to many people, and liked hanging around the tavern and flirting with women. He came from a poor family and this activity showed a wanton disregard for saving money and working hard. Samuel finally lost the last of his meager money at the hands of cardsharks. Rather than face his family in disgrace he headed out of town. Soon word spread through town that Samuel had disappeared after he was "seen drinking and gambling with strangers at the Gast-Haus," or Guest House. Wolf reports that Samuel "worked his way on a sailing vessel to New Orleans," supposedly leaving by way of Hamburg. Whether this means he merely traveled by this vessel, which implies that he earned his fare somewhere in Europe, or that he actually signed on as a sailor on the ship, is not clear from Wolf's tale.

A few years later, in 1806, he surfaced in New Orleans as a partner in an inn on Bayou St. John. His partner in the inn was one H. Labruere. The inn must have been substantial for they publicized private party rooms. It was also said that they had the "finest liquors available." He must have had an epiphany some where in his years of travel and determined to succeed in business. Where he got the money for this venture is not known. Perhaps he assured his success by going into a business that he knew well from at least one side of the bar.

Why or when he came to New Orleans is not known. But he must have been there for a few years, perhaps five. This is probable given that the same year he was at the inn he is found filing lawsuits over considerable sums of money. He may well have sailed directly to New Orleans. This would have given him enough time to learn both French and English, the languages of the city. He would also have to have learned enough of the real estate market and business practices of the city to make informed decisions about which deals were going to pay off the promised return. It can also be assumed that he must have come to know these men with whom he did business on a personal level. Business was generally con ducted on the basis of reputation, there being no credit reports as we know them today.

The earliest record found is contained in a civil suit entitled Samuel Kohn v. John F. O'Neill. In 1806 Kohn hired a man identified only as R. McShane to write his petition. There were also an affidavit of the facts and a summons pre pared. The suit sought payment of two debts owed by O'Neill. One was for $200 and the other $600. Kohn was involved in another civil suit in 1807. This time he was suing Pallus P. Stuart. The dispute was over payment of a promissory note for $1,450 written by Stuart to Kohn on August 7, 1806. There is no record that these suits were successful. In the Loyola Library in New Orleans are more than two dozen suits filed by Kohn during his early years in the city.

These were large sums for the day, equivalent to tens of thousands of dollars today. These loans were mostly for real estate deals of one sort or another. That he was able to lend such sums so soon after his own arrival attests to some high level of business acumen. We must assume that he collected many more promis sory notes that were paid on time and in full for it is hard to believe that these suits comprised more than a small percentage of what he loaned out.

Besides doing business in New Orleans he also bought land in Rapides Parish, a place that was to become a center of Czechs who arrived much later than Kohn. He bought two pieces of land there in 1809 and sold them in 1816 for $1,200 and $1,600. This we know only from notarial records in New Orleans for the parish courthouse in Rapides was burned by the Yankees in the Civil War. Whether he bought land elsewhere in Louisiana is not known.

According to a historian of New Orleans Jews, Bertram W. Korn, Samuel Kohn was involved in many business deals throughout the early years of New Orleans as a new American city. In 1810 he hired a contractor to build two residences in the Fauburg Marigny that were similar to the ones he had just bought next door. He paid $1,200 for the construction and also transferred yet another lot he had in Alexandria, Louisiana, to the builder. Over the years he built and sold many residences throughout the growing Uptown and the established Marigny areas of New Orleans.

Samuel was much consumed by his business interests. He did not appear much in public affairs. He was, though, the treasurer of a Masonic lodge in 1823. On the 19th of May, 1825, he deposited with the well known notary, Hugh Gordon, a development plan for batture property in the Fauburg St. Mary. This area is now known as the Lower Garden District. Batture property was land outside of the levee sysetm along the river. The map does not survive. The very next day Samuel bought a lot on lower Tchoupitoulas Street for $480 cash from John F. Miller.

Over the years he was appointed trustee of many bankrupt firms. He discharged his duties to the continued satisfaction of the courts. In 1829 he was elected president of the Orleans Navigation Company. He then promptly engineered the replacement of the board of directors and tried to sell the business to the state. This same year he sold at auction a lot in the Fauburg de Religienses in what was then Jefferson Parish that he originally sold to Jean Baptiste Thoret. Thoret was apparently unable to make payment for Kohn arranged the sale of the same lot to John Nichelson for $350 just a few months later. The lot was on St. Mary's Road. Kohn bought the land the year previously from the Ursuline Nuns. In the same Fauburg, on Felicite Road, he had two other lots also bought from the nuns the previous year. These lots he also sold in 1829 to Isaac J. McCoy. Immediately McCoy turned the lots over to James Coutts as if he had never bought the property; the act actually transfers the property directly from Kohn to Coutts. The selling price at an auction was $330 for both lots. Kohn held a mortgage for four years.

In an act dated the 21st of January, 1830, Samuel accepted final payment on a loan of $5,000 to James Workman on two lots. One faced Tchoupitoulas Street and the other was on Commerce Street. These were on the batture in Fauburg St. Mary. Given the price they must have had some buildings, perhaps warehouses, on them. This would be right along the wharves and levees of the Mississippi River. They were lots 35 and 36 of the plan "mentioned in said act" but which no longer exists.

Samuel hosted a political dinner in 1831. And in perhaps his only recorded philanthropic move he donated $1,000 to a fund for the widows and orphans of the 1832 cholera epidemic. This was more than any other citizen according to Korn. He did, however, believe that charity began at home and there is much evidence that he sent money to his family back in Horany as soon as he had extra funds. He also made some long lasting and close personal friendships with many of the leaders of the Jewish and Catholic circles of New Orleans.

Between 1827 and 1830 Kohn lived as 65 Bourbon Street. City directories list his place of business at Bienville Street and Bayou St. John. This would apparently mean that he still owned the inn first found in 1806 or at least kept offices in the same building. Being so long in one place of business no doubt ensured his own reputation as a valued business partner. Whether he commuted by his own carriage or one of the public transport carriages can only be conjectured, but it was too far to walk.

In 1829 Kohn and Moses Schiff, another prominent Jew in early New Orleans, arranged a letter of credit for the sum of 10,000 British pounds sterling from the "mercantile house of W. J. Brown" of Liverpool, England, for the benefit of Kohn & Bordier, his brother Joachim's firm. This was an enormous amount of money, over $50,000 in American money at the time, which itself could be valued at more than a million dollars today.

Samuel was well enough situated financially to became involved with Bernard Marigny and later Laurent Millaudon and John Slidell in developing the Carrollton area of the city. On April 20th, 1831, Kohn and Marigny bought one half of the Macarty Plantation from Barthelemy Macarty, son of the original owner. The plantation was 37 arpents in width along the river and ran back 80 arpents to what is now near Claiborne Avenue. It was only partially cultivated; the back portion was swamp. The distance by road to New Orleans was eight miles along the River Road. The plantation stemmed from the claim of a Spanish land grant to Jean Baptiste Macarty in 1795. There was much litigation in establishing the grant but eventually Macarty gained title to nearly 1,300 acres. His sons and daughter inherited the property in 1808, each getting half. The land lay between what are now Monticello Street at the end of the city and Lowerline Street. This is a stretch almost two miles long along the river towards downtown New Orleans. On September 2nd, 1831, Marigny sold his half in the plantation to Millaudon, who received four-fifths interest, and Slidell, who received the remaining one-fifth, These two were now partnered with Samuel Kohn, who retained his half-interest.

Three months later the New Orleans Canal and Banking Company bought the other half of the plantation from Barthelemy's sister Eleanore Mirtile Macarty. The company paid $300,000 for the property which included slaves and "improvements." The company quickly sold everything but the land for $215,000. Presumably Kohn and his partners had done the same. In response to rising land values they hired Charles Zimpel, a German immigrant, to survey a neighborhood. The plan was drawn up by April 16, 1833. It subdivided the land into 650 foot squares. The streets "parallel" to the river were numbered while the streets perpendicular to the river were named after the presidents of the country up to that date. The new town was named after William Carroll, who was a general at the Battle of New Orleans. Many buyers then subsequently subdivided their lots and laid out the streets we know today. Zimpel was to have other notable projects in the city over the next decade.

After the subdivision Kohn, Millaudon and Slidell and others were then involved in organizing the New Orleans and Carrollton Railway Company in 1834. This line was to bring Carrollton into the orbit of New Orleans. It enabled people to go to the new town where there was a race track, fancy restaurants and other entertainments. It was strictly a commercial venture meant to bring people to their new Fauburg where they could sell lots and make more money. The line was to run through the middle of the newly laid out Nyades Street, now the city's famous St. Charles Avenue. An early city law limited the street car to a speed of only 4 miles an hour and the cars had to give right of way to anything that crossed its path. Kohn maintained a majority interest in this venture and was the main figure in developing the street car line.

Samuel began to establish a presence in Paris in 1832. This was the year that he granted Joachim a power of attorney for his affairs in New Orleans. For the next three years he apparently traveled between Bohemia, Paris and New Orleans. 1835 he moved permanently to Paris where he remained for the rest of his life. Because he was in Paris at the time he did not attend Joachim's wedding in 1834. Samuel never did marry. But he did have a long time servant whom he brought along to Paris. Her name was Delphine Blanchard Marchegay. Korn states that she was "probably his mistress." In his will he left her $800 a year for the rest of her life. This was more than enough to sustain someone in a nice life. In the records she is listed as a "free Negress." She died in Paris at the age of 85 in 1877.

We know a little about a trip he made to Bohemia in 1833 or 1834. Again Lucien Wolf is our reporter, though the story may be slightly exaggerated. Samuel is said to have arrived in a carriage drawn by six horses and was attended to by four African-American servants he brought with him from New Orleans. There was much baggage including many gifts for his extended family. His mother was alive, though his father had died in 1831. According to the story he presented her a small cask "full to the brim of newly-coined gold." This might be overstated. Though Samuel was rich enough for it to be true. He sent a letter to his nephew Carl in New Orleans about this trip. Carl makes mention in his own letters of the details provided by Samuel. It is clear that Samuel made provisions for a steady stream of funds to be allotted to his relations in Bohemia.

For the next 18 years Samuel lived in Paris with Delphine and engaged in many business ventures. He brought another nephew, Eduoard, from Bohemia to join him in Paris. Eduoard Kohn was to become a wealthy and prominent member of the Jewish community in Paris. Samuel, Eduoard, Joachim and Carl kept a transcontinental business running for several decades. Their trade extended from California to Mexico to Chicago and New York and over to continental Europe. In the process Samuel became extremely wealthy. His will left $66,500 to each of Joachim's children, a rather large fortune in the days before the Civil War.

An order dated December 10, 1853 was granted on a petition of Joachim Kohn and Carl Kohn, executors of Samuel's last will and testament, to make an inventory of Samuel's property in New Orleans. This inventory was taken on the 16th of January, 1854. About half the estate consisted of property, all listed as "lots." The "lot" that occupied most of the block between Magazine, Gravier, Camp and Natchez Streets in the heart of downtown was valued at $25,500. Kohn originally acquired it in 1835. 12 lots worth $34,000 were between Julia, Commerce, Notre Dame and Tchoupitoulas Streets, (about where the Morial Convention Center is now.) He acquired these at a Sheriff Sale in a case entitled "Kohn v. Joshua Baldwin." There was also a lot valued at $9,000 on the Public Road between Custom House Street and Bienville Street. Kohn acquired this from S. W. Oakley sometime prior to 1835. He also owned a lot in the French Quarter at Royal and Dumaine. This had a value of $19,500. A lot between Royal, Hospital, Ursulines, and Conti Streets, also in the French Quarter, was valued at $6,500. Finally, there were three lots on Baronne Street with a combined value of $10,000. This is a total of $105,200 in real estate. Today these lots would be valued at several million dollars.

Given the values of the properties they were obviously more than just "a lot" as stated in the inventory. No doubt there were buildings on these lots. And these buildings were earning rent for Samuel Kohn for many years, some for nearly three decades. It was Joachim who collected the rents for the many years that Samuel was in Paris. Also in the estate were a "dozen or more" promissory notes all secured by mortgages—being listed as "bills receivable" of $32,512.20. It is apparent from this alone that Samuel was acting as his own private bank even if not in name. There were stocks, too. The largest sum was in Bank of Louisiana stock. This was valued at $9,720. There was $3,500 in the New Orleans and Carrollton Railway. Kohn was the largest stockholder until his death. Another stock series in the Railway was worth $2,205. Plus, there was $2,192 in Old Union Bank of Louisiana stock. This is a total of $17,627 in stocks. A small fortune at the time.

There was also $8,254.37 in "cash on hand." The inventory does not state where this money was being kept. There were two loans to Joachim and Carl. One was a $10,000 loan to Carl Kohn. Another was for "65,000 francs," or $12,500, due by both Joachim and Carl. In keeping with all the suits Samuel filed over the years there were "doubtful claims" of $4,948.94. They were "mostly promissory notes of one kind or another." Finally, there was an "interest in Mr. Gormley's property, worth $10,000." This brings the total of the estate to $201,042, the equivalent of many millions today. This was just what he had in New Orleans. His will mentions another $200,000 in cash, stocks and property in Paris.

He strode across the business world of New Orleans for more than 50 years. As one of the primary developers of Carrollton and the street car he left a concrete impression on the face of New Orleans. He left a family that had an equally large impact on the city. The experience of New Orleans for everyone who lives in or visits the city is the result of decisions that this Bohemian Jew made in the first half of the 1800s. Despite all this his obituary in the Times-Picayune was just one simple line: "Samuel Kohn, long of this city, died at Paris May 18, 1853."

Joachim Kohn

More than a decade after his own arrival Samuel brought his brother Joachim over from Bohemia. The 19 year old Joachim was a passenger on the schooner Daedalus, which sailed from Bremen and arrived in New Orleans on December 6, 1820. One would presume that Samuel should have met him at the wharf but instead we find that Samuel did not arrive in New Orleans from Europe, via Havana, until May, 1820. Joachim most likely had letters of introduction from Samuel and the directions to important contacts as was common in an era before quick communications. In 1823 the two of them were in business at 116 St. Ann Street in the French Quarter. The next year Joachim was in a partnership with John L. Bernard. Over the next few years Samuel set Joachim up in the merchant business with a succession of partners for specific ventures. By 1826 Joachim was teamed with J. A. Bordier. The firm of Kohn & Bordier owned several ships and engaged in a vigorous trade in many commodities, among them "wine, coffee, cigars and dry goods." It had many ventures in Mexico.

The firm also served as agents for a few shipping lines and its business extended up the Mississippi as well as around the world. Both the 1827 and 1830 Paxton's City Directory lists Joachim in business with Bordier in dry goods and merchandise at 103 Chartres Street. This shows some stability for the business. The directory is unclear as to whether this was his residence or not. It is quite possible that he was living with his brother at 65 Bourbon. That would have made his commute just a short walk each way. After his brother started his move to Paris Joachim took over for him. He kept constructing buildings and managing the ones that Samuel had built. Joachim's business dealings benefited from the large amounts of money that Samuel invested and the firm of Kohn & Bordier was one of the leaders of its day.

In 1833 or 1834 he returned to Bohemia to visit his family there. He may have traveled with his brother Samuel on his own trip back home. When Joachim returned to New Orleans he had his nephew Carl in tow. Soon, Joachim and Carl Kohn were at the top of the social pecking order. This was facilitated by Joachim's marriage to Marie Thalie Martin. She was the nineteen year old daughter of a well-situated French physician in the city. Because he was Jewish and she was Catholic they received special "dispensation of the impediment of mixed religion" when they got married at St. Louis Cathedral. The ceremony was held June 22, 1834, and officiated by Abbe Moni. They had three children: Samuel Arthur, Joseph Gustave and a daughter Amelie.

Of Samuel Arthur we have only the barest of information. He was born on November 13, 1835. As a young man he moved to Paris were he engaged in business with his Uncle Samuel and other relatives and died in 1910. Their daughter Amelie married well, to Armand Heine. Armand and his brother Michel had a commission and banking enterprise that was worth nearly $600,000 in 1854. That made it one of the largest in the South. Gustave stayed in New Orleans and set out on his own business ventures.

Joseph Gustave was born on March 18, 1837. In 1861, Gustave, as he was known in the pubic record, was in the dry goods business at 15 Rampart Street near the corner of Canal Street. He was still there in 1866 when the first city directory after the Civil War was published. In 1870 he had a residence on Burgundy Street at the corner of Spain Street in the Fauburg Marigny. 1871 saw some major changes for Gustave. The city directory for that year says his residence was now on Bourbon Street between Dumaine and St. Ann Streets. It also lists his occupation as "capitalist" with an office at 14 Carondelet Street. Just a few years later, in the 1880s, he was back in the dry goods business, at 531 Burgundy Street in the French Quarter. There are two possible reasons for this seemingly backwards step in his fortunes. One is that his capitalist business failed in the financial panic of 1877. The other is that he found his time too limited by his business to pursue his passion for nature.

Gustave died on September 7, 1906. In his lifetime he amassed a collection of 6,000 wildlife specimens. He donated this hoard to Tulane University where it resides today. It includes samples of birds, fish, reptiles, mammals, crustaceans, mollusks, insects and plants from around Louisiana and the Gulf Coast. He was one of the leading naturalists at a time when the systematic study of nature was coming into vogue, particularly following the publication of Charles Darwin's "On the Origins of Species." Gustave must have spent thousands of hours tramping through the arboreal and swampy wilderness that surrounded New Orleans as well as making forays to the southern marshes and the Gulf Coast.

In the mid-1830s there were numerous reports in the New Orleans Bee, the leading newspaper in the city, of the machinations of Joachim and three other men concerning them buying up all the stock of the Louisiana State Marine and Fire Insurance Company and excluding other interested parties. Joachim was elected director of the company in 1836. Probably riding on his brother's good name he established himself in the business circles of the city and served in numerous capacities. He served on more corporate boards than any other New Orleanian Jew of the era. These were good years for the city. There was a booming economy and wealth was readily to be gained. Among the largest companies he was involved with were the Mechanics and Traders Bank, The Carrollton Bank and the New Orleans and Carrollton Rail Road Company. With the latter he was following the lead of Samuel. He also continued to oversee his brother's properties in the city.

Though Joachim's firm survived the panic of 1837 by 1842 it was in some financial trouble. After his wife died in 1843 Joachim mostly retired from his own business affairs when watching over Samuel's became too big of a project. In

1844 Joachim's address for both his business and his residence was 31 St. Louis Street. In 1845 he tried once more to start a business but this was short lived. For the rest of his life he oversaw the disposition of Samuel's large estate. He worked with his nephew Carl on these ventures.

Nearly ten years later, on March 20, 1854, an order was given by Judge J. W. Lew for a family meeting to be held. Five days later there was a family meeting among the tutors of Joachim's children to settle the affairs of their Uncle Samuel's legacy to them. It was decided that the best course of action was to sell all the property and divide the cash proceeds in thirds. Later this same year, on June 22, Joachim signed a power of attorney appointing Thomas L. Bayne as his representative because he "was going to be absent a long time in Paris."

There was so much property to sell that Joachim and Carl had preprinted forms prepared They were among the first to do so in the city at a time when most records were still hand written. These forms were ready for filling in the blanks with property descriptions, purchaser, date and the dollar amount of the sale. This surely means there was more property than Samuel's will inventory suggests. Furthermore, there is no doubt that Joachim and Carl were engaged in many other real estate deals during the pre-Civil War years. Many buildings still stand today that the Kohns had a hand in developing or maintaining.

After 1854 Joachim traveled back and forth between New Orleans and Paris frequently. He died in Paris in 1886. No obituary appeared in the New Orleans papers. There is a portrait of him at the Louisiana State Museum in New Orleans. It shows a very distinguished, even serious businessman of the period, yet with a sly smile of content under eyes that seem to reflect a worldly experience.

Carl Kohn

Carl Kohn's obituary in the New Orleans Times-Picayune of August 28th, 1895, was a lengthy and flowery affair replete with a drawn picture of him. The picture shows him in the style of his day; he had a big a mustache and hair parted in the middle. It appears to be a picture of him in his prime. The obituary bore the headline "The Death of a Prominent Louisiana Financier." He died at his "cottage" at Pass Christian, Mississippi; this was actually a rather large house. At his bedside was his only child, a daughter identified in the obituary as only the "wife" of Mr. Victor Meyer. Her name was Eveline. His "beloved wife Clara had died some years previously." Carl cut his own path through New Orleans business and society but he definitely had the help of his wealthy and well-placed Uncle Samuel at the start of his career. He was extolled as an exemplary man of the "finest character."

Carl was the son of another of Samuel's brothers. He was born at Horany, Bohemia, in 1814. The obituary states that he "received his early education in the excellent schools of his native country." His Uncle Samuel arranged his voyage to New Orleans in 1834 when he was just 17 years old. He traveled with his Uncle Joachim on the ship "Charles Carroll." He spent his first weeks in the New World on vacation with Samuel and Joachim at Bay St. Louis, Mississippi. When he came back to the city he quickly got a job and joined fine society. He first went to work for John A Merle & Company in 1835 on a low rung of the corporate ladder. But he was wealthy enough to take regular vacations at Bay St. Louis. Samuel seems to have rented a house each season and Carl was following in his uncle's footsteps. After a few short months at Merle he joined his Uncle Joachim in a business venture.

In 1837 he organized his own firm, Kohn, Doran & Company. It can be assumed that his Uncle Samuel made a big investment in the new venture. The firm was heavily involved in trade with Mexico. Carl traveled often to Mexico City to bolster the firm's business connections and for a while was quite successful. In 1839 he was elected to the board of the Atlantic Insurance Company. This was not his only such position. During the panic of 1842, however, Kohn, Doran suffered enough to be dissolved. Yet active business continued to call to him and that same year he formed a partnership with Henry Legendre, a money broker. In 1845 he went into business with Julian Neville importing western grown produce to the eastern part of the country. Neville died three years later and Kohn continued on his own.

Over the years since his arrival he became proficient at French, Spanish and English, became comfortable with firearms and learned to play the flute. After several flirtatious courtships with woman from the finer families of New Orleans in 1849 he returned to Bohemia for nearly six months. Upon his return to New Orleans he married Clara White on June 27, 1850. She was the daughter of Mansuel White. White was a major sugar planter and political figure in early Louisiana. The relationship certainly started before his big trip and one wonders if his future father-in-law was not happy with the idea of his very Catholic daughter marrying a Jewish man from a little known place. However, her constant pining for Carl convinced White to give his permission. They were married in St. Louis Cathedral. Like his Uncle Joachim he received special dispensation for a mixed marriage. From the beginning of his time in New Orleans he traveled in high society and from his surviving letters it is evident that he was acquainted with nearly every major family of the time. By the early 1850s he was working in his father-in-law's cotton commission business.

In 1855 he made another extensive trip to Europe. He went first to Paris to take care of his late uncle's affairs and then to Bohemia. It is not knwn if Clara accompanied him. When he returned from this trip he went into the sugar and molasses business with Cornelius Ryan. Ryan died just three years into the new business and Carl carried on the business by himself until he joined the Union Bank.

In 1861 Carl was a sugar broker and commission merchant with an office at 137 St. Charles Street. He and Clara kept their residence at 20 Bienville Street. This was a few blocks from the Mississippi River in the French Quarter. It was the eve of the Civil War and Carl was doing well. He and his wellborn wife traveled among the planter aristocracy that made New Orleans one of the wealthiest cities in the country. He most likely went to visit many of the plantations that are a well documented part of Louisiana's history. He had the money to give his own lavish entertainments. He apparently still had some vestiges of his Bohemian accent according to some reports of his contemporaries.

Despite the turmoil that the war inflicted on New Orleans the 1866 city directory presents the same information on Joachim and Carl as in 1861. It seems then that they made it through the Civil War relatively intact. Though Carl's obituary does note that he suffered the "deprivations and reduced business of the war years" like everyone else in the city. He was exempted from service in the Confederate Army. He was, though, inducted into the Orleans Guards Regiment of the Louisiana military as a private in Company D of the so-called Home Guard. He never saw any active service. It also appears that he was not committed to the Southern Cause and he probably conducted business with any and all comers during the turbulent war and occupation years.

His father-in-law died in 1866 and he lost his mother-in-law in 1867. So these were years of some melancholy. He was appointed as executor of both wills. His obituary notes that he discharged his duties "without legal intervention, to the entire satisfaction of the heirs." By 1870 Carl made his office at 20 Bienville Street, his former residence. His occupation was "Commission merchant." He and his wife had moved to their new residence on St. Charles Avenue at the corner of Julia Street, where they were to live to the end of their lives. Whether he built this house or bought an existing structure is not clear from the known record. The original address of the house was 191 St. Charles Street. After the house numbering system in New Orleans underwent at the end of the century the address became 759 St. Charles. The building is no longer standing.

He became president of the Union Bank in 1871 and quickly set about getting it a national charter. The bank was quickly renamed the Union National Bank. Carl was to remain president almost to his death. He retired in 1894. The bank's offices were first at 3 Carondelet Street. It was a bank known all across the United States as a major financial house. It also acted as the agent for many European companies doing business in America. The bank surely took advantage of the new technology of the telegraph. He was very successful in this venture and made a lot of money. Indeed, he became one of New Orleans' wealthiest citizens.

In 1879 the Soard's Directory for New Orleans printed a half page advertisement for the Union National Bank. The ad has Carl Kohn's name and title as president prominently under the name and address of the bank. Stephen Caloron was named as the only "Cashier." The names of the ten directors of the bank are small under the large word and number: "CAPITAL—$250,000." The bank did a bit of marketing, having "discount days" on Tuesday and Friday of each week. The ad also points out that the bank was "Exchange on New York, London and Paris." This was a day of small, privately run banks that relied on the personal contacts among men who needed financing for deals that came along at irregular intervals and the men who had the means to gather large sums of cash on a moment's notice. By 1888 the ads were stating the bank had "$500,000 in capital and a $100,000 surplus." Doubling the size of the bank in ten years was a sign of Carl's business sense. By this time the bank's offices had moved to 36 Carondelet.

On December 2nd, 1881, Clara Kohn died at the plantation of her brother Mansuel White Jr.'s; it was named "Junior Place." The plantation was not far out into Plaquemine Parish and down river from the city. Her obituary in the Times—Picayune is very brief mentioning only her death. It does not even mention her daughter.

During his entire career Carl was involved with civic and charitable events. Though he never ran for political office there was some pressure on him to do so from his wide circle of business and personal friends and acquaintances. He did serve for many years on the city's Board of Liquidation for city debts. He was also a member of the exclusive Boston Club and was one of the few Jews admitted. He was a vice-president of the Clearing House as well as a visiting member of the Cotton Exchange and other merchantile exchanges in the city.

He probably knew another Bohemian, Joseph Frankenbush, who was also involved in civic and business affairs, particularly the Cotton Exchange. And he probably knew Michael Porkorny, a downtown merchant and landlord originally from Moravia. Whether they shared a few words in the old language can only be speculated. Carl's obituary laments that he never wrote a memoir setting down his interesting life at the top of the commercial world of New Orleans for more than 50 years; indeed that would have been invaluable.

But he did leave a letter book, a common method of keeping track of correspondence in his day. There are 21 copies of letters comprising more than 100 pages of text that he sent to his uncle Samuel in Paris. This bound book of letters is in the possession of the Historic New Orleans Collection (HNOC). Most of them are in English, though a few are in French. They are quite detailed on Carl's life and reflect the social conditions of his time as well as offer political commentary on the events between 1832 and 1833. They were often written just days apart. They are often quoted by students of this period since they are one of the largest collections of surviving correspondence from this time in Louisiana's history. Carl Kohn is, however, misidentified by the HNOC as coming from Bavaria instead of Bohemia despite the fact that in letter after letter he mentions his "relatives in Bohemia."

These letters show that he was present at an endless series of parties and social gatherings. He also kept track of the political situation of the time, especially the election of President Jackson. He was also concerned with the epidemics which raged through the city. In all of his endeavors Carl Kohn could certainly be said to have been a success. It is the proverbial rags to riches story of which historians of America's immigrants are so fond.

Joachim and Carl were not wholly wrapped up in business affairs. They maintained lively personal friendships with others of their class. They served as godparents to more than a few children. Many of these friends were among New Orleans' earliest Jews. Carl and Joachim served as executors of the wills of their fellow Jews and carried out their duties responsibly. They also helped raise money for the victims of this or that disaster and for the orphans of the epidemics which raged through the city. Being so successful of course meant they were well known. Their reputations as highly regarded generous men were well earned.

The historian Bertrand Korn goes into great detail about the interweaving of families in the Jewish community in New Orleans during the pre-Civil War era and Joachim and Carl are frequently mentioned. The two of them were not very religions however. They contributed funds to different synagogues and Jewish charities with no clear allegience to any. Carl mentions the problems Jews had in Bohemia in some of his letters to his Uncle Samuel and compares that to the freedom he experiences in New Orleans. He laments the oppression that the remaining Kohn family still faced in Bohemia. Like many educated people from Bohemia Joachim and Carl had a Freethinking way of looking at religion. They took the parts that were convenient, such as their Catholic wedding ceremonies, and kept parts of their old faith that did not require too many sacrifices from their business and social pursuits. They believed in God and Providence as if success for them was preordained. But they had no time to get involved in the actual practice of religious belief.

So the three members of the Kohn family from the little village of Horany, and Gustave, born in New Orleans, each made their contribution to New Orleans. They were big players in the social and business scenes of their times. They were intimately involved with the plantation econ omy and the related bank ing and the shipping industries. Yet, despite this I found no evidence that any of the Kohns were involved in the burgeoning slave trade that permeated New Orleans before the Civil War. Nor did they own slaves. This trade was no doubt distasteful for Bohemian Jews who knew what oppression was all about. Instead, they seemed to be forever involved in some charitable affair benefiting the poor of society. But they also left some tangible evidence of their contributions that live on today in the streets of Carrollton and the street car system that we enjoy today. Czechs came to be connected with the street car 150 years later, about which more later.

Benjamin Latrobe

Benjamin Latrobe was one of America's most important architects and there are many excellent biographies of him. These biograpies do not dwell much on his ethnicity but this is the very reason he is included here for he was part ethnically Moravian and thus Czech. He was the initial architect for the United States Cap ital and the White House. He helped bring the federal style to American architec ture. His son, also named Benjamin, followed him into the architectural and engineering professions. Together they built public works and buildings and pri vate residences in many places. In all of this they relied on the education they received and were aided by the precepts of the teachings of the Moravian Church. They were to have a lasting impact on New Orleans as well as end their lives there.

Latrobe and his son were instrumental in building the water systems that both protected the city of New Orleans from the river, lake and swamps that surround it and provided its drinking water. Many of the works they built are still surviv ing, merged into an ever more sophisticated system. Benjamin Latrobe also designed and supervised the building of New Orleans' first Federal Custom House in 1807, since torn down. Beginning in 1811 he accepted a contract from the New Orleans City Council to build a waterworks. His contract was renewed every two years until his death. In 1820 his design for the Louisiana State Bank was accepted. This building is now a restaurant on Royal Street in the French Quarter; it was the last building he was to design.

He was descended from a mother who was from the Pennsylvania Moravian community and a father who was a minister of the Moravian Church. The Moravians first settled Pennsylvania in the late 1600s. At this time they nearly were all ethnically Moravian. They were seeking religious freedom in William Penn's colony. Latrobe's mother was a third generation descendent of these original settlers. She was from an old line Americanized family. Yet, there is no doubt that she was of pure Moravian stock. Latrobe's father was descended from French Huguenots, or Protestants, who had escaped France and settled in England. The Moravians had a school at a town called Fulneck, north of London, where many Moravian children went to study according to the educational and spiritual doctrines of the church. Fulnek is also the name of town in Moravia which was the inspiration for the English town of the same name. It was here that Latrobe's parents met and married. He was born shortly thereafter on May 1, 1764, at Leeds, England.

He was sent to the Moravian School at Niesky in Silesia in what is now southeastern Germany. Latrobe arrived at this school in 1776 when he was a young teenager. He was there for a number of years pursuing both theological and practical studies. By 1782 he was in another Moravian school, also in Silesia, on the Czech border. It was here that had more practical experience with the building trades. There is evidence that he apprenticed for short times with various trades. He was, however, deemed unfit for the ministry and he returned to Fulneck. Whether he ever went to Moravia, birthplace of the church, or to Prague, is not known, but they were just a short trip away from the schools. The architecture of the area, however, seems to have had an opposite influence on him. The region is filled with the asymmetry of village houses and Medieval castles as well as the ostentatiousness of palaces built during the Renaissance, Baroque and Rococo eras. The Federal style to which he was to become connected had no place in central Europe.

He returned to England in 1784 and became employed in the Stamp Office. Soon thereafter he became an apprentice of the eminent British architect C.R. Cockerell. In the early 1790s he entered private practice and built a grand country residence in Sussex, England called Hammerwood Park in 1792. This was his first independent work. In 1793 he was the architect for Ashdown House, another large country estate, which was built nearby to Hammerwood. Both houses still stand. He was married during these years but his first wife, Lydia, died in childbirth. She was also a member of the Moravian church. At some point he decided to come to America. He may have inherited some property in the Pennsylvania Moravian settlements from his mother which could have spurred on the move. He arrived in Norfolk, Virginia, on March 20, 1796, at the age of 31.

By 1802 he was designing buildings at Princeton University in New Jersey and became almost instantly recognized as a major architect and designer of homes and government buildings. In 1803 he was asked by President Thomas Jefferson to help design Washington D.C., including the Capital and the White House. Latrobe arrived in New Orleans by 1807 and set to work in sorting out the problems the city faced with its watery environment. He also helped build a better jetty system at the mouth of the Mississippi River enabling more shipping.

He was coming and going from New Orleans attending to his contract and by this time his son, Bejamin Latrobe Jr. was working at his side. The son died of yellow fever in 1817 in New Orleans. The father was not in New Orleans when the sad event occurred; he was at work on other projects and he had left his son in charge of the enterprise in the city. This fact indicates that the son was well educated and had a keen mind. The New Orleans project was a major engineering work. It has been said that without the water protection plan initiated by the Latrobe's New Orleans would not have grown into the city it was to become.

The senior Latrobe came back to New Orleans to finish the work his son had started on several civil engineering works. Despite the tragic event he delved into the completion of the city's water supply and levee system. He also found the time to design and oversee the building of the tower and steeple of St. Louis Cathedral in the French Quarter. This cathedral is the very emblem of New Orleans. He, too, died of yellow fever in New Orleans, succumbing on September 3, 1820. Later we will encounter another major Louisiana architect and engineer who was half Czech. But this Moravian deserves a special place of thanks for straightening out the watery mess in Louisiana's largest city and helping to create the cathedral that no resident or visitor to the city can miss. No history of Louisiana bothers to mention Latrobe's Moravian heritage.

The Pokorny Family

The earliest definite reference we have of Michael Pokorny is in an 1861 city directory where the single line "M. Pokorny, shoemaker, 170 Rampart" appears. He was to establish a long lasting family in the affairs of New Orleans, one that lasts to this day. Nearly 80 out of approximately 150 living descendants recently had its first family reunion in New Orleans. They visited the Tulane University

Manuscript Department where the Pokorny Family Papers are kept. The papers cover the years 1851–1957, with the majority from 1915–1945. The approximately 200 items document the estate of Michael Pokorny and his emigration from Moravia to the United States, his shoe store and real estate businesses in New Orleans. There are many minutes of the family meetings which are filled with mundane details. It is odd to see what was saved and to lament what was thrown out. These few papers, occupying .04 feet in linear archival space, are all we have of this illustrious family in the public record. Two members of this family provided other materials for me to examine.

Michael immigrated from Jihlava, also known by its German name Iglau. It is one of the larger cities in Moravia. He was the second oldest son born to a Jewish family. He was born in 1828 at Puklice (Puklitz) a small village on the outskirts of Jihlava. We think of that as such a long time ago. Consider this though: Jihlava was laid out according to a building code issued by King Ottokar II in 1270. Over the centuries facades were altered to fit the fashions of the time and there was an all-consuming fire in May of 1523. Yet, one thing stayed constant and that was the 36,653 square meter town square. In American terms this is about 40,000 square yards and it is one of the largest in the Czech Republic. Jihlava's population is no larger than 100,000 today. The name of the city roughly translates as the "Southern Main City." Pokorny itself is a surname that both Jews and Christians had and is a fairly common Czech last name.

He left Jihlava to pursue a better life. Jews were circumscribed by Austria's so-called "family laws" that offered marriage rights to only the oldest son. The goal was to keep the admitted population of Jews low. This, of course, did not stop couples from pairing off. Contemplate the lousy situation Michael's sister, Johanna, faced. She had children with Mathias Epstein but they were considered bastards by the state because there could be no legal marriage. Michael, not being the oldest son, faced a similar situation. Not pleased with his prospects he first went to Vienna were he learned the shoemaking trade. It was perhaps as early as 1846 when he took an apprenticeship. With bleak fortunes there he left and went to Budapest, Hungary. It was there that he got married to Fanny Singer in January of 1853. Family history has it that he and his wife Fanny came to the United States in 1856 or 1857, arriving at New York, and got to New Orleans in 1860. They had a young son in tow. There is no evidence of any speical reason that Michael had for moving to New Orleans other than that he might have heard about the booming city and discounted or was not aware of the threat of the war to come.

How soon he learned English we do not know but soon after his arrival in New Orleans he had a shoe store. We do not know where he got the money to start such a venture. No matter, soon the Civil War broke out. We can only speculate what he knew or thought about the war. But he did go to Camp Moore near the city and made boots for the Confederacy. The paper dollars he was probably paid with were to become worthless in just a short while for soon thereafter, in 1862, the Yankees took the city. Afterward he served many a Yankee officer buying new handmade boots. There is every indication that he kept up the shoe business to support his growing family during the occupation.

During Reconstruction Michael and his two young sons, John and David, worked at expanding the shoe business. They opened stores on both Poydras and Royal Streets as well as the flagship store on St. Charles Avenue. This period also saw the beginnings of the Pokorny real estate empire. Ultimately they became one of the largest land owners in downtown New Orleans and there is hardly a street that did not see a Pokorny owned building. Some were existing structures; others they built themselves. Brad Fanta, a great-great grandson of Michael Pokorny, tells me that "for fifty years, the family owned the properties at three of the corners at Canal and Carondelet Streets, as well as a third of the properties on St. Charles Avenue between Canal and Poydras, including the Liberty Theater."

Michael's daughter Bertha was issued a marriage certificate on January 24, 1876; her husband to be was Benjamin Kamien. Three years later his second daughter, Anna, received her marriage license to be married to Alex M. Haas. By 1879 David was a clerk in his father's shoe store. His residence must have been above the store for it was the same address as the business: 103 St. Charles Avenue. The 1888 city directory states that David was only a "clerk," but he actually had the more important position of being the boss's son. His brother John was also a clerk at the store. They both now lived at 358 South Rampart Street. Michael was in the "boots and shoes" business at 20 & 28 St. Charles; he too made his residence at the house on South Rampart.

In 1889 Michael Pokorny bought the entire block bordered by St. Charles and Camp all the way to Common. He also bought Numbers 20 and 22 St. Charles. He bought them from the Beer Family for $54,000. He paid $30,000 in cash and made three promissory notes for $8,000 each. Their riches growing Michael thought he and his family deserved a better home. So in 1897 he bought one of the finest in the city. The Charles Howard mansion was built in 1875 and featured an elevator. Another claim to fame is that the house is commonly credited with having the city's first indoor plumbing. The address was 2113 St. Charles Avenue and family members occupied the house until it was torn down in the 1930s. His succession lists six buildings that he owned in downtown New Orleans, the big house up on St. Charles Avenue and a house on Chestnut, but hidden in the notarial archives are the records for many more property transactions.

Besides selling shoes made by other manufacturers the Pokorny shop engaged in making specialty shoes. An article in the *Daily Picayune* on January 6, 1893, proudly reports that a boxer named Andy Bowen wore shoes "made by M. Pokorny." It is probable that the firm made shoes for other boxers and practitioners of other sports. This was a time of very specialized footwear, with strict social rules about what shoe was appropriate. There were no sneakers as we known them today.

In 1897 the Underwriters Inspection Bureau of New Orleans street rate slips show that "on the Lake Side of South Rampart Street," there were two houses owned by Michael Pokorny. They were later numbered 1131 and 1135 South Rampart. These are near the corner of Esplanade Avenue in the Old Treme neighborhood. Both were 2 bedroom singles. At the rear of 1135 was a "Storage [building] of Trunks & Stable." These houses do not survive.

In a pre-death business maneuver, on the 11th of May, 1901, Michael Pokorny had M. Pokorny Shoes at 124 St. Charles and the Regent Shoe Store at 105 Royal Street dissolved. $20,000 was allocated to each child and the shoe stores and property were made into a family business that is now in its fifth generation. The paperwork notes *"Michael Pokorny, being blind and largely incapacitated from looking after the business of the firm and John and David Pokorny shall have active management consulting with Michael Pokorny in all Matters."* Michael was very old at this point and had been debilitated for a long time. Yet he was so active in his business nearly to the end that he was obviously loath to give up control. What his sons and other family members thought of this control is not known.

In 1902 we know that they employed 12 people in their store. J.A. Abbot was paid $1,800 a month as sales manager. The other salesmen were paid lesser amounts, Norman Mohr received $1,200. Philip Reich earned $1,500. Alfred Betzer earned just $700. James Quirk earned just $600. Whether these were commission salaries is not recorded. Charles Ebert earned $600 as a stockhelper. John Williams was an office assistant earning $700. There was a "colored boy," with no name mentioned, who earned $350 as a porter; he must have been the head porter because there were two other African-American porters earning $250 each. There was a man named Bonec, who was a "shoefitter" earning $1,200 and there was an Italian man named Busciani who was a shoe repairman earning $700. At the other store were Oscar Wintell at $500, Rosneo $700, Henry, $600,

Sam Goldman, $1,500, all salesman, and Quintano for $1,200 and John Acheson $900. No duties were listed for these last two. Why these salesman made less than those at the other store can only be imagined. This was the only detailed payroll saved in the papers. But the Pokornys were definitely paying wages higher than the prevailing wages of the time almost as if Michael was making up for his own poor early situation.

Both Michael Pokorny and Fanny Pokorny had their wills filed on June 12, 1902, according to an article in the New Orleans newspaper *Daily States*. This was when Fanny died. We can learn a lot about the man Michael from his obituary in the June 5, 1903, New Orleans *Times Picayune*. Yet despite his fame and fortune his surname was misspelled throughout the entire piece as "Pokorney." Even the sign hanging over the store on St. Charles Street which the reporter had to have seen read Pokorny. Why the glaring error can only be a matter of supposition.

An extensive excerpt is warranted for no Czech in the state received such a flowery and complimentary life's summation:

> *"He Became One of the City's Leading Men; Afflicted by Blindness, His Undaunted Spirit Achieved Success, Besides Helping Many Others, M. Pokorney is dead. Nearly every one in the city knew him, as he had lived in this city so many years and been prominent as a businessman and in Jewish circles.*
>
> *Mr. Pokorney died yesterday afternoon about 2 o'clock. He has been an invalid for twenty years, but of late had been growing very feeble, and his death was not altogether unexpected, although it was hoped that he might live for some time.*
>
> *Besides having lost his sight by a severe spell of illness in 1863 and 1864, he was crippled and unable to walk, and was wheeled about for years. He was in the habit of many years of visiting his stores, and the old man sitting in the St. Charles Street doorway was a familiar figure to every one. More recently, however, he has been unable to go downtown, and very recently has been confined entirely to bed."*

And:

> *"The first of April last, Mrs. Pokorney died. This was a severe blow to the old gentleman, for she had been his constant companion through all his blindness and illness. With her he had been in the habit of going away on his summer trips, sometimes to the eastern summer places, and sometimes to Europe, the later place his destination almost every year. They were always accompanied by faithful servants, who cared for the old gentleman, and though he could not see, he liked to*

make the acquaintance of people, and was a very pleasant conversationalist, and a very well informed man, because though he traveled so much, that though he did not see the beauties of nature, he knew about people and places for that accurate manner which the blind always acquire."

Another excerpt reads:

"During all the years of his blindness and lameness, Mr. Pokorney bore his lot with cheerfulness and was always in a good humor and full of hope. He was never in this life discouraged by his difficulties or disappointments. Previous to his illness, he had been through many vicissitudes but had overcome all difficulties with his quiet determination.

Mr. Pokorney never held any public position, but devoted himself entirely to business, and had it not been for his personal misfortune, would no doubt have become one of the most celebrated businessmen in this country, for as it was, he accomplished marvels, having begun as a poor shoemaker, though a good one, and acquired a position as one of the leading businessmen of the city, and that with twenty years of blindness, very few men having been able to accomplish so much."

The obituary further notes that at the time of his death all seven of his children were living, "who are his only close relatives." John and David lived in New Orleans as did four of their sisters, "Mrs. B.J. Kamien, Mrs. A.M. Haas, Mrs. M. D. Levy, Mrs. Coleman E. Adler, of this city." The last sister, Mrs. Julius Goldstein, lived in Mobile. The final line of the notice is *"He was a wonderful man in every way, and will leave his imprint on the city's usefulness and the city's progress."*

In July, 1902, M. Pokorny & Sons "carried on" at 124, 224 and 314 St. Charles Avenue and also at 105 Royal. The firm had a net value after debts and obligation of $72,743.80. "David Pokorny as President, John as Sect. Treas. and Benjamin K. Kamien as Clerk shall each earn $150 per month," reads one memo in the papers. Their promotional materials bore the legend "Cordwainers since 1860" They were now in business nearly 50 years and there were few New Orleanians who did not have occasion to shop at this humble Czech shoemaker's business.

During the late 1890s to the early 1900s some of the Pokorny's lived uptown. 2333 Chestnut Street was the home of Mrs. D. Pokorny and her husband David. It had two bedrooms and a front salon and was not that elaborate. Up the block at 2425 Chestnut in a similar house lived "M. Pokorny." This must be Michael, who lived alone while members of his growing family lived in the house of St.

Charles with grandchildren. In 1907 the Pokornys subleased out a building they owned at 1013 Canal Street. No rent was listed. They were, however, receiving $300 a month from the "widow Apon" for 105 Royal Street. They had a lease for the store at 312 and 314 St. Charles Avenue. It ran from October 1, 1908, to September, 1913, for $250 a month; They rented the entire four story building, using the upper floors for storage and offices. During this same time they had to ask the attorneys Rise and Montgomery "to effect collection from Doctors S. and D. Davidson for the rent of the upper floors of 1013 Canal Street."

John Pokorny's obituary in the New Orleans Times-Picayune on Sunday, February 21st, 1915, shows a man who achieved the same heights as his father in the social and business world. His obituary, too, bears extensive excerpts. His actions had affected New Orleans since the start of his business career.

> *"Cold Contracted Last Sunday Develops Into Pneumonia and Causes Death,"* it reads, *"John Pokorny died for his friends, just as he lived for them. He was not feeling well last Sunday, but a number of his friends were here for the Carnival, and he deemed it the duty of hospitality to show them special attention. So he insisted in venturing out in the rain, remained out all day in damp clothing, and contracted a cold. By the time he went to bed that night he was very ill, pneumonia developed despite the best medical skill and the most careful nursing, and early Saturday morning he died. He was always so strong, so genial, so unmindful of self, that his family could scarcely realize that he was no more, and the community to which he had endeared himself will be equally shocked at the news of his death.*
>
> *Mr. Pokorny was the oldest member of the family which has won wealth and prominence here. He was born in Budapest, Hungary, Nov. 12, 1853, and came here with his parents in 1860. All his life he had a keen desire to revisit his birthplace, but something always interfered. Last year, as if by providential urging, he decided to delay no longer, and he and his wife set out for Europe. He was in the ancestral home on the very day that Austria declared war on Serbia, and witnessed the first stirring scenes of the world tragedy before he was compelled to leave while the road to America still was open. But the dawning woe made deep impress upon him, and almost his last words recalled some of the pictures that had touched his heart.*
>
> *The history of the Pokornys is well known from the day when the father, the late M. Pokorny, established a small shoe store in St. Charles street, almost opposite the Orpheum, until they conducted half a dozen prosperous stores and owned some of the finest homes and commercial properties in the city. John Pokorny did*

his full share in building the family fortunes. He attended the Marshall school, and then went into the shoe business, aiding in its expansion, and for years had charge of the store on Royal street, near Canal. Although faithful to his business, he found time for useful citizenship and for broad humanity. He contributed to many good causes, and was a member of every Jewish charitable organization, in addition to Temple Sinai, the Young Men's Hebrew Association and the B'nai B'rith. He was an Elk and a Pythian. His main recreation was fishing and hunting, and he was not only among the first member of the Tallyho Club, but spent many happy days among equally ardent sportsmen there.

In 1885 Mr. Pokorny married Miss Clara Markstein of Mobile, and the union proved ideal, the pair remaining lovers to the last with no children to divide their rare affection."

None of the other Pokornys were to receive such glowing notices of their life's achievements. Though David's obituary is also quite substantial. It is obvious that these three, Michael and his sons John and David, had a significant impact on the development of downtown New Orleans. It is probable that they knew all the great men of the city at the time. They almost certainly had to know Carl Kohn and Jacob Frankenbush, two other prominent Bohemians in their midst. They all traveled in the same financial and social circles for many decades in New Orleans. Yet, there is no direct evidence for this.

Starting in 1915 and continuing through 1949 the Pokorny company bought significant amounts of advertising space in the New Orleans Times-Picayune. The amounts are listed in agate lines which was the common measurement at the time for column inches. It ranged from 25,000 agate lines in 1923 to as little as 5,000 agate lines in the depths of the Depression in 1933. Nearly every New Orleanian had opportunity to see the ads in the daily paper. Indeed, the stores were advertised daily and it would have been nearly impossible to miss them.

On December 2, 1916, Michael's daughter was elected president of the family organization. Meetings were held at the family home on St. Charles. They had their own seal which they crimped on to various letters and papers. They bought liberty bonds and "war savings certificates," in 1916. One of the Pokorny stores was at 109 St. Charles Avenue at this time. On August 25, 1917, the family sold their property at 224 St. Charles Street to the Whitney Central National Bank for $125,000. The Whitney Bank tower we know now in downtown New Orleans was built on this site. On June 5, 1919, they rented 120 St. Charles to Nathan Triven & Bros. for $550 a month; this building still stands.

We know a little about them in the years before the Depression struck. In the 1919 city directory we find that "Mrs. David Pokorny," was listed as president of M. Pokorny & Sons, which managed the family's real estate holdings. She lived in the St. Charles Avenue house. Mrs. John Pokorny also lived at this large house. Her brother-in-law, Ralph D. Levey, was secretary treasurer of the family corporation and whose office was listed as 124 St. Charles Avenue. 1920 saw them selling 1401 and 1403 Baronne Street for $6,250. Bernstein Glenny Buick rented 822–826 Howard Avenue for $275 a month and the right to build two more stories on the structure from the family. In one of the few solid records of charitable efforts that we have they donated a $50 bond to the Tulane Endowment fund on June 22, 1920. On April 28, 1921, Coleman Adler, Michael's son-in-law, rented the St. Charles residence for $225 a month until it was sold. That took nearly ten years. The combined company brought in $14,940 in rents during 1922.

Coleman Adler deserves special mention in our story and presents an odd coincidence. His dates were 1868 to 1938. He was born in Kosice, Slovakia, and came to America before he was 20. In 1897 he married Rosa Pokorny, Michael's youngest daughter. Their first introduction probably came within the confines of their Jewish background rather than as fellow Czechs and Slovaks. Michael set up his new son-in-law in a jewelry store. From this well seeded start up comes the Adler's Jewelry chain with stores across the South. Coleman Adler II, a grandson, today owns the former Louisiana National Bank Building that Benjamin Latrobe, the first Moravian in New Orleans, built.

In more mundane matters there was a letter, dated August 1, 1922, from the Johnson and Murphy Shoe company that severs a "relationship of long-standing due to the insufficient business." The Pokornys reply of August 16 says "for the last quarter century, which have always been pleasing and satisfactory," the two had beneficial business relations and goes on to say that the whole thing leaves "a little bitter experience." In 1924 Pokorny & Sons hired Leon E. Ber for $5,000 a year to manage the stores. That same year Charles Wenar sued M Pokorny, Ltd. for work performed and not paid for and won his judgment of $375 with costs. This was one of the few law suits that the Pokornys were involved with. In 1924 they rented out 116 St. Charles to Mayer the Hatter who is still in the same space today for 5 years at $7,500 a year. In 1925 the family rented out the top 2 floors of their building at St. Charles and Gravier Streets to the Louisiana Club; the rent was $310 per month and was to run for 10 years. They rented the Howard Avenue property to Glenny Buick company in 1926. On June 7, 1926, the family arrived at a plan to construct a building on the St. Charles property with a net lease of $15,000 a year for 99 years with revaluation every 10 years to set increases in the rent. What was built became the Avenue Hotel. It took another ten years to get the hotel built.

On September 13, 1929, the family wrote a letter to the Louisiana Club giving permission for a Mardi Gras "gallery along your St. Charles Street Frontage during Carnival time, providing not before Wednesday preceding Mardi Gras." This was prime viewing space for the parades during carnival. On June 29, 1927, the family purchased the property between St. Charles, Gravier, Camp and Poydras Streets for $142,000; it was divided into seven portions. The family members also had their individual investments. For example "Mrs. Dave Pokorny personally had five 1,000 dollar notes of the Packard New Orleans Company at 1705 St. Charles" according to a note in the family meeting minutes of January 4, 1928. There was also a $5,000 note with Victor Kiam on property at 2104 Canal Street, presumably a mortgage.

In 1929 the company had revenues of $249,402.60 and had a payroll of $6,000. The next year saw sales rise about $7,000. Salaries remained the same. Then the Depression hit. Sales fell to only $200,891.62 in 1931. The payroll still stayed the same, however. On January 29, 1932, at a family meeting, they all agreed that "some temporary modification of rents were suggested for certain tenants until economic conditions became more favorable." And well they should, because in 1932 sales were down to $145,037.76. They reduced salaries by only 250 dollars, to $5,750. On March 10, 1930 the Pokorny company agreed to join a group of civic leaders headed by Ralph Terny to give then Mayor Walmsley a Pierce Arrow car; this was one of the very finest automobiles at the time.

In 1932 they were delinquent on 2 property taxes which they were working to resolve. No numbers or property were given in the notes of the family meeting. This is the only indication that the Depression severely impacted the family fortunes. There is mention of an iron safe in the big house where important family papers were most likely kept. There were two insurance policies, one of $7,500 and one of $5,000 that were taken out by Ralph Levey. There was the odd situation of one share with the par value of $100 in New Orleans Chair Company belonging to David Pokorny; he paid $16 for it. Perhaps he bought it from the man who made the many chairs they needed for the shoe stores. They also owned five lots in Slidell about which nothing more is known.

In January, 1932, they acquired the property at the corner of Canal and Carondelet and they rented the 828–832 Howard Avenue property to Lyons Benton Motor Company. This was the third car dealership on this property. From 1933 to 1936 sales hovered just above $100.000; half what they were just a few years previously. Combined salaries were never more than $4,000 during these years.

The four years encompassing 1937 through 1940 saw a steady up-tick in sales, rising to $145,000 by 1940. The war years were good and sales rose from $187,000 in 1941 to $362,000 by 1943. Salaries paid rose from $4,800 to $10,000 in these same four years. Whether they sold shoes they made to the military is unknown; we know they did it 70 years earlier.

The most complete accounting of the property they owned was taken on May 25, 1936, and was recorded at a family meeting. They owned 300–314 St. Charles Street which they rented out to the real estate company Latter & Blum. They rented out 636–64 Gravier Street to Leo Fellin & Co, Realtors. The 3 story brick building at 116 St. Charles was worth $45,000, as was the building at 120 St. Charles. They owned nearly the entire block front from 438 to 440 to 448 St. Charles. This was a series of 4 story brick buildings. They were each worth $35,000. They owned the 3 story brick buildings at 822–826 Howard; long rented to car dealerships and worth $35,000. The house on St. Charles was valued at $40,000. They owned 132–40 St. Charles. This was worth $110,000. They also owned 316–18 St. Charles; worth $50,000. At 420–22 St. Charles was the Liberty Theater building which was worth $40,000. They also had 405–407 St. Charles Avenue; worth $15,000. Along South Rampart Street they owned the 2 story brick buildings at 308–310 and 336–338, both were worth $20,000. And they owned 814–816 Howard Avenue which was worth $30,000. This is about $400,000 worth of real estate. Even today they would be considered major landowners in the city.

Semiannual family meetings were held over the decades and things went smoothly. The minutes contain very little action. Mostly they say the rents were collected and the taxes paid. Various family members were present or submitted proxies in writing. One interesting fact was that the men acted for the women. Even though it was Michael's daughters who owned the property that he left them it was the sons-in-law who are shown making the decisions and signing the documents and being at the family meetings "acting for" this or that of the sisters. On June 27, 1941, we have the first hint of dissension in the family. We learn that the sisters "no longer desire to remain owners in indivision of said properties but they desire amicably to divide and partition the same amongst themselves." They were apparently talked out of this.

In 1941 the stores employed 18 people, 28 in 1942 and 31 in 1943. But salaries were controlled by an agency called the wartime Salary Stabilization Unit. This information is all from an "employer's application for approval of salary rated for new position" filed by Ralph. On May 31, 1943, there was this self-congratulatory note in the family records: *To be able to gross nearly $400,000 dollars* *sales per annum with rationing of shoes and no change in set up, without the assistance of dept. heads of long training who are presently in the armed forces,"* shows a the business skills of all the children and spouses.

This was part of a plea by Ralph P Levey for salary "adjustments." He lived at one of the city's most fashionable addresses: 307 Audubon Blvd. One can imagine why he felt he deserved a higher salary. We have fiscal year sales from May 31, 1929, to May 31, 1943, and it shows a business that went through ups and downs. At one point Harold Levey was living at 311 Audubon Blvd. When he was approved for a salary increase on February 10, 1945, the war was still raging though victory seemed assured. He had asked for $3,000; he got just a tad more than half, $1,560. In an abrupt ending to war times the Pokornys received a letter from the Office of Price Administration, dated November 6, 1945, stating that "shoe rationing ended last Wednesday." Which was a good thing. For a fire had occurred on the morning of January 23, 1944. Lost and damaged was $1,314 in the stock of shoes and $429 in furniture and fixtures. The company was rebuilding and went on as before.

In 1949 they copyrighted shoe sachets with "created moisture absorbing and deodorizing compositions" as one of the unique aspects of their invention. Ralph Levey was charter member of the Cooperative Club of New Orleans, founded in March, 1950. Long time lawyers for the family were Montgomery, Barnett, Brown, Semins and Reed. They were needed for a suit against Pokorny and the manufacturer of a shoe polish. The suit was brought by a client who purchased "the can of Esquire shoe polish which burst into fire." We do not know the outcome of the suit. Though it shows an early used of the legal theory of suing those with deep pockets.

In all of this we find a well run family organization that managed to hold on for many decades the estate that their father created. There is hardly a visitor or resident of New Orleans who did not have a first hand look at the buildings owned by this family descended from a Moravian immigrant. Given the sales volume of the shoe stores it is obvious that many people reaped the benefits of the hard work Michael Pokorny put into his business. The shoe store is still in existence today and run by his descendants.

One other Pokorny we find in New Orleans in the 1880s was Joseph, a teacher, living at 329 South Liberty Street, though, he does not appear to be related to the Michael Pokorny family.

The Frankenbush Family

For more than 100 years the Frankenbush family has been in New Orleans. Their forefather Jacob Frankenbush came to the United States from Prague sometime in the 1850s. I have heard from some of the descendants of this man. He was a prominent businessman in New Orleans for many decades and was involved in political pursuits at least as a behind the scenes player. He was instrumental in both the so-called Uprising of 1874 and the founding of the New Orleans Cotton Exchange. In the record Jacob Frankenbush is first found in an 1860 Slave Schedule in Port Gibson, Claiborne County, Mississippi, though no mention of the number of slaves he may have owned survives. He is also found in the 1860 Federal Census in the same place. The 1866 Mississippi State Census Index for Claiborne County shows that Jacob Frankenbush had made it through the Civil War in one piece.

The New Orleans Cotton Exchange was initiated by a handful of men and soon grew to 100 members. They formed the exchange because they were conducting business outside on Carondelet Street and moving into nearby saloons during inclement weather. This was deemed unfitting to the growing wealth and prestige of these brokers. It was January, 1871, when 18 men gathered to create the New Orleans Cotton Exchange, Frankenbush among them. They rented themselves a fancy building. From February 6th through the 8th all of the members met and the exchange was formally organized. On February 20, 1871, the exchange held its first business. Edgar Degas was to paint one of his most famous paintings, entitled "Cotton Exchange," which depicts the nascent exchange, during his stay in New Orleans in the 1880s. Whether Frankenbush is in the painting cannot be determined.

During the second half of the 1870s Jacob's son, Joseph Warren, was a student at the Virginia Military Institute. None of the other Frankenbush boys were to attended this bastion of Southern Pride. He graduated in 1878, the 17th of 25 students. He was the roommate of Richard K. Boney and was later the best man at Boney's wedding. Boney was from Duckport Plantation in Madison Parish, Louisiana, and his diaries are well known historical documentation of the period. During his trips to New Orleans to meet Joseph he apparently half-heartedly courted both Bertha and Martha, Joseph's sisters. All three are mentioned throughout the social comings and goings of Boney's diaries.

The 1879 city directory of New Orleans lists several members of the family at work. Jacob was in business as a cotton factor and engaged in "commerce." Joseph was a clerk at J.M. Frankenbush Company, his father's firm, which had offices at 32 Perdido Street in downtown. He had just returned from the VMI. Another son, Albert, was a clerk at Pelican Press. All of them were living at the family home at 313 Second Street.

The 1880 U.S. Federal Census paints a more complete portrait of the family Jacob was married to the former Ellen Graves. He was 52. His birthplace was stated as Bohemia and his occupation was listed as cotton factor. The census says his father's and mother's birthplace was "Germany" and surely Frankenbush is a German name. But Prague was said by officials of America, Austria and Germany at the time to be in Germany—though it never was—it was the Germans who were in the Czech capital claiming it as their own. The Frankenbushes were just among the many Bohemians with German names. Ellen was born in Mississippi. Her father was born in Maine and her mother in Ohio; she was 44 years old .

They had six children by this time. Mary, 22, Joseph, 20, Albert, 18 (these two were clerks with their father) Bertha, 16, was at school. All these children were born in Mississippi. The next child, Sarah, was born in Louisiana. She was 11 at this time and at school. Walter, their youngest, was just 5. Also in the household were Sarah Potts, Frankenbush's mother-in-law. She was a 64 year old widow. Also living in the house were Ellen's sisters, Sallie and Emma. Both were still single at 32 and 30 respectively. The family had three servants: Elizabeth Goette, born in Louisiana of Prussian parents, Ellen Sanders, who was married and 40, and Rachel Jefferson, age 19. The last two ethnicity or race are unknown.

Tragedy struck the family on September 18th 1894: Walter Clement died. He was 20 years old at the time of his death and the youngest son of Jacob and Ellen. His obituary is sad and poignant, reading:

"*Frankenbush Dead. The young man who feel through a hatchway. The young man, Walter Frankenbush, who accidentally fell though the hatchway on the second floor at H B Stevens Clothing store on Canal Street, last Saturday died at the hospital yesterday morning from the effects of his injuries. Deputy Coroner Maylie viewed the body and gave a certificate of death in accordance with the facts.*

"*Mr. Frankenbush was the son of the senior member of the firm of Frankenbush and Borland. In the social circles where he moved the young man was well known and highly esteemed. There were no hopes for his recovery, and from the time of his accident his death was known to be inevitable. His demise on the brink of manhood, when life was unfolding its fairest promise of success and usefulness, was pathetic. It was a severe shock to his family and to a large number of friends.*"

Life went on for the family and on June 29, 1899, Jacob bought the Harriston Oil Works in Mississippi. This firm was probably involved in the cotton seed oil business and not the petroleum business. The firm was originally incorporated with a capitol stock of $20,000. S.R. Ewing was president and W.G. McNair was secretary and treasurer. The reason for this sale was rather simple: *"A large sum of money was borrowed by the company from S. Hirsch of Fayette in 1900 and as the concern was unable to meet the notes, Mr. Hirsch had the property sold at Auction August 5, 1901 at the County Court House in Fayette."* The top bidder was the Frankenbush firm. Frankenbush paid only $5,325 cash. There were other claims amounting to $8,564, that were all satisfied by the Frankenbush firm.

The next year's city directory chronicles the family. Albert Frankenbush was still working at J.M. Frankenbush and Sons and he was living at 1629 Second Street. This is the same house as the one at 313; it was the numbering system that changed. Also living in the house was his father. Joseph Warren had married Fannie Freret and was living down the block at 1721 Second Street. Fannie was from an old line New Orleans family whose ancestor was once mayor of New Orleans; Freret Street is named after the family. Frankenbush & Sons was still a cotton factoring business with Jacob, Joseph and Albert all working at 806 Perdido Street. This was probably the same building previously mentioned but also with a new number. All three gentleman shared the simple phone number 257.

In September of 1901 Frankenbush and Sons incorporated the Jefferson Gin and Oil Works at Harriston, Mississippi. The firm had an initial capital stock of $15,000. The company was set up *"for the purpose of operating a cotton seed oil mill, and public cotton gin; to buy cottonseed for manufacturing cotton seed oil, meal or cake, hulls and fertilizer."* This mill operated until 1911, though it was sold earlier to a Mr. Ewing. It was just one of the many ventures that Jacob Frankenbush engaged in.

His obituary in the *Times-Picayune* was a flowery expose that heaped praised on him. It is headlined *"Honored Veteran and One of Cotton Exchange Founders, And prominent in Patriotic and Philanthropic Movements, passes away."* He was "a businessman and citizen of high character and reputation." The obituary notes that Frankenbush was "a native of Prague, Austria," and that "he was educated in his native city and graduated in the University of Prague." This is most likely Charles University; it was founded in the 1340s. The notice says he came to New Orleans in 1850, though it may have been later. He "engaged in mercantile pursuits and after a few years removed to Port Gibson, Miss." This is probably where he met Ellen, got married, and definitely had his first few children. He served in the Confederate army during the war. He was "first a private in Company Fourth Regiment of Cavalry under Captain J. M. Magruder" and then "in the quartermaster's department under Major W. K. Bennett."

By 1865 he was back in New Orleans; he had became a member of John Burnet Co. He soon was in a partnership: Frankenbush & Borland. Eventually he started his own firm, J. M. Frankenbush & Sons. He was said to be "a Democrat in politics and one of the most earnest patriots in this city." He was the fourth signer of the call to arms for the citizen uprising against Republican corruption and misrule. This uprising took place on the night of September 14, 1874. Hundreds of men angry at the way their city was being disparaged by those in power in the last years of Reconstruction met at the Henry Clay Statue at the foot of Canal and made their grievances known rather vociferously.

The obituary continues *"Broad-minded, liberal in his views, Mr. Frankenbush was eminently charitable and was interested in altruistic work, notably as a member of the Prison and Asylums Commission and as a subscriber to the fund for the support of the Home for Incurables. He was one of the founders and on the first Board of Directors of the Mechanics and Traders Insurance Company."* The Reverend Mr. Miller, Curate of Trinity Episcopal Church, officiated at the funeral This attests to the fact that Frankenbush probably adopted the religion of his wife.

The obituary for his wife was far simpler in keeping with the times: "Frankenbush, entered into rest on Thursday, July 10th, 1919 at 2:30 PM. Ellen Ann Graves, widow of Jacob M Frankenbush, in her eighty fourth year." She was still living at 1629 Second Street near the corner of Carondelet Street.

The 1919 Soards New Orleans Directory lists Albert Frankenbush as a cotton weigher and still living on Second Street. "Jacob M Mrs.," was listed, but she was to die this year. Joseph was a broker who lived at 3812 Chestnut Street. 10 years later, the city directory for 1928 shows that Albert was now a teacher and he had moved next door to 1625 Second Street. Joseph was a manufacturer's agent living at 1623 Marengo Street; about a 15 minute walk from his brother's house. Marguerite D. Frankenbush was a teacher at the Isadore Newman School. She was Albert's daughter and lived with her father.

In 1929 we find Albert's son, also named Albert, working as a "manager" and living at 1126 2nd Street. Albert senior was still at 1625 Second Street, along with his wife, who was a teacher. His daughter Margaret was also a teacher and she lived with them. Joseph had become a "merchandise broker" with the business address of 407 Board of Trade Building, yet the same home on Marengo Street.

The Depression saw major changes in the family fortunes. The 1932 city directory says Bertha Frankenbush was living at 2450 Prytania Street. Around the corner and up the street was Joseph, still a broker, but now at 2520 Robert Street; his son and daughter were living with him. Joseph Jr. was an engineer and Lise

McCall Frankenbush had no occupation listed. Margaret was still a teacher at the Newman School but had moved to 3107 Jena Street. Mary, another daughter of Jacob's, had a house at 4500 Prytania Street.

One record has it that Fanny Salkeld Freret Frankenbush, wife of Joseph, died on November 10, 1937, with interment in Lafayette No 1 cemetery. She was born on January 1, 1866. Another record has her dying on her birthday in 1937. Joseph Warren, whose dates were August 31, 1859, to January 1, 1948, died at the age of 88 and was also buried at Lafayette No. 1. Fanny is also credited with being the first woman with a drivers license in the city of New Orleans.

The 1938 city directory shows more changes for the remaining Frankenbush's. Albert and his daughter Margaret now lived at 2308 Napoleon Avenue while Joseph Jr. was living at 3629 Chestnut Street. On Tuesday, April 18, 1939, Albert Sidney Frankenbush died at his residence. He was interred at Metairie cemetery. A few years later his wife Margaret Darrah died and she too was buried at Metairie Cemetery.

By 1945 the family's fortunes seemed to have bettered because they were now living at some of the most prestigious addresses in the city. John and his wife, also named Fannie, were living at 248 Audubon Street. Next door at 246 Audubon was his cousin Joseph W. Jr., and his wife Lottie. Joseph's occupation was listed as "Examiner US Civil Service Commission," but he had to have inherited money to afford to live in the neighborhood they were in.

On "Sunday, November 28, 1954 Mary T. Frankenbush, of 8313 Panola Street, daughter of the late Ellen Graves and Jacob M. Frankenbush, sister of the late Bertha, Sarah, Albert and Joseph W. Frankenbush, aged 96 years," died and was interred in Metairie cemetery. She had never married. The 1956 City Directory shows Joseph Jr., and his wife Lottie living at 8313 Panola, which he probably inherited from his maiden aunt. His occupation was now listed as "personnel office" at the IRS. 10 years later, in 1965, Joseph and Lottie were still living at the house on Panola Street. Lise McCall Frankenbush, died on Friday, November 28, 1969, "daughter of the late Fanny Freret and Joseph Warren Frankenbush." She, too, was never married.

The Frankenbush's did not acquire a lot of real estate as the Pokornys and Kohns did. They did, however, own their own homes. The family's biggest claim to fame is probably their ancestor's role in founding the Cotton Exchange.

The Laska Family

The first mention we have of the 50 years of the Mathias Laska family, New Orleans' second Moravian family is in the 1879 city directory when we find "Mathias Laska, gunsmith, 148 N Basin." They were the only people listed as Moravian in the 1880 census of the city—and thus Czech. Laska means "love" in the Czech language. Mathias Laska was 43 years old at the time of this census. His wife, Theresa, was 50, which is an odd age difference for a couple. They brought three children with them from Europe: Annie, 19, Joseph, 17, and Mary, 15. Joseph's occupation was listed as a locksmith working with his father. Once in New Orleans they had two more sons. Mathias Jr., born on September 2, 1869 and Frank, born December 23, 1872. While the exact date of their arrival is not known from the births of the two youngest boys it is clear that they were in Louisiana by 1869. Yet, the family is not in the 1870 census.

Their store was in a two story building with the new number of 616 N. Basin Street. At the time it fronted on the water basin at the end of Canal Street which led to St. John Bayou and out to Lake Pontchartrain. The basin was not filled in until much later. The building no longer stands.

The 1881 city directory lists only Mathias Sr. In this directory he was listed solely as a "gunsmith." Two of his sons must have been apprenticed to their father because the 1883 city directory lists Mathias the father and Joseph and Mathias Jr., as gunsmiths. City directories only published the names of people who were over 18. Both residence and store were at the same address. The younger Mathias must have been somewhat of a tinkerer and inventor. On April 20, 1886 he received patent #340,328 for a coffee roaster contraption.

In the sort of detail we obtain from many obituaries we know that Theresa Pavich Laska, died on Monday, January 8, 1894. She was aged 63 years. The notice says she was "a native of Austria and resident of this city for the past twenty five years." She was survived by her husband, as well as her sons, Joseph and Mathias, and sons-in-law Joseph Ezregovich and Anthony Gergurovich, though her daughters are not mentioned. It is interesting to note that two of the daughters married men of Slavic heritage. Both Ezregovich and Gergurovich are from the Yugoslav families that settled in the New Orleans area at about the same time. The notice also shows that once the Laska's settled into New Orleans they stayed where they were and they were successful at what they did.

The 1900 city directory notes that Frank had joined "M.A. Laska & Sons," and that both his business and residence were at 616 North Basin Street. They did not move; the street numbers were changed. Frank was 7 in 1880, so he was

27 in 1900. He took over the old family home. Matthew had Americanized his name and moved to 2536 Dumaine Street. Living with him was his father, now stylized Matthew. Either he or the publishers Americanized his name in the city directory. The father's obituary says that "Mathias," died at the age of 63. Moravia was noted as his birthplace. He died on Sunday, February 11, 1900, and had lived in New Orleans for forty years.

From the Sanborn Directory for the years 1908/09 we know that 616 North Basin was on a cobblestone street facing the still extant basin. There were two buildings 2½ stories high sharing one address and both buildings were 27' wide. They were probably built before the Civil War. From the outline on the map we can tell that there were so-called slave quarters in the back along two courtyards. They were a very typical residence and business at the edge of the French Quarter.

Joseph must have moved to Biloxi, Mississippi at some point and then later moved back to New Orleans. We glean this from the unfortunate event of the death of his son Clifford Joseph on November 2, 1910. The young man was just 19 years old. The funeral was held in the family home at "1123 North Johnson Street, between Ursuline and Governor Nicholls Ave." He was buried at the new St. Louis No. 3 on Esplanade Ave. The obituary asks that the "Biloxi papers please copy" so the family was apparently still known there.

The 1910 census shows that Joseph had changed professions; he was now working as a plumber. He was married for 20 years to Antoinette. She was 42 and the mother of 7 kids, six still living. They were Oswald, who at the age of 19 was also a plumber. Theresa was a 17 year old book binder. Their second son, Wallace, was already working as a telegraph clerk at the age of 13. William, their youngest, was just 11. All four kids were listed as born in Mississippi. Their mother was reported to be born in Louisiana of Austrian parents who spoke German. Somewhat correctly Joseph was listed as born in Louisiana of Bohemian speaking "Austrian" parents. Austria was the ruling power of Bohemia at the time. His parents actually, though, were more correctly Moravian speaking.

The next year, on Thursday, April 6, 1911, Joseph Oswald Laska, "beloved husband of Antoinette Lucase, aged 48 years, a native of Austria and a resident of this city for 44 years," died. His address was given as 1123 North John Street. The funeral took place from this home which more likely on North Johnston Street. His daughters had already married into the Erzegovich and Gergurovich familles.

The 1919 city directory has the many members of the Laska family listed. Frank was a blacksmith whose residence was at 3116 Dumaine Street. An apparently independent-minded daughter was listed as "Miss Hilda." She was a telephone operator in the era when they really did have the spaghetti tangle of wires known from old movies in front of them. She lived at 1014 North Broad Street. Also at this address we find Wallace who was in the army and William whose occupation was "helper." Where or with what he helped is not further identified.

Mathias was the president of Mathias Laska Company and made his residence at 904 North Rampart Street. Mathias was also president of the Lionel S. Boulman firm. This firm were the managers of Automobile Supplies and Auto Repairing at 210 North Rampart. Their phone number was "Main 4055" so apparently they were quite progressive. "Miss T. Laska," was a clerk at DH Holmes on Canal Street. She lived at 904 North Rampart and we can assume she was Theresa, the daughter of Mathias. Edward Laska was a clerk, though it is not clear where, who lived at 7338 Irma. Henry Laska was a bookkeeper at the T & T Cumb Company. He, too, lived at the house on Irma street.

Ten years later Antoinette was still living on North Broad Street. So were Wallace who was now a cabinet maker and Willaim who was a messenger. Frank was a parker at Jabert Brothers, a car dealership, and owned a home at 3116 Dumaine Street. Mathias was now in auto supplies at 1700 Tulane Avenue. He owned a house at 425 South Clark Street.

By 1932 Antoinette had moved to 2718 Aubry Street. Frank was still on Dumaine. Matthias had graduated to owning a service station at the 1700 Tulane Avenue address. He was still living on South Clark Street. Wallace was a woodworker living with his mother on Aubry Street. William, who was now a salesman at Ideal Used Car Company, was also still living with his mother.

William Lawrence Laska died on Wednesday November 25, 1936. He apparently never got married. The only survivors listed are his mother; his sisters (who are listed as Mrs. Emile T Marrero and Mrs. Herbert Harz,) and his two brothers Wallace and Oswald. Oswald was living in New York City at the time. The funeral took place from the Laudumiey Funeral Home. Religious services were at St. Rose De Lima Church on Bayou Road Street. He was interred in St. Louis Cemetery No 3.

In 1938 Antoinette had moved to a house at 1730 North Dupre Street. Everything had stayed the same for Wallace; still a woodworker and still living with his mother and apparently unmarried. Matthew was married to Barbara Crutti, a daughter of Italian immigrants. He worked as a watchman at HG Hill Stores, Inc. They still lived on South Clark. He died at his home at the age of 73 on February 6, 1943. He, too, is buried at St. Louis #3 Cemetery on Esplanade Avenue.

He left just one daughter: Mrs. Roy Lovell, and a grandson, Private Roy Lovell Jr of the United States Marine Corps.

His brother Frank died in 1943 also. Frank also died at home; 3116 Dumaine Street. His wife was born Elizabeth Kirm. He was also survived by a number of nieces and nephews. He was a member of Merlin Grove No. 18 UAOD, and had worked at Jaubert Bros. Inc. for quite a while. He was Catholic at least in name since a Requiem Mass was held at Our Lady of the Holy Rosary Church. He was interred in Greenwood Cemetery.

In 1945 Antoinette was still living on North Dupre Street and she would live there the remainder of her long life. She did not die until October 21, 1954. She was still in the city directory for this year. She had two daughters, Mrs. Theresa Harz, Mrs. Mark Silverberg and one son, Wallace, living at the time of her death. She was also survived by four grand children and eight great grandchildren; her resting place is St. Louis cemetery No. 3, with other relatives.

Elizabeth, the widow of Frank, lived her last year at 613 North Alexander, dying in 1946. This same year Mathias and Barbara were still in their house on South Clark and Wallace was still listed as a carpenter living with his mother. He, too, never got married.

Both the 1947 and 1954 city directories relay the same information: Antoinette and Wallace lived together. In 1947 Barbara is listed as the "widow of Mathias" and still living on South Clark. The family name ends on Friday August 23rd, 1968, when Wallace Andrew Laska, "son of the late Antoinette Lucas and Joseph Laska, brother of Mrs. Theresa Harz, and Mrs. Hilda Silverberg, age 71, a native of Biloxi, Miss and a resident of New Orleans for the past 58 years," died. He was buried in the family plot in the St. Louis No 3 cemetery. While the family did die out in name the daughters had several children among them and they are apparently still in the New Orleans area.

The Pollatsek Family

The family of Adolph Pollatsek were Slovakian Jews. Though no evidence has been found of any memberships in any synagogues nor record of him being an observant Jew. He was the long time head bookkeeper for the Grunewald Music Company. The Louis Grunewald Music Store Company was at multiple locations in downtown New Orleans. They occupied 18, 20 and 22 Baronne Street and 127 Canal Street as well. They were importers of musical instruments. Most famously as being agents for the celebrated Steinway and the New York-made but Czech-originated Matushek line. They were also publishers of sheet music. Their telephone number was the three digit 708 and we can imagine Adolph a frequent user of the instrument with his position in the firm. We first encounter Adolph in the 1870 Census as a 28 year old bookkeeper. We do not know for which firm. However, by 1879 Adolph was with Grunewald; his residence was listed as 369 Canal Street. Also at the same address was George, a clerk, whom we can assume was Alolph's brother. He is not one of Adolph's children.

In the 1880 census he is listed as "Hungarian" but the language he was listed as speaking as a "mother tongue" was actually Slovak. He was born in 1841. Hungary was the ruling country at the time of his immigration and this census. We witness the same thing with the Pastorek family which was listed as Hungarian in early censuses. Plus, the name Pollatsek is definitely Slovak.

A New Orleans City Directory for 1893 lists Adolph Pollastsek as "secretary" of Louis Grunewald & Co. The store at 127 Canal Street was separated by a few blocks from his residence at 369 Canal. He may have taken the trolley or he may have walked on nicer days but in any event his commute for so many years was literally just down the street.

In 1880 we also find an Isadore Pollatsek working at C. Louis Block & Company, though it is not clear what relation, if any, he was to Adolph. The Block company was at 109 Custom and his residence was at 65 Bourbon Street. This is an odd coincidence since this was where Bohemian Jewish Kohn family had lived so many years before.

Adolph's son Maximillian was a clerk; perhaps with his father. Twenty years later in a 1900 city directory Adolph was still secretary of Louis Grunewald Co, Ltd.; this when he was 59 years old. With the new numbering system put in place at the turn of the century the business was at 735 Canal Street and his residence was at 1907 Canal Street. Maximillian, too, was listed in the 1900 at 1907 Canal.

On Thursday, December 20th, 1906, the 65 year old Adolph, "beloved husband of Isabella, a native of Hungary and a resident of this city for the past thirty years," died. His obituary was this brief. Tragedy struck the widow and his sister when "Maxie" died on Friday, August 4th, 1916. In his obituary Isabella's maiden name was said to be "Hahn." This is not a Slovak name and is, in fact, most likely German. In any event, services were held on August 7th at his house on Canal Street. The young man was born and died in the same house. In 1919 Adolph's widow was still residing at the house on Canal. With her was her unmarried daughter Nina. Nina was a teacher at the Benjamin Franklin School at 2101 Dumaine. Isabella Hahn Pollatsek died on Thursday, May 26th, 1927. Services were held at her residence.

Nina teacher was a teacher at the Mc Donogh School #28 and still residing as a single woman at 1907 Canal in 1929. The same year someone else named Adolph Pollatsek is listed at 1907 Canal. Either the directory reprinted some very old information or this may have been another son of the first Adolph and Isabella. This is, however, the only mention of him. By 1956 Nina had sold the house on Canal and moved to 800 Moss Street on Bayou St. John.

On Friday, August 13th, 1965, Sydonia Pollatsek, known as Sydie, another daughter of Isabella and Adolph, and sister of "the late Mr. Carlotta P. Reynolds, Mrs. Gisella P DeWolfe, Ernestine and Max Pollatsek," died. She is not ever listed in any of city directories. She was interred in Dispersed of Judah Cemetery. Nina Pollatsek died on Monday afternoon February 5th, 1968. Apparently she never married. Her obituary also mentions her sisters and brother as all being late. So she is the last of the Pollatsek line. And she too was buried at Dispersed of Judah Cemetery.

Observations on Movers and Shakers

What I have proven here is that 6 families from the Czech and Slovak lands were instrumental in the development of New Orleans as we know it today. Yet, in not one of the histories of New Orleans I have ever read are these facts presented. That nearly ¼ of all the buildings in downtown New Orleans at a certain point in history were owned by Czechs and Slovaks is alone astounding. That the very emblems of the city are connected to Czechs and Slovaks is indeed a major addition to the history of the city. It is almost as if there was a willful ignoring of people who were not French, Spanish or Anglo. Perhaps even more intriguing is that these six families came from various regions of the Czech and Slovak lands and represent nearly off of the religion traditions in these two places. This cosmopolitan reality fits rather well into the cosmopolitan city of New Orleans. One can only hope that future historians of New Orleans no long ignore the contribution of Czechs and Slovaks.

3

Big City Immigrants

This chapter examines 100 years of Czech and Slovak immigration to New Orleans. It is divided into two parts: 1850 to 1900 and 1900 to 1950. This roughly conforms to overarching Louisiana historical periods. While the period of 1850 to 1900 saw the most dramatic influx of Czechs and Slovaks into New Orleans they also continued to come until the post World War II era. Indeed, they are still coming. Only the Civil War years saw no immigration. There were slightly 100 Czech or Slovak families that made a difference in New Orleans during this 100 year period. Several were on a large enough scale that we feel their presence even today. However, there is no overarching theme or narrative to this immigration. This immigration was the product of indiviudal decisions wholly unrelated to any other Czechs' or Slovaks' decisions.

I present these individual stories below in roughly alphabetical order within each 50 year period for lack of any better organizational method. No family or individaul is more important than any other. For some we have but one brief reference while for others we have considerable information. When I heard from descendants I was able to fill in more details than the public record would allow. Those families are presented in their own small sections. None, however, had the impact of those families in the preceeding chapter. These years, however, are inextricably bound up in the conditions and changes to New Orleans that occurred between 1850 and 1900 and then from 1900 to 1950.

This first timeframe is usually divided into four periods: The prewar years, Union occupation, Reconstruction and the Victorian era. For the period between 1900 and 1950 there are likewise four main periods: 1900 until World War I, the war years themselves, the Depression years and World War II and its aftermath. During during both world wars immigration virtually halted but did not stop completely as with the Civil War years. The period between the two wars saw the creation of Czechoslovakia and this had a major downward effect on immigration. With the coming of World War II and its aftermath there are ony a handful of refugees who arrived. Each of these approximately 100 families or individuals had a different reason and experience in coming to and living in New Orleans. There is no "story" as such. Rather there are only individual stories.

New Orleans in the Civil War

It is nearly impossible to give a history of New Orleans and Louisiana and avoid the Civil War. This book is no different. By the time of the Civil War there was a sizable group of Czechs living in Texas. Texas is still the only Southern state with a considerable Czech presence. The basic reason that these Czechs found their way to Texas and ignored Louisiana and the other southern states is that Texas had a homestead program while other southern states did not. That is, the land was essentially free if a family stayed long enough on it. That most of these Texas Czechs are from the Moravian region of the Czech Republic is a historical oddity. The only connection between these Texas Czechs and Louisiana is that they usually passed through New Orleans on the way to Texas. They had no intention of staying in Louisiana. New Orleans was merely their port of entry. However, this means that for many Texas Czechs Louisiana was their first view of and experience in America.

There was one other connection between the Texas Czechs and Louisiana—the Civil War. Texas Czechs were not keen on joining the Southern cause but they had no opportunities to join the Union cause. At least not until New Orleans fell to the Union. Shortly thereafter Texas Czechs made their way to the city and joined the Union army. This fact is recorded in many articles and books by descendants of those Czechs living in Texas. They do not appear in the public record in Louisiana for they never established residency in the state. The few Czech families that lived in New Orleans at the start of the war were quite prosperous. There is, however, no solid evidence that any of them gave money or succor to the Confederate Cause. They also survived the rise and fall of the Confederate currency and economy because their assets were in real estate.

When the Civil War broke out in 1861 it was difficult for many new immigrants of any ethnicity to comprehend the reasons for it. Certainly each individual had his own opinion of the situation and they were probably just as divided as the rest of America as to the cause and solution to the crisis. Most of the Czech and Slovak people in Texas and Louisiana as well as across America were against secession from the Union. They were also against slavery, too. The institution of slavery was contrary to their Freethinking, individualistic ways and anathema to their deeply help theological beliefs. We find only a few Czechs in Louisiana who owned slaves: two of the Touchets in early Louisiana and at the start of the war James Blahut of Houma as well as earlier the Klady family of Monroe. But we also find one probable interracial couple, too, Samuel Kohn and Delphine Marchegay.

It is known that some of the Czechs of Texas were conscripted into the Confederate Army and there are several good books and articles on this subject. The majority who became involved in the hostilities, however, came to New Orleans and joined the Union Army. Those who were in either army probably saw action in the many battles that raged across Louisiana. Many others hid from Confederate conscription patrols in Texas. There are some reports that a few dressed as woman and hid in plain sight in the fields. Some of the Czechs and Slovaks who later settled in Louisiana may have been to the state during the war as Yankee soldiers or perhaps heard stories of the fertile lands and good climate. This seems to be the origin of some immigrants who arrived after the Civil War in Louisiana. In this Czechs and Slovaks were not much different than other Yankee soldiers who stayed in or returned to the South.

Of all the Czechs in Louisiana during the Civil War James Blahut seems to have suffered the most. He surely lost the slaves he had purchased. His plantation was subject to being picked clean by the Yankee army in his midst. He tried to sell his plantation a few times but failed. While he was not living in New Orleans during the war he did significant business with the firms in the city during the occupation. He faced several large debts from the war years.

It is family history that Michael Pokorny sold shoes to the Confederate army but he also probably sold to the Yankees after they seized New Orleans. Absolute proof is lacking. Frankenbush seems to be the one who was most taken up with the Southern Cause. He was involved in politics on the side that wanted to preserve as much of the prewar status quo as they could. He sent his son to a bastion of Southern military pride, the Virginia Military Institute. Considered together, Czechs and Slovaks in Louisiana during the war were just as divided as every other sector of American society. This is perhaps to be expected because every immigrant had his own story of assimilation.

This entire period warrants much further research in regards to Czech and Slovak involvement. Basically, the involvement of people from these lands has been ignored, overlooked or been mere footnotes. But given all the stories and anecdotes and the possibilities there is far more to this story than is currently known.

New Orleans During Reconstruction

The first use of Czech made glass beads for Mardi Gras costumes started soon after Reconstruction was over. Who first obtained the beads has never been determined and there are stories that this or that Krewe, including Rex, Comus and Momus, were the first to throw beads. Nor was I able to locate a company that imported the beads. There must have been at least one or perhaps several. One way New Orleanians could have found about beads is if one of the scions of the city made a grand tour of Europe which include the Czech lands and that is where he first saw the beads. Or perhaps some of the Czechs already in the city mentioned the beads to their neighbors and the clamor began.

The economic and social conditions affecting Czech and Slovak families in New Orleans during the post-Civil War years were as tense and difficult as those facing everyone in the city. The city was long occupied by Union troops. There was a palpable tension between the old line Southerners and the new influx of Northerners after the war. A volatile part of the mix were the freed African-Americans and the Republican political machine behind them. There were Czechs in the city who were clearly involved in the politics of the day; Jacob Frankenbush being the most prominent. However, few of the Czech and Slovak immigrants could hardly have been unaware of the situation. All of this turmoil led up to the Uprising of 1874 which lead to the end of Reconstruction in Louisiana three years later.

New Orleans in the Victorian Era

The economic and social conditions of Czechs and Slovaks in New Orleans from 1877 to 1900 was one of living in a booming city; one of the largest in the country. It was a smart and sophisticated place with two new universities: Tulane and Loyola. There was an opera house and two of the frequently performed productions were Puccini's "La Boheme" and the operata "The Bohemian Girl." I found dozens of ads and reivews for these performances in newspaper of the period. There were cotillions and balls related to the newly burgeoning Mardi Gras krewes. No doubt some of the Czechs and Slovaks went to these early parades. Music of all kinds swirled through the city. This was the dawn of the Jazz age and surely the Laska family, whom we already looked at, was in the midst of it. After all, their shop and home on Basin Street were at the very heart of the public displays of music. They were also on the edge of the red-light district in the city:

Storyville. They might well have provided locks to many of the new houses and even to a few bordellos and gambling houses though no business records survive.

Czech and Slovak families probably installed the new gas lights and heating stoves in their homes. They would have seen the birth of the telegraph and experienced the news that was brought so much quicker to the city. The city was undergoing a great expansion uptown. Whole districts were being built as wave after wave of immigrants from around the world made their way to New Orleans. This was the time when most of the Garden District and Uptown New Orleans were built. This filled in the area between Carrollton and Downtown. Czechs and Slovaks were just part of this trend but they did not come in waves as others did. They were still coming as individual families or alone. The businessmen among the immigrants benefited greatly from this new wealth in the city after the deprivation of the Reconstruction period.

Towards the end of the century there were great new marvels like the electric light and automobiles. We already have seen how one of the Frankenbush daughters was the first woman with a drivers license but we can surely assume that other Czechs and Slovaks made use of this daring new technology. The Pokornys were particularly busy in acquiring real estate during this period and constructing solid buildings a few stories higher than in the past. They did leave a legacy set in stone.

Families from 1850 to 1900

The censuses and city directories for the years 1850 to 1900 give us brief glimpses of Czechs and Slovaks who lived in New Orleans. There are no records from the 1890 census because the originals were burned in a fire in Washington D.C. If there are descendants of these families they have not been heard from yet. If they left papers and photographs they have not been found yet. None of these families stand out in the historical record although some spent a longer period than others in Louisiana. I present here, alphabetically, those I found in the record. I give as much information as I have found.

Edward Adler was listed as a "Bohemian" in the census of 1860. All that is known is that he was 28 years old at the time. His occupation was not listed. Whether he may have been related to the Adlers that came from Slovakia is not known. The Balinka family was in the 1890 census and was one of the few names that survived. Catherine and Leopold Balinka were living with their son Leopold. This is very likely a Czech name since it is the name of a river in the Moravian region of the Czech Republic.

In the 1893 city directory Thomas Cervenka is listed as living at 66 Lesseps Street in the Bywater section of the city. He was a hostler. This is a lost occupation. It is someone who takes care of horses and mules. His wife Katherine Loudova died on Friday November 2, 1902. Her obituary says she was "a native of Bohemia, Germany." The obituary records that she lived at 822 Lesseps Street which was the new number for the same house. Elizabeth Cervenka died Friday, June 17, 1927. She was the daughter of Thomas and Katherine, and "sister of Mrs. Henry Kathmann and aunt of Walter Welbreck and Mrs. Blaise Adous." She was 47 years and a native of New Orleans. This would mean that the Cervenka family was in New Orleans for nearly 50 years. Yet this is the only record of them that could be found. They also had a son Elis. In the 1929 city directory he was listed as a clerk. Cervenka is the Czech word for a robin redbreast and is often encountered as a surname in the Czech Republic. Why this family does not appear in earlier records can only be guessed at.

A single man named Frank Chaloupka lived in the city in the 1880s. He was a foreman although we do not know for what company. His residence was at 1220 Mazant, just a block off of St. Claude Avenue. The only evidence we have of his ethnicity is his surname. It means "cottager" or "one who lives in a cottage" in Czech.

Frances Franek was Acting Consul of Austria in 1880. Franek is a Czech name and we find other Franeks in New Orleans. The consulate office was at 173 Gravier Street in downtown and his residence was 244 Louisiana Avenue. He probably rode the street car to work. He apparently served out his term in the city and returned to Austria. That a Czech man was representing Austria is not so odd. First, Austria was the ruling power at the time. Second, the Czechs were among the most educated people of that polyglot empire.

Adeline Fusniber was a 19 year old seamstress in 1860 New Orleans. Another young woman of whom nothing much is known was Johanna Gruber. She was just 20 years old in 1860 and was a servant in a large home in New Orleans. Both of these woman certainly had some German roots given their last names. Their birthplace, however was listed as "Bohemia" in the census. What happened to them is lost to the past. No evidence could be found that they married any men in New Orleans. It is perhaps possible that they met Yankee soldiers and returned north as the Union Army settled into its occupation of the city.

The Hadazeks were an ethnic Bohemian family. Joseph Hadazek's obituary on Friday, August 10th, 1906, states that he was "a 59 year old native of Bohemia." It goes on to say that he was "a resident of this city for the past forty five years." This means he got to New Orleans in 1861 and was born in 1847. And that means he was 14 when he arrived. We know nothing of his family and though it is possible, it is not probable, that he traveled alone when so young. He married a woman of French heritage, Leonore Mouson, in New Orleans. She died on September 13, 1929 at 55. When Joseph died the relatives friends and acquaintances of the family as well as the officers and members of Guibets Battery Benevolent Association and the Tailors Union were invited to attend the services "from the residence of the late deceased, 515 Madison Street," in the French Quarter. They had a daughter who became Mrs. Bruno Llado.

In the 1881 city directory there are four Hadazeks mentioned. They all lived at 305 Conti Street in the French Quarter but their exact relationship to each other is not known. It would seem that they were brothers or at least cousins. Anthony was a clerk while the other three, Harry, John and Joseph, were tailors. Nor are any spouses mentioned. However, we do know that by 1886 John Hadacek (sic) was a tailor with his shop and residence at 38 South Derbigny Street. The Joseph listed in this directory would seem to be the same Joseph as in the obituary.

John must have died by 1893 for only Harry and Joseph are mentioned in the city directory for that year. Harry was still a tailor although by then living at 59 Palmyra Street. Where his shop was is not clear. This does not seem like a commercial address. Joseph was now a grocer whose shop and residence were at 388 St. Ann Street in the French Quarter. Seven years later Harry had moved to 314 South Roman; he was still laboring as a tailor. Joseph returned to the tailoring business but now was situated at 832 Burgundy Street. Neither the censuses nor the city directories provides any more information on this family. Given that they were around for decades there must be more records about them.

J. Hartman was a 20 year old Bohemian saddler living in New Orleans in 1860. The census provides no more information. This is a German surname. From his profession we can imagine that his skills were needed by the Confederacy and recruiters would have found him at work. He was young enough to enlist or get drafted even if he did not know the reasons for the war. Perhaps he just skipped town to avoid the whole mess. In 1870 we find young Barbara Hartish, just 18 years old, of Bohemia, working as a domestic servant for an unknown family. This the only mention of her and no marriage records or anything else could be found.

Another Bohemian with a German surname was identified only as "C. Hopf." The 1860 census says he was a 46 year old musician with $1,500 in real estate. This was a valuable piece of property. Exactly where he played is not known but this was a time when there were several classical music venues and dozens if not hundreds of clubs in a time when live music was the only entertainment. Besides making sufficient money to afford such a fine house he must have been a good manager of his money.

In 1890 there were two bachelor Slovaks who were living and working at 841 St. Ann Street in the French Quarter. Joseph Horik was just 24 years old but he already owned his own grocery store. He was born in December of 1875 and arrived in America in 1886. He employed an older man named Paul who was born in December of 1868. He was 31. He arrived in America in 1884. What is not known is Paul's exact surname because the name is both poorly written and blotted out and corrected. It is either Julibcik or Fulebcik or maybe even something else.

In 1880 Anthony Junek was a border living at 782 Burgundy Street in the French Quarter. Joseph Junek was in the oyster business and his residence was at 126 North Peters Street. When John Junek died he was said to be the eldest son of "Louise Munch and the late Joseph Junek." He was 54 years old. He was "a resident and native of this city for life" states his obituary. We have no other evidence for this family's Czech roots other than the last name which is clearly Czech.

Thomas Kaniksmark was a 44 year old who owned his own furniture shop in 1860. His wife was the 35 year old Antoinette. They had a son and daughter: Joseph, 14, and Jepista, 12. The census records that he had $750 in personal property which would indicate some level of success. All four were born in Bohemia. The Civil War probably spelled the death of Kaniksmark's shop since furniture purchases were not high on the agenda for people who lost their savings and fortunes and were living through the occupation of the city by Union troops. The economy of the city was dismal for nearly a decade after the war. The family is not in the 1870 census.

The 1870 census shows that a Bohemian named Lawrence Kara was a 32 year old blacksmith. Yet in the city directory for the same year he is listed as Lorenz Kara. Obviously he was toying with the idea of Anglicizing his name. Or the census enumerator changed it for him. In both instances the address for both his residence and his business were listed as 277 Liberty Street near downtown. He was a partner with a German man as Kara & Schlutter, Blacksmiths. He was married to the Bavarian born Margaret. She was 36 years old. This is one of many examples of younger Czech men marrying older woman. This was fairly common among the Czechs and Slovaks encountered in Louisiana.

There being no child labor laws to speak of a Bohemian girl named Susanna Kerr was just 14 years old when she was listed as a servant in New Orleans in the

1860 census. If she grew up to get married and have children it is not recorded in New Orleans. Another tailor in New Orleans was a 37 year old with the unfortunate name of Philip Leper. The jokers of the day must have made light of a man whose name was also the English word for a dangerous disease. He did well enough to have $300 in personal property according to the 1860 census. He was from Bohemia. J. Loring was a 19 year old waiter in New Orleans in 1860. That is all we know about this young person from Bohemia.

John A. Maschek, who had a German spelling for his Czech name "Mašek," was born on January 11, 1874. He is in the 1900 city directory but just his name and no other information. By the time of the 1929 City Directory John was the vice-president of Philip Forschler Wagon and Manufacturing Company. He was living at 215 North Jefferson Davis Highway at the time. He died on January 30th, 1943. His wife was Leonore Adele Ticoulet and he was the father of "Jockey" Francis Julius and Adrian M. These were just two of his sons. He had a third son, John A. Maschek Jr., who was living in Gulfport, Mississippi, at the time of a grandson's death, the third John A. we find in the family. We also learn from the young boy's obituary that John, the patriarch, was born in Franklin, Louisiana. This means his parents had emigrated sometime prior to this but exactly when they got to Louisiana is unclear. He was a member of several lodges and fraternal organizations including the Knights of Pythias and was a Mason. He lived at 1320 Euterpe Street.

In 1897 John Mihalik lived at 619 Bourbon Street in the French Quarter. He ran a fruit stand. Caroline Belak Mihalik was his wife. She died on Tuesday, September 12, 1939. From her obituary it is clear that she was the mother of three sons, John, Paul and Rudolph Mihalik, as well as three daughters: Mrs. W. Hourbeigt, Mrs. R W McCaffrey and Mrs. John H Cook. She also had 11 grandchildren and two great grandchildren. She was 70 years old when she died. Caroline was also said to be a native of Rovne, Slovakia. She lived in New Orleans for "the past 64 years." But this means she arrived in New Orleans in 1875 when she was 6 years old. So who were her parents? This is not known. They had to be Slovakian and somewhere in the city. She was a member of Gold Star Mothers of the American Legion which means she had a son who died while serving in the military; probably World War I. Her funeral was held on September 14th at 9:30 in the morning at her residence at 2716 North Robertson Street. A Requiem High Mass was held at Holy Trinity Church for her.

The city directory of 1922 lists Rudolph Mihalik as a "checker" at Abbott Automobile Company. His residence was still on North Robertson Street. There is mention of the death in New Orleans of a Reverend Irme Mihalik on 25 May,

1995, but we do not know where this person fits in the family tree or even if he does. But the surname is too unusual for their to have been two Mihalik families in New Orleans. Another member of a religious order was Wenceslaus Newman, 53, of the Congregation of the Holy Redemeer in New Orleans. His name was perhaps originally Novak; the literal translation being "Newman." While he changed his last name he oddly kept his Czech first name. He was from Bohemia and appears only in the 1870 census.

There were three generations of the Noha family in New Orleans in the late 1800s to early 1900s. In the 1870 census there is Charles Noha who at 65 years old and working as a "sailor." There was a woman named Mary Noha who was 48. Whether she was the wife or widowed daughter of Charles is not clear; the age differnce is big enough to be either. Also in this household was Otto, 18, who was an "apprentice carpenter" and Adolf who was 10. Not much more is known about this family during these early years in America.

But from an obituary on January 1, 1926, it is clear that Lisette Schneider Noha, the "beloved wife of Otto Noha, mother of Ottelia Noha," died at her residence at 1712 North Claiborne Avenue. In 1922, "Ottillia" was executive secretary to the president of the Interstate Trust and Banking Corporation. This company kept an office in a building at the corner of Camp Street and Canal Street. She too lived at 1712 North Claiborne. Her father Otto was still alive and she lived with him.

Young Adolph grew up to be a doctor. On December 16, 1932, Mary Elizabeth McGrane Noha, "beloved wife of Dr. Adolph Noha, aged 71 and a native of this city" died according to an obituary in the Times-Picayune. In the 1888 city directory Adolph Noha was a druggist on St. Claude Avenue near the corner of Washington Street. Later in the 1890s he lived and worked at 606 St. Claude Avenue. He was a member of the Young Mens Excelsior Benevolent Association. He kept the rather limited office hours of "7 to 9 am and 6 to 7 PM" and also "at C. Gelbacks from 12–1." Though perhaps this was for new patients and other times were reserved for established patients of his. He was also a member of the Southern Mutual Benevolent Association and Knights of Pythias. In 1894 he became a member of the Orleans Parish Medical Society whose directory shows a rather stern photograph of the man. The 1919 City Directory notes that Adolph Noha was a physician with an office at 921 Canal Street and a residence at 726 Mandeville Street in the Fauburg Marigny. In the 1922 city directory he was still listed as "Adolph Noha, physician." His phone number had just four digits, 1229. His office was at 921 Canal Street but he still lived in the same house in the Marigny.

Another Noha in New Orleans appears in a record from 1922: Charles Noha was a tailor who lived at 137 Union Street in the 3rd District of the city. It is not clear how he is related to the other Nohas but it appears he was a son or grandson of the first Charles Noha. What they all share is an odd last name, for one meaning of "Noha" in Czech is "big foot."

Mary A Noziska was just 17 when she was a servant in the home of Thomas Jones in New Orleans in 1860. Her prospects were probably reduced by the onset of the Civil War. The romantic supposition would be that she found a dashing Union officer and went off to live a happy life. Although in fact she simply disappears from the record.

An oplatek is basically a very thin white wafer resembling the holy bread that one receives in church during holy communion. This is a traditional Christmas-time baked food in Slavic countries. In the late 1800s we find a family by this name. There were two brothers, their wives and children. One is first found in the 1870 census: "Oplacack J, 44, harbor master," which is one misspelling of this name. They were probably in the city earlier because we have a record that a 16 year old Julius Oplatek died in December of 1867. It would be sad to think that the young boy had just arrived before succumbing to one of the many diseases that ran through the city periodically.

A few years later Joachim Oplatek is listed in the city directory living at 171 Terpsichore Street not far from the waterfront. He gave up that arduous work by 1879. In that year's city directory Joachim is listed as a travel agent with his residence at 82 Race Street. The same year his brother Victor J. Oplatek was living with him. Victor worked at a commercial printing press. In 1880 Victor was a clerk at Smith and Goldsmith. There is no record if the brothers came together from Europe.

In 1888 Joachim was a broker though we don't know for what commodities. He was living at 12½ N. Galvez. Victor had moved with him but was now employed as a clerk at A. Adler & Co. The firm was comprised of the brothers Abraham and William Adler and their partner, Cerf Hirsch. They were grocers and commission merchants and could be part of the Slovak Adler family. The relationship between all the Adlers is not known. Perhaps Joachim was employed here as well. The firm was located at 22 to 30 Canal Street and they were forward looking enough to have a telephone. They had just the three digits 552 as their number.

In 1893 someone identified only as "J. C. Oplatek" was a clerk at Augustus C. Fowler's drugstore. Fowler was also a physician. J. C. lived and worked in Gretna. It is evident that he changed jobs often. It would be interesting to know if he was seeking out better positions or if he was an undesirable employee. Eventually he came to open his own drug store on Front Street in Gretna using the name Charles Oplatek. His father, Joachim Oplatek, died at the age of seventy four. Joachim's obituary says he was a native of Bohemia. Roberta Weiman Oplatek, "wife of the late Joseph Oplatek and mother of JC Oplatek," died at the family residence which was at 2904 General Pershing Street on June 29th, 1930.

Just two years earlier in the 1928 City Directory J. Charles Oplatek was listed as having his own drug store and living at 4117 Eden Street. Joseph Jr. and his wife lived at 3125 Jena Street among the leafy streets of Uptown New Orleans on a street named by Charles Zimpel. There can be no doubt that he got his training at the hands of Fowler.

Every Southern story should have its crazy uncle and in the case of the Czechs in Louisiana it is Victor J. Oplatek. He was on the list of "Persons Adjudged to be Insane" by the Civil District Court for the Parish of Orleans. In case number 43543, on August, 22 1894, "Victor J. Oplatek 41 M[ale]/W[hite] New Orleans; Austria" was diagnosed with "Monomania, about 18 months. Women & Persecution." He was "delivered" on August 24, 1894 to the Superintendent of the State Insane Asylum at Jackson, Louisiana. When he was 43 he was struck with chronic hallucinations. His committal record for this event says he was from "Austria, Bohemia." It mentions that he was a clerk. He was well enough to get married on Valentine's Day, February 14, 1885, to Jeannette Mayer according to the New Orleans Archdiocese Archives; what his wife did after he was committed is not known. Victor J Oplatek died at age of 51. He was a native of Bohemia and a long time resident of New Orleans.

Living with the Oplateks were the young couple, Phillipe and Lena Pauli as well as their toddler son, 2 year old Julius. They are listed as Bohemians in the census of 1870. How they knew the Oplateks, other than as tenants, is unknown. Though with so few Czechs in the city it is hard to believe that this was just a coincidence.

In the 1870 census we also find the Bohemian Babelon Papelic. He was a driver, though of what it is not known. Yet, it had to be with horse drawn vehicles given the year. He was 50 years old. 50 year old Anna was his wife. They had two sons: 14 year old John and 8 year old Joseph. Both boys were said to be born in Louisiana. This would place the Papelic family in New Orleans in 1866. No record is found of them in the 1860 census which does not mean that they were not there at the time, however. Having been such recent arrivals it is very possible that they did not speak English when the earlier census was taken and thus they weren't counted.

Not far from New Orleans though also in the 1870 census was a Mr. V. Pisecky. He lived in the second ward of St. Bernard Parish. He was a rope maker and undoubtedly found much business among the fishermen who populated the area. He also probably came across some of the Yugoslavs who lived in St. Bernard Parish and was able to exchange mutually intelligible greetings. (Czech and Croatian have some similarities.) He was 38 years old. His wife, Eva, was two years older than him. Their eldest son Joseph was 15 years old. He was a laborer on one of the farms in the area. They had two other sons, Frank, 14 and Vance, 3. All of them were born in Bohemia. By Vance's age it is clear that the family arrived after 1867. It is highly unlikely that Vance was the young boy's original name as it is not at all a Czech name and Vaclav seems a likely alternative. Their daughter Marie, who was 1 at the time of the census, was born in Louisiana.

All we know of John Podeska is that he was a Bohemian oysterman working with "W. Troegel." He lived at the corner of Gravier and South Galvez Streets in the 1870s. One of the other two Bohemians in the city in 1870 was Sophia Semlar. She was a cook in the Dalsemann houshold; she was just 20. The other was Vincello Walker 22 who was employed as a bartender. He must have changed both his first and last names. Neither name is Czech. While the Czech "Prochaska" means something like "walker," and perhaps that was the original, this is not certain. In keeping with common Czech-American habits the untranslatable name Vaclav was often changed to some American sounding name that started with a V. Given the growing number of Italians in the city at this time Vincello may have seemed very American to the new immigrant.

Also in the city in the 1870s was the Bohemian Joseph Prachuski, 35. A man named Prager in the 1879 city directory had a saloon at 184 Common Street. He lived at 372 Felicity Street in the Lower Garden District. Prager is often a name in German denoting someone from Prague, the Czech capital. Another family whom we know as Czech only from their last name was the aptly named Prague family. James Prague was in business as "Prague and Sherman lumber merchants" at 18 St. Joseph Street as early as 1844. Why there were no earlier records is unknown. Perhaps he had a more complicated Czech surname and simply renamed himself after the city of his birth.

He had two sons over the age of 18 who apparently had their own families. Henry T., was a machinist living on Burdette Street and James B. was a clerk at Eager Ellerman & Co. He lived around the corner from his brother on Burthe Street at the corner of Burdette. By the 1850s his widow Rosina was living on 2nd Street near Washington Avenue. From the 1861 City Directory it seems that another brother was John. He was living and working with his brother James at

Mariposa Mills Lumber Yard at 33 St. Joseph Street. There is a big bold listing in the directory for the company. "Mrs. R. Prague" was at the St. Joseph Street address, too. This was probably Rosina. This name is a very common Czech woman's first name.

Another family that we know from their Czech name and not from census or obituary records are the Prochaska family. This is a quintessentially Czech name. John Prochaska Jr., lived from April 27, 1859 to February 20, 1900. His obituary says he was a native of Burlington, Iowa and "long a resident of this city." Burlington has a sizable Czech community. He was married to Mary H. Wilkinson Prochaska. Her date of death was listed in different sources as both October 11 and October 14, 1881. She was a native of Pennsylvania, aged 48. He might have met her in Pennsylvania when he was living among a large Czech community in that state.

The 1879 city directory lists George B. Prochaska as a clerk at the Galbreath company. He lived at 671½ Carondelet Street. Duncan Galbreath was a firm of sugar brokers at 24 North Peters Street. His brother John was a watchmaker at A. B. Griswold; he too lived at the house on Carondelet Street. A. B. Griswold & Company was comprised of Arthur Griswold, Henry Ginder, and Albert Abbot and dealt in watches and jewelry at 119 Canal Street.

Gertrude Ellen Prochaska lived from April 22, 1861 to December 30, 1951. She apparently never got married. She was, however, John Jr.'s sister. They are all buried in New Orleans cemeteries. In 1945 Gertrude was living at 1636 Jackson Ave. When she died she was living at 5121 St. Charles Avenue and was 90 years old.

Another Prochaska in New Orleans died on Thursday December 21, 1893; George B. Prochaska was just 33 years old. The family was struck with tragedy again when George Alvin, aged 9 years and 3 months, died on Saturday, November 17, 1894. He was the second son of the late George and Mary R. Carroll. The elder George was probably John Prochaska's brother. By 1945 Mary was an office secretary at the Grace Line who resided at 1724 Louisiana Avenue. The 1929 city directory records that John Prochaska was a clerk living at 1467 Nashville Avenue. Mrs. J. Prochaska was living at 2814 Robert Street. "Logan, S.," was a salesman who lived at with his father at 1467 Nashville. Down the block at 1448 Nashville lived Mrs. S. L. Prochaska. She was a teacher at MeGehee's School.

Lynette Prochaska painted "Court Tower" [25 x 24, oil painting.] This painting is in the state archives collection in Baton Rouge. The round tower house that is the subject of this painting was, according to more than one source, a "favorite for artists in the 20's and depression days." It was a French Quarter tenement house in the old lower part Quarter. It is situated in a few blocks thickly inhabited by Sicilian immigrant families. Mrs. Prochaska continued her art in New Orleans, teaching art at her home-studio. In the 1945 city directory Lynnette was living at 1911 Broadway in Uptown New Orleans. Both "Saul L" and "Saul L. Jr.," were in the United States navy at the end of the war. Their residence is listed as 1911 Broadway, too.

Samuel Logan Prochaska died Friday, July 20, 1945. He was then married to Katheleen Lackey. This appears to be his second wife. He was listed as the father of "Sam Logan Prochaska Jr., Mrs. Jamie Fitzgerald and the brother of Mrs. James A Walsh and Carroll W. Prochaska." On Sunday, December 14, 1958, Samuel Logan Prochaska III, son of Mary Katherine Beeson (who must have been the first wife of Samuel Sr.) and Samuel Logan Prochaska Jr., brother of James Knox, Lynette Barney, and Susan Prochaska, died. He was buried in Metairie Cemetery. His obituary is rather simple: "Prochaska, of 1726 Prytania Street, on Thursday March 18 1943, Jessie Roemer, wife of the late John Prochaska, sister of Mrs. Agnes Mernier."

Lynette Hoffman Prochaska outlived them all, dying on the morning of Tuesday, March 17th, 1964. She was the wife of the "late Samuel Logan Prochaska, mother of Mrs. Jamie Fitzgerald, and Sam Prochaska, also survived by five grandchildren." She was buried in Metairie Cemetary. The Prochaskas were definitely Czech. They were however, from Czech communities in other states and did not come to Louisiana directly from Europe.

How a young Bohemian girl named Ann Rosiskie, just 14, came to be a servant in the home of James Jones is not known. James Jones was a successful building contractor with a house valied at $20,000 in uptown New Orleans in 1860. This was one of the huge mansions in the area. The exact address is not known and its value is oddly listed in the entry for Ann. The young girl was undoubtedly busy with minor tasks.

John Rouher was a 46 year old Bohemian living with his wife Veronika. She was 30 years old. Thus, 16 years younger than her husband. He must have married her when she was just 17 or 18 because they had a son Frank who was 12. These three were born Bohemia but they made their home in New Orleans in 1860. They also had a daughter named Josephine who was just 1 year old when the census was taken. She was born in Louisiana. This puts the Rouher family in New Orleans in 1859. Living with them was a woman named Barbara Schwade, 43, but we don't know anything else about her. He would have been too old for the Confederate Army but he is another Czech who disappears from the record once the war came.

Joseph Seidel was just 24 when he is recorded working as a "turner" in one of New Orleans factories in 1860. This was a skill using machines to make dowels, molds, buttons and other round things. He worked hard enough to accumulate $200 in personal property. In an unusual circumstance his wife Teresa was 30, or seven years older than him. We lose track of him with the coming of the Civil War but we know that he stayed in New Orleans. Joseph Seidel Sr. born in 1824 and died 1875. He was married to Theresa Reimer. She was born 1830 and died on January 9, 1912. There are several Seidel tombs in the Metairie Cemetery in New Orleans. Seidel Sr. and Theresa had six children: Gustave, 1864 to 1940, Henry (Henrich,) 1866 to 1941, Joseph, 1854 to 1923, Otto, 1857 to 1908, and Mathilda who was born in 1870. Before the second son named Henry there was a child also named Henry who was born in 1859 and died 1865. One date recorded for the wedding of Joseph Sr. and Theresa was September 15, 1864. This date does not seem correct given the birth years of the children. This family still resides in the New Orleans area today. They have only recently discovered their Czech roots.

Tabor was taken as a last name by people who were involved in the Hussite Wars of the mid-1400s. Tabor is a city about 50 miles south of Prague. It was a hotbed of rebellion against the Catholic Church. This is the only clue we have that the Tabor families in Louisiana are Czech. One of the Tabor families stems from Henry Tabor who was born about 1867 in Louisiana. It is obvious from his parents facts that he was at least first generation American. His father, Benjamin Tabor, married Clelie Borne. Henry got married in January, 1886, in Vacherie, St. James Parish. From certain Internet searches being done by relatives we find that there was a Henry Jr. and his wife Eda McNamara in Covington at the turn of the century. Other family members from this time were Paul Butler Tabor of Gretna, Judith Ann Tabor of Farmerville, Ashley Todd Tabor of Pierre Part and Faith Amelia Tabor whose town we do not know.

One of the most extreme examples of changing a Czech name to an American name is Simon Young. He was a 31 year old Bohemian machinist living in New Orleans in 1860. There are many people who are named "Mlada" in the Czech Republic. This is the Czech word for "young." It is quite possible that he translated his name directly into English upon his arrival in the United States. And it is also possible that he left the city as secessionist sentiments began to rise in New Orleans. He is not listed in the rosters of eligible men prepared for the war.

Families from 1900 to 1950

Following are historical snapshots of the Bohemian, Moravian and Slovak families who settled in New Orleans between about 1900 to 1950. Again, for most we have just limited amounts of information. Many of these families quickly disappear from the Louisiana record and most had little lasting impact on the city. Some were, however, in the city for a number of years. For these new immigrants New Orleans was their first taste of America. Why they chose this city is not known. The Depression seems to have driven some out of the city. Yet others weathered the storm. For those who settled somewhere else before choosing New Orleans something drew them south to the city; the best guess is that the grass is always greener on the other side.

Alfred Auffarbor ran a variety of businesses during his time in New Orleans. In the 1919 city directory his residence is listed as 924 City Park Avenue. He owned a saloon just down the block at 902 City Park Avenue. He is in the 1920 census as the 40 year old proprietor of a confectionery shop. That was quite a change in business, one that had to have been brought about by the onset of Prohibition. His wife, named either Anna or Jena, the handwritten record is hard to decipher, was said to be a cook at a restaurant. They had a son named Curt A. Auffhauber, which was an alternative spelling to the name. His nationality and birthplace, however, were listed as Bohemian. In 1929 it is recorded that he was running a restaurant at 141 North Carrollton Avenue and still living in the house on City Park Avenue. When he died he was living at 4110 Iberville Street. In his obituary his wife's was written as Lina. Her maiden name was Becher. The son's name is spelled Kurt in the paper.

The Brada family can be found in the 1893 City Directory. Martin Brada was a painter living at 9 North Lopez Street. This is not far from downtown and nearly at the corner of Canal Street. Also listed was Nicholas. He worked as a barber. He also lived at the house on North Lopez. Nicholas was the son of Martin and had to be over 18 to get his own listing in the directory. The 1900 census lists Martin as a Bohemian. Brada is the Czech word for "chin." He was born in 1848, was 51, and had arrived in 1870. He had been in the United States for 30 years but it is not known where. His wife had the rather American name of Lizzie. She was born in 1850 and was now 49 years old. She arrived in 1869 when she was 19 years old. They were married for 25 years. Nicholas is not mentioned in the 1910 census. Nor can the family be found in the 1910 census, though, they must have been in the city.

Their three daughters were all born in Louisiana. Both Katie and Camille were 18 and they were born in 1882. Obviously, Katie and Camille were twins. Their youngest daughter was Rosa. She was 16, having been born in 1884. Brada's obituary says he died on "Thursday October 17, 19, aged 51 years, 11 months and 6 days," It says he was "a native of Austria and a resident of this city for the last thirty five years." This line of the Brada family ended with the daughters. Exactly to whom they married I could not discover but it is clear from later obituaries that all three married local men.

Nicholas Brada died on June 18, 1914. His wife was Hermine Lehder. He was only forty one years "and native of New Orleans." The relatives, friends and acquaintances of the family, also officers and members of the Journeymen Barbers' Union, No 496, were "respectfully invited" to attend the funeral. He lived at 2823 Bienville Street and was interred in Greenwood Cemetery. How the Bradas avoided being recorded in many public records is not clear.

The next year Lizzie Brada died. She expired on Wednesday, March 17, 1915. "Elizabeth Zobec, beloved wife of the late Martin Brada, aged 63 years, a native of Austria and a resident of this city for the past 40 years," reads her obituary. Given not only her husband but her own last name she was probably Bohemian also. Relatives and family were invited to attended the funeral which took place at the residence of her son-in-law, W.J. Sailor. He lived at 317 N. Gayoso Street and no doubt Lizzie spent time with her daughter at this address.

Another early death was that of Louisa Johnson on December 28, 1920. She was the "beloved wife of the late John Brada" and was just 42 years old. She was a native and a resident of the city. The funeral was at the residence of her sister-in-law, Mrs. E. Johnson, at 3007 Bienville Street. They are buried at St. Patrick Cemetery No 1 in New Orleans.

The family members moved often. In 1929 Frederik Brada made his home at 507 South Rendon Street. He made his living as a pressman at E.T. Harvey & Son. While Martino (sic) was a salesman at the Standard Sanitary Manufacturing Company. He resided at 322 South Miro Street. He was the son of Nicholas and Minnie (Hermina) Brada. He was living with his mother Hermina. She was in the workforce as a machine operator at Foster Manufacturing.

Minnie Lehder Brada, Nicholas's wife, died on Tuesday May 2nd, 1933. She was said to be the "beloved mother of Frederich Brada, Mrs. M. J. O'Conor, Mrs. M. Smith and Martin Brada and beloved grandmother of Elmo Smith Jr." She was a native of New Orleans. Relatives and friends and also members of the Canal Street Presbyterian Church, officers and members of the Lydia Memorial Circle of the King's Daughters and the Ball Society of the Canal Street Presbyterian Church were all invited to attend the funeral, showing a wide circle of friends and acquaintances. The wake was at her residence, now at 318 South Rocheblave Street. Interment was in Metairie Cemetery after services were held at Canal Street Presbyterian Church.

On Monday, December 2, 1954, Frederick M. Brada died. He was married to Caroline Keifer McCarthy. His children were listed in the obituary as Mrs. Wilber Hoyt and Mrs. Andrew Bacos. His obituary was ornate and he was said to be the "brother of Mrs. Edith O'Conor, Mrs. M. E. Smith and Martin Brada. His parents were the late Nicholas and Hermina Brada. Frederick died at age 62 and was a native of New Orleans. He remained a printer for his entire life. Relatives and friends of the family and also employees of Harvey Press were invited to attend the funeral. A Requiem Mass was held at Sacred Heart of Jesus Church. So the Brada family clearly belonged to several different Christian denominations and mostly likely the men adopted their wive's religion.

"Out in the Parish," as they say in New Orleans referring to St. Bernard Parish, we find a "general farmer" named Frank Brabetz. He was 44 in the 1920 census and he arrived from Bohemia in 1907. His 40 year old wife Mary arrived from Bohemia in 1908 They may well have been married in Europe and she followed after he had secured a home. What happened to them is unknown.

We first encounter the photographer Joseph Cermak in the 1919 City Directory. This lists his house as 1200 Burgundy Street near Esplanade Ave. The 1920 census says Joseph was 28. It notes that he arrived in 1913 and that he was a pottery artist. He was still living on Burgundy Street. Sometime after this he married Edna Sykes. They had two children, Helen and Josef; the son having the Czech spelling of the name Joseph. This is what probably led him to more stable employment by 1928 as an "assistant" at the Herbet J. Harvey Company. What sort of company this was is not known. His house this year was listed at 2303 Laharpe. The very next year, in 1929, the city directory has Cermak working again as a self-employed photographer. And he moved his family to 2024 Coliseum Street in Uptown New Orleans.

In the City Archives at New Orleans Public Library in the Mayor deLesseps S. Morrison Photograph Collection there is a typical Louisiana photo of a man and his fish. The man won the City of New Orleans' trophy for the first tarpon caught in the 1954 Grand Isle Tarpon Rodeo. The photograph was taken by Joseph Cermak. This seems to be his only known surviving work; perhaps, though, there are many people in New Orleans with family portraits that were taken at his studio.

In 1900 the Bohemian George Cernich was a cooper, also known as a barrel maker, an occupation long gone. He resided at 1823 North Roman Street. It is obvious that he was Czech only by his last name which means "dark skinned," or "swarthy." Their son William C. Cernich was an electrician living at 1624 Annette Street. In 1919 the city directory records Mrs. Anna Cernich working as a confectioner and living at 942 Verret Street. Also in the city directory for this year is Miss Hilda Cernich. She was a clerk at the well known department store D. H. Holmes. Her residence was 1224 St. Anthony Street. She was probably Anna and George's daughter; George was apparently deceased at this time. William was still listed as an electrician living at 1921 Frenchman Street.

10 years later more evidence of the children of Anna and George is available. The 1928 city directory says Anthony was working as a salesman at EC Palmer & Co. He owned his own house at 2030 St. Claude Avenue. Their daughter Hazel was a bookbinder at the Hauser Printing Company. She had an apartment at 2657 Iberville Street in Mid City. Her sister-in-law Mrs. Mary Cernich was a machine operator at Seet Orr Company. She lived a few blocks away from Hazel at 3015 Conti Street. She is one of the few working women we find among Czech and Slovak immigrants. William H. was still an electrician living at 1921 Frenchman. He had a son living with him, also named William. The young man worked at the Orleans Parish School Board. To whom William was married is not clear.

In 1929 Albert Cernich was listed as a lineman, presumably on a railroad. He lived at 3010 St. Louis Street, while his sister Hilda lived at 2235 Elysian Fields Avenue. By 1936 he was living with his wife Nora at 601 Congress Street in the Bywater neighborhood. Friday, June 19 was a sad day for their daughter Alice Cernich died. She was just 7 months and 10 days old. They did have five other children: Calvin, Dorothy, Albert, Georgiana and Betty. Also mentioned in an obituary was Anthony Cernich, "a native of this city," who died aged forty nine years, and who seems to be an uncle.

Ceska-Srubek-Silkep-Dubovy

This is one family about whom we know a considerable amount even if it is very confusing. Steve (born with the Czech name Stepan) Ceska Sr., was born about 1879 in Lisov, Bohemia and died on January 18, 1958, in Charity Hospital, New Orleans. Lisov is in Southern Bohemia not far from the city of Ceske Budejovice. He was, according to his obituary, "the husband of Albania Hurt (Hurtova,) who died before him. He was aged 76 years and was a "native of Czechoslovakia and a resident of this city for the past 51 years." The obituary notes that "employees of

McKenzies Pastry Shoppes and Schott & Company are invited to attend the funeral." Albina Hurtova was most likely born in 1879 in Bohemia; probably also in Lisov. In the Czech language a woman's last name often ends in "ova"—that is the male surname Hurt has a female counterpart "Hurtova." She used both once she was in America. She married Ceska sometime around 1906 or 1907, probably in Galveston, Texas. She died on October 27, 1912. Apparently she died from complications with the birth of her daughter Camilla. After this sad event Steve Sr., married Marie Srubek on August 23, 1913. He was later divorced from Marie in an acrimonoius split in the late 1920s and that is why she is not mentioned in the obituary. Marie Srubek was born December 5, 1887 and was apparently baptized on December 6, 1889, in Novy Jicin. This is a city in southern Moravia, Czechoslovakia. She died March 29, 1967. How he found a Czech girl in the ethnic mix of New Orleans is not known and perhaps he married her because she was Czech.

There are two 1919 city directories by competing companies. One lists Steve Ceska as a butcher living at 1220 Mazant. The other lists him at residing at 1343 Touro Street. There is evidence that he actually lived at both places and moved in between the compilation of the two directories. In the 1920 census Steve Ceska was listed as 41 year old. The census says he arrived in 1893 and became a citizen in 1914. But there is an existing manifest of the ship SS Koln showing that Stepan Ceska arrived at Galveston, Texas with his brother Frank on August 25, 1905. They sailed from Bremen, Germany, as was usual for many Czechs and Slovaks. Stepan was already a butcher. The next year there is a manifest listing for Albina "Harkal," also known as Albina Hurtova, who came on June 24, 1906. The manifest says she was born in 1888, but we also have a birth year of 1879. On the manifest itself it says she is coming to "meet her intended husband, Stephan Ceska." She came on the SS Cassel to Galveston from Bremen. Why the discrepencies is unknown, but it is the same man and woman, as determined by the family historians.

Also in the 1920 census was his wife Marie, 31, and four daughters: Iola, 11, Marie, 10, Camilla, 7, and Antonette, 5. All the children were born in Louisiana. But these first three children were with Albina, while Antonette is the child of Marie. In 1925 they had a fifth daughter, Beverly. A descendant of Beverly, Kathy Caprio, provided and clarified much of the information on this family for me. Steve was a butcher at a restaurant and Marie was a waitress at hotel. She was another of the few woman who worked outside the home.

Iola was born August 21, 1909, in New Orleans and died March 3, 1991, in Helotes, Texas. She had married Bertrand Hourne. Marie was born June 5, 1911, and died in New Oleans in 1985. She was married to Anthony Cimo. Camilla was born September 17, 1912, and died March 3, 1992. She had four sons with Peter Livermore who was nearly 20 years her senior. They are James, Douglas, Peter Jr., and Carl. After the death of Livermore she married a Mr. Montet. Antonette was born August 15, 1914, in New Orleans and died March, 1992. She lived her entire life in the city. She was married to Scott Reinecke; he was from an old line New Orleans family. The fifth daughter, Beverly, was born October 16, 1925. She married Paul Michael Caprio, Jr. on February 13, 1943, in New Orleans. He was born in September, 1918, in Rochester, New York, and died at Memphis, Tennessee.

In 1928, Marie was the "department captain" at the Roosevelt Hotel. Presumably this was the housekeeping department but that is not certain. She was living at 2212 Gallier. Her brother, Karel (Charles) Srubek, was a salad and meat chef at the same hotel. He had come separately from the Czech lands. Kathy Caprio has his white chef's hat and one of his knives and also his old portable typewriter (vintage 1917 or so.) Their daughter, Marie, was a clerk at Union Indemnity Company. Stephen was a warehouse worker for Schott and Company and lived at 2119 Derbigny Street. The divorce had occurred by now.

Their son, Stephen Jr., was a carpenter and lived with the family on Gallier Street. He was Steven Sr's stepson-and and later adopted son. He was Albina Hurtova's son by a previous relationship and apparently out of wedlock. According to Caprio he did beautiful cabinet work and "my mom's house is filled with antique reproductions that he made for the family."

Steve Jr. also made reproductions for the Louisiana State Museum in the French Quarter which are still there and seen by many a tourist. Steve Jr. was born in the Czech Republic in 1905 and raised by relatives in the old country while his mother left for America. He was apprenticed as a carpenter when just a young man to his father's family. He arrived in America in 1925 after his obligations were met. He died on November 18, 1953, while he was living on Art Street in New Orleans. He had changed his surname from Hurta to Ceska when Steve Sr. adopted him, possibly in 1906, but definitely by 1925 after he came to America more than 10 years after his mother Albina's death. The 1929 city directory says Steve Ceska, Sr. was a butcher living at 618 Louisa.

We can follow the Srubek, Silkep and Dubovy families backwards fairly well for a few generations. Franz Srubek was married to Lucie Cernin in the early 1800s and they lived all their lives in the Czech Republic. They had a son Jan Srubek who married Florentina Silpek. The last name was actually originally Slipek but was changed to Silpek in America; when or by whom it was changed is not known. Their children were Marie Srubek who was born in 1864 and "Rose" Terezie Srubek, born November 14, 1865 in Moravsky Leskovec #28. This is the house number and the street in Novy Jicin, Moravia. Rose married first a man also named Srubek. A srubek is the Czech word for someone who had lived in a "srub," or log cabin. He was either unrelated or distantly related to her. She and Srubek, whose first name we do not know, had two children: Charles (Karel), who was born on August 5, 1895 in Moravsky Leskovec #7, a house just down the street from Rose's parents. She died on October 29, 1938 and is buried in St. Louis #3 Cemetary, New Orleans. (This is Caprio's great-grandmother and she went by the last names Srubek, Dubovy and Silkep in various documents.)

Rose Terezie then married John Dubovy. He was was born April 23, 1872, in Moravsky Leskovec #28, and was thus a neighbor, in Novy Jicin. They were married February 15, 1897. They had several children. Adolphine Dubovy was born on October 25, 1903, in Novy Jicin and died in March 1985 in New Orleans; she married Henry Langhetee, Sr. He was 10 years younger than she was. He was born on March 3, 1913, and this is another example of a reversal of the usual male-female age differences in marriages. He died in December of 1962. They had one son, Henry Langhetee, Jr., who was born March 6, 1941, in New Orleans. He died at just 50 years of age on March 16, 1991. He, too, is buried in New Orleans' St. Louis Cemetery #3. Henry Jr, married Mary Damien Ganucheau, who was born on April 12, 1941, in New Orleans. They were married on May 23, 1970, in New Orleans.

Two other daughters were born to the union of Rose and John Dubovy: Agnes, born in 1902, and Angela, born in 1905, both in Novy Jicin. From family history we learn that Adolphine wound up in an orphanage or girls home in New Orleans and her mother who worked on a nearby farm came just two or three times a month to see her. Apparently Angela and Agnes were in this institution, too, but we lose track of them. It appears that Rose Terezie took her entire family to America after her husband John Dubovy died. She and her brood, both the Srubek and Dubovy children, were listed as coming in 1907 on board the ship Willehad from Bremen to Baltimore. The family is listed as "Mahren," which is the German word for Moravian.

Rose Terezie's other siblings were Florentine, born on January 30, 1868; a sister Frantiska, born on October 10, 1869; a brother, Frantisek, born on July 11, 1871; and Anna, born July 13, 1877; but she died shortly after birth. These people stayed in Europe as far as is known and thus the family extends into the old country. Another branch of this extended family, long lost, has just been located in Texas, where Frank Ceska, Steve Ceska Sr's, brother settled. This family had all the things we think of as so modern: unmarried mothers, single mothers, bitter divorces, lost relatives and family squabbles. Obviously these complications of life have been with people for a long time.

Other Czechs and Slovaks

In 1920 Sineman Electrical Company had a capable worker in the Bohemian-born James Churun. He was 36 and married to Bessie, 32, who born in Illinois. Their son, Edward, was also born in Illinois and was 12 at this time. They must have recently arrived in the city since their daughter Beatrice, just an infant of 14 months, was born in Texas. They lived at 3136 Maurepas Street in New Orleans.

The Drendul family was listed as Austro-Slovak in the 1910 census. The head of the household was John Drendul, 35. His wife Mary was 28. They had two daughters, Pauline, 3 and Helen, just six months old. They were living at 941 Barracks Street. He operated a retail grocery. They all came to America in 1889. Joseph Drendul, John's father, lived with them. He was a 58 year old peddler of dry goods. Also living in the household was another Slovak, Anna Pavur, listed as a "lodger." She was apparently a single mother at 42. She came in 1878. She was laboring as a servant in a private home to support her two children, Joseph, 14, and Annie, 8. All the adults were immigrants but all the children in this family were born in Louisiana. That places Anna Pavur in Louisiana in 1896. Her husband is not mentioned in any record.

Eugene Franek was a grocer who lived at 1041 Marais Street. There was another Franek, Stephen, who lived at 4324 North Villere and may have been a brother. By 1910 it is known that this man was now living at 709 St. Phillip Street in the French Quarter. He had his wife, Maggie, 44, and six children to support. The children were Agnes, 19, Eugene, 18, Rudolph, 14, Mary, 13, Annie, 8, and Josephine, 4. All were born in "Austro-Hungary." Stephen was 49 years old and supported this large family on the earnings from his peddling dry goods. Stephen and Maggie had been married for 25 years at this point. Also in the household was the 24 year old Peter Geribica. He was listed as a "son-in-law." He was married to Agnes and he had arrived in 1903. The census says they all arrived in 1900. This would mean, however, that the two youngest daughters, Annie and Josephine, were born in Louisiana. There is no other evidence for this. Peter Gerabica was later to change his name to Jarabica and run a grocery store of his own.

The Horil family lived in New Orleans for many years. The first notice of them is in the 1900 Census. They were then living at 909 St. Philip Street.

Joseph Horil was a 45 year old grocer who was born in December of 1854. His wife Annie was 45 also. She was born in May of 1855. Their son George was born in March of 1878 and was now 22. He worked as a salesman at his father's grocery. Joseph and Annie also had four younger children. The birth order was girl, boy, girl, boy: Mary, born January, 1885, was 14; Ferdinand, 10, was born in February of 1890; Annie came along in March of 1892 and now was 8; finally there was John who was born 1898 and was just 2 years old. This is quite a spread in ages for any line of children.

Joseph Horil died January 26, 1910, whe he was 54. His obituary said he was "a native of Hungary and a resident of this city for the past twenty eight years." This puts him in New Orleans in 1882. With his death the 1910 the census records that Anna was now a 54 year old widow who had been married for 35 years and came to America in 1888. The census also says that she had her own income though it does not state clearly from what source. Presumably it is from the grocery store she inherited. She is, though, one of the few independent Slovakian women lived in New Orleans.

This same census has the family in the 3rd Precinct of the city at 1003 Burgundy Street in the French Quarter. Ferdinand, now 21, was listed as the head of household. It also reports that he was a proprietor of a grocery store. Still living at the house were his sisters Anna, now 17 and Pauline, 14. There were also his two younger brothers, John, 16, and Paul, 12. In the census these two boys are actually listed as "sons" of the head of house. They are really Ferdinand's brothers. The 1910 census list birthplaces for children which the 1900 census does not. It is here that the only evidence that all the kids were born in Louisiana is given.

George, the son mentioned in the 1900 census, had by this time moved elsewhere, though where is not known. There was another son who was born in Slovakia. He was named Joseph F. Horil. He was born in 1876 and died aged 42 on Friday, March 1, 1918. His obituary goes on to state he was the "beloved husband of Eugenie Vidal, [he was a] a native of Austria and a resident of this city for the past thirty years. Buried in St. Roch Cemetery." She was a native of New Iberia in the Cajun heartland.

By 1919 the city directory listed Ferdinand as a grocer with both his residence and business at 1000 Burgundy Street. Both his brothers, John and Paul, were in the United States Navy at this time. Their address is given as 1011 Bourbon Street. This is where their mother, identified as "Mrs. Joseph Horil," also lived. Joseph F. Horil is listed as owning his own grocery with both the shop and residence at 800 Dauphine Street. It is clear, though, that he died sometime between the gathering of the information for the city directory and its publication.

By 1922 Ferdinand had teamed up with a man named Schulz. They had a grocery store called "Horil & Schulz" at 2901 Tulane Avenue. Ferdinand lived next door at 2903 Tulane. His brother John was in the soft drink business and was working out of 801 Bourbon Street. His own house was at 825 North Claiborne Avenue. Their mother was still living. Only now she was at 905 North Rampart Street. Paul was in the meat business at number 62 Treme Market. He lived down the block from John at 925 North Claiborne Avenue.

The Horil family had grown to 17 grandchildren and four great-grandchildren by the time that Anna Drendul Horil, "beloved wife of the late Joseph Horil, and mother of George, Ferdinand, John and Paul Horil, Mrs. Alex Grisoli and Mrs. Michal Lion and Mrs. Frank Belin, aged 80 years," died. The only concrete clue we have that the family was Slovakian comes from her obituary which states that she was "a native of Rovna, Austria." Rovna is an area of Slovakia which provided more than a few Slovak immigrants to Louisiana. Since we know her son Joseph Jr., was born in Slovakia it is definite that that Joseph, Sr., was born in Slovakia, too. They were also certainly married there. Besides this scanty evidence is the fact that Horil is a fairly common Slovak name. Also, though her maiden name was Drendul, it is not known if she was related to John Drendul.

Some time in the 1920s Ferdinand changed his name to Fred and left the grocery business. In 1929 he was in the oil business with his son Fred Jr. Their establishment was at 5302 Canal Boulevard. They both lived at 5229 Hawthorne Street. This year a Mrs. Jennie Horil is listed as living at 905 North Rampart which was where the matriarch of the family lived. Perhaps she is one of the daughters who changed her first name or she was a granddaughter. It is not clear where she fits into the family tree.

Ferdinand Joseph Horil, Jr. married Cora (Leona) Schulz. She was probably the daughter of the Schulz his father was in business with. He had several children. He was the father of "Mrs. John T Elfer, Mrs. Raymond L Buchert, Ferdinand J Jr (actually the third,) Joseph L. and Herbert H. Horil." His sister, now known as Mrs. M. Lion, was still alive, as were his brothers John and Paul. There is mention of the late Mrs. F. Berlin, Mrs. Grisolis and George Horil, He also was survived by 17 grandchildren and 4 great grandchildren. He was 73 years old when he died and was "a native of New Orleans" according to his obituary.

The 1900 census has the glaring mistake of the Hustava family being counted twice. Once they are listed as the "Houstava" family and the second time they are listed as the "Hustava" family. All the details on the two entries are the same except ethnicity and the spelling. Under the first name they are listed as Bohemian and under the second name they are listed as "Hungarian Slovak." They were living in the 6th Ward according to one of the data sheets. The second is unclear. Did they move between the time enumerators were getting to the individual houses? It is a slim possibility. But why the difference in ethnicity? That is not really explainable except as a mistake on the enumerator's part.

But the family was to have nearly a thirty year presence documented in New Orleans. In that 1900 census Frank Hustava was aged 30. He was born in "Hungary" in April, 1870, which was technically correct. His language was listed as "Slovak." He came 1888 and for the past 12 years was working as a peddler. He and his wife Josephine, 26, were married for 8 years. It is not known if they were married in Louisiana but we do know that all their children were born in Louisiana. She was born February of 1874. Either she was born in Hungary and spoke Slovakian or she was a Bohemian speaking Bohemian. One is on one form and the other form has the other information. It is impossible to determine which census form is correct. Josephine came 1888 and was in the United States 12 years. Their children, ages, and birth month and year are: Annie, 6, born in August of 1893; A son Joseph, 4, born in November, 1895; A second son born in July 1897, named Paul; and finally, there was a third son named Steven who was just two months old after having been born in November of 1899.

The 1910 census says Frank Hustava was now 42, and a "peddler of notions." His wife was now known as Sophie, 36, but this time the census says she came in 1893. This, however, is more likely the year they got married. Perhaps Josephine did not quite understand the question put by the enumerator or the enumerator misunderstood the answer. Anna who was now 15 was working as a billing clerk. Joseph, 13, and Paul, 11, were joined by a son John who was just 8 years old. There is no mention of Steven who would have been 10. It would have been tragic if the boy died but there is no record to be found of this. The boys were joined by Mary. She was 5 at the time of the census and their little sister, Pauline, was just 3 years old. They were living in the cramped quarters of the rear apartment at 713 St. Philip Street in the French Quarter. This is the third Czech or Slovak family living on St. Philip Street at about the same time. If they knew each other no one recorded their friendships.

By 1920 the family was living at 81 Chartres Street. This is the French Quarter. They were still rented premises but it was a larger apartment. Now the 51 year old Frank was listed as a Slovak. He was a longshoreman by occupation. His wife was still known as Sophie; she was now 45. Their son Joe, now a young man of 22, was a car repairer for a railroad. Mary, 15, was a worker in a tobacco factory. Pauline, who was said to be 11, was in school. She must have been two years older, though, for she was 3 in 1910. There were three more additions to the family. Two more sons, Anthony, 7, who was at school, and Adam who was only 5. And finally there was their daughter Agnes, a toddler at 3 ½. What became of the 10 Hustava children is not known. The whole family seems to disappear with the onset of the Roaring Twenties. We can well imagine that supporting 10 children as a peddler or longshoreman must have been very difficult.

New Orleans has always been one of America's most Catholic of cities and in the 1910 census we find to two Czech Catholic nuns. Sister Agatha at Sister of Mercy, 60 years old, and Sister Bertha Sophere, at the Convent of the Perpetual Adoration, 24 years old. Both were listed as Bohemian in the census.

The two story building where Peter Jarabica, who was married into the Franek family, had his grocery store still stands at the corner of Mazant and Burgundy Streets in the Bywater area of New Orleans. The address of the store was 4101 Burgundy. It was a typical neighborhood grocery store, about a 1,000 square feet with two aisles on either side of a center shelving unit and shelves along the walls. It must have been filled with both bulk commodities. That was still the way one "made" your groceries in New Orleans at the time. Modern packaging was just beginning to hit the food industry.

According to a grandson of Peter, Gerard Peter Jarabica of Mandeville, "grandfather started a grocery store and was in business with Schweggman for a while." However, no concrete evidence of this relationship could be found but there is no reason to doubt that two grocery store owners had business dealings with each other. Gerard also recalls family stories that about 1927 or 1929 his grandfather had a pro-ball baseball club or was involved in an important way. He is not sure which was actually a true story. Mary Ann, Gerard's cousin relays the typical immigrant story: "Grandfather said: 'you're not going to speak Czech—you're in America.'"

In the 1920 Census Peter Jarabica, 32, and his wife Agnes, 29, (nee Franek) and a daughter Anne who was just 8 were living in the Bywater. Peter is listed as "Austria-Slovak" They had two boarders, one named Bronislaw Rapiek from Russia and the other Boris Stidne from Slovakia. Both were 24 years old. One can imagine the two boarders happening on the Jarabica family and hearing the accents and perhaps a few words in the old language and then quickly becoming friends. How else to explain their presence?

In 1928, according to the city directory for that year, Peter Jarabica was still a grocer at 4101 Burgundy Street in the Bywater neighborhood of the city. The next year's directory has the same information. 10 years passed with a relative sameness to each day before he died on Saturday September 10, 1938. His obituary says he was living at 2722 St. Ann Street at the time. He was the "beloved husband" of Agnes Franek, and the father of Joseph, George and Frances, and Mrs. Mark Guidry.

He had a brother named Thomas Jarabica but we do not know where he was living; perhaps in Kansas City, Missouri, because the obituary asks that city's newspapers to copy the obituary. Peter was just 52 years old. The obituary says he was "a native of Czechoslovakia and a resident of this city for the past 35 years." If this is correct he arrived in America in 1903. He was a member of the National Slovak Society and Imperial Grove No. 49 of U.A.O.D. There is no Slovak society of any kind ever identified in New Orleans so to which chapter he belonged is not known. The obituary has the added fillip of "from the air conditioned Lamana Panno Fallo, Inc. 625 North Rampart" A service was held at St. Sorse de Lima Church with an interment at St. Roch Cemetery,

In the 1954 city directory George A. is listed as an accountant at A.L. Shaw Company. His wife Rai was a manager at Monarch Sales. They made their home at 1946D Fillmore Street. Besides Gerald another Jarabica descendant still lives in New Orleans. This is Aaron Jarabica. He owns an antique store at 4310 Magazine Street.

Joseph Kabernik is listed in the 1920 census with his family. He became a citizen in 1901 just two years after his arrival in 1899. He was accompanied on the voyage by his wife Mary. Both were 48 at the time of the census. Where they spent the years between their arrival in America and their arrival in New Orleans is not known. They must have been married in the country bearing the made up name "Slovakland" from which the family is said to come because they brought a son named Emile over to America in 1908. This means, however, that the boy who is 12 years old in 1920 must have been 1 year old in 1908. Did the parents go back to have their first child purposely in the old country? That would seem to go against the fact that they became American citizens so quickly. Was the child an orphaned baby of a sister or brother? The record does not get more specific than saying "son." That, of course, does not rule out an adoption. There is also the question of who brought the child to America? He was way too young to travel by himself. We do not know.

Whatever the case, the couple were blessed with twin girls while living in New Orleans in 1911. Perhaps they were born in Charity Hospital as so many of the children of immigrants were. The girls, Pauline and Bertha, were 9 years old in 1920. Joseph supported his family by working with "wirework at wire works." This was probably a skill he picked up in his native land and that he put to good use at the dawn of the new century. Bratislava, Slovakia, had many such manufacturing plants. While in which wireworks he was working is not stated the Slovak Nosacka family did operate such a business nearby. This could point to the two families knowing each other even in Slovakia itself.

At 510 St. Claude Avenue lived Ludwig Klepec who was a 34 year old office clerk. The 1920 census says he was "Austro-Slovak" and came in 1904. His wife Rose was 8 years older than him at the age of 42. She was of English and Spanish heritage. Rodney Brown, 17, Ludwig's stepson, lived with them. What young Rodney though of this arrangement and his step-father's no doubt thick accent has not been recorded.

Also in 1920 a Moravian named Steven Konecky, 43, who arrived in 1914 and was now working in the laundry department at Charity Hospital was recorded. Another Moravian working in Charity Hospital was Antonea Luza. He is listed as 42 years old. His job was listed as "Kitchenwork in housekeeping;" he became a citizen in 1913. Both are mentioned only in this census. Nothing else could be found on them.

The Kundera family is also listed only in the 1910 census. They lived in Precinct 4 on Marais Street. George Kundera, 34, was listed as a "Hungarian" who spoke Slovak. His wife Maria, 28, was also born in Slovakia. They had been married for 7 years by this time. Their three kids, however, were born in New Orleans. Joseph was 7, Paul was 4, and their 3 year old younger sister was named Maria. The parents came to America 10 years apart: he came in 1891 and she came in 1901. By the children's ages we can tell that George and Maria were in the city and married by 1903.

The Lurie family is also found only in the 1920 census. Ignatz Lurie, 65, and his 60 year old wife, Julia, were borders at 1729 Peter Avenue. He was a salesman at a dry goods store who came in 1869 and became a citizen in 1888. He was just 14 when he arrived in America. Thus there is a good chance that his English did not bear much of a trace of his native Bohemian accent. Being just boarders they did not have a strong stake in the city and they do not appear in city directories or the next census.

Frank Mann is yet another of those few people whose birthplace was written as "Slovakland." There has never been such an entity; you will not find such a place on any map. He and his wife, Francis, both 46 years old, were merchants in the 4th Ward. This is also known as the Lakeview area of New Orleans. He came in 1893 while his wife followed from "Slovakland" in 1894. They only appear in the 1920 census.

There was a Frank Novak in the 1910 census. This is the first time we encounter the most common of Czech and Slovak surnames since Jean George Novaque on the German Coast in the 1740s. This Novak was said to be Austro-Bohemian.

He made his living as a laborer at Charity Hospital. That makes him the third such Czech working during this decade at the largest hospital in New Orleans. Then he disappears from the scene. The next census shows that a John Novak, 41, arrived in 1912. His birthplace was written as "Austro-Slovak." He worked on car repair at the "SPRR." This was probably the Southern Pacific Rail Road. It seems obvious that these two Novaks were unrelated.

Nosacka

A family that was to have a long history in New Orleans and at least some of whose members could be said to be "well known" was one named Nosacka. They were a Slovakian family and a few of the progeny married other Czechs and Slovaks. They are first found in New Orleans in 1897 when there is a vague mention of the Nosacka Wire Works in a newspaper. The next mention of the family business is from the Historic New Orleans Collection. The company had an ad printed by an unknown printer for "Iron products by S. Nosacka & Son." The ad is from the first decade of the 20th century.

By 1910 it is known that Joseph Nosacka, 26, was an iron worker at a wire manufacturer. His wife was the 20 year old Pauline. They lived separately from his father. Steven Nosacka was 56 and his occupation was listed as "iron work at manufacturer." He was married to Mary who was 52. The next two children were both sons. They were working with their father as "iron helper[s] at manufacturer." Steven was 19 and John was 17. They had three younger siblings: Amelia, 15, Josephine, 13 and George 10. Also in the household were three Slovak boarders. All of these were also "ironworkers at manufacturer." George Drendul, 66, came to America in 1862 and he may have been Mary's father. Adam Gyurick was 45 and came in 1905. The third was Stepan Kavka, 22, who came in 1903. It is not known if this Drendul was related to any other Drenduls in New Orleans either. This is the only mention of the two workers in any record.

In the 1920 census states that Stephen owned a wire and iron works manufacturing company at 812 Bourbon Street in the French Quarter. He lived above the business with his wife Mary. Her maiden name was Drendul and she might be a member of the Drendul's of New Orleans, but again, this is not for certain. Stephan Jr. was also an "iron work[er] at wire and iron works." Their daughter Josephine also was still living at this home. Showing that the family was becoming more American they named a son George. He was a student at a university in the city; though at which one is not stated.

In the Louisiana State University's Hill Memorial Library in Baton Rouge there is a poster for "Nosacka, S. and Son." The poster advertises metal furniture, flower stands, hanging baskets, animal cages and yard equipment. Perhaps even to this day there are examples of the company's work strewn through the courtyards and hung on the balconies of buildings throughout the French Quarter. The Nosacka ironworks was old enough to be in existence when the city underwent a number system change. The old number for the business was 178 Bourbon Street while the new number was 812 which places it between Dumaine and St. Ann Streets.

On March 27, 1914, John Nosacka, "of Austria-Hungary and brother of S. Nosacka," died at the age of 45. He was a resident of the city for 25 years meaning he arrived when he was just 20 years old. Funeral services were at the home of his brother Steven on Bourbon Street. This shows perhaps that the family was of the Slovak Freethinking religious tradition. He is buried at St. Roch's Cemetary.

The only obituary that places the birthplace at Rovne, Czechoslovakia, is that of Steven Nosacka Sr. He died on January 11, 1927. He was the "beloved husband of the late Mary Drendul." He was apparently 25 when he arrived in New Orleans, probably directly from Europe, which we can deduce from the facts presented in the obituary: "aged 74 years and a native of Rovne, Czechoslovakia, and a resident of this city for the past 49 years." Living were his three sons, Joseph, Stephen Jr, and George. From the last names of his daughters we can see that five married Slavic husbands. Veronica Durich, Mary Kluchin and Amelia Kotisik all married into Slavic families, these last two possibly Czech or Slovak while the first is Yugoslavian. Two married Bohemian brothers, Mrs. Anna Podrasky and Mrs. Josephine Podrasky. This is a family with both New Orleans and Lake Charles connections. The Podrasky family were owners of shoe stores in Lake Charles and will be looked at in the next chapter. The only one who married outside of the Slavic race was his daughter Mrs. Catherine Preto who seems to have married an Italian.

In a son not mentioned in Steven senior's obituary and virtually 10 years later, July 13, 1937, John J. Nosacka died. His wife was Bertha Chrestien and obviously from a French family in the city. He was the father of Steven, George and Hazel who were all still single. He had two other daughters, Mrs. Frank Restivo and Mrs. John Mutti. This is a clear indication of ethnic intermarriage in the second generation. All his siblings were still alive; the three brothers, Joseph, Steven and George Nosacka, and the six sisters. He was just 43 "and native of this city." He lived 1840 Pauger Street. From his obituary we learn the names of five of the sister's husbands: George Podrasky, Steven Kluchin, Paul Durich, Frank Preto and Louis Podrasky; though not of "Mrs. H. Kotisik."

George P Nosacka, John's brother, also died young. He was only 44. He was living at 3110 Derby Place with his wife Jesse Franek. She was a member of the Slovak Franek family already looked at above. The remainder of his siblings were still alive. On January 13, 1954, Stephen Nosacka Jr. of 1533 Music Street died. He was survived by his sons Stephan A. and Raymond. And also one living brother Joseph and one living sister, Mrs. Louis Podrasky. This means that George and Anna Prodrasky, Mary Kluchin, Veronica Durich, Catherine Preto, and Amelia Kotisik all were dead by this time. Their obituaries were not found and nothing is known of the circumstances of their life or death.

The penultimate member of this large brood of children to die was Joseph Nosacka who succumbed at 80. According to his obituary he "designed head-dresses for Kings and Queens of Carnival krewes." He lived at 623 Andry Street but had kept the family business at 812 Bourbon Street. The same notice gives a little description of how he worked: "After he had designed the supporting wires rhinestones were placed on the headdress." He was well enough known as a professional at what he did that he also "designed funeral wreaths for many of the city's florists." His obituary is a more prominent article than the brief funeral notices of other deceased. No doubt he was well known among the city's Mardi Gras participants. Nosacka had been retired for 15 years before he died but his fame was still quite apparent given the size of his obituary. He left a daughter known only as Mrs. Albert Jones and a son Paul J. Nosacka and a sister Mrs. Louis Podrasky.

One last member of the family whose obituary we have is Frances Nosacka. She was the wife of the Joseph Nosacka and at the time of her death lived at 2811 Magazine Street. For many years Joseph "was the operator of a general merchandise store at Jonesville." Whether this means in the town of Jonesville in north Louisiana or some other location is not clear. She had two sisters living but they had no children and that brings to an end the Nosacka family in New Orleans.

More Familes from 1900 to 1950

There is the odd situation of one Frank Owen down in Plaquemines Parish who was a 47 year old roomer. His occupation was listed as "common laborer." Though he is listed as Slovak in the 1920 census his language was listed as "Turkish." Perhaps he was a Gypsy. In any event, Owen is not a Czech name and we do not know what the original was. This is the only record of this man.

In the 1910 census in the 3rd Precinct of New Orleans at 720 Dumaine Street lived the Panywalny Family. William, 26, was already married 8 years to Clara. She was 40 years old. They had 8 kids but only four still living. One was Adam Hasker, 17, a step-son. Hasker is most likely an Americanization of "Haska." Willaim's own children were Anny, 6, Mary, 3 and Josephine 2. All were born in Louisiana. There is no information about the parents in the census; all the columns were left blank. Adam was a helper at a saddler shop. This was the biggest age difference between married couples that I found. Or it was a huge mistake. If it is true it seems odd even by today's standards and must have really stuck out in that era.

At 2340 Frenchman Street lived Frank Pavelka and his wife Veronica in 1920. They were Slovaks who arrived in 1888. They became citizens in 1900. He was 58 and she was 59. We do not know their occupations as none is listed on the census form. If they were retired they must have made some money somewhere or perhaps they were both unemployed at the moment. Where they achieved citizenship is not clear.

Isaac Philip was 31 and married for 3 years when he is found in the 1910 census. He was not Czech or Slovak. He was born in Louisiana of an English father and Louisiana mother. He was, though, married to Edna who was 28. She had been born in New York of Austro-Bohemian Parents. They had a daughter named Evangeline who was just 2 at the time of the census. She had been born in Louisiana. This is one of the examples we have of early Czechs marrying someone of a different nationality. All we can do is speculate about this family but if they met in Louisiana, that means there was yet another Czech family. We do not know Edna's maiden name and I could not figure out if she was one of the few Edna's we find in the records of Czechs and Slovaks in Louisiana. It is possible that they got married in New York and then left for Louisiana though this seems unlikely given the birthplace of his mother. It is an odd situation altogether.

The 1910 census records that living behind the same Horil family of which we already spoke, in the rear apartment at 1004 Burgundy Street in the French Quarter, was the Pilak family. The head of the household was Andrew, 66. He was a salesman for a jewelry store. He came to America in 1890 but did not get to New Orleans until after the turn of the century. In a reversal of the usual immigration order his wife, Anna, 69, came to America in 1889. Their daughter, Mary, who was 31, also came in 1890, probably traveling with her father. All three were born in Slovakia. The parents were married for 40 years. This is the only record of the Pilak family in New Orleans.

The only thing known about the Bohemian Louis Podkrivacky was that he was engaged in the dry goods trade at 1401 Pauline Street where he also kept his residence. He is only found in the 1929 City Directory. Another Czech man found only in the 1929 directory is Edward Polasek. He was working at H. M. & Wm. Bartels Company. He lived at 127 Camp Street. It is only clear that they were Czech from their surnames and there is no other information about them. Perhaps they both failed in the Depression and moved on before the 1930 census. Another Czech whose nationality is clear from his surname was Wenzel Ptack, (sic.) He was 42 and living in the 3rd Ward of New Orleans. A "ptak" is a "bird." (Yes, ptak is a real Czech word.) That someone "Anglicized" it by adding the "c" seems rather pointless. Czech has more than a few words starting with the letters "pt" but this is virtually unheard of in English other than Ptolemy the Pharoah. He is, however, listed in the 1910 census as "Austro-Bohemian." What became of "Mr. Bird" is not known. Perhaps he finally completely Anglicized his name.

William Povolny was a city policeman with a surname that is the Czech word for "compliant." This is perhaps an ironic name for a policeman. The 1920 census states that he was 36 and married. No wife, however, was listed on this census form. We only learn her name from his obituary. They had three children. All were born in Louisiana and presumably New Orleans, though that is not clear. They were Annie, 16, Mary, 13, and Josephine, 11. Their father came to America in 1901 and was a citizen by 1906. This would imply that he made his way to New Orleans very soon after his arrival in America. The family lived at 741 Burgundy Street in the French Quarter.

William was just 41 when he died on September 21, 1924. His obituary says he lived at 741 Bourbon Street. Could he have moved his family exactly two blocks over between 1920 and 1924? It is possible at least, though odd. In any event the obituary was correct in saying he was "a native of Bohemia and resident of this city for 23 years." Members of the Police Mutual Benevolent association and the National Slavonian Society were invited to attend the funeral. Services were held at St. Louis Cathedral pointing to the Povolnys being Catholic.

His widow, Clara Klenica, aged 66 at the time of his death, died in the 1940s. She was the "mother of William and Anna Povolvny, Mrs. Mary Reilly, Mrs. Stephan Nosacka and Adam Hesko. She was "a native of Rovne, Czechoslovakia and a resident of this city for the past 45 years." There was a good chance that William and Clara were married in Slovakia and came to America as a newly married couple. That their daughter married into the Nosacka family shows that at least some Slovaks were aware of each other in New Orleans.

Anna Povolny was living at 720 Almonaster Avenue when she died on June 19th 1943. Her survivors were listed as "sister of Mrs. John Edmonds Mrs. Josephine Nosacka and William Povolny. Stepsister of Adam Hesko." She was born in New Orleans. This family died out on November 30, 1959, when William A Povolny beloved "brother of Mrs. John Edmands, Mrs. Gene Pierpont and the late Ann Povolny, half brother of Adam Hesko, son of the late Clara Klenica and William A Povolny," died. Despite these many children who no doubt had their own children no descendants could be found in New Orleans.

In 1900 and even further down the river in the 10th Ward of Plaquemines Parish was Luke Ramadan. He was born in Bohemia in 1844 and emigrated in 1862. In the household were a woman named Julia who was 25 years old and a girl of 6 named Leontine. Both are listed as being born in Louisiana. There is no evidence of the relationships of these people though they all bore the surname Ramadan. Either this was his daughter-in-law and granddaughter or he had an extremely young wife, less than half his age.

One Czech who had already been in America for a few generations and was making his way in Louisiana was John Roberts. He was 53 years old. He was a furniture maker who was born in Georgia of Bohemian parents. His wife Mary was 42. She was born in Wisconsin of Kansas born parents. She was probably Bohemian, though, which we can determine from two probabilities. One is given the large numbers of Czechs in both those states it would seem likely that she could be also. The second is much more clear. Apparently her first husband was Czech because this couple had two children listed as foster kids who bear a Czech surname: Helen Krecek 13, and Frank Krecek 10. Also living in the household was Jenny Johnson, 45, listed as a sister-in-law and apparently widowed. This was 1920. He, too, might have had a business go bankrupt in the Depression. Hand made furniture was surely a luxury item that many people made newly poorer passed up. Also, Roberts must have been Anglicized from a Czech orginial for it definitely is not a Czech name. What the original could have been can only be conjecture.

The 1920 census for Orleans Parish shows that a Bohemian named Marie Schyder was living at 6018 Chestnut Street in the Uptown section of the city. She was the 50 year old mother-in-law of George Davila. He was a 26 year old public accountant married to her daughter. She was also named Marie and was the same age as her husband. It is not clear what nationality George was; his name could derive from any one of several heritages including Czech.

In the 5th Precinct of the 8th Ward of New Orleans in 1910 lived Cedonia Seperovich and her 22 year old son George. She was the owner of a confectionery shop. This makes her one of the few businesswomen we will encounter in this history of Czechs and Slovaks. She was a widow who had come to America in 1884. She was listed as a Hungarian-Slovak. George was a postal clerk for a railway company; he was born in America.

935 Barracks Street in the French Quarter is a 2½ story Creole house. It is a typical example of early 1800s New Orleans architecture. For a brief time it was the home of the Slecko family. This was also in 1910. George, the father of six living children, was 37. He arrived in America in 1889. He is another of these immigrants who supported his family by working on a railroad. He was listed as a laborer. He was married to his wife Marie, 31, for 18 years. The census bears the sad news that they lost a child whose name we do not know.

The living children were divided equally between three sons and three daughters. The oldest, Magdalene, was 15. The census says she was born in Louisiana; probably New Orleans. This means that the family was in the city as early as 1895 unless they were living somewhere else in the state and only moved to New Orleans later. They are not, however, in the 1900 census anywhere in the state. Valdimar, 13, bore almost a Czech name though he was born in Louisiana. Vladimir would be the proper Czech but the change could have been made by him or the census taker. His 12 year old brother Rudolph also had a typical Czech name even though it was spelled in the American style. Following him were two daughters, Elenore, 8, and Anna who was 5. Their last child was a son named Joseph who was 4 years old in 1910.

The parents are listed as "Austria-Slovak" on the census form. The form also says that the Slecko's had four "lodgers" living with them, a Spaniard and 3 Louisianians. They probably took up the slave and work quarters along the courtyard of this old home while the Sleckos lived up front. None of the Sleckos are in the index of obituaries kept by the New Orleans Times-Picayune.

Another "Austro-Slovak" family in the 1910 census was a steam engineer named Stephen Stranich. He arrived in 1901 and was now 27 years old. He was married to the 24 year old Mary for 4 years. They already had two daughters: Evelyn, 3, and Annie who was 1½. Living with them was Annie Cernizen She was Stephen's 50 year old mother-in-law. It is not clear when the two women arrived. Nor is it known what happened to the family.

In 1920 John Vanek, who came to America in 1888, lived at 2514 Orleans Street in the Mid City section of the city. He became a citizen in 1895. His wife, Josephine, also came in 1888 and swore the oath of citizenship in 1895. He had a tailor shop which he apparently operated from his home. Could this be yet another family forced out by depression? Once again only speculation can give an answer.

The Vetas family was also from the semi-fictional "Slovakland" They lived for more than 20 years in New Orleans. They are first encountered in the 1910 census. Anthony arrived in 1903 and his wife Marie arrived ten years later in 1913. He was 34 and she was 22. They both became citizens in 1917. This would seem to indicate they were married before this date. They had a daughter named Josephine whose age is listed as "2 5/12." This was the interesting way that census takers meant someone was 2 years and 5 months old.

At the time of the 1920 census Anthony had established himself at 923 Dumaine Street. He owned a French Quarter retail coffee shop. One can imagine his customers puzzling over his accent and asking him where he was from. His wife now bore the Americanized name of Marian. Their daughter, Josephine, was an only child at the age of 13.

In a case of one of the few criminals founds among the Czechs the 1910 census of New Orleans says that Oscar Wocet was an inmate at a correction facility in the city. He was Bohemian. What crime he committed we do not know. Wocet is not a normal Czech name in that the letter 'w' is not used in Czech or Slovak. What the original was can only be guessed at.

Zelenka is a common enough Czech name that we find several people with this last name. Though it is not known how or even if these people were related. One was listed as early as 1880, when Leopold Zelenka was a carpenter living at 316½ Lafayette Street; he might be related to the Zelenka family of Houma but that is not clear. He did, however, start his own family in New Orleans.

In the 1886 city directory Charles Zelenka was listed as a carpenter living on Euphrosine Street between Magnolia and Clara Streets. That same year his brother Leopold Zelenka was bartender and his wife "Mrs. A Zimmerman" were living at the same address as Charles. On November 27, 1906, Leopold sought a bar license for the premises at 1239 and 1241 Liberty Street. On December 3, 1906, a request was made to repeal the permit at the behest of a concerned neighbor.

The 1919 New Orleans city directory records that Charles was now a switch tender for the railroad. He was living at 2328 Melpomene Street. His son, Charles Jr., was a clerk at "S Bonart" at 500 South Rampart Street. He lived with his father. The 1929 city directory reveals that Charles was still a switchman but now he made his home at 2806 General Ogden. His sons Emmett, a clerk, and Walsh, a laborer, were living with him. His brother "Leo" was now in soft drinks; no doubt driven there by prohibition. He had his own house at 1769 Julia. When

Leo died April 8, 1936, he was 70 years old and lived at 747 South Claiborne Ave. He had been married for many years to Wilhelmina Ruthenberg. Besides his brother Charles he also had a second brother, Matthew, of whom nothing more is known.

Charles Zelenka died March 1, 1944. His obituary notes that he was the "beloved husband of the late Irene Walsh, father of D. Walsh, Emmett G. and Mathias F. Zelenka, brother of Mrs. Ella Strausser, and the late Mrs. Katie Schriener, aged 47 and a native and resident of this city." No mention is made of his late brother. Irene Walsh Zelenka had died on August 13, 1937. So for a number of years he was a single father. She was a native of New Orleans.

The last mention of the Zelenka family is in the 1954 city directory. D. Walsh and his wife Marie were living at 8734 Apricot. He was a clerk at Dixie Mill. His brother Emmett was married to Caroline. Emmett owned the Apricot Street food store but still lived at 2806 General Ogden. Running a neighborhood grocery was a drudge of continual work and small problems. He had at least two children older than 18 since both Emmet Jr., and Irma were listed in the city directory as students.

There is mention of "brother" Mathias who was married to Blanche. But it is not clear whose brother he was. He was, though, a ship fitter at Alexandria Ship Yard and she was a saleswoman at Woolworth's. They lived 2818 Holly Grove.

Another Zelenka was Bernard. He was married to Mina. They made their home at 142 South Clark Street as did their daughter Bertha. The young lady was a clerk at Capital Stores #23. It is not known if they are related to the other Zelenkas.

Observations on New Orleans

Among the vast tide of immigrants from Italy, German and Ireland who made New Orleans their home in the early 1900s we find just approximately 45 families and individuals comprising about 200 people from the Czech and Slovak lands. They joined the descendants from the previous 50 years of Czech and Slovak immigration to make a total community of no more than 500 people in 100 years. This is an incredibly small number in a city with more than 200,000 people. Yet, with the Pokorny sign hanging on St. Charles Avenue and the Laska sign up on Basin Street all the Czechs and Slovaks had to know they were not alone. Especially among the immigrants who lived and worked in the French Quarter it is impossible to think that they did not encounter some of their fellow countrymen. It is clear that some families intermarried. There may have been others who did so though the records found are not clear on this. The children were in school with each other. Surely they recognized the Czech and Slovak names around them. The French Quarter is a small place and it does stretch the imagination to think that the Czechs and Slovaks did not encounter each other regularly.

Czechs in Post World War II New Orleans.

Francis Soyka

Any one who went to the Isadore Newman school in uptown New Orleans during the years from World War II until the 1970s came across Francis Soyka. He was the tennis coach at this school for nearly 40 years. His life in America begins with an affidavit of good character which was notarized at 55 Wall Street, New York. In "a true translation of the Czech" documents Max Holan stated that "I am conversant with the Czech and English languages." He then provides the English translation of a Czech language document; Holan's letter was signed on 12 December, 1940: "Frantisek Sojka, was born in the Karlin Section of Prague on April 25th 1892, with right of citizenship in Prague. This is in support of an application of extension of passport." He was living in a house in an area of Prague known as: Praha X [ten,] Karlin, Pobřežni. The translation and the original are just part of the rich trove of materials related to Soyka that are in the Historic New Orleans Collection.

Francis was a Czech Jew whose father owned a wine and champagne wholesale and production company. He was raised in the privileged atmosphere that wealth brought to a young Jewish man. He served in the Austro-Hungarian cavalry during World War I and received a decoration for service personally from Emperor Franz-Joseph. It was said in his eulogy that he kept a picture of the old autocrat in his bedroom. After the war, in a newly independent Czechoslovakia, he worked for his father and worked on his tennis game. He invested enough time in the game that he became the captain of the country's Davis Cup team, a position he held for ten years from 1925 to 1935. He had games with kings and queens and other potentates all around Europe. It is recorded that he often graciously played a little less capably than he was able to and allowed the titled players to "win" the game. In 1939, two months after the beginning of the German occupation of Czechoslovakia, he got permission to go to Holland. He never looked back and left for England from there. It was extremely prudently that he decided not to go back. His brother, Hugo, among many other relatives who stayed, perished in the Holocaust.

Francis wound up in New York with tennis racket in hand and where he took care of his immigration situation. Then he landed a job at a summer camp in Maine. Winter was setting in and the camp was closing. He was once again without good prospects. At the invitation of Ruth Dreyfous, a former student at the Newman School, he headed to New Orleans. One story has Ruth explaining to him that he "could play tennis all year round" in the balmy climate of the city. That gave him a great incentive to try his luck in the Deep South. He spent the rest of his life in New Orleans. He lived for a long time at 2108 Palmer Avenue not far from the school.

Francis had already changed his name from the Czech "František" when he came to America. He also changed his religion. When asked why he was not a practicing Jew he answered "being Jewish almost got me killed once, I don't intend to try it again." But he was involved with his Jewish roots for a long time. On November 21, 1960, Francis started litigation to try to get his ½ of the value of his father's business which he had already inherited along with his brother. He sets out the details of how his family was killed by the Nazis and mentions that his brother, Hugo, and he were "members of the lawn tennis club in Prague VII," as a testament to the claimed value of the estate. He estimated that the company's production was about 20,000 bottles a year.

His uncle, Camille Soyka, had made it out of Hitler's Europe and settled in London. In the early 1960s there were a series of letters from Camille to the English law firm of Pritchard and Englefield. One dated February 27, 1962, pertains to the maintenance of the graves of his parents, Markus Soyka and Josepha. They died in either 1920 (or 1921) and 1895 respectfully. They were "buried in a Jewish Cemetery in Vinohrady, Prague or perhaps at Volsany." There are no cemeteries in the Vinohrady section of Prague so it was Volsany or perhaps even somewhere else.

Plus, Camille was looking for his brother Ernst and wife his Paula, his sister Karolina and her husband Moritz Singer, and another sister Ottilie and her husband Ludwig Kapper. All were presumably killed during the war. Why Camille contacted this particular law firm is unclear; perhaps the firm had a practice in solving such problems. In any event, he forwarded copies of all this correspondence to Francis, who kept it to the end of his life.

According to the terms of Camille Soyka's will Francis received "platinum and diamond cufflinks of Knights Cross of Emperor Franz Josef Order and the letter patent thereto." He also left "to my said nephew, Francis, and to my great-nephew Georg (Jiri) (sic) Soyka, Four thousand British pounds each." Actually on the 11th of May, 1962, Francis inherited nearly 9,000 British pounds. At the time there were about 5 American dollars to each British pound. He took this approximately $45,000 and invested it. Given inflation this was like inheriting several hundred thousand dollars today.

Still trying to gain repossession of his family's business he filed a petition with the Foreign Claims Settlement Commission. This United States government agency tried to help displaced Europeans and especially its Jews regain possession of their assets that they lost to the war. In his application he states: "M & J Soyka had a value of about $50,000; wholesalers and manufacturers of wines, Champagne, liqueurs and fruit juices was recorded in the local (Prague) commercial register since 1885." It further states that Francis owned ½ since 1928. Whether he was successful in this suit is not known.

During all of this he quietly educated generations of Newman students in the finer points of tennis. But he was also a very creative man. In the materials at the Historic New Orleans Collection are many surviving examples of his creative output There are copies of his whimsical drawings and Christmas cards that he made each year. He published a cute little cartoon-like book on tennis tips, dedicated to Thomas Masaryk, Czech patriot and politician, entitled: "Tips on Tennis." Only 500 copies were published and he used a vanity press. On April 26, 1974, WWL, the local New Orleans TV station, broadcast an editorial "celebrating the life" of Francis Soyka on his 82nd birthday. Clearly he was a well known and respected citizen of New Orleans. It is effusive in its description of this Czech immigrant. It notes that he was "bright and witty and original," as well as "an accomplished artist, a most civilized conversationalist and best of all, simply a nice, warm, humorous, lovely man." It finishes by noting that "he ornaments our city by his presence."

His eulogy was just as laudatory. It was delivered by a fellow teacher on October 8, 1979, two days after his death at 87. Still another article about him says this: "he was a fascinating raconteur, one so witty that he could draw wit from his listener in turn, like a magician drawing cards from the pockets of an ingenious volunteer." He never, though, lost the thick and to some "impenetrable" accent he brought to America. In 1973, 6 years before his death, he donated his investments, worth between $300,000 and $500,000 at the time, to the Newman School. At the time it was the largest gift the school had ever received.

Frank Cernicek

Frank Cernicek taught ninth grade social science at the Isadore Newman School in New Orleans in the 1950s and 1960s. He was from Czechoslovakia; having come after the war. He earned a mention in the New Orleans States-Item for

November 6, 1958, when he became a United States citizen. He took the oath of citizenship before Judge J. Skelly Wright. This was not so remarkable except that the entire ninth grade class of the school took a field trip to the courthouse to witness the swearing in. They charted a special bus to ensure their arrival. He may well have taught about the virtues and responsibilities of being an American citizen and inspired the gathering which the paper says was "probably one of the largest numbers of well-wishers for such a ceremony." Also being naturalized that day were 33 other immigrants, mostly from Germany, but three from Japan and a handful from Great Britain.

There is every probability that Cernicek and Soyka knew each other since they worked with each other. Their accents alone would naturally spur their colleagues to introduce them to each other. Yet, whether they were friends can only be surmised.

4

Commercial Relations

Bohemia Plantation

By the mid-1840s Bohemia Plantation was a major sugar plantation on the east bank of the Mississippi River south of New Orleans. The exact founding date of the plantation is not known. However, in 1844 its only neighbors were a Mr. Osgood and his brother at 45 miles downstream from New Orleans. Bohemia was just a little further than that. In fact, it is the last piece of arable land on the east bank of the Mississippi down river from New Orleans. How this agricultural outpost came to be called Bohemia is a mystery. There are no recorded Czech settlers in Plaquemines Parish until the 1920s when the lonely Emil Marek shows up in the census. The only person with a Czech connection known to have been in the area was Benjamin Latrobe when he was working on projects at the mouth of the Mississippi some 30 years before the plantation appears in the record. And even he had only distant Czech connections. It is doubtful that he had a hand in naming the plantation.

Different planters were listed over a period of a few years prior to the Civil War. P.A. Champomier published a statement of sugar made in Louisiana for the years 1849–1859 and from this we learn that in 1849 through 1850, J & D Urquhart owned Bohemia Plantation. It was 47 miles from New Orleans and they produced 360 hogsheads of sugar. A hogshead is an old measurement of liquids containing roughly 60 gallons; it is abbreviated as "hhs." There can be no doubt that they did this with at least 100 slaves and maybe more. This number was about the complement of slaves on plantations with this level of production, though no records of slave schedules for this plantation could be found. In 1851–1852, the owners are listed as Mr. Urquhart and Mr. Milligan producing 230 hhs of sugar. This partnership makes it unlikely that this was the romantic vision of a plantation house and southern belles. This far removed from any town; the closest being Point A La Hache 5 miles up river. It is unlikely that this was more than strictly an agricultural enterprise. There are at least no records of any great house here in any book on Louisiana plantation homes.

In 1853–54 it was owned by Urquhart and Milligan but production had greatly increased, more than doubling to 520 hhs of sugar. Perhaps they had brought in many more slaves to increase their yield. They had also brought in as partners two other gentlemen, Moussier & Cornen. Once again only J & D Urquhart are listed as owning the plantation in 1855–1856, Chapomier lists J & D Urquhart as owning the plantation in 1859–1860, too, this time with production of 400 hhs of sugar. With the coming of the war production was drastically decreased to only 166 hogs heads of sugar in 1861–62. Throughout the record there is no mention of what the J and D stood for.

The plantation made it through the Civil War intact enough to still be a workable enterprise but obviously the owners were distressed financially as they had to sell it at auction in January of 1866. Messers. J. B. Walton and Deslonde conducted the auction. The newspaper notice gives no other information. The next time we encounter Bohemia the plantation is listed in Murray's Planters' Directory for 1871—72. This publication gives no evidence of its owners or its production. Carl Kohn, in his capacity as a sugar merchant no doubt knew of this plantation named after the place of his birth but whether he did any business with it is unknown.

In 1886 the newly incorporated New Orleans and Gulf Railroad Company acquired rights to build a rail line paralleling the Mississippi from New Orleans to Bohemia. The 48 miles of track were finished being laid in 1887 connecting the plantation directly to a depot on Elysian Fields Avenue in the city. Regular freight and passenger service was established when the line was complete. From this we can gather that the plantation was still producing significant amounts of sugar. Why else build a railroad all the way to the end of the marsh?

The post office at Bohemia lasted from March 24, 1893, to just March 31, 1896, when it was closed down. The first and probably only postmaster was Numa M. Hebert. The population was said to be just about 90 people. Perhaps it closed because of an 1893 hurricane that was said to have nearly wiped the small community off the map and the town never recovered. Like today after a disaster relief poured into Plaquemine Parish and no doubt the residents at Bohemia received some of the $46,000 raised and distributed. The name has stuck through the centuries. In 1916 the Bohemia Planting Company was formed and it wasn't dissolved until the 1990s. This was the entity that ran the farming operation during the 1900s. Today there is the Bohemia Spillway there which is part of the flood control system at the mouth of the Mississippi built in the 1940s. Bohemia

Bayou wends its way through the nearby marsh. There is also a small settlement of perhaps a few dozen houses spread along the river and bayou that still appear on current maps of Louisiana as "Bohemia."

The plantation made the news just twice over the years. A tragic event happened on Saturday night, April 11, 1908. Thomas Encalade Jr., was murdered at the Bohemia landing by his brother-in-law. Another person with a connection to Bohemia was Louisa Evans—"Aunt Louisa." She was a former slave on the plantation who died at the supposed age of 110 and she received an extensive obituary in the New Orleans Picayune.

A drive through the area today shows the remains of fields of sugar cane and citrus orchards. From recent reports Hurricane Katrina virtually destroyed the place. The connection to our story is that it is one of only three places in Louisiana with a Czech name; the other two being Libuse and Kolin. The English word "bohemian" is a possible name source. "Bohemia" has long been used in English as a synonym for an arty, cosmopolitan, perhaps funkily downtrodden atmosphere. Many cities today claim to be the "new bohemia." The owners and those who lived on the plantation must have had limited access to these cultural entertainments. Perhaps it was an ironic name bestowed on a far away place. It seems unlikely that any one who established the plantation had been to Bohemia itself. Plus, there are few places more different than the marshy subtropical flatlands at the mouth of the Mississippi than Central Europe.

Czech Glass, Ceramics, and Crystal

All the people of New Orleans were exposed to Czechoslovakia for several decades from the beginning of the use of throws in Mardi Gras parades until World War II. The use of Czechoslovakian made glass beads in the parades of New Orleans began sometime in the late 1800s. Though, the majority were in the late teens until 1938. Quite a few of these beads survive. And there is an active community of collectors of the beads. In the years after World War I every parade was throwing bead strands with tags that read "Made in Czecho-Slovakia." Nancy Campbell is a collector of antique beads with almost 10,000 in her collection. She is a native New Orleanian and recalls how "as children, she and her friends would follow parades, crunching the discarded beads underfoot." She runs a bead shop on Magazine Street in Uptown New Orleans that features many of these Czech beads. At those parades the frolickers were often holding a beer bottle produced in Czechoslovakia but filled with Dixie or Jax Beer or one of the other New Orleans beers. Many breweries imported their bottles from "Czecho-

Slovakia," which is written on the bottom of the bottle. There is one example in the Historic New Orleans Collection, though there are many in the hands of private collectors. They are, however, collected for their labels and not for the fact the bottle is Czechoslovakian.

Czech crystal and china is recognized as some of the finest in the world. The first Czech factories for making china were started in the late 1700s. There is anecdotal evidence that a fair number of woman in Louisiana got their first sets of china for their weddings from Czechoslovakia. In the course of my research I ran across more than a few people who told me they have china from Czechoslovakia handed down from their mother or grandmother The country made many ceramic and porcelain items for export, too. They did a particularly brisk business in the canister sets that were popular in the pre-Depression years. They were marked in English, "Made in Czechoslovakia." The Czechs and Slovaks were so much involved in ceramics that there was a Czecho-Slovak American Pottery Company in New York at 10 West 19th Street that also produced items for the American market. The company hired Czech-American craftsmen, my own grandfather among them, to hand paint the designs on pottery and ceramic pieces. (In an odd coincidence I wound up working at this same building while I was in college.) These items also made their way into Louisiana stores and homes.

Czech crystal, or as it is more commonly called, "Bohemian Crystal," is considered the finest in the world. This is partly due to its high lead content which in turns lends itself to being cut and shaped easily and dramatically. The crystal industry started in the mid-1300s in the Czech lands and by the turn to the 15th century there were 20 manufacturers that were well known. They produced hundreds of items that graced the tables of royalty and other rich people across Europe. There is proof that glass was being produced in what are now the Czech lands as early as the 3rd century B.C. some 600 years before the arrival of the first Czechs. Newly arriving Czechs quickly learned the glass making process and began to add their own twists to the primitive industry. New innovations were slow in coming but by the 900s the craftsman were churning out glass jewelry as well as glass encrusted goblets and bowls. These products were purchased by the growing middle class of the Middle Ages who could not afford real gemstones.

The first written proof of Czech glass making prowess is recorded in 1276. This is when the makers of stained glass windows across the Czech lands were using colored glass to build their masterpieces for the churches and palaces of the Medieval period. Much of this production was in the hands of Benedictine monks. The earliest extant records of exportation of Czech glass to the rest of Europe is from 1376. There is a factory that was started in 1515 that is still producing glassware in Northern Bohemia. Over the centuries there were hundreds of small workshops with artisans who perfected their own signature approach to blowing the glass by hand, and then etching their own distinctive patterns into it. The art has not changed much in the last 600 years. Though some of the process has been automated and helped along with new machinery at least half of the process still used today is done by hand.

More than a few Louisiana planters were ordering Czech-made china and crystal to grace their plantation homes during the pre-Civil War years. Some of this survived through the Civil War intact and can be seen at a few plantation homes today. These objects were among the first items imported directly from the Czech lands to Louisiana though not on a truly commercial scale. That was to come with the rise of a new middle class and the new found wealth of the Victorian era after the war saw a fresh impetus to import these fine products. Today, a few fine hotels and restaurants in New Orleans tout the fact that guests will be dining under Czech crystal chandeliers and drink from Bohemian crystalware. One thing for certain is that Czech crystal, glass, beads, china and porcelain have long had a place in Louisiana.

The Gathering Storm

On September 3rd, 1931, the Times-Picayune reported that Dr. Franz Karl Sprinzels had arrived in New Orleans to talk to port officials about "Czechoslovakian Shipping Via the City," as the article is titled. Sprinzels was on his first trip to America. He had a tight schedule of visiting many of the larger cities of the nation but seems to have spent his most extended period in New Orleans. He was gathering a wide variety of information about American "manufacturing, marketing and export methods" which he hoped to turn into a Czech language book to help his country's "business interests." The article notes that he "registered at the Hotel Monteleone" a few days prior to the article. So at least we know where he slept. It also notes that he was a "doctor of chemistry and physics, graduate and degree man" from the "University of Prague," which is properly called Charles University. The paper got it right when it said the university "was one of the oldest educational institutions in the world."

While there is nothing concrete reported about his talks or any arrangements made the article does relay some interesting quotes about his views of America. Quotes which foreshadow the events which overtook Europe in just a few years and then lasted for decades after. The article said he "was unstinting in expressing his admiration for American organization in factories and industries." Then quoting him directly, "I find a great many Americans lamenting business conditions and hear a great deal of talk about unemployment conditions, but conditions here are so much better than they are in certain parts of Europe that it is refreshing to view them." This was when the Depression was at one of its lowest points. "Also, with your two party system you are not confronted with all sorts of coalitions which are formed in political life" in Europe he noted. This fractured political scene enabled Hitler to be elected Chancellor with just 33% of the vote two years after Sprinzels was in New Orleans.

Sprinzels "declared that economic conditions in Czechoslovakia are better than in other adjoining countries. Germany and Austria are in the throes of the European Depression, while in Hungary conditions are also bad." Czechoslovakia was sandwiched between these three and thus "feels the effects of these conditions." Germany was perhaps the worst off. During the late 1920s and early 1930s inflation raged in the 10,000% range each month. It literally took shopping bags full of money to buy a few groceries. Currency and postage stamps were just rubber stamped with more zeros to reflect the ever falling value of the currency; they couldn't print it fast enough to reflect the changes. At one point the Deutschmark was trading at over 1,000,000 for each United States dollar. A loaf of bread could cost one or two *million* Deutschmarks. Hitler was to use this situation to come to power and then as an excuse to gather ever more power into the Chancellor's office. Austria and Hungary also experienced this hyperinflation while the Czechoslovak currency remained fairly strong and stable at about 100 korun (crowns) to the dollar.

Once in power in 1933 Hitler launched a remilitarization in Germany. This employed tens of thousands of people which certainly helped him cement his position. Almost immediately upon taking office Hitler made a demand that portions of Czechoslovakia's territory be turned over to Germany. While Sprinzels could not foretell the future he surely pinpointed Hitler's reasoning with this comment: "Czechoslovakia is one of the largest iron manufacturing centers in Europe." And Hitler needed iron. Sprinzels was also prescient when he said, "America has little to contend with from her Communistic element in comparison to some European countries." This was when Stalin was first gaining power in Russia, a country which was to cast a dark pall over Czechoslovakia after World War II.

Directly relating to Czechoslovakian exports to America Sprinzels noted "my country is a big exporter of glass and porcelain to the United States." These would include the Mardi Gras beads and dinnerware that Louisianians were lapping up but also industrial items made of these materials. Perhaps the biggest loss to Louisianians was this: "We also export a great deal of beer. I am sorry to say our exports to your country of this product are no more." No one in Louisiana would be able to enjoy a good Czech beer again until the early 1990s. How did we survive?

In the mid-1930s New Orleanian and Louisiana businessmen and farmers were treated to the efforts of Sam E. Woods to bolster trade with Czechoslovakia. He was the commercial attaché at the American embassy in Prague. A trade conference was held in New Orleans in March of 1936. The meeting was held at the customs house under the auspices of Colonel James E. Edmonds. Woods explained that Czechoslovakia wanted to import cotton and rice and manufactured goods including typewriters and adding machines. In return she wanted to sell to America shoes and her own manufactured products. He expressed concern that because "America does not buy enough Czechoslovak goods they are instead trading with Egypt, exchanging cotton for beet sugar, bypassing Louisiana farmers and businessmen who could benefit from the trade."

This was a continuation and building on the trade in glassware, china, jewelry and the beads used in Mardi Gras parades that was already vigorous even if not very large. These relations were to see a low point during the Cold War before resuming in the 1990s. What became of his efforts is not exactly known though trade did continue. Unfortunately, the Time-Picayune index covering this time is not as adequate as I would have liked and it only gives references to a few specific meetings involving local people and visiting Czechoslovaks. Since no article mentions specific companies I was unable to determine exactly which New Orleans concerns were involved with this trade.

On December 4th, 1937, the Times-Picayune reported that Dr. Jaroslav Kose was in New Orleans to consider "the first branch office of the Czechoslovak Export Institute." He was the deputy director general of the Institute. The purpose of this organization was "to stimulate trade between the United States and Czechoslovakia." New Orleans was the preferred site for the first office for two reasons according to Dr. Kose: "The first is the large amount of cotton imported annually by Czechoslovakia, the second is the large Czechoslovak population in the United States centered mainly in the South and the Mid-West." By the "South" Dr. Kose meant Texas, which has one of the largest Czech populations of any state. There are no large Czech or Slovak populations in other states of the South. The Midwest states along the Mississippi River are the other large centers of Czech immigrant settlement. It was, however, Texas, Louisiana and Mississippi that produced most of America's cotton at the time of Dr Kose's visit. Since

New Orleans was the leading cotton port it was the logical place for such an office.

He probably was wholly unaware of Libuse and Kolin in Central Louisiana as they were forgotten outposts of Czech culture by 1930. I will digress here, but given Dr. Kose's comment long ago, this is perhaps as good a place as any to note another distinction between Czechs and Slovaks versus other immigrants. During its time of independence between the two World Wars and then again after 1990 the Czech and Slovak governments (as one country or two) have always tried to maintain and foster relations between those who immigrated to America and the old country. In fact, there is a current well-funded program by the Czech government today to catalogue and preserve every aspect of Czech immigration to America. It is probably one of just a few, if not the only, countries in Europe with such a coordinated outreach program. Most European countries view their emigrants as long-time Americans with perhaps only a passing interest in genealogy and other family oriented projects. Today there is certainly some level of assistance for Americans trying to find their roots in the hands of those governments. Nothing I could find, however, matches the Czech effort.

For a long time most European countries viewed those departing as a welcome removal of discordant elements from their populations. Indeed, France, England, Germany, Spain, Russia and Italy in particular emptied their prisons, poor houses and other undesirables into America. In stark contrast, Czech and Slovak officials in Europe viewed their emigrants as long-lost brothers and sisters who were forced out first by the Germans and Austrians and then the Russians. They did not throw people out.

Dr. Kose met with leaders of the New Orleans Association of Commerce and leading local businessmen and shippers. They met at the office of Harold Jacobson. He was the local district manager of the United States department of commerce. Also joining them was Gordon Boswell who was the honorary consul of Czechoslovakia in New Orleans. This office closed in 1938 when Hilter seized North Bohemia just three months after Dr. Kose was in New Orleans as he had been threatening to do since 1933. That ended any plans that Kose and New Orleanians may have decided upon. There was not to be another Czech honorary consul office in New Orleans until the 1990s. In early 1939 Hitler invaded the rest of Czechoslovakia and dismantled the counrty.

A Czech Jewish Rabbi named Lazar Eichenstein visited New Orleans in February of 1938. He came to raise money for the Mizrachi movement which wanted to settle Euroepan Jews in Isreal. There was a Mizrachi organization in New Orleans which helped arrange the visit. Rabbi Eichenstein was from a 400 year long line of Czech Rabbis. He did, however, give his presentation in Yiddish and not Czech. He spent at least two weeks in New Orleans speaking to small groups at Jewish homes and also at Beth Isreal Synagugue and the Menorah Institute on Euterpe Street. As part of his plea he noted that while Czech Jews were living in one of the most liberal countries in Europe there was "a gathering storm coming from both Germany and Russia." Living between the two, "we are no more afraid of war than other nations, but most of us think most of the trouble…will come from Germany." He was prescient. In November of 1938 Hitler began his "final solution" against the Jews.

Another Rabbi, Nathan Krass of New York, had come to New Orleans in 1920, speaking of the plight of Jews throughout Europe. He brought the news of pogroms and starvation amoung Jews in several countries and the poor Jews of Czechoslovakia. These were perhaps the best off of their fellow Jews in Europe for though they faced poverty there was no pogrom or strong ant-Semitic feeling among the Czechs and Slovaks. It was in Germany and Romania, Russia and Poland, that the Jews faced the toughest conditions. He pointed out that many people in Europe had received letters from family in America that spoke of money being enclosed but the envelopes had been ripped open and the money stolen. He raised more than $25,000 in one meeting with the Jews of New Orleans. Gifts ranged from $10,000 from Sam Zemuray to the 50 cents from a young boy who had saved his pennies. What became of the Rabbi and his efforts is unknown.

Czech and Slovak immigration to America was to virtually cease with the German invasion of 1939. Only one of the few who got out before the war was to settle in Louisiana. Francis Soyka of Prague arrived in New Orleans in 1940.

The Czechoslovak Trade Exhibit

The Cold War spilled over into New Orleans in April of 1949. That is when a trade exhibit was set up by the Czechoslovakian government at the city's new international trade mart. It was the third nation to open an exhibit. Just 1,500 square feet, it featured Czechoslovak made "textiles, glassware, metal and engineering goods, toys, jewelry, beers and liqueurs." Mayor deLesseps S. Morrison gave keys to the city to Dr. Evzen Loebl and Dr. Karel Fink, representatives of the Czechoslovak ministry of trade and commerce division of the Embassy, respectively. The mayor declared them honorary citizens of the city. Over 100 businessmen and public officials from around the New Orleans metro area came to the opening, listening to statements of "friendship" and "economic opportunity," by various local and foreign speakers. One can imagine the ribbon being cut to sustained applause from content, if calculating, people. After this auspicious and promising opening the situation fast declined.

Almost immediately, on April 30, Ivor Trapolin, of the "un-American affairs committee" of the New Orleans Young Men's Business Club called the exhibit "a meeting place for Communist forces in New Orleans to build up the Communist cause." He was adamant in his extensive remarks about the dangers of allowing communists, "and they must be," to work in the city. Dr. E. Rudolpher, head of the exhibit retorted "I am the only representative of the Czechoslovakian country in New Orleans. Who will I have meetings with, myself?"

Barely a month later, on May 3, William Kirn, speaking for the Knights of Columbus, called the exhibit a "real danger." He went on to point out that the exhibit was only aiding and abetting a communist regime which "is riding roughshod over the God-given rights and freedoms" of the Czechoslovak people with whom he pointedly stated "he had no quarrel."

On June 2nd there was a long debate between Clay Shaw, manager of the trade mart and Trapolin at the Roosevelt Hotel about the relative merits and demerits of a resolution calling for the removal of the Czechoslovakian trade exhibit. Shaw tried to point out that there were other such exhibits in the United States. He noted that this was strictly about trade as well as pleading that the matter should be left to the State Department which had already approved of the exhibit. Shaw called the proposed resolution "pernicious." Another speaker, Wren Anderson, with the city's department of commerce, pointed out that the United States was actually importing 20 million dollars in important metals from Russia itself. These were manganese and chrome which are used in making steel. Trapolin kept up the steady drumbeat that it was contrary to America's national interests to give support to Czechoslovakia. He accused supporters of the exhibit as working to "build up a country that will seek to destroy this nation." The resolution was passed.

There were many column inches of newsprint devoted to the controversy. On June 24th the West Bank Lions Club also called for the "immediate removal" of the exhibit. Whatever continued to take place both in support and in opposition to the exhibit it was off the newspaper's radar for the next year. The exhibit continued to operate, though what deals were struck are unknown. Then on April 29, 1950, it was abruptly announced by the Czechoslovakian Federation of Industries that the exhibit would close on May 1st. Clay Shaw said that the lease was up but that he had been surprised by the decision. But it was clear that Czechoslovakian-American relations during this period were worsening and that the exhibit was untenable. This episode is the lowest point in direct Czech—Slovak relations with Louisiana.

1950 to today

According to he U. S. Census Bureau the total number of those with Czech heritage in America in 2000 was about 1.3 million while there were 850,000 of Slovaks heritage. These all lived primarily in five midwestern states and Texas. Since the 1950s the number of people listing Czech or Slovak as their "nationality" in the United States decennial census for Louisiana has hovered at about 5,000 people. On average, 2,500 say Czech, 1,250 claim Slovak, and the last 1,250 chose Czechoslovakian as their heritage. All we know are the broad numbers. There is no further breakdown provided by the Census Bureau. And the latest census available is the 1930 census. We can assume that these are people who self-identify as Czech or Slovak and it is probable that they have an ancestor who arrived more recently than some of the people seen in this book. We know now that all the Touchet's have a trace of Czech blood yet are mostly unaware of it. There are many people who may have a trace of Czech or Slovak heritage and are aware of it; they are perhaps either wholly subsumed by another cultural heritage or just thoroughly Americanized.

Immigration Through New Orleans

Some 4,000 Czechs and Slovaks passed through the port of New Orleans. For these immigrants this was their first taste of the New World. That they landed in perhaps the most European of American cities probably escaped their notice.

Anyone researching their Czech roots has a man named Leo Baca of Richardson, Texas, to thank for the incredible job he did of assembling lists of Czech immigrants over more than 60 years. There are seven volumes that cover the years from 1852 until the early 1900s. He lists thousands of immigrants, both parents and children. In his research he complied their port of embarkation, as well as their port and year of arrival, where they were going to settle, and the ship they came over on. There are other details as well. These books were invaluable in learning more about some of the Czech immigrants who are mentioned in this book.

Other than this the books can give us a fairly clear picture of Czech immigration through the port of New Orleans. Nearly 4,000 Czechs, both Bohemians and Moravians, immigrated through the port. These families first saw the New

World up close at the mouth of the Mississippi. They had to fend their way through the hustle that imbued the port with an organized chaos. One wonders what a group of Czech immigrants from the frozen center of Europe, and after what was no doubt a harrowing passage across the stormy, wintry North Atlantic, thought when they disembarked at the balmy wharf in New Orleans with the palm trees and banana plants still in their prime, flowers blooming where they could. The flatness of the place, as well as the assault of French, English, Creole, and the slave patois, perhaps Spanish and Italian and a dozen other languages, must have been a bit overwhelming. There is no record of ships being met by Czech speaking agents or family members, though it is possible that this was the case. Perhaps they found only some Germans they could speak to. On any given day 15 to 20 ships were docked at the wharves along the river where the Czechs disembarked after the long journey. This is where they met the ship that was to carry them up river or to Texas. One wonders how many missed the boat because of language difficulties.

About half of these immigrants went north to settlements in the states carved out of the Louisiana Purchase; mostly the Bohemians. The other half went to Texas; mostly the Moravians. Czechs stayed in New Orleans for just a few days before boarding steamers, paddle wheelers or trains for the final leg of their journey. During a time when Louisiana saw just a handful of Czech immigrants states like Texas, Oklahoma, Nebraska, Iowa, Minnesota, Illinois and Wisconsin saw thousands of Czech immigrants. They joined settlers who came not only through New Orleans, but also through New York, Baltimore and later Galveston, Texas. This influx was to have a later effect on Libuse and Kolin, but for now we will discuss their impact on the old Louisiana Purchase and Texas.

It is an odd fact that the majority of Czechs in Texas are from the Moravian region of the Czech Republic. Indeed, of the 300,000 Czechs in Texas some 80% claim Moravian heritage and particularly from the eastern portion of this province. There are many Czech settlements in Texas. All were supplied with a steady flow of new immigrants through New Orleans, and to a lesser degree Galveston, during the time after the Civil War and leading up to the creation of Czechoslovakia. These Czechs took ocean going vessels to New Orleans where they switched to either the train or coastal schooners to make the rest of the journey. According to many Texas Czech historians many Czechs turned down job offers in Louisiana and made their way west.

In the states that were carved out of the Louisiana Purchase tens of thousands of Czechs settled in small towns and big cities. In fact, there are Czechs who settled the area when it was still known as the Louisiana Purchase territory, before any states were created, forming settlements and beginning the process of assimilation These Czech settlements were to form a population base that provided a backflow to Louisiana, particularly to Rapides Parish. Many of these people became farmers and there are dozens of communities with a strong Czech presence throughout the Midwest. They sent their produce south to New Orleans and thus the city was to have a lingering connection to the Czechs and Slovaks who passed through her.

Decade by decade the immigration flow through New Orleans can be seen. Strangely, virtually none of the people who listed New Orleans or just "Louisiana" as their destination seems to have stayed. For others only conjecture at the relationship can be made; no records could be found to make the direct connection. Other than the year 1852, when it seems an entire ship's passenger load stayed in New Orleans, the 1850's saw just a few people stay in New Orleans. There is little that we can surmise about why.

On December 13th, 1860 a handful of Czech families listed Louisiana as their destination. From a granddaughter we know that the Barchick (Bacik) (alternate spellings are sometimes indicated in records) family wound up in Ohio; Joseph & Anna—plus five unnamed children. Other individuals or families were Johann Beranek who just 20 years old; The Bushta (Buska) family, Frantz & Maria—plus 4 kids; Wenzel & Marie Gerack (Gerik,) ages unknown; a youth of 17 named Wenzel Jezellineck (Zelinek or Jelinek;) Frantz & Katherina Kotnaver and their young daughter; The large Puvet (Pivetz,) family consisting of Joseph & Teresia—plus 6 children; and another youth, named Franz Sapitz (Zapitz.) Either the record is wrong or the day before the Bram family, consisting of Franz & Maria—plus 4 kids—arrived on the 12th of December, 1860. On the same ship was Johann & Katharina Heismann and their one child. This was the last ship with Czech immigrants until after the Civil War.

By the 19th of December, 1865 the war was virtually over; the conclusion known. New Orleans was long in the hands of the Union when Louis Rose (Hrozen), then 25 years old, landed at the newly reopened port of New Orleans. This young man Anglicized his name and quickly blended into the society. Well he should have since his Czech last name is derived from the word for "terrible." And he changed it to Rose which is such a sweeter thing and more in line with the wide open future he faced in America as a young man. On the same ship were four other Czech immigrants. Salomon Ehrmann (Hermann,) was 35 years old. He was most likely a Bohemian-German Jew. The other three were Anton & Margaretha Kudela (Kubela,) and their one son.

On the 25th of October, 1867, M. Konvicka, a 30 year old man, listed as intending to settle in "Louisiana or Texas," arrived. Whether this man is related to the Tom Konvicka who is the long-time weatherman on an Alexandria, Louisiana, television station is not known. Tom says his family was from Texas and this person is listed as going there so there is the possibility.

The majority of years in the decade of the 1870's saw just seven immigrants who claimed Louisiana as their destination: Joseph Smutny, 30 years old when he landed on January 18th, 1870; Adolph Wildner was 25 years old when he arrived on December 22, 1870. There was a single mother named Rosalia Deutschman, 33 years old—plus 2 children—on April 1, 1871. Josephus Mojzicheck (Moziček) was 32 years old and who may be the start of the Motichek family in Madisonville. He arrived on December 1, 1871. Johann Miculka arrived on September 10th, 1873. This happens to be the same last name as the man who currently runs the National Park Service office in New Orleans and who is a native of the city and yet a relationship cannot be established. Paul Cabanowich arrived on May 10th, 1876. On April 1, 1872, the 56 year old Rosalia Sohele—and Anna, 9 years old—landed at New Orleans.

The 18th of May, 1872, most likely dawned warm and humid in New Orleans. 330 or so other Czechs had already passed through New Orleans to other locations so far this year. But on this date 14 Czechs told the immigration officials that they were staying in Louisiana. What led this group to stay here? Why so many on one ship on one day? And why did no one seem to stay? These are questions that have not been answered yet and may never be. These people were the Wotruba family consisting Carl & "Wife"—plus 7 children; the teenage Ignatz Zitek who was just 19 years old; Antonie Uhlia (Uhla), 22 yrs old; the Slinka family, Wenzel & Anna—plus two children, a young lady named Vinzena Pajer, 18 years old; another young woman, Maria Schatra (Satra,) 19 years old; a young man, Wenzel Ryska (Riske,) 24 years old; a middle aged woman, Anna Kozab, 31 years old; A young childless couple, Mathias Krejci, 24 years old and his wife Marie, 25 years old; another teenager, Joseph Charybar (Srvbar,) 19 years old; Joseph & Maria Hejna (Hejny) plus 1 child; Franz & Ana Hejna (Hejny) plus 1 child; a mere wisp of a woman, Josepha Hlavacek, 16 years old; and even younger Mathias Jelinck (Jelinek,) 15 years old; and still another young man, Josef Krinawok (Krivanek), 19 years old. None of these people are in any other record that I could locate in New Orleans or Louisiana.

Besides New Orleans, and before Ellis Island was to become the leading immigration processing center in 1897, many other ports accepted new arrivals. Baltimore was one such major immigration hub and thousands of Czechs and Slovaks came through her. Galveston, before the hurricane of 1900 which destroyed the town, was a major port of entry for Texas and the West. New York, when they were still using Castle Clinton on the Battery in downtown Manhattan, saw many Czechs and Slovaks start their American journeys. Eventually, Czechs and Slovaks who came through these ports were to find their way to Louisiana. That so many Czechs are documented coming though New Orleans is a starting point for more intensive research, I was unable to locate any of these people in any other record.

Current Czech and Slovak history

The Velvet Revolution of 1989 and the divorce of Czechoslovakia in 1993 led to both the Czech Republic and Slovakia joining NATO and the European Union. Czech military units participate regularly in NATO exercises in Fort Polk in west-central Louisiana. Czech police have had training in Baton Rouge. Louisiana lawyers helped the newly freed countries develop a Western legal system based on Louisiana's Civil Code. Czechoslovakia went through the same sort of "people's revolutions" as the rest of Eastern Europe after the Berlin Wall came down. The so-called Velvet Revolution of 1989 removed the Communist Party from power after weeks of peaceful protest in Prague and other cities. There was no violence. Basically, the party was hounded out of office through ridicule and mass disbelief that it had the power to control society never mind the right to do so. The famed dissident, Vaclav Havel, poet and playwright, statesman and philosopher, became president of the newly free Czechoslovakia. There were tensions between the Czechs and the Slovaks almost from the beginning of the newly liberated country. This led to the divorce of Czechoslovakia in 1993. In one of the only peaceful divisions of a country the world has ever seen the Czechs and Slovaks agreed to form two independent nations. They divided the weapons of the army and the power plants and the other state owned properties on a 2-to-1 basis. This is because the Czech Republic has 10 million people and Slovakia has 5 million. There are still a warm commercial and familial relationship between the two countries; there is an open border between the two.

Today, the Czech Republic is a country being thoroughly integrated into the European Union. Democracy and the freedoms it brings are in strong force. The Slovak Republic has had a few more problems particularly under one nationalist leader who thought the country could make it on its own, but this country, too, is being brought into the greater cooperation of a modern Europe. Louisianians have had a hand in helping this progress though this story strays from the focus of this book.

The Honorary Czech Consulate in New Orleans

On November 2, 1998, New Orleans became the ninth American city to get a Czech diplomatic mission. The Honorary Consulate of The Czech Republic was formally instituted with Kenneth Zezulka, a Metairie lawyer, as the first consul. While Zezulka was born in Detroit to Czech parents, he came South as a young man and has made his home in New Orleans for over 30 years. The opening of the consulate was attended by Ambassador Aleksandr Vondra. Mr. Vondra, then still in his late teens, signed what came to be called Charter 77. This was a call for substantial changes in the Communist regime then in power. For his efforts he served several years in jail. After the Velvet Revolution, Vaclav Havel, the first president of the free Czechoslovakia appointed him as the country's ambassador to the United States.

The opening of the Consulate was attened by members of the Czech expatriate community in New Orleans. Also making the event were members of the Czech community in Rapides Parish as well as myself. This was the greatest surprise to both Vondra and Zezulka. They had no idea that there was a functioning Czech community in Louisiana. Zezulka is still in his position of helping Czechs who come to the state to visit or for commerical purposes.

Czechs at Wal-Mart

In a classic case of immigrants working hard in low positions during their first years in America, Czech men and women worked as the overnight cleaning crews in Wal-Marts across the state from about 1997 to 2004. I found them from Chalmette, near New Orleans, to Baton Rouge, to Lafayette, to Lake Charles and on to Alexandria, and in every Wal-Mart in between. I discovered this quite by accident; one day I was in one of the Wal-Marts in Baton Rouge late at night and asked a woman cleaning up where something was. As she answered me in halting English I immediately recognized her Czech accent. I exchanged a few pleasantries with her in Czech, which lit up her eyes. Her name was Eva and she quickly introduced me to her five co-workers. We sat around the breakroom table and in a conversation half English and half Czech had a grand old time. They told me this was the first time they ever met an American who knew even one word of

Czech. And they told me about the many Czechs in Wal-Marts around Louisiana, which was a great surprise to me.

After this first encounter, I made special trips to Wal-Marts around the southern part of the state to find the Czechs working late at night. I met dozens of them (but no Slovaks.) They were sweeping, washing and waxing the floors, picking up garbage and moving pallets of merchandise on to the floor. They were always vague about who hired them. They spoke limited English, if any at all. It sure surprised them every time when when I walked up to them and asked "Jak se maš?" (How are you?) I visited with several at their homes. They were bunked 6 to 8 people in two bedroom apartments in not-so-fine apartment complexes. None of them drove and they were picked up and dropped off by their crew boss. He would translate the manager's orders for the night to the workers. These shadowy figures whom no one wanted to talk about, like Harry Potter's Valdemort, were Czech, but apparently spoke English well. They lived in their own apartments, but I never met even one of them. They arranged for the rent and utilities to get paid; they arranged shoping trips. Otherwise the workers were on their own, though barely venturing outside. In late 2003 legal actions were brought against Wal-Mart for hiring illegal Czech workers which put a stop to the practice; afterwards there are no more Czechs doing this work. But it was a thrill for me and them during this brief time. Every Louisianian who shopped at Wal-Mart for these six years had these Czechs to thank for clean stores.

Current Commercial Relations

The resumption of trade between Louisiana and the Czech and Slovak republics was in full swing by the mid 1990s. In 1996 the Czech Republic imported over $1 million in products directly from Louisiana, mostly industrial and electronic machinery. Louisiana imported a similar amount from Czech companies. Another $7 million in goods went to and from the Czech Repulic and the United States through the port of New Orleans. This is, of course, a very tiny amount considering the amount of trade the United States is engaged in. Yet it is significant given the near 70 years of isolation and repression that the Czechs and Slovaks endured under the Nazis and then the Russian Communists. One small, but vibrant, area of importation was in Czech glass, crystal and china. More than a few New Orleans restaurants and hotels, including Victor's and the Windsor Court, advertsised that patrons could dine on Czech china and drink from Bohemian crystal under Bohemian crystal chandeliers; there was a certain sense of cachet and panache imparted in doing so.

The World Trade Center and other organizations in New Orleans cosponsored a luncheon on "Doing Business in the Czech Republic" on Friday, December 5, 1998, at the Plimsoll Club. The conference featured three speakers: Aleksandr Vondra, Ambassador of the Czech Republic to the United States, Martin Jahn, who is the Director of CzechInvest in Chicago, and Robert Doubek, who was the president of the American Friends of the Czech Republic which is an organization based in Washington, D.C. Czech music was performed by LSU's European String Quartet during the networking reception immediately prior to the luncheon.

As the Czech and Slovak republics joined the economy of Europe after the fall of the Communists the country became a darling of many Americans and other Western Europeans. Soon the streets of Prague, Bratislava and other cities were filled with people looking to teach English and capitalism and also learn about the Czechs and Slovaks themselves. The University of New Orleans Prague Studies Program was started shortly after the liberation. This program offers Americans the ability to study at Charles University in Prague as well as helps Czech students at UNO and other New Orleans area universities.

The New Orleans street car story with Czech made parts.

The story of the street cars of New Orleans has been intertwined with Czechs and Slovaks since the beginning. When the Bohemian Jew Samuel Kohn and his relatives were involved with the creation of the system in the 1830s street cars were new to the world. They were the latest technology. By the 1940s they were considered old fashioned. The machinery to build the parts for street cars was sent to the newly freed Czechoslovakia in the late 1940s. Then the stagnation of the Soviet era settled on the country. This had the effect of preserving the old knowledge and parts. In an odd twist of fate, now in the 1990s and 2000s, as New Orleans begins to reinstitute the street car line up Canal Street it had to go to the Czech Republic to get the parts. While the bodies of the streetcars were replicas built from scratch at the Carrollton Shops in New Orleans, they were fitted with the what are refered to as "old PCC-type running gear" from the Tatra trolley factories in the Czech Republic. Every person who rode the street cars in New Orleans was riding on Czech made parts.

The Favor Repaid

When Hurricanes Katrina and Rita hit Louisiana the Czech and Slovak governments, non-govermental organizations and individuals in both countries did not forget the help that Louisiana and her people gave to their own emerging democracies. These two countries were among the first to offer aid, assistance and money to Louisiana and all the people that suffered in the twin disasters. One of the odd circumstances of both hurricanes is that this book became a link between Czechs and Slovaks and Louisiana.

As part of my effort to find information about the families in this book I had set up a website that lays out the gist of what is in it. As Katrina was swirling in the Gulf of Mexico Czech and Slovak news organizations wanting to cover the story turned to the internet to find any Czech and Slovak citizens in New Orleans or the rest of the state. What they found was me. I began what were to become regular live reports to the Czech and Slovak media on the approaching storm. When it hit and the horrendous aftermath followed I continued to give reports every few hours. The Czech and Slovak people were well informed of what was happening in Louisiana. I have been told that these two countries were among the few in the world who had a "reporter" on the scene and were not relying strictly on the American media. The reporters and I would speak in English but their questions and my answers were translated live on the radio and television.

When the reporters came to Louisiana they stayed at my house because there was no where else to stay—people from the New Orleans area had filled all the hotels in Baton Rouge. I escorted these reporters into New Orleans just days after Katrina struck; thus Czechs and Slovaks were among the first in Europe to get a first hand look at what was happening from their own reporters in their own languages. The reports were filed each evening with the dateline of my name and house in downtown Baton Rouge.

Once these reports began both republics' embassies contacted me to ask if I could help some Czech and Slovak citizens who were stuck in New Orleans in the rising waters. Since the Honorary Consul's office in New Orleans was out of commission my house became, in effect, the temporary consul's office. I assisted dozens of Czech and Slovak tourists and students in getting out of the disaster zone. Indeed, more than a few stayed at my house for lack of any other shelter. Not one of them was less than surprised to find an American who could speak some Czech as well as landing in my little outpost of Czech and Slovak culture.

As the disasters unfolded and Czechs and Slovaks at all levels of government and life rallied to help Louisiana the two goverments were faced with a bureacratic nightmare at the federal level in Washington. So I simply provided the names and contact information of counterparts in Lousiana who, while surprised indeed at this unlikely source of assistance, were more than happy to accept the proferred help. When the various Czech and Slovak entities found out that their country-men had been coming to Louisiana for nearly 300 years they were equally sur-prised. That there are two Czech town in the middle of Louisiana was even more astonishing. These facts, I do believe, spurred the Czech and Slovak goverments and other entities to even greater measures of assistance. It was like they had found long lost family.

Tens of thousands of dollars were raised at events in both republics and sent directly to small organizations in Louisiana. One example is the $90,000 that a Czech group called ADRA gave to a Baton Rouge organization that was assisting displaced children replace their school books, clothes and even toys. Another example is the concerts that the City of Prague organized for musicians from New Orleans in venues around Prague. Czechs paid the way for these musicians to continue bringing their music to the world even if that was half a world away. No doubt few of the Louisiana musicians were entirely sure of where they were—but music always draws people closer.

The Tatra Motor Works is helping the New Orleans Regional Transit Authority get the street car lines back up and running. Charles University, one of the oldest in the world, is assisting the University of New Orleans rebuild. Czech and Slovak engineers are working with their Louisiana counterparts to rebuild the many parts of the public infrastructure that were destroyed by the hurricanes. The City of Prague is working with the City of New Orleans in preserving his-toric structures. This is all being done on the basis of friendship and a shared humanity. It is not at all a commercial or for-profit effort. While not in the fore-front of news in Louisiana, since as was the case with the people in this book Lou-isianians still have a difficult time grasping who Czechs and Slovaks are and where they are from, it is happening.

While there is credit enough to go around, this book, my website and my efforts, did indeed help bring Louisianians of all heritages closer to the Czechs and Slovaks in Europe.

5

Farmers & Tradesmen

Czechs and Slovaks in Rural Louisiana

The social and economic conditions that all Czech and Slovak families faced in rural and small town Louisiana in the second half of the 1800s were not at all different than those faced by other pioneers in the area. There was a major change as people went from a slave based agrarian economy to the beginnings of the industrial revolution. The war years traumatized society at every level imaginable. Much of the land was still virgin forests, though lumber companies moved in after the end of Reconstruction in 1877. Roads were dirt, and the cliché "dusty in dry weather and mud when it rained" is true in this case. Towns were a day's journey from each other. In the parishes in the center of the state, away from the Mississippi River, small farms were sprinkled through the countryside, wherever someone was able to clear some land and plant some crops. Along the big rivers and bayous were old plantations that had long been in agricultural production.

Most people lived a subsistence life and money was used in the rarest of instances. Average yearly incomes rarely topped $1,000. Life's machines and way of doing things was closer to the time of the American Revolution than to the industrial revolution that was sweeping Northern Cities and Europe, including the Czech Republic. Horse or mule were the usual land transportation or you walked. There were many river boats plying the rivers and bayous of Louisiana. This was the primary means of getting crops to larger markets and for bringing in the supplies that they could afford. Other than the Blahut and Klady families there were no Czechs or Slovaks in the planter caste that was growing rich off of slave labor.

Towns were rarely more than 1,000 people. There was generally one store for each type of human endeavor, that is, one hardware store, one saddler, one doctor, in each town. Life was limited. Entertainment was basic. It was common, however, among the Czechs and Slovaks for the men to play musical instruments, mostly horns and the accordion. Waltzes and polkas were the basic folk forms for Slavic music, and the word "polka" itself is Czech. How much of this music they shared with their neighbors is unknown, but it was not that much different than the two-step and accordion based waltzes of Cajun music. Any Czech or Slovak musician would have been able to quickly pick up the music of the surrounding culture and join the fun.

Czechs and Slovaks, like the French when they originally came, would have had to drastically change the diet they were used to. Though there is evidence that they quickly planted dill, caraway and poppy, the traditional Czech and Slovak spices, among the spices in home gardens. They often bought the seeds through the Czech language newspapers that they received. There was a tradition among the Czech and Slovak farmers in Europe to carefully manage their lands and take advantage of the latest developments in farm practices. The farmers among the immigrants would have taken this attitude with them to their new ventures.

What follows in this chapter is basically a list of all the families and individuals that I could find in the rural areas of Louisiana outside of New Orleans. I divided this chapter into the usual sections of the state that are still used by Louisianians today. Within each geographical region the Czechs and Slovaks are presented alphabetically, again, for the lack of a better way to present them. There is no evidence that any of these families or individuals knew each other, other than the Slovaks in Cameron Parish. They each came of their own accord. They worked at assimilating into the larger culture around them. Some changed their names to more Americanized versions, though most kept their surnames in the Czech and Slovak forms.

Houma

Houma was a city of less than 1,500 people when the first Czech immigrants arrived in the city. Two of the families were to make a significant contribution in the history of the city, but two just surfaced briefly and then disappeared. In this section I will look at the trajectory of these families as they came and went through Houma. The city was on the verge of a boom brought about by the plantation economy that was spreading in the former wilderness surrounding the city in the 1850s when James Blahut first appeared. The city was prosperous and growing during the last decades of the 1800s when the Zelenka family made their mark. The city was enjoying new found oil wealth when the last members of the

Blahut and Zelenka families either died or moved away, but they did leave an indelible trace on the face of Houma.

The Blahut Family

The story of the plantation owner James Blahut and his family's 75 years in Houma begins with a record in the Terrebonne Parish Court House: James Blahut, "native of the city of Prague in the Kingdom of Bohemia, age 31 years, and emigrated to the United States in the month of March, 1851," applied for naturalization on April 21, 1853. James could not have been the name he was given at birth. Immigrant naming conventions of the time dictate that James was most often the translation for the Czech Vaclav. He quickly moved into the social scene in the area. James Blahut was a master mason at Houma Lodge No 139. He was initiated in 1854 and became a full member in 1855. He was treasurer for the lodge in 1864, 1865, and 1866. Prague, where James Blahut was born in 1822 or 1823, was a major city of the Austrian-Hungarian Empire and had several hundred thousand residents.

In the 1850s his residence was listed as Houma. His occupation was recorded as "merchant." And we have one odd transaction confirming his job: on the 23rd of October, 1855, "Blahut and Wright" sold a "mortgage recording book" for $15.50 to the Parish police jury. Blahut was in business with his brother-in-law, Abraham Wright. In 1854, the year before Holden Wright was to become his father-in-law, Wright produced 146 hogsheads (hhs) of sugar. So James was making a good economic step when on July 25, 1855, he married Maria Elizabeth Wright, Holden's daughter. She was born January 28, 1829. The nuptials took place at the Bayou Black residence of her father; a Reverend Wilson did the honors. The marriage record says he was "the son of Mathiew Blahut and Marguerite Fomayer." The marriage was short lived as Maria died on April 15th, 1858. They had one son, William Holden Blahut.

Things could not have been good between the young couple for a petition for divorce was filed at Houma Civil Court, in an action titled "James Blahut vs. Maria Wright." It was dated June 22, 1857. This was not the first litigation that James was involved in. The record is unclear as to whether the divorce was granted, though it did not matter for Marie had died. A year after Maria died, James Blahut married Madeline Zulinda Porche. His new father-in-law, Evariste Porche, was producing 225 hhs of sugar. In 1859 when Holden Wright produced only 98 hhs of sugar James Blahut is mentioned for the first time as a sugar producer with a paltry 12 hhs. In the record his name is misspelled as "Blaut." All three plantations were adjacent to each other. Could Blahut have been carrying on an affair with Madeline while he was still married to Marie? Is this the reason for the divorce? There is no clear evidence.

In the 1860 Slave Schedule for Terrebonne Parish James Blahut is listed as owning 3 slaves in Precinct 11 of Houma's 6th Ward. There is also a record seeming to indicate that Blahut rented out 6 slaves that he owned to a Mr. N. B. Neal, but that record is not clear as to exactly what happened. Some of the planters were listed as owning as many as 200 slaves so Blahut was not in their league. For the following year there are sugar records, this being 1861 to 1862, stating that James Blahut, spelled Blaut again, produced just 12 hhs. Holden Wright produced 117 and Evariste Porche 236 hhs of sugar.

The 1860 Terrebonne Census shows that James Blahut was now 36 years old and married to "Zulinda Porche." They were married on April 27, 1859. She was born on November 27, 1833 and was 27 years old at the time of the census. His son, William, whose birthday was October 2, 1856, lived with them. He was eventually married to Josephine Theriot on February 19th, 1878; he was just 22 years old at the time. He died on March 1st, 1926, in Hot Springs Arkansas. Also in 1859, the will of John Thuer, left "to his friends James Blahut and Valentin Berger" his property on Little Caillou Bayou, 22 miles below Houma.

Blahut entered the Civil War years owning at least two plantations, and a handful of slaves, as well as a merchant business in Houma. Things seemed to be going well for this Czech immigrant. He and Zulinda had added a daughter to the family. Marguerite was just one month old when the census was taken. According to the 1860 census he was worth $43,000 in real estate and $11,700 in personal property. This was a huge amount of money for the times and shows a very successful business man. He traveled in the exclusive circles of people at the top of the social order. Terrebonne parish had 110 plantations with 80 sugar houses through the 1850s and into the 1860s. He clearly owned slaves.

But the ravages of the Civil War befell Houma. The slaves were freed and the Yankee armies took what provisions and stock they needed from the plantations. There is an extant letter from "W. J. Minor, et al. to Major Genl. Banks" from January 14th, 1862" signed by 170 leading citizens of Houma, including presumably James Blahut. This letter from the owners of the plantations surrounding Houma asks the Union commander of the district to restore some of the property looted and to force freed African-Americans to get back to work or the region would face "dire straits and even catastrophe."

Blahut faced these trials and tribulations as best he could. But he did not fare well economically. In a suit titled "Oliva Theriot vs. James Blahut," which was filed December 24, 1866, Theriot claims "he was employed as an overseer on James Blahut's plantation on Bayou Dularge." He was suing for $500.00 wages that were unpaid. He also claimed a share of the crop. But Peet, Simmes & Company had already seized the crop in their own suit against Blahut and Wright. The date of that suit is not recorded. But on January 12, 1869, judgment was made against Blahut for $500. Witnesses summoned to record the event were B. F. Bazet, who was a leading citizen of Houma and who was to become the father-in-law of another Czech in Houma, and Lucien Arcenaux.

A second suit recorded was "Gaune & Eichelberger vs. Blahut & Wright." Filed in December, 1867, the suit says Guane & Eichelberger, a commercial firm in New Orleans composed of Peter Guane and Edwards Eichelberger, was suing Blahut & Wright, a firm in Terrebone Parish, composed of James Blahut and Abraham Wright. Wright was James's ex-brother-in-law. The suit concerned an overdue account of $442.90 for goods delivered on credit. The account dated from September, 1861, at the beginning of the war.

The Terrebonne Parish Census for 1870 has James Blahut in Ward 14. His wife was listed as "Maddlin." She was now 36. Besides their son, William Holden, they were joined by five daughters: "Elmise," 10, really Elmire Marguerite, born June 14, 1860; "Mary," 8, real name Marie Elfride Alida, born December 12, 1861; "Emily," 5, who was born Emilie Barras on April 10, 1864; "Anna," 3, born as Ann Georgina on November 15, 1867; and Alice Elizabeth, born on February 20, 1871. There was a sixth daughter, Franklina Wilhelmina, who was born November 22, 1865, and died on May 22, 1866, aged just 6 months. None of these daughters were to marry.

There are three "Emancipation from Parental Control" petitions listed in the 1870s and 1880s against James. The petition of William Holden says that John P. Vigurie was appointed as a special tutor for the young man. The abstract states "William Wright, his maternal uncle testifies that he [William Holden] has been supporting himself for the past two years. James Blahut is now residing in Texas." I could find no evidence that James Blahut ever went to Texas other than this document. If he had gone to Texas it could not have been for very long. Mary Alfrida and her sister Emily Barras also filed for emancipation. These were done while the children were still considered minors, but they had to be at least 18 or 19 when they sought this. They were all filed before James Blahut died on the 18th of April, 1875. He was 53 years old.

We must move to Arkansas to follow the family of William Holden Blahut. He must have died before the 1910 census, because that records that Isaac W. Hill was married to Lettie C. Blahut. They had two children in the household.

Isaac Wayne Blahut, age 7, and Frank Blahut. Both were listed as grandsons. In the 1920 Arkansas Census we find Frank Blahut, age 22, born in Arkansas and Agnes, age 23, born in Missouri. They also had a son Francis, aged 2 months. Living with them was "Wayne Blahut, aged 17 and born also in Arkansas." According to what was found in the census of Arkansas, William Holden Blahut was a farmer. Josephine Theriot was the first 1st wife of William Holden, (and she may have been the daughter of the overseer who sued James Blahut,) so Lettie must have been his second wife. He died and was buried, possibly in Hotsprings, Arkansas. But it surely brings to an end the Blahut family name.

In the 1900 census the five Blahut sisters were recorded as all working as milliners with their own store in downtown Houma. This census erroneously lists Germany as the birthplace of James Blahut. The five woman went by the names Alice, Emily, Mary, Elizabeth and Elmire. The 1910 Census lists only Mary and Alice. Also in the household was Alphonse, listed as an "adopted son" He was a 25 year old dentist. They also had a "helper" named Nara Parchic. As the years rolled by nothing much changed for the sisters and in 1920 Mary and Alice where still in the census. This time their father was listed as born in Prague, Austria. Also in the household were Alphonse Veret, now listed as a 34 year old cousin; he was, though, still a dentist. He was married to the 25 year old Lillian, identified as a "cousin-in-law." She worked at a shoe store which was probably the Blahut sister's store. They had a daughter Marie who was 4 years and 5 months old. Also in the house was Lydia Wirth, a "friend," who a 59 year old widow. It was obviously a crowded house and perhaps they all lived together to share expenses.

There is still a two story large brick building at the corner of Main and Roussell Streets in downtown Houma which housed the store of the Blahut sisters for more than 50 years. It was known as the Blahut Building for many decades because the sisters built it. That five spinster sisters built one of the biggest buildings in town was surely an eye-raising situation. Their store sold the usual items required by women of the era: bolts of cloth by the yard, feathers, hats, notions and other household wares. "They were the fashionable milliners of their day" according to our best source on the Blahut sisters, Helen Emmeline Wurzlow. She wrote a series of newspaper articles which were later joined into serveral volumes called "I Dug Up Houma." The other Czech in town, Rudolph Zelenka, had built a building with the Blahut sisters. It was torn down shortly after a major fire in 1892 destroyed several blocks of the downtown area.

The Wurzlow series is sprinkled with references to the Blahut sisters, mostly how this or that important and fashionable woman had their wedding dress, hats, and other clothing made or finished by the Blahuts. There was also a Blahut shoestore. One clerk was Albert Chauvin. Several other businesses were at one time or another in the Blahut Building. One was the office of the well respected Dr. Collins. He was known for making people feel better "before they swallowed their pills." Charles Daspit ran his drug store, called the Standard, out of one side of the lower floor. The Theriot drug store also apparently occupied this space for a short while. So the ladies owned the building, owned the store on one side of the building and rented out the rest of the space. This was quite enterprising for women of the era.

Elmira Blahut died in a tragic accident when the horse pulling her buggy went wild and overturned it and dragged the unfortunate victim and the buggy for several hundred feet. This accident happend on School Street, not far from the sisters' home on Belanger Street.

Mary Blahut died at Hotel Dieu in New Orleans on Monday, September 7, 1936. This was actually a hospital and not a hotel at all. She was survived by her two sisters and also "adopted brother, Dr. A A Verrat of Houma." Religious service was held at St. Francis de Sales Church in Houma. On Friday, January 8, 1954, at the residence of Mrs. Mamie Toups at 433 Columbus Street in Houma, Alice Elizabeth Blahut, died at the age of 83. After a funeral at St. Francis De Sales Catholic she was buried in the church cemetery. The last Blahut sister to die was Sister Mary of St. Theodora MBC, "in the world, Annie Blahut." She died at the Marianite Provincial House at 3523 North Rampart Street in New Orleans on Tuesday June 22, 1956. She had been a resident of New Orleans for 6 years, working at the Holy Angels Academy. Interment was in St. Vincent De Paul cemetery No. 2 in New Orleans. None of the daughters had gotten married and this spelled the end of the promising start of James Blahut and his family in the New World. But the Blahut building still stands in downtown Houma, a legacy set in stone and brick.

The Zelenka Family

The Zelenka family's experience in Houma parallels the Blahut's. They were related. Louis Zelenka's father had married James Blahut's sister in Prague. In 1860 "L Zelenka, 23," was a professional musician with a wife named Georgiana who was 20 living in New Orleans. They had $200 worth of personal property He was recorded being from Bohemia; she was from Terrebonne Parish, Louisiana. From the sacramental record we know that Louis G. Zelenda (sic) married Georgiana Bedford either on the 8th or 23rd of May, 1859 in Houma, both dates are given in the record His parents were John Zelenka and Madeleine Blahut. Her father was George C. Bedford and her mother Francoise Benoit. Both of them were of long time Houma families.

Shortly after his marriage he moved his new bride to New Orleans. The 1861 city directory says Louis Zelenka was working as a clerk while living at 41 Chartres Street in New Orleans. They must have lived in New Orleans for a number of years, but in a document dated March 21st, 1870, and recorded in Donation Book A in the Houma Parish Courthouse, there is a transaction where "Mrs. Francaise Bezaline Benoit, widow of George Bedford," gave to her daughter, "Mrs. Georgiana Bedford, wife of George L Zelenka," a lot in Houma. Why Louis was recorded as "George" is not at all clear. Their son Rudolph Louis was born on June 3, 1868, in Houma. In 1878 "L. R. Zelenka" was still eligible at the age of 44 for militia duty according to a roster drawn up by the local military office. He apparently, though, never served any time in the armed forces.

On March 15, 1890, Rudolph Zelenka was named as the publisher of the Houma Courier, the city's newspaper. A. F. Champeau was editor. The 1897 Rogers Parish Directory for Terrebonne Parish, published in New Orleans, says that Dr R. L. Zelinka (sic), had an office on Roussell Street in downtown Houma and that he was a "specialist in Gold Teeth." On February 27, 1897 Rudolph married Eva Bazet, the daughter of the owner of the Courier. Eva Bazet, was the fifth child of "Lafayette" Filhucan Bazet. Bazet had been born in Lassere in Gascony, France and took Lafayette as a nickname. Eva lived all her adult life on Roussell Street in Houma. She and Rudolph had four kids: Thelma, Rudolph Jr., Bernard, and Louis. Eva died at the age of 84 and rests at the Zelenka family tomb in the Catholic Cemetery in Houma.

Bernard Zelenka was born December 21, 1902. He was a captain in the United States Navy during World War II. He died February 10, 1957. He had the rather romantic wedding locale of a ship at dockside in San Diego. He married Mina Jewel of New Iberia on June 12, 1926.

It is always odd to see which facts were preserved through no special effort about people in the past. One such odd fact is that Dr. Zelenka and W. C. Comean attended the Annual Meeting of the Clinic of the Louisiana Dental Society on May 5, 1927, in New Orleans. That same day one Mr. H. L. Bourgeois entertained the 500 Club, a group of important citizens of the Houma. Prizes were said to be "won by Mesdames R. L. Zelenka and C. X. Henry."

Rudolph L, Jr., was also midshipman at the United States Naval Academy at Annapolis. He enlisted on June 25, 1918, and resigned April 19, 1919. Which means he served in the last days of World War I and shortly thereafter. The military was downsized after the war and nothing should be thought amiss about his brief sojourn in the navy. Thelma went off to school at the Louisiana State Normal School in Nachitoches, Louisiana (as teacher's colleges were known then.) There she married into the Kyser family. Her husband became president of Northwestern State College in Nachitoches. All of the Zelenka children eventually moved away from Houma, but they apparently still own property in the city, including their parents' original house and one other house, both of which are just a block from the courthouse square. They are around the corner from the Blahut's house. So at least four buildings that stand today in Houma are connected to Czechs.

The most interesting story about the Zelenkas does not really involve them, other than it happened on their front porch. "In those days," as Wurzlow says, "bakers delivered fresh" bread to each home at the break of day. A man named Fane Bourg was working for Sam Achee, a local bakery owner. It was Bourg who related the story to Wurzlow: The two men were uneventfully making their rounds when they got to the Zelenka house. Achee stepped down with a loaf or two in hand, ready to put in the bread basket on the front porch. He walked up to the gallery and "he was greeted by a lion, yes a real live lion," Bourg is quoted. Wurzlow quotes Bourg at length: *"The lion was waking up from a nap. He stood up and looked at the baker. Achee was so startled he backed away. He backed down the steps all the ways across the walk and right into the wagon, still clutching the loaf of bread."* Achee yelled to get the chief of police. Bourg continued, *"the lion was not ferocious. He did not try to attack the startled baker. He just stared at him."* Apparently, the lion had escaped from the traveling circus in town, which was set up a few blocks away. Police Chief Zeringer got a rope and "lassoed the lion and led him back peacefully to the circus." It is not clear which year this happened, but given the details it was the late 1890s. But as even Wurzlow wrote when she recounted it, "the story is too good to miss." I share her feeling on this point.

The Mayer & Rose Families

P & M Mayer were confectioners in Houma according to the 1860 Terrebonne census. They were recorded as Bohemian. They were in a business that relied on the disposable income of their customers. The Civil War eliminated this source of business and the Mayer's and their concern disappeared, though this census does list $200 in personal property which was quite substantial for the times.

Also in the 1860 census of Houma there was one Valentin Rose, 34, a farm laborer, and his 30 year old wife, identified only as D. Rose. They had four children, Valentin, aged 7, Ernest, 5, Ernestine, 3 and Caroline just six months old. All from were born in Bohemia and this means that the Rose family essentially stepped out of the frying pan of Austrian dominated Bohemia into the fire of the Civil War Louisiana. They did not stay in Houma more than a few years. Where either of these families went is not known.

The Horecky Family

John Horecky was born January 3, 1868 in a town called Velka Bytca in what is now the Slovak Republic. The surname was origianlly "Hvorecky," but he changed it sometime after his arrival. He came to America in 1886 with a cousin for what was supposed to be a one year trip. He stayed; the cousin returned. He was just 18 years old when he settled down in America. They came through New York, but made their way to the Slovak community in St. Louis, Missouri. John engaged in the tinsmithing trade. He made his own wares. Not liking winters he started to make trips down the Mississippi River to Louisiana, then he would travel by boat to the small town of Washington, at the edge of the Louisiana prarie. He would walk the countryside selling his wares and each night he would stay at someone else's house. He always left a small gift of a thimble or cup. He returned to St. Louis each summer to make the goods he would spend the following winter selling in Louisiana. In a sign of the times, he kept his savings in cash in the safe of Homer Barousse in the town of Church Point on nothing more than a hand shake and trust. On one of his trips to Church Point he met his future wife, Julia McBride. She was a friend of the family where he was staying. Soon he decided to make Church Point his home and he asked for Julia's hand in marriage.

They were married on February 25, 1892. John bought the cloth for the dress in New Orleans, along with an amethyst engagement ring and two gold wedding bands. Soon after the wedding he purchased a horse and buggy which made his trade easier and more far ranging. He had also been learning French and English during his travels, but still spoke them poorly. His goods must have spoke for themselves in order to make the sale. He felt he spoke English poorly enough that he decided to go to a school with mostly small children of immigrants of other nationalities to learn English better. At the turn of the century business was good enough that he was able to build a small retail store in Church Point. While he continued on his forays for a few days each week, his wife and her sister ran the store. Aurelia McBride, Julia's sister, lived with the young couple in a few rooms at the back of the store.

He was a very good business man who added a second horse and a bigger wagon to peddle the wares door to door through the rural areas outside of town. He also built a separate small house behind the store to serve two purposes. One was to add space to his store by using the former rooms they had lived in. The other was because he and Julia were building a family. Their first child, a daughter named Delia, was born in 1893. Sorrowfully, she died of diptheria at the age of 2; the house was quarentined and the family and friends did not get to mourn properly. Following the young girl's death in 1895 they had a son they named Conrad. The next year a daughter they named Nita was born. Then there was a another baby who died shortly after birth. Following that tragic event was Hester.

The family was struck with further tragedy when they lost 8 month old Colton. But they were soon blessed with another son, Roy. A daughter Jenny was the youngest surviving daughter, her proper name was Genivive. Actually, from the information in the 1910 census the young girl was also known as "Joseviva." And Nita was listed as "Nisa." In this censu John Horecky was recorded as a 42 year old merchant living with his 35 year old wife and five children: Conrad, 15, Nita, 14, Hester, 12, Roy, 7, and Jenny, 5. Their home address, as well as that of the store, was 47 North Main Street in Church Point. Shortly after this census they also had a tenth child who died at childbirth.

As he was growing his family he was growing his business. He hired Sidney Beaugh to run the peddling route while he worked the store. Sideny lived with the family and the young Horecky children thought of him as a brother. In another bit of a "company town" feeling, a man named Dave Marshall came to live with the family. He took over the traveling sales when Sidney moved full time into the store. Dave and Sidney were to spend many years with the company. As the business grew John added more personnel.

According to Mary Alice Fontenot in her history of Acadia Parish, John Horecky served on the town council in the 1910s. The councilmembers were all Democrats who normally faced no opposition in their campaigns. When Horecky was building his buinsess Church Point was a very small town, in 1900 the population was only 278 residents. By 1910 the town had grown to 481 inhabitants, yet by 1920 it had fallen to 393. In 1902 Horecky built his first warehouse and by 1905 he was the first to bring ice to town to keep his perishables fresh. In 1902 there were several stores in competition with him. Daigle's General Store was one; Guidry's Hardware and Grocers was the biggest business in town at the time. Guidry manufactured shoes, harnesses and saddles, too.

Despite this competition he continued to build his business and in 1914 he built a warehouse on 3rd Street. The building had a galvanized iron frame and roof and was built on a brick foundation. This was a very modern building for the times. It was during this era that he bought a wholesale company started by Leo Franques and Emile Daigle and combined it with his own store. Together they became Church Point Wholesale. This company exists today.

He also was able to build a bigger house for him and his family; it was completed in 1911. He designed the floor plan himself. The house still stands. There was no central hall as was common in Louisiana homes, but instead a foyer opened to a staircase to the second floor and large formal parlor. There is a unique triple fireplace in the house that allowed them to heat the dining room, family room and parlor at the same time. There were 12 foot ceilings. Four bedrooms were upstairs. Still, it must have been a crowded house. In another inovation, the house had electricity provided by its own generator. After this house was built he moved the old house so he could build a bigger warehouse behind the store.

In another inovation, one way John increased his business was to institute a "frequent shopper card." Just like those used today, John punched a card he gave his customers each time they made a purchase. After ten purchases they were able to choose a small item such as picture frames, crockery or wicker chairs. This kept up a loyal clientelle. John kept growing the business and his family. He traded goods from his store for chickens and eggs and dairy products from his mostly farmer customers. By 1922, when his son Roy joined the business, he was shipping a train car full of chickens and eggs to New Orleaans about every other day. Roy was only 20 years old and had run the business on his own for a few months while his father was ill. At this time they were also bringing in 300 pounds of ice nearly every day to keep the perishable items cool. Within a decade the company was to buy ice by the train car, at 30,000 pounds per load.

Thoughout his years in America John had kept in touch with his family in Slovakia, but with the coming of World War I his letters were returned as "undeliverable." He had estalblished contact with an old friend, John Grunik in Cameron Parish, who had come over on the same boat with him. This was both a business and personal relationship. When Grunik went to Slovakia after the war he was able to meet some of Horecky's cousins and other family. Horecky had been so long without conversation in his native Slovak that he was unable to translate the letters, so Grunik had to help him read them. Horecky had planned just once to return to his homeland, but he never did so. After Grunik contacted the European relatives, Horecky found out that he had a cousin in Chicago. He tried to get a passport to go with her back to the old country, but he could not get it in time.

He did, though, send money to his relatives, and one of the letters from his Slovak relations mentions a gift of $50. He did this both before the war and after he reestablished contact in the post war years. There are several extant letters that decry the fact that John never made it back to visit his hometown. The letters are filled with family woes of untimely deaths, and peppered with allusions to what could have been had they gone to America, too. There are also references to many of the sons of the village going to America. One letter, dated January 24, 1901, says "10 men from our street are leaving for America." Most of the letters are addressed to John using the original spelling of the name, Hvorecky. One letter is addressed simply "John Hvorecky, Church Point, America." It was delivered.

Instead, John concentrated on his business. There are stories that during the Depression he would leave baskets of food on the doorsteps of those he knew were too proud to ask for help yet were struggling. He extended credit to many of his customers. He kept people employed, even if in so-called make work jobs. The company in some ways acted like a private social service agency. The wholesale company kept up a healthy business despite the lean years. It even grew in a time when other companies were in retrenchment. Many citizens of Church Point and the surrounding area were indebted to Horecky for his help during the Depression years. They repaid that loyalty by faithfully shopping at his store when times got better for them. And for reelecting him, and later his sons, to the town council.

John died on October 3, 1941. At the time he was a member of the Knights of Columbus and the Woodsmen of the World, both civic improvement organizations. Indeed, it was said that John was involved in every civic improvement project that Church Point saw during his years living there. He was the richest man in town and that certainly led people to respect his opinion. He owned not only several cotton farms but also a cotton gin. He served as a director of the Commerical Trust Bank. A notice in the Opelousas Daily World said that he was "one of the most widely known men in Southwest Louisiana." He never did lose his Slovak accent and that must have puzzled the many people he dealt with.

His sons Conrad and Roy were actively involved in the business, as were the sons-in-law. Roy had perhaps the most success. During World War II, when there were no cars being sold, the family was able to buy the local Ford dealership, which they renamed Horecky Motors. It lasted until the late 1980s. In 1943 the family was able to start their own bank, the Farmers State Bank & Trust Company. Roy was one of the directors; Edward Diagle, his brother-in-law, was another. They kept expanding the wholesale business as well as being involved in many other ventures. Roy served as a Church Point city councilman for 16 years.

The Horeckys were the most important family in the northern reaches of the parish. In one of those quintessential Louisiana moments John's granddaughter, Jean Horecky, was the first Louisiana Yambilee Festival Queen in the 1950s, in St. Landry Parish.

Over the decades all the family members of the first generation, and quite a few from the second generation, were to work at the company. It had grown to a many-armed conglomerate, at one time even including Schlitz beer distributorships in Opelousas and Monroe. The company was supplying many small groceries throughout the state, as well as having a hand in many enterprises in Church Point. It grew to be the largest food wholesaler in Louisiana. Yet, typically with family businesses, as time went by divisions were sold off, and descendants pursued their own intersests. The wholesale company was finally sold after the turn of the millennium. There are now plans underway to build a small memorial to the founder of this dynasty in the new building for the company. There are approximately 200 descendants of John Horecky, immigrant from Slovakia, living in Louisiana today.

Rosalie Beer

The Church Point Wholesale Company engaged in the liquor trade, both before and after Prohibition. They even had their own house label wine called "T & T," for Tried and True, which was not discontinued until 1993. They also sold beer and this is when we come to the story of Rosalie Beer. 500,000 cans of Rosalie Pilsner beer were produced and only 6 survived to our day. There was a brewery in Chicago called the Manhattan Brewing Company. It was alleged to have been owned by gangster Al Capone. One legend related to this beer is that Horecky gave a deposition on behalf of Al Capone regarding sugar prices that Capone paid. Whether Horecky went to Chicago to testify is not known. To return the favor Capone made Rosalie Beer (the rose taken from a period wine bottle) for Church Point Wholesale and shipped it south. Whatever the story, Capone's company was also known as Malt Maid Products Co. & Malt Maid Co.—during Prohibition this is where he made bootleg beer. The firm lasted from 1893 to 1947, brewing private label beers.

In the late 1930's, well after Prohibition had ended, Manhattan produced three brands of beer in cans that were sent to Louisiana. They were Rosalie Pilsner Beer; Tiger Beer; and Autocrat Beer. Rosalie was sold exclusively by Church Point Wholesale. Tiger Beer was sold by the Piggly Wiggly supermarket chain and was purple and gold for the LSU Tigers. Autocrat Beer was sold in New

Orleans. These cans are very sought after by collectors. There are 6 Rosalie's known to exist, just 1 Tiger Beer can known—it was found in the Chicago brewery in the early 1970s. There are 4 known Autocrat cans. Such rarity of course leads to great values. In the late 1990s there was a new record price set for a beer can. A Rosalie Pilsner flat-top can sold for $10,300 over the internet service eBay. Perhaps ironically, this lone can, with a rose on the label, sold on Mother's Day, when roses are such an appropriate gift. This means, of course, that the most expensive can of beer ever sold is connected to a Slovak immigrant to Louisiana.

Czechs and Slovaks in Acadiana

On the eve of the Civil War in 1860 Catherine Tonsek headed her household according to the census of Lafayette Parish. She was a seamstress with $450 in real estate and personal property, which put her in the middle class of the times. She was recently widowed, and the poor woman was left to raise six children on her own. They were Francis, who was 14, John, 12, Rebecca, 10, Zacavia, 8, Thomas, 6, and James, 4. They are not in the 1870 census and what happened to them either during or shortly after the war is unknown. Perhaps she got married to a local man and her and the children adopted his name.

In the Fourth Ward of St. Landry Parish, according to the 1870 Census, there was a tanner named Joseph Kohler. He was 70 years old and was born in Bohemia. His wife Rosina was 61. She was of German heritage, born in Baden, Germany. She took two children from a prior marriage to her union with Kohler. They were Edward Grisman, who was 15, and Casinetta Grisman, 12. Once again, there is just one reference to another Bohemain family in Louisiana.

Peter Labriska was a Bohemian who was living in Point Coupee Parish. The 4th ward where he lived was mostly farms when the 1890 census was taken. He was a bachelor farmer.

These three were the only Czech settlers to Acadiana during the second half of the 1800s.

Among the tens of thousands of Cajuns spread across the 22 parish area of South Louisiana known as Acadiana only 7 other Czech and Slovak families, besides the Cameron Parish Slovaks, can be found. Five families were farmers who spent some time in the area before moving on, one was a lone man in a small town and one family, the Podraskys, had an 80 year presence in Lake Charles. There were 42 people in these 7 families. Of course, the Touchets had by now 100s of family members in the area and it is quite possible that the newly arrived Czechs and Slovaks met one or two Touchets in the course of the their daily lives.

It is doubtful that the Touchets knew anything of their Czech heritage and it is equally doubtful that any of the new Czechs and Slovaks could figure that out either.

The 1920 census of Vernon Parish, out on the Acadian prairie, shows that a farm laborer known only by his surname, Belohradsky, made his home. He was a 45 year old widower. His four daughters were all born in Illinois. They were Josephine, 20, Rose, 16, Louise, 14 and Marion, 9. If they stayed in Louisiana they probably married into some of the very numerous Cajun families living around them. The family name died out with the four daughters. Their mother, Josephine "Belohradzlty" in her death record, died August 12, 1918. She was 41 years old. The youngish couple was starting out in a new land and all of a sudden the father was saddled with four girls to raise by himself. It must have been a difficult time for him. What happened to them is unknown though it could be possible that he took his family to another state with more Czechs to remarry. This was an era, after all, when single fathers simply could not make it on their own.

In neighboring Beauregard Parish lived Charles Lorenz. He was 40 in the 1920 census. He arrived in 1880, meaning he was just an infant when he arrived. His wife Josephine was 34. They had eight children, 6 born in Kansas, and 2 in Louisiana. They were Theodore, 14, Anna 12, Angleina 11, Charlie, 10, Ladislav, 8, Mary, 6, Joseph, 4, and David, 1, the last two born in Louisiana. By the ages of Mary and Joseph it is clear that the family arrived in Louisiana sometime around 1915. A cemetery inscription in that parish records that "Charlie" Lorenz was born on July 5th, 1909 and died December 17th, 1977. He was married to a woman named Helen, whose dates were August 21, 1916 to April 4, 1973.

At the turn of the century the Lovas family was recorded in the 1900 census of the town of St. Martinville, deep in the heart of Cajun Country. Joseph Lovas was born in 1851 in Bohemia. Now he was a 48 year old merchant, presumably with a shop in downtown. Mary, who was 41, was born 1859. The parents both arrived in 1890 and apparently settled in Louisiana upon their arrival. But two children born in Bohemia arrived later. Annie 16, born 1884 and Joseph 10, born 1890, arrived in 1892. They were very young, but it is not known who they traveled with. Then the Lovas had three children in Louisiana: Mary, 7, born 1893, Vencenne, 3, 1896, and Paola, 1, in 1898. Only one obituary for this family could be found, that of Loula Lovas Bernard. She died at the age of 86 in her residence in St. Martinville, on Sunday, May 11, 2003. She must have been a daughter born after the census was taken. This also perhaps indicates that the Lovas family had a long sojourn in St. Martin parish.

Out in the rural 3rd Ward of Vernon Parish lived a farmer named Joseph Smudrick. He was born in Bohemia in 1855, though his age is erroneously listed as "43" in the 1900 census. He arrived in America in 1880. His wife Anna, was much younger than he was. She was born in 1879 and was just 28, but she, too, was born in Bohemia. They had a 2 year old toddler named Olin who was born in Louisiana, putting the family in the state no later than 1898. This is the one record of this family.

From the immigrant book by Leo Baca of Czechs who landed at New Orleans we find Johann and Theresia Sterba plus 1 infant arriving on July 12, 1852. Whether these were related to the Sterba family in the 1920 Census is not clear, but it seems likely. In that census a Bohemian named John Sterba, just 35 years old, was a farmer in Beauregard Parish. The farm lay between DeQuincy and DeRidder. John's wife Mary, 35, was also born in Bohemia; her maiden name was Caithaml. A wedding picture of them shows a serious man with a bushy mustache and a pensive woman who seems to have no idea what the future would hold. They had three children, George, 8, Richard, 6 and Vlasta, 5. All the kids were born in Nebraska. According to Barbara Edmon, the granddaughter of Vlasta, the family had some hard knocks. One family story is that her great-grandfather, John, was gored by an ox and died soon thereafter. Another family story is that the farm was destroyed by a hurricane. By 1930 the family had left Louisiana for Texas.

A Slovak named Frank Pastorek lived in St. Landry Parish in 1910. He was 41 years old and he came in 1888 when he was a little boy. His wife, Julia, was a 41 year old Slovak. They must have come to Louisiana in 1895, because their oldest daughter Mary was 15 at the time of the census and she was born in the state. Their sons were John, 13, and William, 11. In a somewhat confusing situation William had a twin sister, Willie. Their youngest daughter was Cecelia, 8 at the time of the census. He was a farmer. There is no evidence that they were related to the Pastorek family over in Tangipahoa Parish. Pastorek is one of those more common Czech names.

Of the bachelor Albert Wingler it is known only that he arrived in 1880 from Bohemia and he was 51 years old in the 1910 census. He was living in Westlake, Louisiana, near Lake Charles. Wingler is not at all a Czech name, nor is there a translation from a Czech word or last name. Perhaps he just picked it out of thin air as more than a few immigrants did to make them seem more American. He, too, simply disappears from the records.

The Podrasky Family

For many decades the Podrasky family lived and worked in downtown Lake Charles, the parish seat of Calcasieu Parish and the largest city in Southwest Louisiana. The family is first encountered in Lake Charles in the 1900 census living in the 2nd Ward of the city. Henry, who was born in 1869 and was now 31, was recorded as a dry goods merchant. He arrived in America in 1882. He had been married 4 years to Annie. She was ten years younger than him. She had arrived in 1886. They had at least two children George, born 1897, and Marie, born in 1899. There is definite evidence of a third child, Fred, that we get from many sources, including a tombstone in Consolata Cemetery in Lake Charles. That stone says he was born January 14, 1896 and died the 16th of June, 1986, at the age of 90. Why he is not listed in the census is a mystery.

Ten years later we find Henry listed as "George Henry" Podrasky, now 41. The census says he was "Hungarian Slovak." He was still a retail merchant of dry goods. Anna, as she is known in this census, was now 31. Besides George Jr., now 12 and Mary, 10, from the previous census, they had four more children. Joseph was 9, Anna was 7, Helen was 3 and they had a two month old infant named Frederich. If this is the same Fred recorded on the gravestone than one or the other ages must be incorrect.

In 1934 Fred H. Podrasky was a clerk, though it is not clear where. His brother, George Henry, was the owner of Podrasky's Men Furnishings at 539 Ryan Street. They both lived at 625 Mill Street, just a few blocks away from the store. In 1941 a new store and alterations to the existing store were made at Podrasky's. That same year, Dunn and Quinn, architects for the store also built a wood frame residence for George. The drawings are dated May of that year. Later that same year, in October, drawings were submitted by the same architects for a residence for "Mr. and Mrs. Fred Podrasky." These houses are still standing and in the historic district of Lake Charles.

By 1942 Fred was married to Delila and he is still listed as a clerk. They were making their home at 1000 7th Street. They were sophisticated enough to have a phone, with just the four digit number 3538. His brother George was now married to Anna and they lived at 919 Cleveland Street. This couple already had a son who was at least 18, named George Jr., which was the minimum age to get listed in the city directory where he is first recorded. Tragedy struck the family when the infant daughter Elizabeth of Fred and Delilah died. The only date on her tombstone in Lake Charles's Graceland—Orange Grove Cemetery. is October 3, 1943.

Their sister Helen was a saleswoman at Podrasky's. Her address was not listed, but she had a home phone number: 9554. She may well have been living with one of her brothers but had her own phone. Now the store where they worked was called Podrasky's Shoes, though it was still at 539 Ryan Street. You could call the store by dialing 3924. By 1952 Fred and Delilah had built their own house at 1021 7th Street. George was still at 919 Cleveland as was Helen. She was still a saleswoman at the family store. Which itself had morphed once again, this time into Podrasky's Shoes for Men, Woman and Children. The address and phone number were the same as in 1942. 1963 saw all of the same information repeat it self, only by then Fred and Delilah had a daughter named Mary, who had to be over 18. She was listed as a student, probably at McNeese State University. The Podrasky family was actually quite ahead of its time to have telephones at both their houses and at work. There are many listings in these cities directories which contain no phone number for either home or work.

1966 saw big changes in the family. Fred and Delilah closed the shoe store and opened River View Nursery. They were still living, though, at the house on 7th Street. Fred's sister, Helen, was now a saleswoman at Newstadt's Shoes, which was just down the block from the old store. It was at 727 Ryan Street in downtown. 1972 saw another change for Fred and Deliliah; they moved to 1921 7th Street. They still had the River View Nursery, however. Helen was still living on Cleveland, but was retired. Helen died on December 17, 1994 and is buried in Consolata Cemetery in Lake Charles. She never married. From her tombstone we know that her birth date was January 12, 1907.

Our final record of the family is the obituary of Delila Podrasky on March 3, 2000. She was 81 years old and had died the day before. Her full name was Delila Monica "Dee" Ardoin Podrasky. The Ardoins are an old Cajun family mostly from Lacassine, about 20 miles east from Lake Charles. She lived in Lake Charles for most of her life and was well established in the community. She was a member of Immaculate Conception Catholic Church, as well as of the Friends of the Library and of group called Very Important Christians. She was survived by her daughter Mary Ann Podrasky Hay of Beaumont, Texas. From this history we can see that the Podrasky's had a long term impact on Lake Charles for they were one of the few shoes downtown during these years. There were generations of people from Lake Charles who bought their shoes at the Podrasky store. Due to the lack of sons, the family name, though, has left the scene.

The Pohorelsky Family

World War II was a force of dislocation for many people. The Catholic Relief Organization was resettling thousands of refugees from Europe across America and through the efforts of Father Theodore Hassink in the Diocese of Lake Charles Louisiana received its share. Among them were the newly married couple of Eugene and Jana Pohorelsky. They came to America in 1948 with their young son Viktor and an unrelated woman, Natalie Cechova. They were settled with a farming family near the town of Iowa, about 20 miles distant from Lake Charles. Alas, the plantation mentality still existed, and this family thought they were getting cheap labor. "That lasted but two weeks," said John Pohorelsky, Eugene's son.

Jana, later known as Jane, was born in Prague in 1926 to Marketa and Jan Poucek. Eugene was born in Moscow in 1912. He and his parents were not Czech, but Russian. Eugene Pohorelsky was living in Prague after the Second World War, which is were he met Jana. The political situation was precarious. John relates: "my parents escaped the Iron Curtain in 1948 after the Soviets took control of Czechoslovakia." He adds, "Father Hassink was a Dutch immigrant and probably understood my parents need and desire to come to the states." Father Hassink was a short fat man with a thick Dutch accent, according to people who knew him. But he was a tireless ball of energy on many fronts in Catholic life in Lake Charles. "He was a man of big passions," I was told by someone who knew him.

In 1955, Gene and Jane were living with Natalie Cechova at 602 Clarence Street. He was the parts manager at Radford Buick. They had Americanized their names, other than their son Viktor, all their children bear American names. Viktor is now a federal magistrate in Long Island, New York. The 1958 city directory has both Gene and Natalie owning Joe's Drive In at 1840 Bilbo Street. In a bit of what we would now call sexism, he was listed as the primary owner. In fact, there is much agreement among people who knew them that she was the primary owner. When it moved to the corner of Ryan and 7th Streets, Natalie became the sole owner. This is probably because Gene was busy with other endeavors. In 1960 he also owned the Quality Service Grill at 924 Ryan Street downtown and the Snow Cap Cafe at 107 City Services Highway on the edge of the city. He was living with his family at 1018 Holly Street. Over the years Gene and Jane raised their five children, all of whom would go on to earn college degrees. These children and grandchildren live in several cities around Louisiana.

Cechova

Natalie "Tasha" Cechova. came to the United States after World War II as a displaced refugee. She was fleeing both the devastation and the looming Communist regime. She arrived in 1948. She came to America with the Pohorelsky family, who were no relation, but just good friends in Europe. She lived briefly in San Antonio and then joined up with the Pohorelsky's in Lake Charles. Their lives were to stay entangled. She ran Joseph's Drive-In on Ryan Street until 1999. John Pohorelsky, a Lake Charles lawyer, told me "her restaurant became something of an institution in Lake Charles during its heyday." For many years it was one of the most popular restaurants in Lake Charles. Nearly every hip kid in the city had occasion to eat at this establishment. Most people probably thought of it as a Cajun place. There were, however, a number of people I know who knew that it was run by a Czech immigrant.

In 1955 Natalie lived at 602 Clarence Street with Gene and Jane Pohorelsky. She operated a restaurant called the Hob Nob at 1416 Broad Street. Gene was the parts manager at Radford Buick so we can assume he worked there for a number of years, probably since his arrival in Lake Charles. Sometime in 1958, at the height of the drive-in restaurants of the sort featured in the movie America Graffiti, Natalie opened her own restaurant. She was in business briefly with Gene Pohorelsky as co-owner, but it was her place. He probably helped with the financing. In 1960 Natalie Cechova was living at 1807 Bilbo and operating Joseph's Drive Inn Restaurant by herself. The city directory for this year does not give an address for the restaurant, but it was already at its permanent location at Ryan and 7th Streets. She ran the restaurant until 1998 working virtually every day it was open as the chief cook and bottle washer.

Natalie was from a town with an ancient history, Skrben, Czech Republic, in the Olomouc region of Moravia. It was known by a Latin name, Scriben in 1174, which by 1263 was changed to the old Czech Skrbyn before taking its "modern" form. The Czech name for the town was formalized in 1438. In German the town was known as Khurwein at first, and then Kirbein as early as 1521. In 1771 it was bestowed with the German name Kirwein. It has less than 30,000 inhabitants today. Interestingly, she kept the feminine Czech form of her family name. Her father, as all the male members of the family, would have had the last name "Cecha." Natalie, and all the female members of the family would have the surname "Cechova." This is just a convention of the Czech and Slovak languages. Most Czech and Slovak women who came to America adopted the American style of identical last names for men and women. She died in Lake Charles on

May 12, 2001, when she was 95 years old. Her obituary says she was "an entre-preneur in Prague." Nothing is known of this period. In Lake Charles she was a member of St. Louis Catholic Church. She had never married and left no descen-dants. No one seems to know who Joseph, the namesake of her restaurant, was.

Czechs and Slovaks in North Louisiana

North Louisiana was not without its Czechs and Slovaks. Though they were of a slightly different character than their countrymen in the rest of the state. There were more German-Bohemian families and more Czech Jews than in the south-ern reaches of the state. Though, there were also a few ethnic Czechs and Slovaks practicing their native religions, too. Only one family made a major or continu-ing mark on the area and that was after 1950. Most seem to have left the area with the coming of the Depression. The oldest family, though, comes early in the settlement of North Louisiana in the 1820s. North Louisiana is mostly of Anglo-Scots-Irish heritage, then and today. It was never a magnet for immigrants of any other heritages like South and Central Louisiana were. The predominant religion is fundamentalist Protestant of various denominations. Other than Shreveport it is a very sparsely populated region even today. Czech and Slovak immigrants must have stood out like the proverbial sore thumb.

The Klady Family

Klady means "merit, virtue, strength" in Czech, and is a word used as a part of the Czech version of the English phrase "pro and con:" *klady a zapory*. Klady is also a Czech surname and in the early 1800s a family by this name lived in Oua-chita Parish in the far northeast corner of the state. The first reference found is that one James Owens married a Maria Klady on July 29, 1816. We know noth-ing more about him or her. Then, in the 1820 Federal Census for Ouachita Par-ish we find a Jacob Klady. His first name is another pointer towards Czech origins as this has always been a popular boys name among Czechs. It was unlikely that there were two unrelated people with the surname Klady in this wil-derness area, but how they were related is not known. Perhaps they were brother and sister or father and daughter.

The "Washita Gazette" of June 21, 1825 has this obituary: *"On the 25th ultimo, [May 25, 1825] Jacob Klady, of this parish, died, aged 63 years; The deceased was active and bore a conspicuous part in that revolution that gave a guaranty to the enjoyment of equal rights: He was moral, a peacible and industrious citizen, highly distinguished for those virtues that do honor to the most honorable, and but seldom united to man."* The war refered to is probably the American Revolution. From the laudatory tone of the piece and the mention of community involvement it can surmised that Jacob was in the Ouachita area for quite a number of years.

Another Jacob Klady, probably a son, married Rachel Faulk on February 19, 1833. The final record we have of the family is a listing in the 1830 census. It says that Samuel Klady, perhaps another son of the first Jacob, had 15 people in his household. There were the six members of his family and 9 slaves. The census only gives ranges for the ages, and it does not list relationships. But we know that there was one teenage boy between 15 and 19. There were four adult men, two who were in their 20s and two who were in their 30s. There was also one woman who was in her 60s. This woman could be the widow of the elder Jacob. For the 9 slaves only age ranges were given. There were two boys of less than 5, 2 boys between 5–10, 2 teenaged children between 10–20, 2 men between 30–40, 2 girls less than 10, and one woman between 10 and 20. Their relationships can only be guessed at. Other than a few of the early Touchets, and later James Blahut, the Kladys are the only other slave owning Czech family found in Louisiana.

How a Czech family came to be in Ouachita Parish is perhaps forever beyond our reach. Jacob Klady seems to be the patriarch of this family and once he got to America he kept heading west. Fort Miro (the present day city of Monroe,) in 1820 was nothing more than a collection of log cabins within a stockade. The Spanish and the French had given out land grants in the area and there were people every few miles along the waterways. By the time the Kladys are in the record Louisiana was a new state in the Union. The area was seeing the beginnings of the Scots-Irish influx and every other of the 200 names or so of people at Fort Miro reflect this. Klady stands out in the list. After these few references, however, the family disappears from the record in Louisiana; perhaps they headed further west. They apparently spent at least 20 to 25 years in the area and were seemingly well known and integrated into the local community. This means, though, that a Czech family was one of the first families of Monroe.

Other Czechs and Slovaks in North Louisiana

There was a trickle of Bohemians who settled in the towns of North Louisiana. These people are known only from the census reports. No other information was found on them. In the small town of Bastrop in Morehouse Parish, in the far reaches of North Louisiana, a Bohemian named Antonio Falcone, was a 22 year old confectioner. The 1870 census does not say if he owned his own shop, but he may well have, because there was probably just about enough business to support a one man business in a town of a few hundred people. Bastrop was not a rich town and the people who were eking out a living in the piney woods would not be buying confections very often. What Falcone had to offer, though, were just maybe treats far out of the plain and ordinary, especially if he had learned his trade in the old country. Neither of his names seems Czech or Slovak at all. Either he changed his name rather drastically or he was mislisted as Bohemian by the census taker.

In the same year that Falcone is found in Bastrop the family of Jacob Heller also lived there. Heller was a harness maker, which was a very valuable trade to have in the era of horse and buggy. His wife, Babette was born in Bavaria. From this Czech-German mixed marriage came two daughters. Leonora was 2 at the time of the 1870 census, while her sister Clara was just 7 months old. Both were born in Louisiana. Their father was 38 years old and their mother was 23. The census records that there was also a 15 year old named Abram Isaacson living with them. Perhaps he was Babette's younger brother, though that is not clear.

Farrow is an English surname. But in the 1870 Census we find a widower from Bohemia named Fred Farrow. This is obviously a name change situation. The original Czech name could not be learned. However, the word for a farrow in Czech is "Vrha" and this could very well have been a last name an immigrant would want to change. Vrha also would not have been unusual as a Czech name. He was a 40 year old farm laborer living in Tensas Parish with his four children. His three sons were John, who was 18, Frank, 12, and Albert, 6. His only daughter, Anna, was 8 years old. Their mother's name was not recorded. All the children were born in Louisiana, though, placing the family in Louisiana as early as 1852. With a name like Farrow they would have quickly disappeared into the surrounding culture.

In Shreveport nothing more is recorded than that one J. P. Hockson, a 28 year old woman from Bohemia was living in the city in 1860 and working as a servant. Her name last name is not Bohemian and there could be any number of reasons that she spent just a short time in Shreveport as well. With her was a woman we know only as E. Rauman, 30 years old, also said to be from Bohemia. Rauman could be a Czech name of German origin. They were both working at the residence of the Winter family in the capital city of Caddo Parish.

The Kanka family is unfortunate to have a surname that is the Czech word for "stain." They came very early to North Louisiana. This family history is also confusing because we have two H.A. Kanka's in the 1880 United States Census. One was born in 1845. He was 35 and working as a laborer, probably on a farm. His wife, Mary, was born in Louisiana in 1850. She was now 30. She was one of the few women with an occupation; she was listed as "laborer," though no details were provided as to what kind of labor. The other head of household bearing the name H A. Kanka, was married to Jenny Kanka; she was born in 1855. They had a daughter Emma in 1979. All of them were living in the 10th Ward of entirely rural Catahoula Parish. There, of course, several possibilities, including that two brothers shared initials.

A 37 year old merchant known only as R. Rubenstein came to Shreveport from Bohemia shortly before the 1870 census. Virtually nothing was recorded about his early years nor is it clear even if later Rubensteins in Shreveport are related to him. But it is clear that in 1926 Rubenstein's Department Store purchased 517–519 Milam Street which was constructed in 1915 on the site of a defunct hotel. They remodeled it as their new store. The four story building is opposite the Caddo Parish Court House. The odd thing is that the Rubenstein family didn't seem to show up in any other census. One conclusion is that this mysterious R. sold the store to owners who kept the name, another is that he only had daughters to carry on his legacy, as with the Pokorny's. It would not have been that odd, though, for a Czech Jew to have the name Rubenstein. This was also an era when many small southern cities and towns had a Jewish merchant such as Rubenstein's.

In 1870 there was a laborer in a Stein's Dry Good Store in Farmerville, Union Parish, named Rhinehold Snyder. He was sharing his labors with 8 other workers who were not Czech. He is listed as Bohemian in the census and was 28 years old. Whether this Stein's is related to family in the next paragraph could not be determined.

In the 1870 census for Ouachita Parish a couple identified as C. Stein and his wife H.C. Stein were living fairly well. He was a thirty-year old retail merchant in the city of Monroe. He was born in Bohemia in 1837, most likely of the Jewish faith. Bavaria was listed as the birthplace of his 33 year old wife and she, too, was probably Jewish. This can be gleaned from the names of the four children in the household: Mark 15, Frances 12, Solomon 11, Julia 7. All four were born in Louisiana and their last name was Gersenberg. Clearly a man named Gersenberg was her first husband. This is one of several instances of step-children among Czech and Slovak families in Louisiana. It also shows that Stein was willing to take on some big responsibilities and had the means to do so. This is reflected in the fact that the census also lists Roy Constance and Adam Sloping as a cooks in the house. Also listed in the Stein Household was one "H. Weiskoph," also from

Bohemia. He was a 29 year old clerk in the Stein store. If he was a relative it was not recorded.

A cemetery with the odd name of St. Rest Cemetery is located on Louisiana Highway 146 in Lincoln Parish. This road is also known as White Lightning Road and it does not take much of an imagination to guess the origin of its name during Prohibition. It is approximately 4.4 miles east of the Claiborne Parish Line between Homer and Vienna, Louisiana. In the cemetery there are four tombstones pointing the way to a Czech family about whom nothing more could be learned. Julia Tabor was 79 years old. Her dates were given only as 1820 to 1899. A person named only as L.P. Tabor had the dates July 24, 1810 to July 23, 1885. These two were probably married. There was a Tabor with the male Czech first name Lovic who was probably their son. His dates are October 10, 1860 to June 26, 1928. Finally we have Ora Caver Tabor, whose dates were July 18, 1872 to September 19, 1968. Lovic and Ora were most likely husband and wife. Tabor is a Czech name that has origins in the Hussite Wars of the early 1400s when the city of Tabor was a flashpoint of revolution.

Ruston in 1910 was a small town of less than 2,000 people when Joseph Brichacek was a 47 year old laboring as a boiler maker at a foundry. He was from Bohemia where iron works and machine shops were a major industry. We can guess that he learned his trade in Europe. He was married to Anna, who at 38 was nearly 10 years younger than he. Their son Frank, 17, worked as a machinist at a foundry, presumably with his father though that is not clear. They had a second son named Harry who was 15. The census is not clear as to where the boys were born, but it appears to be somewhere in America.

Not far away, but 10 years later in the 1920 census, there is a man named Frank Fuhrer in Caddo Parish. He was a 58 year old musician in the Shreveport Shriners Band. Shriners are a part of the Masons; their focus has been on operating children's hospitals all over the world for nearly 85 years. He no doubt played at the opening of the world's first Shriners Hospital in Shreveport in 1922. We do not know what instrument he played, but Bohemian music does have a propensity for the use of horns and perhaps he played one of these. His wife Anna May was 48. This was yet another example of men marrying significantly younger women. She was born in Ohio to Bohemian parents. They had two sons. The eldest was Frank W., 20; he was a cashier. He was married to Fay Edith. She was, at 22, two years older than he was, another out of the ordinary marriage situation for the times. She is listed in the census as "daughter-in-law." Their daughter has the rather interesting name of Dorothy Mickado; she was not even a half year old at the time of the census. The other son was Leonard, 18. All three were born in Missouri.

Alexandria in 1920 was a small but bustling town in the center of the state when John Heidelberg made his home here. He had arrived from Bohemia in 1906 and was now 33 years old. When he was thirty years old in 1917 he became an American citizen. His wife was 10 years younger than he was. Her name is written as "Tele" on the census form. She, too, came from Bohemia. They had two children. Their youngest daughter was named Libi and she was two and a half. Their older daughter was given the very Czech name of Vlasta. She was 5 years old and was born in Louisiana, putting the family in the state about 1913 or 1914. Since we know she arrived in 1914, it would appear that as soon as John and Tele got married they moved to Louisiana. This was earlier than the soon-to-be Czech communities of Libuse and Kolin which were to be founded near the city. There is every indication that they came before these communities were conceived and were completely unconnected.

The Heidelberg family lived on Bogan Street in 1920. The next record of them is in the 1938/39 city directory for Alexandria. John Heidelberg is listed as owning John's Tin Shop. Both the residence and the business were at 2137 Lee Street, which is one of the major thoroughfares in the city. He would have been fifty one years old, his wife 41 and his daughters would have been 23 and 22. Because the Alexandria newspaper is not indexed, and no tombstone has been located the date of John and Tele's deaths cannot be determined. From those obituaries we would likely have learned who the daughters married.

Another Czech who seems to have arrived independently of the creation of the Czech farming communities in Rapides Parish was Rudolph Hlobil. In the 1920 census it is recorded that he arrived in America in 1912 and was a citizen by 1917. He was just 22, but he was already married to a woman named Mary. She was born in Nebraska. There is a significant Czech population in state and there is the likelihood that she was of Czech heritage, too. Their son Elbert was just three months old and born in their new Louisiana home. In the actual pages of the census the Hlobils are not grouped together with the colonists at Libuse and Kolin and it seems unlikely that this family was connected to the two colonies to come. Rudolph supported his young family by working as an oar finisher in an oar factory. This was a far different profession than the farming work of his fellow Czechs that would move into Rapides Parish.

For about 15 years a Bohemian man named Charles Holman lived in Lincoln Parish in the far reaches of North Louisiana not far from Arkansas. He was married to a woman named Anna who was born in Louisiana. He was 33 and she was

31. Her father was from South Carolina and her mother was from Louisiana. Their daughter Ethel was 9 years old. They are first recorded in the 1910 census and also appear in the 1920 census. He earned his living as a foreman as a "stationary engineer." What exactly this profession was is unclear, but perhaps it had to do with steam engines or foundries or even the infant oil industry. In any event, it would appear from his position that he was both skilled at his job and at it for some time. After what must have been at last a little more than a decade in Louisiana they disappear from the record.

Another skilled worker in North Louisiana was the Bohemian Alfred Matyska. He was a baker at a shop in Cedar Grove Village in Caddo Parish. He was in the country just a year, having arrived in 1919. How and why he chose a place very distant from Czech communities across America is a mystery. Perhaps he just wanted to get away from it all. This is the only record of him.

The Rudy family was already first generation American, but of Bohemian heritage. The patriarch, Mathew, was 48; he was born in Wisconsin to Bohemian parents. It was probably in a town rich with Czechs of which there are more than a handful in that state. At some point, when he was just past 20 years old, he made his way to Texas. He apparently went to another Czech community, perhaps in search of land he could afford. He met and married Addie who was just one year younger than he was. She too was born of Bohemian parents, but in Texas. Their son Cecil, 21, was also born in Texas. Exactly when they came to Louisiana is unknown but they were living in Ward 4 of Spring Hill, Caddo Parish, in 1920. The two men were farmers.

Just across the Red River in Bossier Parish, in the same census, a man named Frank Silhavy was another Bohemian farmer. At the age of 35 he already six children with his wife Rosa, who was 34. He, Rosa and the two oldest children arrived in 1912; Mary was 10 and Helena was 8. The next four children were born in Louisiana. Adolf, the first born in America, was 6, so that puts the family in the parish in about 1913. Following in quick succession was a daughter, also named Rosa, aged 4, and twins aged 2, Paula and Frank Jr. They apparently made their way immediately to the area upon their arrival though why cannot be ascertained. The Silhavys chose names for their kids that were from their Czech heritage.

Rose Silacek, at the tender age of 15, was a servant working at 125 Washington Street in Alexandria in 1920. She was born in Nebraska. She was working for Morris and Gertrude Michel and their four children. Her parents are listed as born in Bohemia. She spoke English. She is not related to any of the people in the Czech Colony. She is listed as "Bohemian" in the Census. Whether she came because of the ads others saw is not known. The surname does not appear in earlier or later city directories. She may have married locally or she may have moved away.

In the 3rd Ward of Caddo Parish in 1900 lived the Unger family. John Unger was born 1843 and he was now 57. He was a farmer who arrived in America in 1895, obviously making his way to the Shreveport area almost immediately on his arrival. He was a widower with two children. His son Fred was born in 1874, and was now a 27 year old farm laborer. His daughter was named Louiza, was 17, she was born in 1882. She was also working as a cook at a hotel in the city. All were born in Bohemia .

On the other side of the state in 1920 John Vargo was living in Ouachita Parish. He was a Bohemian who arrived in 1905. He was now a 32 year old boarder working as a watchman on a steamboat, a quintessential Louisiana occupation. Back on the other side of the state in Caddo Parish, was another Bohemian, Joseph Waven. He was a 21 year old with the prosaic work of carpenter. Both of these last names had to be changed from the original Czech and we can only guess at the reasons and the original version.

A Czech family named Liebrech traces itself to the Moravian town of Jevícko (Gewitsch in German,) in the Chornice (Kornitz in German) region of the province near the Austrian border. They were Jewish in the old country, but somewhere between there and Ouachita Parish they became Christians. The men of the family retained typically Jewish names, so the switch would appear to have come on this side of the Atlantic. Another branch of the family settled in Konigsberg, Germany and stayed Jewish. Those of them who did not escape to England suffered the ravages of Hitler. This is a family whose descendants are tracing their roots, but have come up with precious few details. So we are not sure exactly when the Moravian Liebrech's arrived in America, nor what brought them to Louisiana, and at least some members of the family lived for awhile in Texas. Most of the family that lived in Louisiana are buried in the Rosena Chapel Cemetery near Monroe, though one is buried in Pineville in the center of the state.

Pincus Liebrech was born in 1853 in Jevicko and died 1911 in Louisiana. From his birth year it seems he was the father of the brood. Florence Liebrech was born in 1860 and died 1937, so it seems she was the mother. Carrye Liebreich was born March 18th, 1884 and died January 11th, 1969. She married Sigmund Haas. She is the only one buried in Pineville. It is not clear where Haas is buried. Ellen Haas is probably Sigmund's sister, but she is buried in the Liebrech family plot in Ouachita. She was born August 31st, 1885 and died March 22nd, 1972. Francis Henry Liebrech was born August 20th 1917 and died at the age of three on October 1st, 1920. Hyman Liebrech is recorded in the 1920 census in Texas, so sometime after this the family arrived in Louisiana. He was born October 31st, 1881 and died October 17th, 1944. Isador Liebrech was born June 7th, 1889 and died July 29th, 1940. He was a member of the American Legion, which means he was a veteran, probably of World War I. The 1910 census shows him living in Smith County, Texas, but the 1920 census does not. So perhaps he was the first to arrive in Louisiana and the rest followed. Of Maurice Liebrech we know only that he was born in 1892, no other information is available. Rosalind Heninger Liebrech was born November 8th, 1890 and died November 20th, 1989. Whose wife she was is not clear. I could not find them in the Louisiana census, and other than Isador and Hyman, not in Texas either, but if they moved in 1920, those not recorded may have been missed by both counts. Nor is it clear where the children were born. Some or all may have been born either in Moravia or here. We do not know anyone's occupation. Or where exactly they lived. Indeed, we do not know much at all except that a Moravian family is laid to rest in Ouachita Parish.

The Holoubek's of Shreveport—Post World War II

Alice and Joseph Holoubek have been practicing medicine in Shreveport since the mid-1940's. Joseph was born into a Czech family in Clarkson, Nebraska. His wife was born in Arkansas. He served in the army corps of engineers in World War II.

Joseph was the leader of the committee which raised more than thirty million dollars for the Louisiana State University School of Medicine in Shreveport, bringing a much needed facility to the area. This follows in the tradtion of all Czechs to be involved in education wherever they settled.

Joseph has just recently retired from his position as Clinical Professor of Medicine at the Louisiana State University School of Medicine in Shreveport. He also has served as the president of the National Federation of Catholic Physicians Guild and the Louisiana Heart Association and the Governor for the Louisiana American College of Cardiology. He was honored by Pope John XXIII with the Knight Commander of the Order of St. Gregory the Great.

The Holoubek's most lasting concrete contribution to Louisiana is the Alice Holoubek Theater at the Shreveport Catholic Center. It is a 619 seat theater, with a 1,100-square-foot stage, 2 dressing rooms and 3 rehearsal classrooms. Shreveport is surely lucky to have had this illustrious couple for so many years, and the people of Shreveport certainly owe a lot to this couple.

Czechs and Slovaks in the Florida Parishes—1850 to 1900

There were a few Czechs and Slovaks who settled in the Florida Parishes of Louisiana. These are the parishes that are north of Lake Pontchartrain and east of Baton Rouge and the Mississippi River. They are called the Florida Parishes because for a brief period they were the Republic of West Florida, stemming from their time as part of the Spanish territory of Florida. These parishes were not part of the Louisiana Purchase. They were settled primarily by the Scots-Irish that were leaving the states along the Atlantic Seaboard. There is also a significant French-Creole-Cajun contingent in these parishes. There are also two other major ethnic concentrations in these parishes different from the usual mix in rural Louisiana: Italians and Hungarians. Both of these, however, have far fewer members than the predominant ethnic groups.

The next three families to be looked at all still have descendants living in Louisiana. I learned of them because family members contacted me first after hearing of this project. It was only later that I was able to track down more details. All three are actively engaged in searching for their roots, two more successfully than the third. They are all proud of their Czech and Slovak ancestry. I let them mostly speak for themselves here, because it is often family members who can provide the stories not found elsewhere, while the researcher can only find the dry details. Hopefully the merging of the two will give these families a better understanding of their provenance.

The Pastorek Family

John (Jan) Pastorek married Rosalie Schloegel (Schlögel), a first generation German with roots in Bavaria. Her father was from a town called "Neuburg an der Gamal," near Munich. These two Europeans, settled in the midst of French-Creole Southern Louisiana, became the root of the Pastorek family In America.

The Pastorek family first settled in New Orleans, but over time came to settle in the Covington area. Guy Pastorek, a descendant, provided many of these details, which are in quotes. Sometimes a descendant can tell the story better than I can, but my reading of the situation is in parentheses. *"Jan Pastorek was born April 17, 1839, in Velke Rovne, near Zilina, in Slovakia."* (This is the same region that provided so many Slovak immigrants to Louisiana.) *"He departed Bremen, Germany, aboard the SS Hohenzollern,"* (which went straight to New Orleans.) *"He traveled with a cousin, by the name of Podravcky, who had relatives in New*

Orleans." (I have found a family named Podrasky in New Orleans, and later of Lake Charles, at this time, but not Podravcky, so this may be the same family, but whose name may have been misspelled or simplified somewhere along the way.)

"*John arrived on November 1st, 1881 and was processed through the Customs House on Canal Street. He became a citizen October 4, 1889 in New Orleans. The family today has a copy of his naturalization papers. He died June 30, 1915 and was buried in St. Roch Cemetery in New Orleans. He brought with him a bible written in Czech.*" (perhaps Slovak, which is a slightly different langauge, which the family also has.)

"*Jan was a tinker.*" Guy relates that "*according to his eldest son Joseph, when he first came to Louisiana, he traveled in the country areas as a peddler selling pots and pans. Tinkers, drotar in Slovak, from Velke Rovne, had as their craft the repair of metal articles like pots and pans. The Slovak term drotar means tinker or metal worker. In Louisiana they referred to themselves as tinkers, which in English also means peddler. So in Louisiana they were sometime referred to as peddlers, which they were, but they were also skilled workers with metal, particularly with wire.*" (Witness the Nosacka family) "*Later he worked at a brewery in downtown New Orleans.*" One anecdote that survives in the family concerns a snowy day which paralyzed the New Orleans: "*Being from the mountains, Jan was at home in the snow and volunteered to deliver the beer and succeeded in getting it out to [the restaurants in] Milneburg on Lake Pontchartrain.*" (Leave it to a Slovak to get the beer through!) "*He was member and officer of the National Slovak Society,*" (but this group did not have a large membership in New Orleans, nor a lodge or meeting hall.)

This is what I discovered: the 1900 census reports that 37 year old John Pastorek was a day laborer who was born in December of 1863. His wife, Rose (in the census) was born in May of 1869. They had four children living with them. Annie, who was 9, was born in August of 1890. She died on May 5th, 1973. Joseph was 7, and born in March of 1893. Both of them were reported being in school. Alma, 4, was born October, 1895 and a son, August, was just 2. Also living with them was a boarder named John Bellas.

A few generations of Pastoreks are buried in Lafayette Cemetery #3 on Washington Street in New Orleans. August lived from August 26th, 1897 to April 17th, 1976. Marie Aida Hymel Pastorek was born October 4th, 1896 and died on June 12th, 1987. Rosalie Schloegel Pastorek's dates are May 27th, 1869 to August 23rd, 1936. She was not buried with her husband, who rests alone in St. Roch's. A member of the third generation who died recently was Rene August

Pastorek, who lived from November 28th 1930 to February 5th, 1997. Given her middle name, she was probably August's daughter.

In the 1945 city directory for New Orleans there are these family members. August Pastorek and his wife (Marie) Aida lived at 7734 Cohn Street (Which was named after Samuel Kohn, who had developed this part of New Orleans.) Their son Richard was in the United States Navy and used their house as his domicile. Joseph G. Pastorek and his wife, Aimee, lived at 1020 Marengo Street. Given her first name she was most likely of French heritage. He was a jeweler with the firm of Leon Kroner. They had two sons, John and Richard, both of whom were living with their parents, and both were in the navy. Since this was the last year of World War II it is likely that the two brothers and their cousin were all veterans of the war. Other family members had already moved across the lake, but there were no city directories for this area at that time.

Guy Pastorek relates this next story best, and it gives not only some interesting details of the past, but a heartwarming story of reconnection to the old country: *"Jan's 15 minutes of fame came when, on April 28, 1884, he accidentally shot himself in the abdomen with a .38 caliber revolver at his home at 99 St. Peter Street in the French Quarter. It was reported in the Picayune on May 25, 1884 that this had occurred and the article describes how Dr. LeMonnier, a local physician, removed the bullet which had perforated his kidney and liver, finally lodging near his spine. The operation was a success and he made a full recovery. Our family owes a debt to the doctor, for without his skill the Louisiana Pastorek line would have died out prematurely. We have been very fortunate because several of my extended family, including my wife and I, have returned to the town where Jan came from and visited our relatives there. One of the highlights of my trip was to eat dinner in the dining room of the small house where he was born. My late great-uncle John, (named after Jan) was instrumental in finding the town and locating our relatives there."*

There are now many descendants of this lucky immigrant from Slovakia living in Louisiana. All have achieved the American dream and many went on to college and have good positions and are active in their communities.

Another Blahut Family

There is another Blahut family in Louisiana. No relation to the Blahut family in Houma could be found and it seems unlikely given the number of years that separate them. If they were related the connection had to be in the Czech and Slovak lands long, long ago. This Blahut family is still active in strawberry farming between the towns of Springfield and Holden. This is at the western edge of what could be called Louisiana's strawberry belt. Somehow the Blahuts came to settle among the ethnic Hungarians near the towns of Albany and a town called, appropriately enough, Hungarian Settlement. These four small towns form a rough square centered on Highway 43. There are two exits from Interstate 12 a few miles apart which lead to all four towns. Ponchatoula, a little further east is, of course, the buckle of this belt.

I dwell a little on this family of whom so little is known to help clarify a point of confusion that often surfaces when discussing Eastern Europeans in Louisiana. That is, Louisiana has so few immigrants from Eastern Europe that most people simply lump them all together as if they were one big ethnic group: Yugoslavs, Croats, Serbs, Czechs, Poles, Slovaks, Ukrainians and Bulgars are indeed all of the Slavic language group—but they are all very different. Hungarians are unrelated to any other ethnic group in Europe—they are not Slavs, or Germanic or Romantic (The French, Spanish, Italians and Portuguese mostly.) They are simply where they are and their most famous son is Attila who wrecked so much havoc on the Roman Empire. Another group that stands out in the region are the Romanians. Strangely enough, they are the descendants of Romans who settled in Eastern Europe far from Rome in order to stop the invading Hungarians. While this is all ancient history it does lead to much confusion when discussing this region of Europe with Louisianians.

I suspect this Blahut family came to settle here because the family's origins are in Slovakia and they knew some of the Hungarians who settled here. I was often pointed to Hungarian Settlement during my research by well meaning people who thought that Czechs, Slovaks and Hungarians are related ethnicities. Yet, the only connection between Hungarians and Slovaks is that the Kingdom of Hungary ruled Slovakia for centuries and now the two countries share a border. In Slovakia today about 5 to 7 percent of the population are ethnically Hungarian. Likewise in Hungary 5 to 7 percent of the population are Slovaks. Hungarian and Slovak are simply unrelated languages and peoples. They cannot speak to the other unless they translate from one language to the other like from Chinese to English.

The Blahuts are not the only Slovak family that I heard about in this region of Livingston Parish. None of them, though, are in any census as Slovaks. Indeed, they do not seem to be recorded at all. However, I discovered them through a descendant of one of these families. I received this email from Nick Benyo concerning Slovaks in Livingston Parish:

"I've also done some Slovak research in the past and noted that the "Arpadhon" Hungarian settlement near Albany appears to have included a substantial number of

Slovaks. For some reason these Slovaks lost their identity and assumed a Hungarian ethnicity. The surnames from St. Margaret's church cemetary include some names very likely to be Slovak in origin: Barbuscak, Palascsak, Maruschak, Gubancsik, Spisak (from Spis county, Slovakia,) Vassil, Blahut, Ivanyisky, Matusicky (refers to Slovak place names,) Haluska (Slovak pasta!) Hudak (Slovak for musician) Sziszak, Bayus, Kluka, Kopcso, Resetar (Slovak for sieve-maker,) Gaydos (Slovak for piper.) Also I believe these Slovak families also settled in Louisiana: Drendul, Gasperecz, Kurucar, Mihalik, Lacinak. Klobucky, Cimerak and Repak are all possibly Slovak.

This is most intriguing, yet leads to a dead end. These names do appear to be phonetic transcriptions of Slovak names into the Hungarian language. The few family names that I knew, such as Drendul and Gasperecz, are well accounted for in other parishes, but not in Livingston. There are several possibilities for this situation. Chief among them is that these immigrants arrived sometime after the 1920 census, therefore missed being recorded in that one. Because Hungarian Settlement is extremely rural it is quite possible, too, that any census taker simply missed these people living far off any main roads. But if Mr. Benyo's research is accurate this means that there is a rather significant Slovak presence in Livingston Parish that has yet to be explored. This is quite possible. Given the propensity of Louisiana record keepers in any capacity to simply ignore those who were not the known ethnicities, French, Cajun, Irish, etc, it is quite possible that these families were simply misidentified in any records or just not recorded.

It was Kathleen Blahut who was searching for her family roots who contacted me about her Slovak family in Livingston Parish. Alas, she could provide no definitive information. Though Blahut is definitely among the surnames of Slovakia, as well as being Czech, it is not Hungarian. It is interesting to note, however, that of the small ethnic groups in Louisiana who fill one town the Hungarians maintain the second strongest cultural connection to their roots, after the Czechs of Rapides Parish. Within the last decade a Hungarian festival has been started in the settlement named for them.

In St. Margaret Catholic Church Cemetery in Albany are the graves of a number of Blahuts. The patriarch of the family was Joseph Blahut. He lived from 1857 to 1944. His wife, Elizabeth Blahut, lived from 1863 to 1940. Since they are not in the 1930 census, it would seem they arrived just about this time, which is also the tail end of the influx of Hungarians to this area. They were certainly born in Europe, however. We know they had at least one son, for alongside of them in the graveyard is one Julius Blahut. He lived from January 1st, 1887 to December 4th, 1981. His wife, Katherine N. Blahut, lived from March 26th, 1893 to April 12th, 1980. Julius and Katherine had at least two daughters.

Cecilia Blahut sadly died young, living from 1916 to only 1924. Another daughter may still be still living. Virginia Blahut Duczar was born in August of 1919, but no death date could be found. She married one of the local Hungarian boys, Alex Louis Duczar, whose dates are February 28th, 1916 to October 5, 1987. A recent obituary in the Baton Rouge Advocate stated that Doris Rae Blahut was a co-owner of Blahut Strawberry Farms in Springfield. She was a native of Hammond and married into the Blahut family. She was apparently married to the Julius Blahut who still runs the farm. He is the son or grandson of the deceased Julius. As with so many American families, assimilation has cast them apart and only now are these relationships and this history being explored. We shall have to wait for the release of the 1940 census to get a clearer picture of this family and perhaps the other Slovak families who lived in this area. In the meanwhile, however, you can buy some Slovak grown strawberries.

The Felicianas

Somewhere in East Feliciana Parish in 1860 lived a Bohemian we only know as G. A. Guldon. He was a 32 year old jeweler worth $650 in real estate and who had $200 in personal property. This was a sizeable amount for the day. Also with him were people we know only from their first initial: S., who was 22 and A., who was 12. Though no relationships or sexes are given, this is problaby his wife and child. S was born in New York City. In 1860 the big towns in East Feliciana Parish were Clinton and Jackson, just like today, and we can assume that he had his jewelry business in one of two, though the census is not clear which one. The Civil War had to have brought misfortune to his business and the young couple apparently moved on.

The Motichek Family

The Motichek family settled in the Madisonville area of St. Tammany Parish. They lived on Turnpike Road. They were Slovaks, whose patriarch Jacob came from Petrovice, Slovakia. He married his first wife, Mary Komich Motichek, in Europe. She died in childbirth giving birth to her son Louis. Jacob married a second time in Slovakia to a woman named Mary Jancik of Velke Rovne, Slovakia. Mary arrived in Madisonville in 1897. Their oldest son, Joseph, was born in Slovakia. The couple had eight children all together.

Jacob supported his family as a tinsmith. He made his own pots and pans and peddled them around the Madisonville area, walking door to door. He was known throughout the area as "Jake the peddler." Sometime after 1900 he stopped making his own wares and sold only those that were made elsewhere. Jacob died August 26, 1924 in a drowning accident.

The eight children of Jacob and Mary all stayed in Louisiana. Joseph was married to Veronica Druzgala and was probably Hungarian. Veronica and an infant daughter were killed in a house fire in 1923 while Joseph was away in the merchant marine. John Bernard was born March 17th, 1897 and died August 26, 1983. He was married to Beatrice Heider. Thomas was born in 1902 and died at the age of 10 on June 22, 1912. Jake was born March 19, 1903 and died February, 1983. He never married and had no children. A daughter Estelle was born on April 11, 1905. She died in April of 1972 and she, too, never married nor had children. Another son was Andrew Thomas, born April 9th, 1907 and died January 14th, 1998. He was married to Alma Frederick and they, too, had no children. Ferdinand and Albert Louis were twin boys born August 15, 1909. Ferdinand died in June of 1983. He was married to Clara B. Olman and they, too, had no children. Albert Louis died May 19, 1992. He was married to Estelle Frederick and they also had no children. It would seem that the family would die out, but one last son kept it going.

It was Louis, the son by the first marriage that spread the family name. He had several children. Oddly, he began having children while his father was still creating his own family, thus the generations seem a bit skewed. One son of Louis, James Jessie, who was born in 1904 and died in 1956. James was married to Mary Jane LeBlanc. James and Mary lived in Ponchatula where he ran a shoe repair shop in the front of their home on West Pine Street. Another son of Louis was Louis Francis, Sr., who was born on April 6, 1908. He was married to Mary Matheis. Yet another son was Othmar Henry. He was born on July 19th, 1919 and died on March 9th, 2000. He was a retired tug boat captain and he had also been a ferry boat captain for the state ferry system earlier in his carreer. He was a veteran of World War I, attaining the rank of corporal. His children were one son, Robert Othmar Motichek; and four daughters, Marcia Ann Motichek, Lynn Motichek Novick, Terry Motichek Guillory and Wendy Motichek Singleton; there were also 10 grandchildren and five great-grandchildren.

Louis had another son, known as Uncle Placide, who had his own shoe store in the 1940s and 50s at the fork of Turnpike and Covington Highway in Madisonville. He was not married. Following him was a daughter Katherine who married Joseph Plescia. Peter Motichek was another son of Louis. Peter's own son Peter died fairly young. In the Wagner Cemetery in St. Tammany Parish are the graves of Louis's son Peter A. Motichek, 1931–1977, and his wife, Marian Motichek, 1932–1993. There was a daughter named Elizabeth who married Joseph William Quave. And finally there was a daughter, Louise Motichek.

Besides the published record we know this little amount about the family from Kelly Motichek, who maintains his own website about the family. The family, as most American families of the post World War II era, grew apart and the history was lost. It is only in the last few years that the fourth generation of Moticheks in Louisiana are tracing their roots. There are nearly one hundred decedants of this family in the state today.

Czechs and Slovaks in the Florida Parishes—1900 to 1950

For more than 30 years the Chabrecek family made their mark on St. Tammany Parish. Appearing first in the 1900 census in Ward 9 of the parish was Simon, patriarch of the family. He was born in 1862, and was 57 when he was listed as Hungarian in this census. This was technically his country of origin. But he was Slovak as revealed in later censuses of the family. He earned a living as a peddler. He married a local girl named Eve, 40, who was born in 1860 in Louisiana. They had five children and from the age of the oldest Peter, who was born in 1889 and was 10 years old at the time of the census, it can be calculated that Simon was in Louisiana at least by 1888. A second son, Paul, was born in 1892 and thus was 7. Their third child was a daughter named Anna. She was born in 1894 and was now 6 years old. Next was Mary, just three years old, having been born in 1896. Their third son was John, born just two years before the census, in 1898. All the children were born in Louisiana.

Alas, all did not work out well for the family, because the 1910 census shows that Eva Chabrecek, now 50, was widowed. Peter was no longer living in the household and there is no record of where he went. He is not in the census with his own family. Paul had grown to 17 and was doing odd labor jobs, no doubt to help support the family and that must have been difficult. Anna was 16 and Mary 13. A son, Adam, 11 years old, was not listed in the 1900 census but appears in 1910. John was 9 and he was followed by three more children: Joe was 7, Charlie was 6 and Josephine was 4. It is obvious from the ages of the youngest children that Simon died just a few years prior to the census so the wound in the family was fresh. All the kids' father was listed "Hungarian Slovak." 1920 finds Eva, 60, still living in Tangipahoa, but with just Joseph, 17 and John, 14, at home. This census records the father as strictly Slovak. The family were farmers and since these children lived on the farm they most likely had chores and duties to keep the family in food. What happened to the Chebreceks is unknown, they simply disappear from the record.

About 80 miles to the west, in Livingston Parish's Second Ward, lived Henry Exner. He was born in 1873 and was 26 at the time of the 1900 census. He arrived in America in 1896. His occupation was listed as jeweler and his ethnicity was Bohemian. The census says that while his mother was born in Germany his father was Bohemian. Also found in the 1900 census is John and Josephine Exner. He was born in 1849 and was 51. She was born in 1847 and was 53 years old. They both arrived in America in 1882 and were now in Ward Two working as farmers. They seem to be Henry's parents, though this is not definite. This family also spanned a 30 year period in Louisiana. By 1910 Henry, now 36 and listed as "Austro-Bohemian" in this census, was a merchant at a retail store with a 27 year old Bohemian wife named Angela. They had three children, John, 4, Ruth, 2, and James who was said to be 11/12 months old.

In 1920 Henry Exner was still in Ward Two which was then further identified as Denham Springs. Now he was a 46 year old merchant "with" a general store. Only now the census records his wife as Rosalie, who was 48. She too was Bohemian, but she seems to be a second wife. The three children from the earlier census was joined by Ester, a seven year old. After this there is no record of the family. Perhaps the depression put him out of business and they moved on.

Itinerant Slovaks in Livingston Parish

Somewhere out in the woods of Livingston Parish's Ward 7 lived Matt Ganosh in 1910. He was the 29 year old leader of a camp of stavemakers. He arrived in 1903 and was listed in the census as Slovak. His wife was Emmie. She was 29 and born in Mississippi. Also at the campsite was George Zagar, 35, who came to America in 1898, and Joseph Gasperecz, 48, who also came in 1898; both were Slovak. Matt's 38 year old brother John was also in the camp. He, too, arrived in 1903 and perhaps the brothers traveled to the New World together. Finally, we find a pair Croatian brothers, George and John Klepac, who were campmates of the Ganosh's. Croatia is a land several hundred miles away from Slovakia. On the actual census form all the names are listed in one record one after the other as if in one household. The Klepacs would have been able to converse with some limitations with the Ganoshs and the others because Croatian is a language that shares many root words with Slovak and many other similarities. Still, complete communication would have been problematic. Being just such a short time in America everyones English must have been somewhat limited.

In another camp in the Seventh Ward were four other Slovak men: Antoinie Stempal, 47, Joe Pojak, 24 Antonie Tomle, 38, and Joe Cap, 25. All were campmates at a stavemaker camp in the woods. In yet a third camp were John Kaderbin, 45, who emigrated in 1904, and the brothers Frank Troha, 25, and John Troha, 21. All three were Slovak campmates. As the trees were cut down they were processed into intermediate or even end products right on the spot so these bands of people moved with the timber companies as they logged new lands. Thus we lose track of these people who contributed an important task to the lumber industry in the state.

The only thing known about a Moravian man named John Lonezer was that he was living in the 6th Ward of Livingston Parish in 1910. He may have been one of the logging camp followers, but that is mere speculation, the census is silent as to his profession.

In the 1910 census Frank Patecek, 27, is listed as living at 306 Rempert Street in Covington. He was a retail merchant in the "gentlemen's clothing" line. His wife Pualine was 27. He had two small children: Bertha, 2, and Frank Jr. just four months old. In the Theodore Dendinger Memorial Cemetery in St. Tammany Parish there are four Pateceks buried. Jerry Louis Patecek was a corporal in the army during World War II; his dates were August 12, 1924 to March 21, 1970. A man named Anton H. Patecek has the dates "1919–1963;" he was probably Jerry Louis' brother. The parents seem to be Anton Patecek, 1895 to 1974, and Adelie Peter Patecek, 1886 to 1968. Frank would have been old enough to be an older brother of Anton or they might be somehow else related. The only way to determine that the Pataceks were Czech is simply that their last name is a fairly common Czech surname.

In any event, the Patecek family left a legacy in brick and mortar. The Patecek Building at 301 Columbia Street in downtown Covington saw a total restoration in 1995. The tourist information for the city touts the Patecek building: *"Built shortly after the Great Fire of 1898, the building provides a beautiful example of turn of the century commercial architecture. For more than 60 years, 301 Columbia has housed retail stores and holds the distinction of its second floor being Covington's first telephone exchange."* One assumes that the first retail store in the building was the Patecek gentlemen's clothier. Oddly, no one in any organization that would deal with the history of the town was remotely aware of the Patacek's Bohemian roots. That one of the major structures in town was built by a Czech surely warrants some attention in future histories and promotions of the town.

In the 8th Ward of East Feliciana Parish were several Slovaks and others who were all recorded as living near each other, but not really with each other. One was a Slovak man, Antonio Poyer. Living with him was Verona Collins. She was also recorded as a Slovak though Collins is not at all a Slovak surname. They were boarders and she was 44; his age was not recorded. There was also someone known only by his last name: Posvan. The census form is damaged at the spot on the page were his first name would be. Also in his household was Albert Collins, 24. The two Collins were likely related, but the census records no relationship. Plus, Albert was not recorded as a Slovak. Something is incorrect in these entries but it is impossible to determine with certainty what was wrong. The men, however, were all stavemakers, just like the other Slovaks working in lumber camps were. They, too, could have been merely itinerant in the area and were caught up in the sweep of the census.

George Racik was running a grocery story in the town of Independence, Tangipahoa Parish, according to the 1920 Census. This town has a large Italian community and he would have stuck out. He was 63 and born in "Czechoslovakia." Nothing more is known about him and he disappears from the record. It is entirely possible that his grocery store failed when the Depression hit in 1929 and 1930.

In another example of a Bohemian changing his name to a completely American one there is a Ben Russell recorded in the 1900 Census living in St. James Parish's Ward 1. He was a 34 year old track boss; he arrived on these shores in 1883. His wife, Mary, was born in 1870 and so was 30 years old. She was a Louisiana native. Their daughter Mary was born in 1888 and was 11. Since Russell would have to have been in Louisiana to sire a daughter he clearly arrived before 1887. They were well enough off that they had a live in servant named Lizzy Maler who was just 17. Her nationality or race is not listed. There is no way to determine what his original Czech name could have been. There are simply no counterparts to Benjamin or Russell in Czech.

In the 1920 census in Slidell in St. Tammany Parish a man was identified as a 51 year old Bohemian with no name more American than "C.M. Smith." He was an agent for the Singer Company, presumably the sewing machine company, though that is not certain. The Czech word for a smith is Kovař, pronounced "KOH—varzh" and it is entirely possible that Smith changed his name to a completely American name shortly after he arrived. Though whether it was actually the Czech variant is not known. He arrived in 1883. He was married to Marie, 43. She too was identified as Bohemian. She arrived in 1887. They both got citizenship in 1899. This is the most extreme name change that I found among any Czechs in Louisiana in the sense that there are few names more quintessentially American than Smith.

Also in 1920 St. Tammany Parish a Slovak named Andrew Trasak was earning a living. The penmanship on the census register is unclear but it looks like he lived on Old Clanse Road. No such road or one with a similar name could be found on modern maps. He was a 47 year old "general farmer." His wife was 41 and named Mary and their daughter was the 17 year old Mattie. What happened to them is a mystery. They disappear from the record.

These 40 or so Czechs and Slovaks made their way in the Florida Parishes, some a bit more settled and successful than others. This area had seen little change over the decades since the end of the Civil War. All the towns were small, less than 2,000 people. Slidell and Baton Rouge, at opposite ends of the area were the only large cities and even that pushes the definition of "large." In between them was Covington, which had something resembling what could be called a Czech "community"—with just three families. Of course, there were the congregated Slovaks if the records are to be believed.

Life in this time and place was simple, basic and near subsistence. Farms were along the few roads that ran through the surrounding wilderness. This was the same time that several dozen Hungarian families settled in Livingston Parish. Any one of the Anglo-French neighbors of the Czechs and Slovaks, upon hearing the accents and learning the last names, might well have concluded they were the same as the Hungarians. They were not. But how these few people from three distant lands in Central Europe, the Czech Republic, Slovakia and Hungary, wound up in the piney woods north of Lake Pontchartrain is a mystery. There was no advertising of these places as great farmland or the ideal place for new immigrants to move. Somehow the all seemed to have just wandered into the region. Most of them wandered out with as much stealth as they came.

Post World War II Baton Rouge

The Kalivoda family in Baton Rouge are a recent arrival of Slovak heritage in Louisiana. Nick Kalivoda, who currently hosts a Biblical Studies radio show, was for a long time involved with running the Louisiana State University press office. He was instrumental in bringing new promotion ideas to fruition, including films about the university. These were used as models for many other universities over the years. His sons are engineers and designers with the Louisiana State Department of Highways, and many a Louisianian has driven on a road or interchange that they helped design. While recent I bring them up to show that those of Slovak heritage are still drawn to Louisina and are still making their mark.

The Navratil family of Baton Rouge were directly involved in the creation of the public radio station in the capital city, WRKF. They are long time benefactors and participants in the classical music scene. Boris was born in Czechoslovakia while his wife Constance was born in England. They came after World War II. They are a well known couple in the city though his Czech heritage is often missing from accounts of he and his wife while her English heritage is brought up.

The Demko Family

The Demko family is also new to Louisiana and they are first generation American. This is another person who heard of this project and contacted me. It is current events, but it shows that Czechs are still arriving in Louisiana. This brief story was told to me by Marie Demko Mentzer: "My father, John Demko, emigrated from Czechoslovakia when he was 9 or 10 years old, in 1920. He traveled via Belgium—where he had his first ice cream cone. I have his original 'Rodny List,' that is, family information, dated 1910: Jan Demko, from the town of Lastomir, father Juraj Demko, mother, Maria rod. Tomasova." (In "rod. Tomasova" the 'rod.' is the Czech abbreviation for family, Tomasova is the possessive form of the surname, that is, she was Marie Tomas.) "His parents arrived prior to his coming here. His citizenship papers are dated 1934. My daughter and I followed our roots a decade and a half ago. We met family in Humene (a town in the Czech Republic,) one being Dr. Marta Sevcikova. She is a delightful person, and made our journey into the past quite memorable." Ms. Mentzer also wrote to me that she makes "great Cabbage Rolls!" They are a Czech delicacy called "zeli rohliki." Not only a Czech favorite, but I may just have to get Ms. Mentzer to make some soon for they are not available in any Louisiana restaurant.

John Desmond

Few people in Baton Rouge have not had the opportunity to experience a building by noted architect John Desmond. That experience may have been just passing by, but there are also thousands of people who every day use the structures he designed. From the LSU Student Union to the Baton Rouge Centroplex, the Louisiana State Library to the Louisiana State Archives, the Catholic Life Center to the Pennington Biomedical Research Center, the USS Kidd Memorial to Baton Rouge City Hall, as well as many churches and schools, Mr. Desmond has been an active force in the city and state for over fifty years. His work is sprinkled throughout southeastern Louisiana in places such as Hammond, Convent, Ponchatoula and New Orleans. His buildings have won awards from many organizations.

But his story is part of the Czech contribution to Louisiana despite his Irish surname. His mother, Rose, was born on October 11th, 1886 into a Czech family on a farm in South Dakota. Her father was Jacob Dvorak. He was born in July of 1848 near Budweis in the Czech Republic. Budweis is the German name for a town whose Czech name is a mouthful: Česke Budějovice. It is in this town which the original Budweiser beer was first made and is still made to this day. (But it is not connected to the American beer of the same name. Anheuser-Busch took the name of the best beer they could find and applied it to their strictly American product. There is continuing legal action between the two companies related to the use of the name.)

Jacob was educated at a Catholic School in the village of Dobra Vodem, which translates as "Good Water." In 1865 his parents and their five children landed in an America fresh from the horrors of the Civil War. The family settled in Iowa in an area already thickly populated by their Bohemian brethren. Dvorak is a name derived from the word for a farmyard—dvur—and living up to that his family became involved in farming. Jacob was 17 years old when he arrived. After a number of occupations including railroad worker, brewers assistant and baker he settled on farming. Prior to farming he took work where he could and it apparently was never quite enough to satisfy the young man.

St. Wenceslaus of the Christmas story The Good King Wenceslaus has a day, September 28th, set aside for him by the Catholic Church. It was on this day that Jacob met his wife, Rozi Zima. They were married November 12, 1877, in Calmar, Iowa. It was in the years following the birth of his son James and his daughters, Anna and Mary, that he began dreaming of his own farm. He heard about homesteading on the prairies of South Dakota and wanting to live the American dream he set off with his wife and children to build a farm. His son James, an uncle of John Desmond, wrote a family memoir which sets out the difficulties they faced. Jacob was lucky that many of his neighbors in South Dakota were people he had been acquainted with in Iowa. They were pioneers in the growing Czech community in Brule County, South Dakota. They helped each other break the tough sod of the prairie and lay down seed while building sod homes, ever wary of the winter they knew would come. It was a fall day when James, just 8 years old, was helping his father plow a field when the midwife called out that the time of birth was nigh. Jacob ran to the house to assist in the birth of John Desmond's mother, Rose. It was the first time that James ran the plow himself.

He remembers that he was scared out of his wits, but he continued to farm for the rest of his life.

After more than a decade of hard work in South Dakota Jacob made the decision, together with a neighboring Czech family, to move to Minnesota, where the farming was easier; the land a little better. During their time in South Dakota the Dvorak family continued to speak Czech since few of their neighbors were English speaking. All around them were families with good Czech names like Noska, Helma, Viskocil and Mucha. The country was settled nearly entirely by Czech immigrants. They went to school together, played together and worked together. It was as if a bit of Bohemia was transferred to the great prairie of North America. It was very similar to other Czech farming communities that were in the states that had been carved out of the Louisiana Purchase: Nebraska, Kansas, Missouri, Minnesota and Iowa. These states today still have large Czech communities. It is at Cedar Rapids, Iowa, that the National Czech and Slovak Library and Museum is located. It is the largest Czech cultural center in the United States. The library and museum are filled with the stories of families like the Dvorak's.

James relates the story of how his father joined the other men in the community in building the school house. With typical Czech frugality they built the coal bins under the school and thus saving the expense of a second building for this purpose. In the first years of school there were fourteen students, all Czechs save one student from a "Yankee" family. "As there was no school before, all of us just talked Bohemian," wrote James. "The new teacher knew no Bohemian and as we knew just a little English we had to learn to speak English." It was this teacher who anglicized the names of the children. James was born Vaclav—and the teacher simply proclaimed him "James," not knowing that Walter or Wesley would be a more correct translation. However, it is an historical reality that many Vaclavs became James in America. There is no known explanation for this.

Despite a promising beginning by 1889 the weather had taken a continual turn to the worse and farming in South Dakota became very difficult. The move to Minnesota saw the slow assimilation of the family into America. All the children, Rose included, began to speak English regularly after having learned it at school. However, they were still speaking Czech at home. With families of other nationalities in the new Minnesota community all the children were shifted to English. This is not much different than any other group of immigrants to America, and John Desmond's mother was part of this changing.

His father, Timothy Desmond, was born in Ireland and came to America as a young man. He worked as a newspaper circulation manager and thus moved quite a bit, opening up new areas for distribution. Along the way he met Rose and they were married on the 29th of December, 1919 in Salinas, Kansas. While there is little record of the event it is probable that the festivities included a mix of cultures still unusual in America at that time: Irish and Czech, no doubt united by the love of beer.

By the time John was a little boy they settled in Hammond, Louisiana where his father worked for the New Orleans States-Item and his mother was a teacher. During the depression Rose ran a boarding house to make ends meet. As John grew up he was aware of his Czech roots, visiting cousins, aunts and uncles who had stayed up in Minnesota. He had contact with the food, the music and the language of his Czech forefathers annually. Timothy and Rose, though, now had a new culture to contend with: South Louisiana. The Czech part was slowly fading, though Rose tried to keep some of the holiday and food traditions alive for her children.

John obtained a scholarship to Tulane University by the chance meeting between his father and the local state representative at the post office. The politician mentioned that he did not know any one to give the scholarship to. Seizing the moment, Timothy said "I do." Had that meeting not occurred, John might have gone into a different profession. During his college years he lived under the cafeteria and ran it when he wasn't in class or studying. During these difficult times he was assured of an education, housing and food at virtually no cost. This was no mean feat. From there he went into the architectural profession.

All told, Desmond was the architect or on the team of architects for nearly 700 buildings in Louisiana, East Texas and elsewhere. The vast majority of them are in Louisiana. Yet, the only way I learned of his Czech heritage is because he came to me after having heard of this project. He contacted me within 24 hours of reading about it in the Baton Rouge Advocate and immediately made time to meet with me. He is proud of his Czech heritage and eagerly spoke to me about it. He said he had brought it up countless times during his working years in Louisiana but simply could not explain it enough to the people he was meeting who were unfamiliar with this part of Europe. Though perhaps, he admitted, he had been too quiet about it, too. He told me that his mother never wholly lost a slight Czech accent in her English, which no doubt intrigued her students in Hammond. Desmond provided me with both his uncle's memoirs and his own catalogue with a great sense of satisfaction that the Czech Dvorak side of his family history would be recognized. "For too long the Irish side has predominated," he told me.

While it is impossible to list every building here I will list some of the more outstanding, award winning and well known buildings. Some I have already mentioned briefly, but deserve a little more notice because of various accolades. After reading this list there will be few Louisianians who can say they have no connection to Czech heritage. Nor any who can deny the lasting impact that the son of a Czech immigrant family to America has wrought in Lousiana.

- In August, 1987, The Louisiana State Archives was placed in a state of the art facility. The building has been hailed as one of the foremost archival facilities in the nation.

- Site plan and buildings throughout the entire Baton Rouge Centroplex, including East Baton Rouge Public Library downtown branch, the Baton Rouge City Hall, the performing arts theater and the convention facility.

- Louisiana State University Center for Engineering and Business Administration.

- Corporate headquarters for Blue Cross of Louisiana in Baton Rouge.

- Southern University Civil and Mechanical Engineering Building, Baton Rouge.

- Lindy Clairborne Boggs Center, Tulane University, New Orleans.

- The Fifth Circuit Court of Appeal building in Gretna, Louisiana.

- Independence, Louisiana High School

- Loranger, Louisiana High School

- His Catholic Life Center on Acadian Throughway in Baton Rouge won a Regional Honor Award from the American Institute of Architects (AIA)

- Louisiana State University Student Union Building won a Regional First Honor Award from the AIA.

- The Myra Clare Rogers Memorial Chapel, Newcomb Campus of Tulane University, New Orleans.

- St. Alberts Catholic Student Center on the campus of Southeastern Louisiana University in Hammond won a Regional Honor Award from the AIA.

- The Universtiy Cafeteria on the same Campus won five awards, including the AIA National Merit Award and the National Competition for School Design.

- Tangipahoa Parish Courthouse won the National First Honor Award from the AIA.

- The Louisiana State Library in downtown Baton Rouge won three awards: Regional Honor Award and National Library Award from the AIA and the Progressive Architecture National Award Citation.

- Miller Memorial Library in Hammond won the Regional Honor Award from the AIA.

- D. C. Reeves Elementary School in Ponchatoula won the AIA National and Regional Honor Awards as well as the Louisiana Architects Association Honor Award.

- Among his church related projects which have won awards are St. Thomas More church, school and administrative buildings; Holy Ghost Catholic School; Chapel at Greenwell Springs Sanitarium; and Broadmoor Methodist Church, as well as additions to Grace Episcopal Church in Hammond.

- He won National Merit Award from the Liturgical Conference for his remodeling of St. Joseph Cathedral, Baton Rouge.

- Among other churches he designed are First Christian Church, St. Paul Lutheran Church, Florida Boulevard Baptist Church and St. Pius X Church in Baton Rouge, and the Wesley Methodist Church on the campus of LSU, and St. John the Evangelist Church in Prairieville, Louisiana.

- Two of his residences have won awards, his own in Hammond, and the Duncan Residence in Covington.

- He designed the entire master plan for the campus of Southeastern Louisiana University in Hammond.

- He was commended for the "preservation of a historic monument converted to modern use" for his remodeling of the Warden House in downtown Baton Rouge, the building which served as his office for many years.

- Among other historic structures that he worked on are the Old Plaquemine Courthouse and the Illinois Central Depot which houses the Louisiana Arts and Sciences Center in Baton Rouge.

- He also received a Special Award from the Foundation for Historic Louisiana. He was a visiting lecturer at a several universities and architectural institutes. He has been published in numerous professional journals and general interest magazines.

This legacy is enormous and to the benefit of every Louisianian. Just recently Mr. Desmond donated his papers and drawings to the Hill Memorial Library on the campus of Louisiana State University in Baton Rouge. Now all can see how his mind worked and his hand put pencil to paper. But they should know that it would not have been possible without an immigrant from Česke Budějovice, Czech Republic.

Cameron Parish Slovaks

Cameron Parish is in the far southwestern corner of Louisiana. It is made up almost entirely of water in the form of marshes. The little land there is actively farmed with truck crops, cotton and cattle. Some time at the turn of the century a Slovak named Elizabeth Cason found herself in Cameron Parish. How or when she got there is not know. The story from descendants says she contacted people she knew up north in Slovak communities and lured them down to the fertile farms and marshes of Louisiana. One thing for certain is that within a few years time a handful of Slovak families moved to Cameron Parish. Given the small numbers of people in the parish all of these people must have known each other. Their descendants are now all over the parish and up in nearby Lake Charles. There was no conscious effort to preserve the culture and indeed, those descendants with whom I communicated were baffled about most of their Slovak origins and the nation itself.

One family was the Buris family, headed by Adolph, 43, and listed as a "Slovak." He had two young children with him; he was a single parent. Mary was his 10 year old niece, and George was the 9 year old nephew. They are only in the 1920 Cameron Parish census.

The Canik family arrived sometime prior to the 1920 Census. In this year Paul Canik, 49, had a wife named Pauline who was also 49. They had a daughter Veronica who was 21 and a son named Johnnie who was 20. Both of these children were born in Slovakia. Paul and Pauline had five children in Louisiana. Stephen, who was 19 in 1920, and his brother Joseph, who was 17. Then they had three daughters in a row, Georgia, just 15, Caroline, 12, and Gertrude, 8.

We know the two oldest children were born in Slovakia and thus the Canik's were married there from "civilian registration cards" completed in 1917–1918. These were draft cards. One reads that John Canik was born 9 February 1889, in "Roune Trenchin Austria." This is really Rovne, an area of Slovakia were many Slovak immigrants to Louisiana came from. The other two cards list Frank, who was born November 22nd, 1895 on Grand Chenier and Steve Francis who was born March 29th, 1900 in Cameron, Louisiana. The Caniks still live in Grand Chanier and neighboring communities. They run a store called "Canik's V & S Variety" on the Oak Grove Highway in Creole. Anyone going through this small town cannot miss this quick stop store on the main highway. There is a Canik Road in the town of Grand Chanier; it is most likely not even two or three blocks long.

Of Elizabeth Cason we know the least. She was from Slovakia, perhaps Rovne, since she brought people from that area to Cameron. She lived with the Grunik family. Several of the descendants with whom I spoke recalled her thick accent. Though, unfortunately, no one among them took careful note of her stories. She died sometime in the 1990s and is mostly forgotten.

In 1920 Stevan Danko and his small family were in Cameron Parish. He was 51, and had arrived in 1888. He was born in "Czechoslovakia" but spoke Slovak. The census lists him as a general farmer. He was married to a woman named Verona or Veronica, the form is hard to read. She was 46 and was also born in Czechoslovakia. She spoke Slovak, too. Their two children had typically America names Joe, 13, and Mary, 17. The census says they were born in Louisiana. Though this puts them in the state in 1903, it is not known if the kids were born in Cameron Parish.

The 1910 census is almost impossible to read but it still deciphered that John Grunik was a merchant in Cameron. His son Joseph, 24, was a bookkeeper. He had four other children: George, 20, Anna, 15, Helen, 13 and Mike, 12. The first two kids were born in Europe, the last three in Louisiana. The home country is listed as Hungary, which was technically correct. The language was listed as Slovak. There was also a 10 year old adopted son named Joseph. His last name was either Jananka or Janouka, or possibly something else. The original document has poor penmanship. Helen, who was born in 1897 died in 1919 at the young age of 22. Annie, who was born on December 19, 1892, died March 17, 1989. She married a man with the last name of Paris. They are buried next to each other at Sacred Heart Cemetery in Cameron.

The World War I draft registration lists for 1918 has Michael Henry Grunik. He was born on December 10th, 1898 in Cameron. The 1920 census reveals that John, now 61, came in 1880 and was a citizen by 1890. He spoke Slovak. He supported his family by farming. The census says he was married to Mary, 52, who also came 1880 and was a citizen by 1890. Mike was now 21. He now had two adopted sons, Joe, 19, who was in the previous census, and now George, 17. The three kids were all born in Louisiana. As was custom at the time the three boys were helped their father on the farm.

Anna Tabachiek Grunik, John's wife, had the dates 1867 to 1929 and John was widowed in the 1930 census. Anna and Mary must be the same person, perhaps she was using the American name Mary instead of her native name. She is buried in St. Eugene Cemetary in Cameron. His son Joseph was now 49. He got married at the rather late age of 35 to Minie who was 36 in the census. She was married at 25 and born in Texas to "Czech" parents who spoke Slovak. They were all living together in one household. It was a crowded place because also in the house were George Duris, listed as a "border." He was a 28 year old, born in Missouri of Slovak parents. Another was Adam Durinik, 40, a Slovak who came to America in 1923. And there was Carrie Koson, a 19 year old Slovak. She may have been related to Elizabeth Cason. All were laboring on John's cotton farm.

In a separate household was Joe Grunik, 29, married at 26, and listed as born to Czechoslovak parents. He was married to Hasel who was just 21. They were married when she was just 18. She was born in Louisiana to born Louisiana parents, meaning she was a local girl. They had a daughter named Sheila who was just 4 months old at the time of the census. A new generation was being added to the parish.

The last name Grunik is derived from the hills of Rovne. The family was living down in Cameron Parish for thirty years and spreading roots into the community. John Grunik had a long commercial relationship with another Slovak, John Horecky, in Church Point.

Louis Labochik was a lonely 21 year old Slovak doing odd jobs according to the 1910 Cameron Parish census. We know nothing more about him except that he was living by himself.

John "Picknic," really Pichnic, was born July 15, 1861, and was listed in the 1910 census as being from "Austria-Hungary" He was married on July 11, 1884 in Cameron Parish. He died on April 8, 1917. His wife was Mary "Delicia" (Delescar) Peshoff. She was born in October of 1867 in Cameron Parish. Mary died on December 15, 1950. Her parents were Edward Peshoff and Marie Emma "Laurmie" Daigle. This is clear evidence of another Eastern European in Cameron Parish, Peshoff probably being Russian. In the 1920 census she was listed as "Laurmie," and "mother" of Mary Pichnic who was the 55 year old "head of household." There were two boys in the house, presumably Mary's sons: Nick, who was 23, and Harvey who was 20. Harvey was married to Emma who was 20.

The 1920 census is confusing on one major point. One listing in the census says Mary was a widow. Another entry says that there was a Harry Pichnic who was a 50 year old widower born in Louisiana of Louisiana parents. He is recorded having two children Harry, 26, and Nick, 23, who was married to Emma. Both boys' mother was said to be born in Bohemia. Eventually Nick and Emma's daughter Iris Pichnic was to be a 3rd grade school teacher in Cameron Parish for many years. Could this be two different families? It seems unlikely that two families both had boys named Nick who were 23 and married to an Emma who was 20. It is a mystery, then, as to why there are such divergent census entries.

The Mary above could have been an aunt for John and Delicia had a daughter in March of 1887, named Mary. She married Sidney DeBarge. Sidney was a 46 year old Louisianian who wife was quite younger than he. She was only 31, born in Louisiana of Bohemian parents. They had four children listed in the 1920 census, Lee, 16, Earl, 11, Irvin, 5 and Flora, 13.

John and Delicia also had a son named Harvey, who was born May 31, 1892, in Cameron. He married Emma James and died in Calcasieu Parish in August of 1973. Nick Pichnic was born on September 17, 1894, and lived all his life in Cameron Parish; he died there on August 18th of 1979. He was married to Elizabeth Alberta "Bessie" Kelley. She died on September 14, 1987. They are buried in Wakefield Cemetary in Lake Charles. She was born on September 21, 1896, the daughter of Daniel Webster and Georgiana (Rogers) Kelley.

Joseph Sedlac was 18 years old when he arrived in 1892. In the 1910 census he is listed as a 36 year old general farmer whose last named had morphed to Sedlack His wife was Maggie, 26. Both were listed as being born in Czechoslovakia but spoke Slovak. Their son Joseph, 5, was born in Cameron Parish as was their daughter Elizabeth, 2.

In 1920 the census says he was 49, but he was really 46, and that he was a widower. He was born in Czechoslovakia and still spoke Slovak, though no doubt he had some command of English. The census says he was a laborer and family history has it that he made and sold fishing equipment and nets. Elizabeth, now 12, is listed as being born in California of a mother who was Czechoslovakian, but who spoke Slovak. Joe, Jr., was 15. They had two more sons at the time, Buster, 7, and Steven, 6. It appears that Maggie died sometime after 1916. Perhaps she died in the flu epidemic of 1918. But since her dates are not known it cannot be stated for sure.

The 1930 census reveals that Joe became a citizen in 1903. He was now a 56 year old cotton farmer. Helping him with this were his two sons, Buster, now 20, and Steve, now 19. Also on the farm, living as a boarder, was a man with the charming Cajun name of Arestile Galian.

Supposedly all the Sedlac men died before they were 55 from weak hearts. According to Marilyn Delauney, a descendant, her grandfather's casket was lost during Hurricane Audrey. She also mentions that there was a daughter named Azora who died from Cat Scratch fever at age 6 months.

The 1930 census for Cameron Parish lists Laurent Miller, a 49 year old "Doctor of Medicine." He was from a longtime Louisiana family, but he married a woman born in Czechoslovakia whose mother tongue was Slovak. Annie J. came in 1893. They had three daughters, Emlie, 19, Annie, 11, and Marilyn who just 1 year and two months at the time of the census. Living with them was Klemenia Tabachnik, listed as a mother-in-law; she spoke Slovak. Could she have been the mother or aunt of Anna "Tabachiek" Grunik? Given that Grunik was bringing family and friends over it is quite possible. The handwritten census is hard to read in both cases. This is a case where an American had married a Slovak woman, when she was about 20 and he was 28, which can be determined by the birth year of their first daughter.

Adam Snatic, whose name is hard to read on the census form, but confirmed by a descedant, was a share cropper. He lived in Cow Island with the Caniks. From a great-granddaughter of Adam Snatic we learn that he immigrated to the U.S. on August 5, 1888, coming through New York from Rovne, Trencin County. He came over with the Canik family. In the 1900 census he appears as a hired hand on the farm of Delma Marceaux. He also appears on a Baptismal Record for one of Delma and Camielia's children the same year. That record is in the Church of St. Mary Magdalen in Abbeville, Louisiana. His name is spelled Snatick by whomever wrote it. In the 1910 census he is a hired hand of Paul Canik, the man he came over with. The 1920 census says he was living with Ozone Dartez at this time. Unfortunately, the records of the church in Abbyville burned in a fire. The descendant is not sure if Adam ever married the woman who was to bear his children.

Also in 1930 there was a Slovak man, recorded as being born in "Austria," named George Wilfer. He was 60 now and had been married since he was 26. He arrived in America in 1870 and was now a general farmer. He was married to a 56 year old Slovak woman named Josephine. Their five children, Larina, 16, Anna, 15, the twins Florence and Lawrence, both 13, and Pearl, 9, were all born in Louisiana

For thirty years Cameron Parish attracted a handful of Slovak families. They all lived near to each other and operated in the small population. The total parish population was less than 3,000 people at the beginning of the 20th century. There were 37 Slovak people in seven families in the 1930 census. They had settled in Cameron Parish beginning in the first decade of the 1900s. Their descendants are still a part of this rural parish. This was the largest collection of Czechs or Slovaks in Louisiana outside of Libuse and Kolin.

Where they were born was listed in several different ways depending on the census taker and the year. In 1910 it was mostly by the old country name of Hungary, which had ruled the Slovaks for a 1000 years. Then, in the 20 & 30 census they listed Czechoslovakia as their country of origin. There were also a few other country names used, as noted above. But in all cases they listed Slovak as their language. Their surnames are typical Slovak names. It also appears that most, if not all, came from the villages of the Rovne area of Trenchin County in Slovakia. Their families may have known each other in the Old Country.

At around the same time in Calcasieu Parish, probably Lake Charles, Agnes Cherrow Varon was married to Peter Varon of Louisiana. He was in the stationery business at the age of 52. She was ten years his junior, and she was born in Bohemia. They had an 18 year old son named Edward. This Czech lineage disappears in a sea of Varons, a common Cajun name.

Cameron Parish has always had a small population and most people in Louisiana think of it as a mostly Cajun place. Now it should be recongized that a Slovak colony has helped make it what it is today. It is even perhaps odder that most of these Slovaks settled in the community of Grand Chenier. This supposedly quintessential Cajun town was actually nearly 1/3 Slovak. This had to be apparent to any Cajuns and Anglos living in the same area. What they thought of the foreigners in their midst is not recorded. Alas, Hurricane Rita dealt the parish a severe blow. It destroyed nearly every building in the parish. So what will become of this conglomeration of Slovak descendants cannot not be foreseen.

6

On Name Changing

There are many myths and realities concerning immigrants changing their names when they came to America. The most common myth is that it happened at Ellis Island or some other port of entry when the immigration officer and the immigrant couldn't communicate. This was not true for a variety of reasons. First, and the most obvious, is that immigrants knew their own names and could probably write them. Education had advanced far enough in Europe by the time of the great waves of immigrants that began after the Civil War that even the poorest of classes were able to at least read and write their native tongue at an elementary school level. This was particularly true for the Czechs and Slovaks who exhibited a 96.8% literacy rate according to some statisticians and historians who have studied immigrants.

Second, immigrants were required to carry many papers, including their identification papers, travel documents and other items that all would have had their name written out. The immigration officer would have asked for these papers and seen the name written as it was supposed to be. Third, Ellis Island and other points of entry employed many translators to keep any problems to a minimum. Finally, the ships' masters and captains had a complete roster of those who were on board, including proof that the person had paid his or her fare and thus had a ticket in his or her name. There was the added incentive for the shipping lines to make sure all was in order because it was they who bore the expense of transporting back to Europe anyone without the proper documents. These are but four reasons for debasing the myth that names were changed at Ellis Island or other points of entry.

However, name changes did occur. And that is were myth does contain some reality. For arrivals prior to 1850 this well defined system of immigration was not in place. We can see from many early French and Spanish records in Louisiana that names were spelled multiple ways. This stemmed from two or three factors. One was that spelling conventions were still not set down in iron clad rules as they are today. Any reader of English literature in the original from the 1400s to 1800s will notice the multiple spellings of many words, often in the same book or document. It was Noah Webster in the early 1800s, among a few others, who first set about formalizing the spelling we use today in English. Other languages had their own moments in history when spelling was formalized.

Another was that many early immigrants were illiterate, as exemplified by the many "ordinary marks" put down as signatures in the early documents of Louisiana's notaries. Thus, the notary was required to make up a spelling to write the appropriate names into the records of land and slave sales and other instruments of life and business. That resulted in all sorts of permutations as different notaries were used, or the notary forgot how he spelled the name the last time he wrote it. For the name we now know as Touchet there are nearly a dozen variations: Touchec and Touchex, Toutcheque and Toucheque, Toutchique and Touchette, Toutcette and Toucet, Toupchek and Toupcheque, as well as Tutzek. For another early family we have Novark, Novak, and Novaque; we have Louchetik and Louchetique. Every genealogist knows to look under multiple spellings when researching their Louisiana roots.

By the 1850s immigration policies were being formalized and names were more unforgiving to alteration. Documents were required; more and more immigrants were at least semiliterate. This process accelerated over the course of the century. There were some glaring examples of necessary changes in this general trend towards getting an immigrant's name right. Obviously Chinese and Japanese, as well as other Asians, with their character-based languages, required transliteration into English. But even for that there were systems in use to assure conformity. Russians and some other Slavs faced the problem of transliterating the Cyrillic alphabet into the Latin letters of English, though for this, too, there were established conventions; the ship captains had the names in Latin letters along with the original.

Besides these orthographic difficulties there were both the pressure and desire, twin forces acting on immigrants, to assimilate into America as quickly as possible. First names were more frequently changed from obviously European ones to American names like John and James for men. More than a few women Anna and Marie became the more American Annie and Mary. This was easily accomplished because there were not as many rules and regulation regarding names. That only changed as the nation grew. On official documents an immigrant may well have used his native name, but in everyday usage in the community he would use an English variant. We find this in the many Czech and Slovak men named František becoming Frank, Vaclav becoming James or Walter and Wenzl becoming Wesley.

Czechs and Slovaks faced the issue of the haček and the čarek. The first is a little "v" over certain letters that soften its sound. The second looks like an accent mark but actually serves to lengthen the vowel, not stress it. (All Czech and Slovak words are accented on the first syllable without exception.) These two marks are strewn through Czech and Slovak names with liberality. The easiest solution, and the one most commonly found, was simply to drop the marks. The Czechs and Slovaks could keep pronouncing their names as in the old country and the Americans around them could read and write them clearly. Some immigrants added an "h" after their letters with hačeks to make the Czech and Slovak sound apparent to the English speaker. Some did not and the letter was now pronounced as in English. We find examples of both methods.

There are many examples of Czech and Slovaks changing their names, ranging from the subtle to the extreme. Russell, Roberts, Smith and Young are the four names I encountered of Czechs going for the radical extreme. Motichek is one that added the "h" after the c, because originally the name was "Motiček," or perhaps even "Mozíček," representing two changes. Hazmuka, without any marks, was changed to Hazmark, which was not as far as it could have gone. Sedlec, in Slovak pronounced "SED-letz," was to become Sedlock in America, with the stress on the second syllable, "Sed-LOCK." Končinsky (KON-chin-sky) became Koncinsky (kon-SIN-sky.) Another major change we encounter is Welcek, still pronounced "well-check," in Libuse, but it was originally Vlček. Still another is Vostrčil, which became Wostrchil and then Westerchil. Few Czechs and Slovaks escaped some sort of name change; nearly fifty of the settlers at Libuse and Kolin dropped a haček. And thus for the Czech and Slovak immigrants to Louisiana both the myth and the reality merge together.

These name changes also presented several difficulties in tracking people down as they were recorded with one name in one place and another name in a second. One thing I hope that will come from this book is much more information as other historians and researchers use the information here to trace the history of these families in Louisiana and wherever else they might have lived in America.

One other problem encountered in tracing Czechs and Slovaks in Louisiana is the incredible number of country and language names that were used over more than 250 years of settlement in the state. There were nearly 40 different variants used. It seems as if few record keepers at any level of government could agree on one name for either group. Plus, this changed from census to census, record to record. This is part a problem of the history of the area. The Austrians, Germans and Hungarians had ridden rough shod over the Czechs and Slovaks for centuries. The United States wanted to have good diplomatic relations with these countries so called all the people from them by the larger country's name. However, Czechs and Slovaks are not Austrian, German or Hungarian. These two are separate and distinct ethnic groups with their own languages and culture who had to fight off their larger neighbors for centuries. It is perhaps understandable that less knowledgeable Louisiana historians could not trace a family identified as Austrian in one census and Bohemian in a second and Czechoslovakian in a third—but since this is my heritage it was not difficult at all for me.

Final Thought on Part One

We can see from all these people spread over 250 years of Louisiana history that there was no great concentration of these Czech or Slovak immigrants in Louisiana, except maybe the Cameron Parish Slovaks. Instead, we find Czechs and Slovaks in every corner of the state, from rural farmland to big city offices. They originated from every corner of the Czech and Slovak Republics in Europe. They ranged across all walks of life and came from many different world views. They practiced the multitude of religions that are present in these two countries even today. If they had all arrived together they would have made a complete community, with someone for every human task. They worked hard at assimilating into the larger culture around them. In this they became thoroughly a part of Louisiana, losing most, if not all, of their Czech and Slovak heritage.

In recent years there has been a resurgence of people searching for their Czech and Slovak roots and their connections to Louisiana. I ran across many of them. The future is sure to bring new stories to light and provide those all important written documents and letters and the old photos still in the shoe box that help make history more complete. All of this is to be eventually catalogued and preserved in a Louisiana Czech & Slovak Museum, the seeds of which have been planted. The museum itself will be in Libuse, a Czech town in the Bohemian Colony of Rapides Parish. And it is to this Colony that next I turn. While the Czechs and Slovaks previously examined were dispersed, Libuse and its sister town of Kolin were thick concentrations of Czechs who came with one purpose in mind: to establish a Czech town where they could remain Czech in the midst of America. The second half of the book is dedicated to these two communities.

Joachim Kohn's portrait in the New Orleans Museum of Art

A Daguerotype of Michael Pokorny taken in 1875

A late 1800s portrait of the Pokorny family

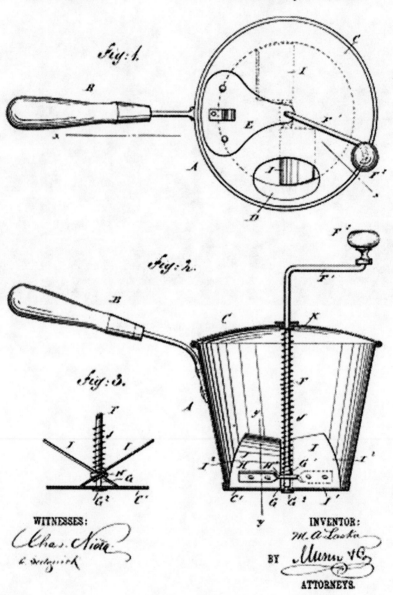

Patent drawings for Mathias Laska's coffee roaster

A 1930s photo of John Horecky

A late 1800s photo of John Pastorek

Andy Gasparecz and wife with their automobile, 1920s

Turn of the century photo of the Motichek family

The Sterba's in their wedding portrait

A strand of Mardi Gras beads made in Czechoslovakia, 1920s.

LSU Student Union building, designed by John Dvorak Desmond

The Stuchlik family in holiday costumes in the Czech Republic

Opening Day of the Czech Republic Honorary Consul's office in
New Orleans; left to right: The author, Libuse postmaster Caroline Tuma
Honorary Consul Kenneth Zezulka, Libuse pioneer George Tuma and
Ambassador Aleksandr Vondra of the Czech Republic

Bohemian Colony Department,

Louisiana Investment and Securities Co.

EDW. J. BALEJ, Secretary,
Lock Box 106.

ALEXANDRIA,
LOUISIANA.

Edward Balej's business card, given to first Czech colony property buyer
Rudolf Stuchlik

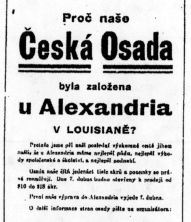

A flowery ad with drawing of the proposed school and testimonials for the Czech Colony at Kolin published in Hospodar

An ad touting the great weather and price of the Czech Colony in Louisiana

An ad showing a typical farm and extolling the virtues of Kolin.

One of the early Bohemian houses

A Bohemian family working the plot in front of their first Louisiana house

A Bohemian family posing on their farmstead

Early Bohemian Settlers at the Libuse Hotel (note African-American cooks)

The first Bohemian retail store on the Holloway Road

Mary Richter's well developed farmstead

The Libuse Czech Hall in 2005

Members of the Louisiana Czech Dancers in 2004

PART II

Preservation

Introduction to Libuse And Kolin

This is the story of the establishment and settlement of two Czech communities in the middle of Louisiana. They are unique in Louisiana as planned ethnic communities, and perhaps in all America. Out of thin air came a grand plan to create a "Bohemian Colony" populated only by thousands of Czechs. The actions of 10 or so Czech men, a handful of native Louisianians or their companies, and several men who were both out of state and not Czech converged. They simply announced that there were two new cities and thousands of acres of available farmland surrounding them. They, along with the first colonists, expected this colony to blossom. They named one of the cities Libuse for the legendary first Queen of the Czechs and the other Kolin after a city in Bohemia. Their centers set down about four miles north and south of each other, and about 10 miles to the slight southeast and northeast of downtown Alexandria, they were to form a haven for Bohemian farmers and tradesmen finally free from centuries of oppression in Europe. Here, in the midst of the piney woods of Rapides Parish, the founders dreamed of two purely Bohemian towns that would preserve forever Czech culture.

The founders created several operating corporations to buy and sell property and manage the birth and growth of the towns. They called one "The First Bohemian Village of America Corporation." They drew up and legally filed plat maps of the new cities and farming colonies. The maps of the cities show hundreds of lots centered around a central square with locations singled out for schools on wide streets at right angles. Surrounding the two cities were ever larger lots, first by small acreage then up in increments of 40 acres until an entire section of 640 acres; this was modeled directly on the development of towns in Bohemia. They promoted the colony exclusively in Bohemian language newspapers that were published in America, but never in English. And they spread the word through purely Bohemian organizations. No effort was made to reach Moravians and Slovaks, who share a common culture, but maintained their own American based publications. Only 250 Bohemian families ultimately answered the call; just five were not Bohemian. These people comprise half of the Czech immigrants to Louisiana. Though never approaching the size planned, Czech culture and a

213

strong sense of community still thrive here. Today you can even attend just one more of the hundreds of quintessential Louisiana festivals—The Louisiana Czech Festival.

This history is unfolded chronologically from the first germ of an idea all the way to today. In six chapters I present the flow of events, good and bad, and the lives of the colonists and their descendants. The chapters cover distinct periods of the communities. They are: the Idea—1908 to 1914, which will look at the formation of the idea, the primary men involved, their promotion efforts, and all of the legal entities involved in buying and selling the land, along with descriptions of the cities and plat maps. The First Years—1914 to 1919, covers the conditions that the first families discovered and how they started the communities. The Reality of the 1920s relates how many families were moving in and out and the hard work of establishing farms and businesses was completed by those who stayed. Following that is the Survival during the 1930s as the Depression came and the remaining families realized that they were going to be the only colonists. The Americanization from 1940 until 1965 details how the second, and then third generation, moved into the American mainstream. Finally, the Reawakening beginning in 1965 and continuing until today catalogues the efforts made to preserve what was left of Czech culture and reconstruct what was lost.

Throughout the history of these town the words *Czech* and *Bohemian* were used interchangeably by people both inside and outside the community. In the earlier years they are more often refered to as Bohemians. In the later years they are more often refered to as Czechs. The words *colony* and *community* were both used by the Czechs to refer to their area. I also use these terms interchangeably or one or the other when being more specific clarifies certain facts or events.

The Bohemian settlements of Libuse and Kolin were very similar to other Czech immigrant towns around America. Except that in Louisiana these were formally planned cities while those in other states grew more organically. There are nearly 300 Bohemian dominated towns still in existence across America, and a few Moravian towns in Texas. These towns are still predominately Czech. They were mostly created just outside of existing culturally American towns. Their purpose in every case was to preserve Czech culture and avoid assimilation into America. Visiting these towns today one would think one stumbled upon outposts of recent immigrants or even a foreign land. They are all that different than American towns.

In Louisiana, like in the other 300 Czech towns in America, the colonists formed their own schools based on the precepts of the great Czech educationalist, Jan Amos Komensky. The elders continued to speak the old language, and many still do. They attempted to teach the language to their children, though only vestiges remain. They read only Czech language newspapers. Both cities had their own post offices. They established stores and businesses. They constituted social organizations, formed fraternal lodges, organized theaters and musical societies and engaged in Scientific farming, all of which served to preserve their Czech heritage. In the beginning, at least, Bohemians married other Bohemians; many families in the community are related through marriage. They built civic buildings, called *Narodni Budova*, or National Halls; these still survive. They established their own cemeteries where the vast majority of the gravestones are engraved only in Czech. Even today, they are known as a distinct and separate group of people among the many ethnic heritages in Rapides Parish; they remain insular and apart. During my times of research in Alexandria I heard "oh, those people" uttered over and over again by non-Czechs. The Czechs still think of themselves as a separate people.

Whether the founders were being nationalistic or were engaged in purely a real estate venture is hard to determine. Surely they sought to make money, but they also expressed high ideals while doing so. There is a strong belief among descendants that the whole thing was a real estate scam from the start. One thing for certain though, is that with much work and perseverance these intrepid colonists carved a prosperous farming community out of the poor soils of the harsh cutover pine forests in Central Louisiana. Later, they established more than a few successful commerical enterprises in Alexandria. Besides Libuse and Kolin, and outside of the mainstream Anglo-French and African-American cultures that predominate in Louisiana, there were only a handful of other single-ethnic group communities established in Louisiana.

These were places where immigrants attempted to preserve a slice of the old country. Among them are Germantown and Robert's Cove for the Germans. The town of Independence in Tangipahoa Parish has its Italians. Hungarian Settlement in Livingston Parish is aptly named (and is considered the largest rural Hungarian settlement in the United States.) New Iberia saw its Canary Islanders, Calcasieu Parish is thick with Lebanese, the Yugoslavs settled in Plaquemines and St. Bernard Parishes and the Belgians filled the westside of Alexandria. A place named Polonia, south of Alexandria, for the Poles who were to settle there, never got off the ground. Out of all these it is the Czechs who have maintained the strongest sense of the old culture.

Any history is, of course, only as good as the quality and quantity of the source materials used. The facts and stories on these communities come from two broad categories. One is objective, including those which are officially recorded, documented, accessible and existing—as they say, "you can look it up." The other is subjective: the stories and recollections of descendants of the original colonists as told to me—and those which are included in three sources published by two community historians.

First, the objective: I went page by page through more than 850 property records in the Rapides Parish Courthouse. Starting with the Vendor and Vendee indices, I found every Czech-related record on file in the courthouse from 1913 through roughly 1940. I arbitrarily stopped my research at this point—anything later I considered current events and private matters. I compared the records with the plat maps filed in the courthouse. I examined the 31 naturalization applications of Czech settlers, also at the courthouse. I found every obituary of a Czech that was published in the Alexandria Town Talk between roughly 1925 and today—in the earliest years of the community Czechs did not have obituaries published in the local paper. I believe I found every article on the Czech communities in this newspaper published between 1913 and today. I accessed the complete 1920 and 1930 census records. These are the only two available on Libuse and Kolin (we shall have to wait until 2010 for the 1940 census.) I went through many city directories. I found complete transcriptions of the gravestones at the Czech cemeteries posted on the Internet. All of this is a matter of public record and is essentially unassailable.

On the subjective side, I spent countless hours talking with most of the elders and many of the second generation in the community during visits to their homes, businesses and farms, as well as at social gatherings in the Czech Halls. Further, I organized more than a few well-attended community meetings to discuss the proposed Louisiana Czech Museum. Here I heard the stories and recollections which are only as accurate as memories can be. The elders of the community today were only children at the time of these events. These stories also, quite obviously, only include what people chose to tell me. There is still a very strong adversion to sharing with outsiders; some people simply refused to speak with me. There are also what can only be called "factions" in the community, stemming from feuds and rivalries of long ago, that color these stories. To loosely quote one resident: *"Libuse and Kolin are separate, aren't they, from each other, different characteristics as communities. One being grounded by the WFLA and the other by the Hall, they attracted different sorts of people, who have to a degree isolated themselves geographically at a very visceral level, down to the square inch."* Yet, for this reason, and perhaps oddly for a history book, I sometimes slip into a First Person narrative.

In addition, there are several "published" community histories. One is a self-published folk-history of the men who served in World War I. It was written by Frances Hazmark, a copy of which is in my possession. The second is the Louisiana Czech Heritage Association newsletter. As any community newsletter is it is a combination of objective facts and subjective stories. Hazmark is the long-time editor and primary writer of this newsletter; though there are many articles in it written by others. They are on file at the Alexandria Genealogical Library; I made a complete copy of these quarterly newsletters with her permission. Ms. Hazmark is a serious and studious person who has worked diligently to preserve the history of the communities. She often says things like "this is only what was told to us," or "I don't know this for a fact," but given that she spent her life in the community and countless hours researching and listening her work is mostly a reliable source.

The third "history" is the doctoral dissertation written in 1986 by Dr. Rosie Ann Walker entitled "The Rural Schools of the Czech Communities of Rapides Parish." The only publicly available copy is at the Hill Memorial Library on the campus of Louisiana State University in Baton Rouge. I spent many hours with this dissertation. It was the most complete history of the Czech colony and its schools until this book. She claims to rely on information perserved in early records and minutes of community meetings. I have not seen copies of these. The Rapides Parish school board says they have no records remaining from this period. No one I ever spoke with in the community admits to having these records. Indeed, many people say no records or minutes of meetings were kept at all. Yet, Dr. Walker presents some rather detailed information—and I can only assume that at least in 1986, when she wrote it, they did exist and she did see them. In my time spent with her I perceived her as a serious scholar. The facts she presents mostly coincide with what I was able to find, though some significantly differ. Still, there is ultimately no reason to doubt the majority of her work.

I located two Works Progress Administration reports in the State Library in Baton Rouge, however, they can only be characterized as subjective histories. There are also a handful of one page "histories" or "remembrances" written by community residents that are found in various places. I also looked at many recently published articles in the Alexandria newspaper and other Louisiana newspapers, magazines, and websites—all of which rely mainly on the same subjective sources. There is another potential, and purported, treasure trove of information that I was unable to access—the archives of the Heritage Association. They are said to comprise personal letters, documents and photos, and originals of the minutes of the early community meetings. Anyone who may hold these claim they contain nothing of importance, or deny possessing them, or worse from the historical perspective, claim they no longer exist. Even Ms. Hazmark lamented to me that she is unable to pry loose any original source materials from people who may have them (indeed, the newsletter contains pleas for people to share this information, all to no avail.) My hope is that this book encourages these materials to become available even if it means correcting my own work.

I took the public record and created several databases of this objective information—and then I compared that to the subjective community histories, stories and recollections. What I discovered is that many of the stories that have come down to this current generation are only loosely based on the objective facts; some are just plain wrong. Where necessary I allude to these subjective histories, recollections and stories—and then give the objective facts. My purpose for doing so is only gentle correction, for many of the current generation have relied on the subjective.

I am not maligning anyone who wrote a recollection—at least they put something to paper. Nor will I disparage anyone who told me a story. It is just that the people who tell the stories are relying on what they learned from their parents and grandparents. They are the cherished stories of a tight knit community. This is what they believe; but they are, after all, just memories—and memory is faulty. And I certainly do not mean to criticize either Dr. Walker or Ms. Hazmark—they are to be commended for their diligent work and I rely on them for much. My goal is only to establish the facts as found in objective sources. Finally, I hope that what I present here is taken by the Czechs of Libuse and Kolin, and every other reader, for what I intend it to be—a celebration of a unique Louisiana community. Here, then, for the first time is a comprehensive history of the Czech Colony of Louisiana.

7

An Amazing Idea
1905–1914

John Rosicky's Hospodar

More than other ethnic groups in America the Czechs had the desire to create their own communities and remain separate from the larger American cultural current. While members of many other ethnic groups settled near to each other in established towns and in certain neighborhoods in cities throughout America they worked at assimilation. The Czechs, on the other hand, tended to form their own towns just outside of established places. Throughout the states of the Upper Midwest and in Texas you will find towns with two distinct halves—the American side and the Czech side. Assimilation and Americanization were not their goals. Of course, they weren't the only European immigrants who predominated a town, nor were they ultimately successful in preventing assimilation, but Czechs stand out as being separatists. No other ethnic group in America engaged in a systematic effort to establish single-ethnic heritage towns. Libuse and Kolin are inescapably bound up in this movement and one man stands out as their progenitor.

John Rosicky, the son of Czech immigrants, was one of the prime movers of this separatist movement. He came to America in 1861 as a fifteen-year-old boy and settled with his parents on a farm in Wisconsin. As a young man he opened his first store in Chicago. He lost this to the Great Chicago Fire of 1871. Undaunted by this reversal, Rosicky continued to engage in a diverse range of business pursuits. He first opened a general store in Omaha, Nebraska, then other stores in other towns, but always in Czech communities. He had a vision of promoting Czech culture. To facilitate this he bought a few small newsletters and tried to build them into larger publications. One was Pokrok Zapadu (Progress of the West,) another was Kvety Americke (American Blossoms,) and a third was Osveta Americka (American Enlightenment.) He worked tirelessly for decades to promote and preserve the Czech heritage, but like most visionaries he was less a businessman and more of a catalyst. He translated Nebraska's school laws into Czech. He helped establish Czech libraries and language departments at the universities of Nebraska and Minnesota. The Western Bohemian Fraternal Association was founded at his instigation; he is considered the "father" of this venerable organization. Traveling far and wide, he helped people create fraternal lodges in Czech towns throughout the Midwest. In the last active year of his life, 1909, he attempted to gather copies of every single Czech-American publication, book and cultural artifact and transport them to the National Museum in Prague, Czech Republic. His vision did not bring him wealth. In fact, the opposite is true: he lost money at virtually everything he tried. He had but one lasting success.

In 1891 he founded a newspaper called Hospodar. Orginally published in Saline County, Nebraska, then in Omaha it ceased publication for a brief while when Rosicky's daughter died. A Czech man in West, Texas then bought the name and subscription list and started to publish it again. Its name means "Farmer" and its main purpose was to advise Bohemian immigrants how to buy land, build homes and plant crops in their new homeland. It is now 115 years old and possibly the longest running Czech language publication in America. It is distributed in all 50 states.

In the pages of this newspaper Rosicky editorialized about the need to preserve Czech culture. He continually published information about opportunities for new Czech towns and did his best to promote them. Many previous attempts had failed. Between 1905 and 1909 he was involved in plans to formalize this effort. An even more concerted effort was the result of a 1908 letter by Wesley Wostrchil published in Hospodar about the need to be more organized in founding Czech towns. This was already an idea that was floating around for several years, but was not as organized as it was to become. In November, 1908, this effort was formalized in an organization called Czech Colonization Club (Cesky Kolonizacni Klub) in Omaha, Nebraska. Wosterchil eventually was one of the first settlers in Kolin, Louisiana.

Prior to the formal establishment of the Club, the founders heard of new opportunities for development in Idaho and Montana. They made several exploratory journies into the region to find suitable land to host a Czech community. Three new towns were created but did not survive. The land was ultimately too arid. John Zpevacek, writing from Rupert, Idaho in 1905, gives a realistic picture of the area: "I am not encouraging the countrymen to come, because the countryside is not pleasant at all: it is very dry, trees are in the distance of 50 miles; summer temperatures reach up to 106." In early 1909 they explored the region near

Klamath Falls, Oregon as a site for a Czech town. On September 21st that same year, they chartered a Southern Pacific Railroad train to carry some 66 Czech families out to Oregon. Here is where a Czech community named Malin (the Czech word for horseradish that also grows wild there) still struggles to survive. After the death of Rosicky in 1910, and as 1910 rolled into 1911, and then 1912, the remaining Club members traveled through at least 20 states in the Union, mostly to the west of the Mississippi River.

All locations were found wanting or at least a decision could not be reached by the members. There are no known surviving records of this effort and no hint as to why a location could not be procured. Though it is known that Wesley Wosterchil was joined by two men known now only as F. J. Posvar of Wyoming and A. J. Sobatka of Nebraska; others may have joined them. It was after this fruitless search, sometime in early 1913, that a new group was founded. It is not entirely clear who all those involved were. In the original documents related to the founding of Libuse and Kolin, however, a few men stand out as ringleaders. After Libuse and Kolin were founded they looked no further.

The Bohemian Colonization Club

The known founding members of the new Bohemian Colonization Society (Ceske Kolonizacni Spolecnost) of Omaha, Nebraska were Joseph A. Ubl, Frank G. Dobrovolny and J. Emmauel Kroupa; if they were joined by others we do not know their names. This organization was not much different than the original organization in either purpose or membership, it was more a psychological boost for a fresh start on an old idea. Ubl, Dobrovolny and Kroupa may well have been on some of those trips around the country. Posvar and Sobatka may have come to Louisiana. They all probably experienced some level of frustration at the inablity to achieve consensus and chose a location for a new Czech Colony. So they set out on their own. Sometime in mid to late 1913 they made a decision: Louisiana was their choice.

They got to work immediately. The three Society founders were joined by Joseph Kadlec, James Vorisek and Josef Legner in creating two corporations. One was called the Libuse Townsite Company. The other was grandiously entitled "First Bohemian Village of America Corporation." Who named these is not entirely clear, though presumably it was these men. Why these names and not some others is not known. If they considered other names that is lost to history. Surely they were chosen to induce settlers to come. Eventually these founders were joined by Edward J. Balej and his brother Frank and also John D. Hasik.

These men are not listed in any of the incorporation papers, rather they seemed to just work as real estate agents. There was another corporation created to guide the new colony: the Louisiana Investment and Securities Company, but it was not owned by Czechs.

Why this place can only be guessed at, but we know that lumber companies were trying to unload lands that they had stripped of timber and they now considered worthless. We do not known if they looked at other locations in Louisiana. How these men learned of the availability of this land is not known. Ultimately, only Joseph Ubl and the Balej's moved into the communties. J. Em. Kroupa bought lots in the Libuse Townsite, never any farms; but is not otherwise recorded as living there. Frank Dobrovolny bought one piece of land and that not until 1918; but he also apparently never lived there. Edward J. Balej was joined later by his brothers Frank and Albert and other family members in living in the community. John Hasik also bought land, but he, too apparently never lived in the community. He did form a partnership with Edward Balej to sell land.

Many of the Czech residents of Libuse and Kolin today tell the story that these men and companies bought land for fifty cents an acre and sold it for 10 to 15 dollars an acre to their forefathers. They supposedly bought 10,000, or 15,000, or 20,000, or 22,000 acres—depends on the story teller. This story is repeated in many of the written or published histories of the colony. But none of this is true. There is no evidence that these men bought such large tracts of land from the timber companies to resell. Only two pieces of evidence were found that anyone bought significant amounts of land from the timber companies to resell: Louisiana Investment & Securities Company bought just 7,188 acres from the Alexandria Lumber Company and a man named Albin Cecha bought 4,000 acres from Lee Lumber Company. Of all the founders only Ubl, the Balejs and Cecha lived in the community for many years. Soon they were joined by Ernest Jilek in the real estate game.

Three non-Czechs started Louisiana Investment. The purchase price for the land it bought, if certain conditions were met, was never to be less than $1 an acre. In reality it was never less than between $5 and $6 an acre; there is some confusion as to exactly the lowest price. Just about a year later this property was foreclosed on by the Alexandria Lumber Company when payments were not made. The lumber company then proceeded to carry on sales of this land to the Czechs. Cecha, who acted alone, paid $5 an acre for his land. Ubl, Kroupa, the Balejs and Hasik seemed to act more as real estate brokers, though no record of any contracts or payments could be found and only vague references are made in a few property records to commissions being paid.

In the first year of its existence, 51 colonists bought from Louisiana Investment. A few bought from the Libuse Townsite Company and land that was supposed to be Kolin. Following the foreclosure on Louisiana Investment subsequent purchases were made by the colonists directly from five different existing Louisiana companies or from Cecha. Of the companies three were timber companies: Lee Lumber Company, Alexandria Lumber Company, and the Union Land & Timber Company. Two of the companies were banks: Guaranty Bank and City Savings Bank & Trust. Cecha operated on his own. Oddly, the records in the Rapides Parish courthouse show that these five entities seemed to only sell land to Czechs—there are just a handful of non-Czechs recorded buying land from them. This was the pattern for the first few years. After that, the remaining purchases were made by one Czech family from another.

Another commonly told and written story in the community is that these men sold the land for $25 down with payments to follow. In fact, more than half the colonists paid cash and the majority of the rest put down upwards of 50% of the purchase price. Only 12 put just $25 down. 8 of those were purchases from City Savings Bank and not from any Czech man. The other four were odd examples. There are many stories of people "walking away from their deposits." I could not find any document that shows where anyone walked away from land they bought. In fact, of those who purchased all paid off their mortages on time. They usually made three annual payments; though this was not really unusual for farmers of the period anywhere in America. When the crops came in farmers had a large amount of money that could be applied to their mortgages. While there were many who bought and never moved in, or stayed briefly at most, they all sold their land—and some not until many years later.

The Czech men and Louisiana Investment did not tell anyone that the land was cut over pine forest. Indeed, the ads and testimonials in Hospodar are glowing about the land and the climate and the community. The actual purchase documents, however, almost all state that the land was "cut-over pine forest." The lumber companies made no bones about that and indeed, they usually reserved the right to harvest the remaining timber in the three years of the outstanding mortgage. That these Czech men were in it for profit there can be no doubt; the companies were stictly about profit. But they did lay out the plat maps for what they promised would be two vibrant towns. And it was Hospodar, carried on by Rosicky's daughter Rose and others, which promoted the two towns.

As mentioned, one other man was involved in the creation of the Czech Colony: Albin Cecha. But he was a lone operator. At some point in 1914 he determined that this colony would be a good investment and he bought 4,000 acres directly from the Lee Lumber Company. He went on to resell it to Czech colonists. He established what he called "Colony B"—it was not a part of the original plan. These purchases, too, were either for cash or substantial down payments. It is not known how he promoted his land for no ads in Hospodar could be found with his name on it. He was also somehow involved in the mapping out of the town of Libuse; one of the streets there was named Cecha Street.

Wesley Wostrchil's letter in Hospodar decried the quick assimilation of some Czechs and how a colony to preserve the community and culture was necessary. Ironicly, it was his name that was already Americanized from Vaclav Vostrčil to Wesley Wosterchil. It was further anglicized by the next generation to Westerchil. The Balej family anglicized their name to Baley, then Bailey. Albin Cecha supposedly remainded in the community until his death, or almost—depends on the source.

Some say it was just a swindle by the Czech men; it was at least a case of gullibility by the colonists. In any event, it was on the wrong side of the river. It was not the rich farm land that Louisiana is known for. Instead, it was piney woods with poor soils. Out of the thousands hoped for only some 260 families and about 60 bachelors are recorded buying land or moving into the colony. 92 families are in the 1920 census and only 88 families are in the 1930 Census. Many did not stick around long enough to make the census. There was enormous turnover in the early years of the community. Some were from big cities wanting to escape to a rural setting. Some were on Midwestern farms as hired hands now looking for their own place. Some sold their farmland and moved south for what was promised to be better conditions. Many came from Czech communities in northern states. Some apparently came directly from Europe.

Like many Czech settlements around the country these two were formed with the express idea of keeping the old traditions alive and to keep the ethnic puresness that they had back home. They were trying to escape the Germanization that they were experiencing in Europe and they were determined to avoid assimilation here in America. This was a very common thread among Czech settlers across America. Slovaks were less inclined to set up their own towns and they gravitated towards the cities. One thing for certain, this shifting group of men were finally on track to create what they called a Ceske Osada—a Czech Colony—in the middle of Louisiana.

8

The Beginning—1914 to 1919

Alexandria when the Czechs settled

When Alexandria was first settled in the early 1700s it was called Post du Rapides. It lay at the head of navigation on the Red River until Henry Shreve was able to clear the enormous log jams that clogged the river all the way to the present city of Shreveport. It was known as Alexandria by the time of the Civil War, though it was not incorporated until 1888. The city and parish saw several skirmishes between Union and Confederate forces. The Yankees were able to seize the town late in the war. Following William Tecumseh Sherman's model in Georgia they burned nearly the entire city to the ground. They made particular care to burn the government buildings, including the courthouse, so there are no surviving property records from prior to the war.

After the war the city languished until the timber industry got under way in the late 1870s. By the turn of the century the city had about 5,000 inhabitants. During the last two decades of the 1800s and into the beginning of the 20th century lumber was about the only industry. In the 15 years between 1900 and 1915 the city doubled in size to about 11,000 residents. It was at the end of this period when the first Czechs arrived in the area. What they found was a city that was about a third French, a third Anglo-Scots-Irish and a third African-American. There were only a scattering of other nationalities, including, a bit surprisingly, a significant number of Belgians on the westside of the city. As mentioned in Part One, there were rumors of an earlier Bohemian settlement, but they were not really Bohemians. The city was still riding the timber-financed economic boom of the late 1800s, though the boom was quickly declining. The city leaders continued to have great hopes of an ever growing city. But the Depression was to put a stop to the growth. It was and is a quintessential sleepy small southern city.

There was apparently only one Czech person in the rural area outside of Alexandria before the founding of the Bohemian Colony. As with many situations in the beginning, there is a bit of confusion. There are two documents related to the same purchase by George Hlavaty. One is dated June 6th, 1912, the other January 16th, 1913. That they are in the conveyance book consecutively does not clarify the situation. There are slightly different details in each. Yet, it also appears that the latter document is a correction of the terms of the first. But it is clear that he bought 40 acres for $600 cash. This works out to be $15 an acre; there is no mention of "improvements." The purchase was from M. Leigh Alexander; he was an officer of Lee Lumber. In the later document the company reserved the right to take "all merchantable timber" for a period of three years, which points to it being raw land. But the sale itself is from individual to individual. The plot's legal description is: Southwest ¼ of the Southeast ¼ of section 41, township 5. This land is right in the middle of what was to become the Bohemian Colony.

Hlavaty and his wife, Josephine, came from Guernsey County, Ohio, about 60 miles to the east of Columbus; she's only mentioned in one document. This is, of course, no where near Omaha, where the Colonization Club began. Josephine's name is in the earlier document. Her maiden name is given as "Kracscyich," which appears to be a misspelling or alteration of the Czech name Krejcik. It cannot be determined if this was the man who alerted the Bohemian Colonization Club to the availability of land in the area. No Hlavaty was recorded being involved with the Club. What happened to him is also unknown; he is not in either the 1920 or 1930 censuses. Nor is he ever mentioned in any stories. He did not disappear entirely, though.

In September of 1925 he sold an oil lease on the property to A. L. Johnson. How a man from central Ohio came to buy land in central Louisiana is a mystery. It is definite, however, that he kept this land for nearly 35 years. On October 29th, 1947, he sold it to Anne Marie Peros, who was not Czech. She was from Guernsey County, Ohio, too, so they probably knew each other. The price was astonishing: exactly One Dollar. There also was a John Hlavaty who bought land in 1918, well after the founding of the colony, but it is not possible to determine if he was related to George. John's purchase agreement says he was a resident of Rapides Parish, but he never appears in any other record.

The first mention of the Bohemian Colony in the Alexandria Daily Town Talk, the daily newspaper of the city (then and today) occurs on December 23rd, 1913. How the paper learned of the plan is not clear, but Donald Despain, president of Louisiana Investment, is quoted in the article. It was published 2 months before the incorporation of Louisiana Investment. The editors apparently considered the story significant enough that they placed it at the top of Page 1, right smack in the middle. The article is entitled "New Bohemian Colony" and it is just three paragraphs long. It contains one major bit of wrong information: that the Investment company had "a tract of 22,000 acres" on which to settle—there was no such tract. In a bit of disinformation Despain is also quoted as saying "the colony will be operated on a basis whereby it is proposed to take care of and over-look the colony until it is on a firm footing. This care of the colony will extend over several years time." The article implies the Investment company will "super-vise" the colony. While this was the stated goal of the First Bohemian Village Despain was not involved with it. Perhaps Despain himself was to be this agricul-tural specialist, though he never moved into the colony. No one was ever appointed or elected to "take care" of the colony. The colonists were left to fend for themselves.

The First Bohemian Village of America

May 6th, 1914, a corporate charter was filed in Rapides Parish creating the First Bohemian Village of America. The charter was not filed with the state until August 1st of that year. It was formed with the express purpose of buying and reselling "about 10,000 acres." It was supposed to buy this land from the Louisi-ana Investment Company. No such property transaction ever took place. Indeed, there is no record that this corporation ever made a purchase of any property. The capital stock of the corporaton was set in the amount of $120,000. One fourth was to be paid in cash up front, the rest paid in over time, though in what time frame was not fixed. There were six men who had shares in the corporation: J. Emmanuel Kroupa, Frank G. Dobrovolny and Joseph A. Ubl had 300 shares each. Joseph Kadlec, James Vorisek and Josef Legner had 100 shares each. What happened to the money paid in is unknown. Kroupa was president, Dobrovolny was vice-president and Ubl was secretary and treasurer; they also were the Board of Directors.

The dream as laid out in the incorporation charter is quite expansive: *"to pro-mote the general prosperity and agricultural interest of the said Parish of Rapides and State of Louisiana, by selling the said land in subdivision to a colony of Bohemians; to assist them in making settlement thereon and in cultivating the said land; the rearing of stock and hogs; planting of fruit tress and crops of berries; to encourage the estab-lishement of dairies, and generally to make said land productive, useful and remuner-ative (sic); and generally to manage, foster and protect the interest of the said colonists."*

Further, the charter states that the company was to *"aid in the sale, cultivation and encouragement of the said colonists; to lend money thereon; to take and receive cash from said colonists... To make with them contracts for the purchase of said lands, partly for cash and partly on terms of credit; to take and accept mortgages and vendor's liens... To secure good titles for said colonists and settlers for the lands... To supervise the assessment of said lands for taxation and the payment of taxes thereon, and generally to take concerted action for the common good of the corporation and of such real estate owners and for the promotion of public enterprises."* (Elipses are for repetitive language.)

Lofty goals, for sure, but there is no evidence that this corporation did anything. Indeed, the only reference to this corporation is the charter itself; its name does not appear in any of the more than 850 documents in the courthouse relating to the Colony. No evidence, either factual or anecdotal, was found that meetings were held or actions considered. Oddly, its corporate charter was not revoked until October 21st, 1985, and then only for inactivity—and this is the date that Louisiana's Corporation Office cleansed its records of hundreds, if not thousands, of inactive corporations. So it appears that this corporation sat around basically dormant for nearly 70 years; its dream dissipated. While the dissolution of the corporation required the actions of the shareholders, all were long dead before its own demise. It is still in the Louisiana Secretary of State's corporate database.

Creation of the Town of Libuse

There are few towns in Louisiana for which we know the very hour of their creation. Libuse is one of them. There are, however, probably none with such a contradictory and convoluted recorded set of transactions leading to its establishment. First I will give the recorded dates in sequential order of these related events. All of these are in 1914. The rest of the story starts in mid-1915 with the real first land sales in Libuse to Czech Colonists. Here I also give a few quick and odd details. Then I will present some conundrums. Only after this will I try to sort it all out in much greater detail in the sections on the Libuse Townsite Company and the Louisiana Investment & Securities Company that follow this brief recounting. Forgive me if I repeat some of the information here a little further on—but the events of 1914 are truly one amazing bit of history.

On February 2nd Louisiana Investment & Securities Corporation is officially incorporated in Baton Rouge; no Czechs are involved. Of its three incorporators, one lives in Chicago, one in Omaha, Nebraska, and one in Baton Rouge.

On February 5th Louisiana Investment enters into a contract with Alexandria Lumber Company to buy 7,188 acres of land in Rapides Parish.

On March 25th Louisiana Investment passes a resolution authorizing sale of its land; which it had not bought yet.

On April 10th Louisiana Investment makes its first recorded sale—to Rudolf Stuchlik.

On April 18th a plat map for the proposed town of Libuse is filed in the Rapides Parish courthouse; it shows the town on 80 acres in Section 2, Township 4, Range 1 East.

On April 30th J. Em Kroupa is recorded buying those 80 acres in Section 2 from Louisiana Investment; he is the only recorded purchaser.

On May 1st a plat map showing 11,280 acres and marked "owned by Louisiana Investment" is filed in the courthouse; Section 2 is on this map.

On May 2nd the Libuse Townsite Company is recorded at the courthouse; of the four Czech incorporators none live in Louisiana.

On May 15th a second plat map is filed showing 10,040 acres and marked "owned by Louisiana Investment;" this land is adjacent to the land on the previous map.

On May 21st the purchase of 7,188 acres by Louisiana Investment from Alexandria Lumber is recorded at the courthouse; while this purchase covers some of the land on the first plat map there is no land in Section 2 listed in the purchase agreement—and none of the land on the second plat map.

On May 23rd the board of directors of Louisiana Investment adopts a resolution to buy the land it is recorded as buying two days earlier—it is the same document—the recording date was placed *on* the document by the courthouse, the resolution date is *in* the first paragraph.

On August 1st the Libuse Townsite Company is recorded in the state corporations office in Baton Rouge.

On September 2nd the Libuse Townsite Company buys a 2/3rds interest in those 80 acres—less the lot "the hotel" sits on—bought by Kroupa alone in Section 2; the sellers are listed as Kroupa and Joseph Ubl.

Consider these conundrums: Louisiana Investment not only filed plat maps for huge swaths of land it claimed to own yet never purchased, but recorded the maps before it bought any land at all. Stuchlik bought his land from the corporation a full six weeks before it purchased any land. Eight other Czechs also bought land from Louisiana Investment in the weeks before the first recorded purchase of land by the corporation. Plus, Kroupa not only bought land from Louisiana Investment before it is ever recorded buying any land, but the land it did purchase does not include the land Kroupa bought. Either the Libuse Townsite Company or Kroupa filed a plat map for land neither owned at the time; no name of the owner is on the map. Not only that, there is no ready explanation for the three month delay between Libuse Townsite's corporate filing in the courthouse versus the corporate filing with the state—you could walk from Alexandria to Baton Rouge quicker. Finally, Libuse Townsite bought land from Kroupa, now joined by Ubl, for which there is no record that Ubl ever came into any portion of ownership by any means—he simply appears. I can, however, grant that of the two dates on the Louisiana Investment purchase agreement one is a typographical error.

Even more amazing is the rate at which the value of the 80 acres of the town escalated within a matter of months. Louisiana Investment bought its land at $6 an acre. Kroupa bought the 80 acres of the proposed town for $14.96 an acre. Kroupa and Ubl sold this land to Libuse Townsite for an astounding $60 an acre. Considering that they only sold a 2/3rds interest in the land, it works out to an even more astounding $88 an acre. And they essentially sold it to themselves!

Now, before the reader wonders if I have all this straight, I can tell you that I searched high and low in every place conceivable in the Rapides Parish courthouse for any records whatsoever that would shed light on this situation. I went repeatedly page by page through the conveyance indices—both by Vendor and Vendee. I looked for any possible misspellings of corporate names (such as "Labuse" for Libuse) and personal names (among them "Korupa" for Kroupa; "Abl" for Ubl,) misfilings of documents (by both altering the number sequences of book and page, that is, both "67" and "76," and looking at five or so documents before and after each record,) wrongly alphabetized listings (of which there are many for Czechs,) and alternate spellings or abrieviations (like "La." for Louisiana.) I looked to see if transactions were listed by the name of the incorporators of Louisiana Investment and not the corporation itself. I double and triple checked for misstated dates in the documents themselves. I went through the plat map books several times looking for anything. I consulted one of the professional abstractors who work daily at the courthouse (and on whom I relied on more than once during my trips to Alexandria to clarify confusing situations.) I checked with the clerk of court to see if I followed the right procedure and if there were any other alternatives. I repeatedly returned to the same documents to see if I missed something. And I repeatedly returned to the Internet website which lists Louisiana corporations, both active and inactive, and tried this all again.

Yet, that is it. Just these 13 recorded events in 1914 relating to the founding of Libuse and the Czech Colony of Louisiana. (21 if you count the other eight sales to Czechs before May 23rd.) Out of all the research I did for this book this situation consumed the most time. Yet it remains the most confounding. Fortunately, after May 23rd, 1914, everything straightens out, and the two companies actually sell land they own. On this date Joseph Hrachovina bought for himself 320 acres from Louisiana Investment—and a ½ interest in the land that Stuchlik had bought on April 10th! On May 25th, now officially two days after Louisiana Investment made its purchase, Donald Despain, the company president, signed another resolution authorizing the company to sell land.

Libuse Townsite Company

The Libuse Townsite Company was incorporated at 11 AM on the morning of May 2nd, 1914, according to the filing in the clerk of court office in Alexandria. Yet, the Louisiana corporate database says it was incorporated on August 1st, 1914. There is no obivous reason for the delay of nearly 3 months time; even in those days it was possible to get from Alexandria to Baton Rouge in two days, or three at most, whether traveling in person or sending a letter by mail. Two weeks before the recording in Alexandria, on April 18th, 1914, Robert W. Bringhurst, filed a map laying out the townsite of Libuse. He was the longtime Rapides Parish surveyor and recorder. It can can be found in Plat Book 2, page 63, at the parish courthouse. So the founders filed a plat map before they were officially a corporation, why this two week difference is not clear. But it is clear that Libuse was created out of whole cloth in the middle of what was basically uninhabited wilderness. It was not on a bayou or river as are virtually every other town in Louisiana. Even the railroad that ran through the property was more of a temporary lumber train than an established line.

The Libuse Townsite Company was headquarted in Alexandria, though no specific address is listed anywhere. There were four incorporators and they were the only stockholders. J. Em. Kroupa and Joseph A. Ubl each owned 24 shares. F. K. Vondries and Frank G. Dobrovolny owned 1 share each. The shares were valued at $100 each. The paid in capital was thus a total of $5,000, so $4,800 of it was money put in by Kroupa and Ubl. Kroupa was president of the corporation, Vondries was the vice-president and Ubl was the secretary and treasurer. Dobrovolny had no official position. In two of the sales documents a man named Joseph Padrnos signed for the company, but he did so from Douglas County, Nebraska. From which city in that county is not stated but Omaha is a possibility

These are the only references to this man. Who he was and what other part he played is a mystery; he is not listed anywhere in the incorporation papers or any other document.

There is no evidence that any more shares were ever sold to anyone. Nor is there evidence that any board of directors meetings were ever held. This was another corporation that seemingly languished in oblivion until October of 1985. One interesting thing is that though the town never came to be the name "Libuse Townsite" was the official property description for many lots sold over the years.

As noted, this corporation did buy 80 acres. On September 9th, 1914 it bought a 2/3rds interest in this land from Kroupa and Ubl for $4,800 cash. However, there is no record of Ubl ever buying an interest in the land from Kroupa, or in fact, any sort of transfer. The first time Ubl shows up in a property record as buying or taking possession of land is in 1915. That was when he bought 80 acres in Section 1 from Louisiana Investment—land that there is no recorded evidence that the company ever bought. It was Kroupa alone who had bought a 100% interest in the townsite land on April 30th from Louisiana Investment. Now the two of them were selling it. They were also essentially selling an interest in the land they already owned as individuals to a company they also owned. They bought the land from Louisiana Investment for $1,192.23, so they were making a tidy profit—and keeping a 1/3 interest in it, too.

The "objects and purposes" of this corporation was *"to buy eighty or more acres of land…On the Holloway Prairie road, about seven miles from Alexandria, near the tramroad of the Lee Lumber Company, and at or near the Bohemian Colony Settlement, from Joseph A. Ubl and J. Em. Kroupa; to sell the same to such persons as may wish to buy lots and acreage property; which shall be known as the Libuse Town Site, as a settlement for such of the Bohemian Colony member or other persons."* Further, the charter states that this corporation was "to build, lease and rent dwellings;" "take concerted action for the common good of the corporation" and "to construct buildings."

So, Libuse was to be centered on the Holloway Prairie Road, now Louisiana Highway 28. The road was little more than a half-gravel track that the map shows pretty much ending in the middle of town. It was no more than a dirt track where it exited towards the east. This street was going to be 60 feet wide and it ran diagonally through the middle of the city. Running north to south were five streets and east to west were four streets. These streets were mapped out as 84 feet wide—which is as wide as most major boulevards in Louisiana cities. 126 lots were laid out facing the main streets. Alleys were laid out behind the lots within each block, with 12 lots per block. The lots were 50 feet by 140 feet. Along the southernmost street in town were 36 lots that were 25 feet by 140 feet. Surrounding this dense core were 18 parcels ranging from 1.44 acres to 3.10 acres.

While the first map filed did not have the names of the streets written in a subsequent revision did show the street names. This revision was actually filed 10 years later and shows the same basic layout of the town. Yet, by this time, it was pretty much known that there was not going to be a real town here. Why the revision was made is not clear. The biggest change shows the Holloway Prairie Road continuing out the other side of town and the addition of the Philadelphia Road forking off of it. For a town that was supposed to be the center of an effort to preserve Czech heritage most of the street names are quintessentially American. The north-south running streets were named Gum, Industrial, Main, Oak and Pine. The east-west streets were Ceter, Cecha, Cook and Flaggon. Cecha was most likely named after Albin Cecha. Flaggon was named after a bayou that coursed along the northern edge of the property that the Louisiana Investment & Securities Company bought; it was a name long established in the area, though the bayou's name is spelled "Flagon" on the townsite map. Where the names for Ceter and Cook came from is a mystery. Ceter is not a Czech word and no one by that name could be found in any records I looked at. There was a family by the name of Cook who had long owned property in the general area, but not in the colony lands themselves.

The revision was drawn up in April of 1924, but it was not "filed" until May 3rd, 1925, and not "recorded" until May 10 1925. I could not ascertain the difference between "file" and "record," even after asking the parish clerk of court and the professional abstractors that I met during my research. Both maps show the Tioga and Southeastern Rail Road running down the middle of the Hollaway road. This railroad does not exist today; nor is there any sort of rail line in the vicinity. The revision also caused 31 of the neat rectangular lots to be made into irregular trapazoidal lots each with different dimensions.

Only a handful of lots were sold by the corporation so the town never got started and none of streets, except Industrial and Main were laid out. These last two still exist, but are just a few hundred feet long now. Only Industrial Street is paved; it dead ends in a parking lot for the Libuse Czech Hall, which is one of only 4 structures on the street. Main—which was at some point changed to "Maine"—is unpaved. Indeed, Maine Street is more of a driveway to several homes belonging to the extended Tuma family than an actual street.

In its first "sale" the corporation donated lots 8, 9, 10, 11 and 12 of Block 6 of the townsite to the Rapides Parish School Board. This donation was nearly a year after the corporation was formed. The donation was on June 6th, 1915. There is a record that the parish at least nominally accepted the land, but no parish school was ever built here. What was built here was the Czech operated Komensky School, which I will discuss later. The land never seems to have been owned by the parish at all but instead remained in the hands of the Czechs. All that the corporation did between September, 1914, and the 1915 donation is apparently wait for subscribers to the colony and purchasers of the land, neither of which materialized.

Other than the school board donation there are only six property records showing that the Libuse Townsite Company sold land and a seventh document shows a correction. Bohous O. Vonasek purchased two lots: lot 11 in block 18 and lot 18 in block 19. He paid $125 cash for each on August 25th, 1915, fully a year after incorporation. For $50 cash on November 11th, 1915, Martin Cizek bought lot 9 in block 18. This purchase was corrected to lot 9 block 15 on February 11th, 1916. No reason was given for the correction. Charles Pecinovsky paid $60 cash for lot 8 in block 18 on November 23rd, 1915. Four years later, on December 22nd, 1919, Joseph Melichar bought lot 12 in block 18 for $100 cash. That was the entire extent of sales and transactions in the Libuse Townsite until September 1st, 1923. On this date, a bachelor named Ernest Jilek bought what remained unsold, undonated and "less the land the hotel stood on"—basically the entire town, for $800 cash.

One last bit of historical oddity is that Walker, in her dissertation, says that the community founders had a plan to give a lot in the Libuse Townsite to the first born girl and boy in the community. If this was the plan it never came to pass. But I was not able to find any evidence that this was actually the plan. There is, at least, no mention of this in any property records. Once again, it seems as if the stories handed down by the early colonists were more apocryphal than real.

Libuse is named for the First Queen of the Czechs, a legendary woman from more than a 1000 years ago. While today the town name is pronounced "Lih-boose" (the last syllable rhyming with caboose,) the Czech name is actually Lib-uše—pronounced LIH-boo-shay. Many a Czech girl was named Libuse. As you drive east from Alexandria on Highway 28 you enter into downtown Pineville and the road is lined with the typical buildings of a Louisiana town. Most date from the early 1900s and later and they hug the sidewalk along the street. It is two lanes, one in each direction through downtown. Soon it opens up to a four lane modern highway, replete with a center turn lane, and the sidewalks disappear. The further east you go the more modern the buildings become until finally there are strip malls, gas stations and supermarkets—the structures of modern

America. The development is actually fairly dense, with no unused land. Finally you come to the Libuse townline marker put up by the state; one of those green signs with white lettering.

And then development just stops; the road immediately narrows to two lanes again. You are immediately in a rural community at the snap of the fingers. It is also immediately clear that the town of Libuse is just a few businesses and a scattering of houses. The two most prominent buildings are the Gunter Library branch of the Rapides Parish library system at one end and the post office at the other. There is much undeveloped land here and after the post office you enter the beginning of a long stretch of pine forests. The town, however, is clearly marked on maps of Louisiana. One claim to fame for Libuse is that it is the only town in the entire United States with this name.

The Creation of Kolin

The founding of Kolin is not nearly as confusing as that of Libuse. No incorporation papers of any kind could be found for Kolin so there are no land purchases or sales with its name. No entity was called Kolin except the proposed town itself. The plat map for the "City of Kolin" that was filed and recorded shows a similar grand plan like in Libuse. Only in this city a large public square was to be placed in the center. That they styled it a "city" shows the aspirations of its founders. The plat map is dated April 21st, 1915. It was recorded by Bringhurst on March 14th, 1916. It is recorded in Plat book 2, page 65. In a quaint mistake the name Louisiana is mispelled as "Loisiana" in the heading of the map. There is a second version of the plat map though no official recording information is on it. It is not dated nor is it in the plat map books of Rapides Parish. I only found it in Walker's book. Where she got it is unknown. The two plat maps differ slightly in the placement and size of some of the smaller lots and the larger "acreage" parcels that surround them.

The town is on maps of Louisiana but there really is no "town" here. Kolin was to be just off The Old Marksville Road, which was also known as the Centerpoint Road and is now Louisiana Highway 107. At the time it was little more than a dirt track through the wilderness. The plat map actually does not show the highway. This town, too, had quintessential American street names—Oak, Pine, Beech, Magnolia and Hickory streets ran east to west and the prosaic 1st, 2nd, 3rd, 4th and 5th streets ran north to south. Not one bit of this town was ever built. Instead, development occurred primarily along the Marksville Highway and the farm roads that splayed off of it. Before World War II there were a handful of businesses along the highway, but they are long gone. Highway 107 starts in Pineville, where it is lined with businesses and industrial operations. After a mile or so, it is rural land, until you come to Kolin itself. It is the main highway between Pineville and the next sizeable town: Marksville.

Kolin was named after an ancient city in Bohemia. Kolin in the Czech Republic is about 50 miles to the east of Prague. Eerily, Kolin today is actually about the same size, industrial composition and even shape of the city limits as Alexandria. Both the Czech and Louisiana Kolins are pronouced "KOH-leen." Why it was named Kolin is a mystery. Of all the historic and fantastic places that tourists to the Czech Republic aspire to go Kolin is not on the list. As an added filip to the possible story of its naming: maybe the Czechs were celebrating one of their biggest military victories against their oppressors. Frederic the Great, king of Prussia, had his biggest defeat at Kolin, Bohemia. But the Louisiana "town" is really just a thin scattering of businesses, the Ruby-Wise school and a few houses; perhaps about a mile and half long. It is entirely rural in character, with fields and woods and undeveloped land between the few structures. The only Czech related buildings remaining besides some Czech-descendant owned homes are the Kolin Hall and the Sts. Francis and Anne Catholic Church and they are on the side roads. There is also the Kolin Cemetery where many Czechs are buried. Oddly, most of the roads with Czech names in the entire colony area are in what is considered Kolin and not Libuse.

It is one of just two towns in the United States with this name. Nearly 1,900 miles away sits the tiny settlement of Kolin, Montana. Hard to imagine, it is actually smaller than its sister city in Louisiana. The Montana town is about 30 miles to the west of Lewiston as the crow flies, in Judith Basin County, but it takes a 40 mile road trip to get there. It sits at the end of some twisting, barely paved county roads, though there is an active railroad line running along its edge. This town has exactly three streets: Main, Railway and Hruska. This last name points to its origins. In an eerie coincidence, it was founded by Czechs just a few years before Louisiana's Kolin. Its post office operated for nearly the exact same years as the one in Louisiana, starting two years earlier and closing four years earlier. It had a rural school during the 1920s which also closed for lack of students. Only instead of being gobbled up by suburban growth like the Kolin here that town in Montana has dwindled to just about 100 residents, miles and miles from anywhere.

Pictures of the school and early settlers in Montana, posted to the Internet, could easily be substituted for early pictures of Louisiana's Kolin without anyone knowing the difference. A modern picture of the Montana town shows a place radically different from Louisiana. There are maybe 10 buildings, including a barn which is the largest, clustered on a windswept, seemingly barren and definitely treeless plain (that this picture was taken in the dead of winter doesn't help.) One of the front ranges of the Rocky Mountains rises some miles in the distance. The only thing I could not find out was if this town, too, was a project of the Bohemian Colonization Club. It is certainly in the right time frame and the founders of the club did explore this region of the country before they chose Louisiana, but other than this coincidence we cannot be sure.

The Louisiana Investment & Securities Company

Bringhurst also mapped out and filed, or at least approved, two other plat maps. It is not clear who drew the maps, evidence points to several hands. They are for large swaths of land. One was roughly rectangular, comprising approximately 10,640 acres and recorded May 1st, 1914. The other was irregularly shaped. It comprises approximately 10,080 acres and was recorded May 15th, 1914. The land was broken down into what are called sections of 640 acres. These are further subdivided into 40 acre lots. This was at the behest of the Louisiana Investment & Securities Company as is clearly indicated on the maps. The only problem was that Louisiana Investment apparently did not own these lands. At least there is no record of any such purchase.

The only recorded property purchased by this company is detailed in a document dated May 21st, 1914. It states that only 7,188 acres were actually purchased from the Alexandria Lumber Company. These acres are roughly centered in the area covered by the first plat map but do not conform completely to the borders seen. The purchase price was $43,073.28. They put down $1,500 and had seven payments due over five years to pay it off. The mortgage shows irregular payments: $1,000 on June 1st, 1914, $2,500 on July 1st, 1914 and $2,178.88 on August 1st, 1914. $7,178.99 was due on March 1st, 1915. The same amount due on March 1st, 1916. Following that were two equal payments of $10,768.38, due on March 1st of both 1917 and 1918.

Just more than a year later the Alexandria Lumber Company was forced to foreclose on the property. The document which makes the transfer back to the lumber company has a succinct reason: *"Whereas the Company [Louisiana Investment] has not complied with the condition of the said deal, and has become delinquent in the payments and cannot remove the encumbrance placed on the land by the mortgage."* Whether any payments at all were made is not known.

According to the state of Louisiana's records the company was incorporated on February 2nd, 1914. It was yet another of these companies that was not officially disbanded until 1985. It was headquartered in Baton Rouge and was not controlled by Czechs, but only sold to Czechs. How these men got involved is not known. Though its president, Donald Despain, was from Omaha, Nebraska, and may well have known Czechs there. The January, 1914, article in the Town Talk says he was "formerly comissioner of agricultural statistics" for Nebraska and that he "has had wide experiece in the handling of immigrants." According to the article "he has associated with him H. Lahroy Slusher, formerly of the Louisiana Delta Lands Company." His office was in the Hotel Bentley. The company supposedly had offices in Chicago, Omaha and New Orleans; no such offices could be found in the city directories for these cities.

Walker has a footnote in her dissertation claiming that when Despain "left the area many of the records and deeds also disappeared causing some to lose their land." Despain may have taken his copies of the records, but the originals were all officially recorded in the courthouse and there is no evidence that anyone ever lost their land due to his disappearance. Everyone who bought land had their corresponding record appropriately filed in the court house. Also, it can be assumed as certain that the purchasers kept their own copies. They may have been immigrants, but most were in the country for at least five years or more. They spoke reasonable English and either they, a family member or at least a friend had owned land in their home states; they knew what was required. Given the Czechs' love of, and desire for, land, they could be considered astute about property transactions. Further, it is highly unlikely that any who bought would simply have taken this lying down—surely they would have filed some sort of lawsuit seeking to claim the property they purchased with their hard-earned cash and no such lawsuits were ever recorded.

Another man involved with this company was Clarence Y. Smith of Chicago. Smith was the secretary-treasurer of the company and often signed the sales documents. How he came to be involved in this venture could not be determined. He is not Czech and he had no other known connections to either Louisiana or Nebraska. He also wound up owning at least six pieces of property in his own name, for there are at least that many property records of his *selling* land on file. I could not, however, find any corresponding *purchase* records. However, in one of the documents, for a sale he made to Joseph Ubl, it is noted that the 85 acres involved was acquired by Louisiana Investment on December 17th, 1913 and that Smith bought this from the company on February 18th, 1916. There are two mysteries here. One is that there is no recorded purchase by the company in

1913, only the one from 1914. Second, Alexandria Lumber had already fore-closed on Louisiana Investment in 1915—making it seemingly impossible for Louisiana Investment to sell land it no longer owned.

There is another record of the legal problems of Louisiana Investment. On May 1st, 1916, Lee Lumber Company filed and won a civil suit seizing 849 acres, divided among three parcels, that Louisiana Investment had owned. They bid $8,000. This was part of the land that Alexandria Lumber had foreclosed on and the payment was actually made from lumber company to lumber company. Why this transaction took place could not be determined. It would seem to make no sense since Louisiana Investment never bought from Lee Lumber Company and thus owed it no money to haggle over.

The Plat Maps and Colony B.

A look at the Libuse and Kolin plat maps show grand plans; neither city was cre-ated. Only Libuse was incorporated, but not as an actual town, just as a regular commerical company. Only four of the roads that are in the colony area today even approximately follow the routes laid out in these maps. There are two ver-sions of the Kolin map, but only one was ever filed in the courthouse. One has the filing notations and surveyor's signature required with such filing. The other is devoid of these markings. There are two versions of the Libuse Map. The sec-ond, filed 11 years after the first, surely shows that the dream was dying hard. Other than Industrial and Main Streets none of the streets that were on the maps of these two towns were ever laid out. The only two roads that exist from the Libuse maps are the Holloway Prairie Road and Philadelphia Road. Holloway Prairie was the only road existing in this area in 1914, for it was the main east-west road, such as it was, in this part of Louisiana. The Philadelphia Road was built later, and only appears on the revised map. It follows the high ground and it grew organically and not according to the plan of the town's founders. It was apparently only added to the revised map because it simply became a reality.

The two plat maps that show the lands that Louisiana Investment & Securities Company supposedly owned are the source of actual property descriptions, but the company never bought the entire 21,320 acres that are depicted. One of these plat maps is listed in the plat map index at the courthouse as the "Bohemian Col-ony." The other has no description other than the name of the company. The Bohemian Colony map contains 282 forty acre plots totalling 11,280 acres. The other map shows 251 forty acre plots totalling 10,040 acres. These two maps are almost certainly the source for the 21,000 or 22,000 acres that is talked about in the community. These maps, however, do not reflect the actual 7,188 acres purchased by the company. They show two huge unbroken swaths of land. The purchase agreement describes parcels that are either entire sections or fractional sections, but they are scattered across what are depicted on the two plat maps and not contiguous. A few of the purchased parcels are outside of the area depicted in the maps. These plat maps are, after analysis, wholly fiction. How they ever came to be filed is a mystery since there could not have been any supporting documentation that the company owned these lands. There was no plat map for Colony B that Albin Cecha founded; there is just a complex legal document with a detailed list of the lands purchased.

In any event, what Bringhurst thought of this rather astonishing idea expressed in the four original plat maps was not recorded. All the other plat maps that Bringhurst recorded in his many years as Parish Surveyor were merely for "suburban" additions to the existing cities of Alexandria and Pineville adding a few streets at a time; there were dozens of such additions. A man named W. J. Daigre was the parish surveyor at the time of the revised Libuse map. He had to know there was no town there. He must have been at least perplexed.

The important part played by the original plat maps of 1914 is that they are the maps on which all the subsequent property descriptions are based. Czechs did come to own much of the land depicted, but they bought from the lumber companies, the banks and from private people. There are, however, eight other maps of the colony area that are in the courthouse. Several are readily explainable; several are not.

In 1939 and again in 1964, Emil Tuma subdivided property he owned into smaller parcels. In April of 1939 he took three lots of the old Libuse Townsite which he had purchased in 1936 from the Ubl family and subdivided it into 15 smaller lots. While the five lots fronting the Holloway Prairie Road are easily accessible, the 10 lots behind them have no apparent access roads to them (in fact, the road shown on the map along the east side of these lots does not exist.) In May of 1964 he sliced off a small trapazoidal section of 40 acres he owned on the Holloway road and subdivided that into 5 small lots. The Tuma family tells me that each of the various children came to own these lots. They are not developed yet. But the map has the heading of "Louisiana Investment & Securities Company Lands" as its heading.

In November of 1968 Emmett Lahoda had a gracefully curving road mapped out through a thirty acre lot he owned. No lots are depicted, just the road. This map, too, has Louisiana Investment's name on it. However, not only was this road never built, Lahoda's story is interesting. He purchased this land in 1918 from Herman Sostak for $1,200 cash and kept it until he died in the late 1990s. Then, in an odd coincidence, I learned about the dispostion of this land from the man who bought it from Lahoda's son. John Wakeman is a property abstractor at the courthouse who I met while I was doing my research. He tried to buy this land for years from Lahoda, but Lahoda would not sell. Lahoda never lived in Louisiana, he lived in the Czech Colony at Malin, Oregon, from World War I until he died. He is the only person I could find who bought land in the two Czech colonies set up by the Bohemian Colonization Club. Wakeman courted Lahoda and met with him several times. Lahoda would actually come to Louisiana every few years to look at his land. He would spend a week or so in the area before returning to Oregon. After his death his son finally sold the land to Wakeman.

In 1969 Frank Reichl partitioned the land he bought in 1917 from Union Timber into several large lots. Once again Louisiana Investment's name is part of the plat map description. While he is not in the 1920 census, both he and his wife, Jennie, are in the 1930 census. They lived on this land for the rest of their lives. Frank Reichl died in 1974 and is buried in Libuse Cemetery.

It is the last four plat maps found that are confounding. On these four Louisiana Investment & Securities Company is listed on the maps as the owners of the land being subdivided. On the first, in 1960, the signatures are unreadable; just faded into oblivion. This land is now the Holiday Park subdivision in Pineville. On the second, dated July 6th, 1961, the signatures are very clear: Barbara Filipi and George Koncinsky. This map shows the Forest Park subdivision. As does a map dated November 21st, 1961, and an addition to Forest Park, but there are no signatures on it. The fourth is dated May 19th, 1964, also with no signatures, for an unnamed subdivision. By my definition, this is current history, so I did not do any further investigation, but it is strange to say the least since Louisiana Investment was basically a long defunct company which lost this land to foreclosure.

Promotion of the Colony

A look at some of the founders' hype and testimonials shows that they were not coy about their plans. Nor did they shy away from hyperbole. There is much circumstantial evidence that the founders continued to promote the colony with these glowing reports through Bohemian newspapers, especially the Hospodar. I present here rough English translations of these testimonials as they appeared in several advertisements; they were only published in the original Czech. I also give my take on the realities and truth behind these claims. At best, to be charitable, the founders were putting the best face on the prospects. A more cynical person would conclude that they were espousing blatant falsehoods.

"Come yourself presently, as long as you have time, to check over yourself our good soil and examine all the colonies. How one eats here shows and you will see what we are saying to you ."

The problem with this claim is that the lands are not "good." Louisiana is filled with very productive farm land, however, the area that the colony occupied was red clay and sand, highly acidic after centuries of pine forests and in general poor farm land. Had they settled on the south side of the Red River this claim would have been true, but the north side of the River is different geologically.

"This is best locality for keeping horses, cows, sheep and pigs, livestock. The best weather on earth for keeping poultry and beekeeping. Ideal weather for people all year. Two crops of corn and potatoes each year. All other crops here flourish excellently, to the nines."

The claim that this is "the best weather on earth" would surely be contested by many people, Louisianians included. Southern Californians would definitely dispute this claim. Anyone enjoying winter sports is, of course, wholly out of luck in Louisiana. The heat and humidity of a Louisiana summer—and this is really a 7 or 9 month period here not just the traditional June to August—is considered by few to be the "best…on earth." This claim does not take into account the violent thunderstorms that can destroy a crop in an afternoon. Nor the not infrequent periods when it might rain for literally weeks at a time, making fields impossible to work and drowning what is growing in them. Louisiana farmers, when not worrying about too much rain are concerned with long periods with no rain at all. As for two crops a year, this is also not true; the intense heat and blaring sun of the summer is inimical to the growth of new, baby plants. The biggest problem during the period of colonization was the total lack of weather forecasts—and thus the vagaries of the unpredictable weather played havoc with the farmers.

As for "all crops flourish here excellently," this is untrue as any one who has tried to grow tomatoes and other vegatables here knows—once again the searing sun, heat and humidity works against what are called truck crops. Besides that, the fruit trees that Czechs knew from Bohemia and northern states, such as peaches, plums, apples and similar fruits, do not grow well at all south of what is now Interstate 20. It is too hot and the soils either too wet or have too much clay. On the other hand, citrus and similar fruits do not grow north of New Orleans. Louisiana is known for some great foods—fruit orchards are not one of them.

"We have for sale also lots, then, 5, 10 and 12 acre parcels in town. Which gives the highest value for you, when you apply yourself as a chicken farmer or beekeeper. Here we are selling, too, cultured and uncultured farms from 60 to 640 acres."

The colony was built in raw wilderness; there were no "cultured" farms—everything had to be started from scratch. The phrase "uncultured farms" would seem to imply land pretty much ready for planting. Instead, the colonists had to clear thousands of pine stumps and the thick tangle of roots they left, not to mention the thickets of thistles, nettles, palmetto palms and scrub brush that seem to spring up virtually overnight. A plot left unattended for just a month becomes nearly impassable with weeds and trash plants.

"Mr. Karel Kazda recently sold his farm in Minnesota, from where he went to New York and other places, where he investigated many different farms. But never had he anything good to speak of, wherefore he came to Kolin and here he bought the first day. He lives for only dear Kolin; you will like Kolin when you visit."

Mr. Kazda bought 40 acres in November of 1914 for $1,250 cash. He sold these forty acres in August of 1915—barely 8 months later—and was never heard from again. He did make out on the deal though, he sold for $2,000—accepting $1,350 down and a payment one year later for the remaining $650.

"Mr. Wosterchil writes: O how it was like to wander the plantation and gather beautiful berries and mushrooms. There is nice green grass at the end of November. The scent of woods and the song of birds are all over the place. When here, a man recalls the tough weather which he must experience there in the north. So blessed that he finds at this time in the landscape, were life stands for living. Not to be those of mindless futures, and yet more mindful of the company in this local country, where here could be located many Czech families in a good home."

Mr. Wosterchil was surely the most poetic. Alas, most of those "beautiful berries" were probably inedible and some poisonous. The same went for the mushrooms, not to mention the hallucinagenic ones. While there is no snow, a winter rain in Louisiana can be just as bone chilling. And, again, that heat, humidity and searing sun the rest of the year. The "scent of woods," is perhaps alluring, if you were able to clear the underbrush to get through them. Maybe there "could be located" many families—but at least in the first five years they were moving in and out at a rapid pace. The majority of people who came did not stay. The first "homes" were little more than shacks. Poetics aside, it was a difficult time in a difficult place; at least the Westerchil family stayed—though they got out of farming quickly.

"Mr. Brozik writes: I came for one future in the best colony in America, few have left or didn't buy."

Mr. Brozik engages in hyperbole at the very least: the colony is actually one of the smallest Czech communities in America and most early settlers did indeed leave; and quickly. How many came to examine the colony and did not buy can only be guessed at.

John D. Hasik placed his own ads in the Hospodar. The translation is this:

"Why was our Czech Colony chosen to be founded near Alexandria in Louisiana? Because on our land investigating journey we found near Alexandria the best land, the best economy, living, schools and the best climate. The colony will be situated on a tract of land that by survery measures to be 11,000 acres. On April 7th [either 1913 or 1914, no year is actually given] land will be sold for $10 to $18 an acre. The real estate agents will be in Alexandria on April 7th. For further information contact the organizer: J. D. Hasik."

There was no single tract of 11,000 acres—certainly Hasik never bought this amount. As noted previously, the biggest tracts were the nearly 7,200 owned by Louisiana Investment and the 4,000 of Albin Cecha. While this did total nearly 11,000 acres, Cecha was a lone operator. Nor was his land ever "surveyed," it was simply described parcel by parcel in the purchase agreement. Indeed, surveys are specifically dispensed with and waived in many of the purchase contracts. The land that was alleged to be owned by Louisiana Investment for the Kolin colony was never purchased by them. I have already looked at the claims about the "best land" and the "best climate."

As for the "best economy," this was perhaps somewhat true in the sense that Alexandria profited greatly from the timber boom, but this was dying out as an industry—the pine forests had been stripped bare. Alexandria's economy was beginning to stagnate by 1915. The final claim by Hasik to be the "organizer" is wholly misleading—he organized nothing but a real estate commission business.

Another promotional piece was published by J. Emmanuel Kroupa; it is undated:

The Town of Libuse in the Czech Colony will be measuring out before you know it. It will be the first Czech town and large Czech colony in the state of Louisiana. The colony has already been organzied. 10,000 acres are broken up into forty, sixty and eighty acre lots and some even into one hundred sixty. Let us now part to the richly, thickly planted land populated with our kinsman. Several families and single men are already settled there and working on their land. A hotel, restaurant, and several stores have been started. With a large settlement there truly will be the need for other various stores. Here is a healthy environment, high ground, good permanent water, two crops per year, natural beauty, and excellent climate throughout the whole year. Anyone who wishes additional information concerning the plans of the town, building a store or home, and so forth, will receive this information free of charge by writing to J. Em. Kroupa. 4113 South 9th Street. P.O. Station C, Omaha, Nebraska.

Yet another figure given for the amount of land; and not true. This is more of the same hyperbole about the "best" land, natural surroundings and two crops a year. As for "good permanent water," this was only true if you dug a deep enough well at great expense. No one could drink or otherwise use the water in the few bayous and creeks that course through the area. "Healthy environment"?—only if you do not count the mosquitos and myriad of bugs (at least there were no fire ants yet.) This ad is probably from 1914 or 1915, and the hotel, restaurant and businesses were indeed started—before they were dismantled and moved from the "downtown" of the town that never was "thickly, richly planted land populated with our kinsman." No large settlement ever existed and there never was a "need for various other stores."

The only thing really true about this ad is that it was certainly the "first Czech town in Louisiana." And in contrast to Hasik's claim, Kroupa could actually claim to be one of the organizers of the community since he was one of of the stockholders of both the Libuse Townsite Company and the First Bohemian Village of America.

Now we come to Mr. Krejzl, who is quoted saying *"chief [land] forms in the neighborhood of Kolin demonstrates the potential that there will be found gas or oil. That is why it foretells that not so far away in the future we will be pumping petroleum in Kolin."*

Not only was oil and gas never pumped out of lands in the Czech colony, this is actually one of the few regions in Louisiana where oil and gas is not found at all. Once again, it was on the wrong side of Red River. The colony actually sits on a sort of clay highland between the rich alluvial soils of the Mississippi River bottoms and the fertile farmlands south of the Red River—which is where the oil and gas are found. Where he got the idea that oil and gas were in the vicinity is a mystery. Oil had just been discovered in Southeast Texas and Southwest Louisiana and there was probably exploration of some sort elsewhere in the state, but this area was not a high priority. But where would a Czech immigrant get this information? While Krejzl was wrong about petroleum, his record in the community is complicated. While unrelated to the promotion I present his situation here.

The last record of him is in a document dated August 2nd, 1919. Here it is said that he was married to Fanny Mitcherling and that they resided in Cedar Rapids, Iowa. That is when he bought the 40 acres, defined as lot 3, section 7, for $555.05—payable in 3 payments, the first of $215.18, followed by two annual

payments of $107.59. However, now it really gets confusing, because in two pre-
vious property purchases Krejzl is said to be married to Julia Vagner and they
resided in Marshall, Texas. Now, it is possible that he was widowed or divorced
from Julia and remarried to Fanny, but all such similar situations were noted in
other property records. That is, a wife was recorded as "second wife," or a document says, "once widowed and now remarried," or some such similar language:
no such notation is made for Krejzl.

Of those two previous transactions the story is even stranger and involves
more people. There are six separate property records concerning lots 7 and 8 in
section 41, totaling 80 acres. This exact same land was purchased by Krejzl (and
Julia) and two other men, both bachelors, from three different corporate sellers,
all in rapid succession. In fact, this land was purchased twice in 1914, once in
1916 and seemingly three times in 1917. No documents could be found where
the men sold the land to either the companies or to each other and no documents
could be found were the companies bought the land from each other or the men.
No documents relating to any forclosures could be found, or any other type of
transfer, nor any corrections. I looked multiple times through the indices and the
documents—there are just the six property records here:

Sobeslav Cerny, a bachelor of Guerniville, California, bought the 40 acres of
lot 7 from Louisiana Investment in September, 1914 for $462.30 cash. Two
months later, in November, John Krejzl and his wife "Julia," bought this exact
same lot 7 and lot 8 from the exact same company for $1,440. They put down
$360 and had a 3 year mortgage for annual payments of $270. Two years later, in
October, 1916, the same Sobeslav Cerny bought the same land—only this time
from the Lee Lumber Company—and for only $200—for which he arranged a
two year mortgage after putting down $150. Then in May of 1917 a bachelor
named George "Petresek" (sic, really Petrasek,) whose residence was listed as
Kolin, bought this same land from the Alexandria Lumber Company for $1,200
payable in two equal payments of $600. But in another document dated five
months later, in October of 1917, George Petrasek (correct spelling in this document,) is said to have paid Alexandria Lumber $1,200 cash for this parcel. Yet,
one month later, in November, 1917, John and Julia Krejzl are documented as
buying this land again—from Alexandria Lumber! They paid $1,440 cash
according to this document.

Cerny is not in either of the censuses; he simply disappears. The Krejzl's are in
the 1930 census, but not the 1920, only his wife is listed as "Josephine," not
Julia, and she is said to be born in Ohio, but Krejzl descendants still live in the
area. Of George Petrasek we know that he married a Czech gal named Minnie

Stegner in April of 1919. The 1920 census says he and his new wife lived on their own farm, (the census says he owned it free of a mortgage.) Presumably it is this land, especially since we know that his father, Frank Petrasek, owned the 160 acres in lots 3, 4, 5 & 6 of section 41—i.e. the farm next door. But that leaves us with two conundrums. One is why there would be two nearly identical documents for the same land just five months apart in 1917. The second document does not say that he paid off the mortgage early. It states that he bought the land for $1,200 cash in October and it does not mention either the $600 he is recorded as having put down in May or that this is a satisfaction of the outstanding $600. The second, is, of course, the Krejzl purchase in November—just a month after the documented Petrasek purchase in October. We can imagine that one or two documents were in error as to their dates or land descriptions, even names—but five or six? That is hard to imagine. However, Petrasek and Krejzl are clearly identified as owning the same land and Petrasek lived on it in 1920 and Krejzl lived on it in 1930—how this was resolved cannot be determined.

While we can perhaps forgive the claims presented in the ads here as hopes and dreams not realized and as part of any good real estate promotion effor, we should also recognize that the colonists who did buy into the scheme were definitely misled—or very gullible.

The First Year

The Alexandria Daily Town Talk documented the arrival of the Bohemians on January 12, 1914. The most interesting sentence in the article is this: *"The idea is an innovation in Louisiana, being the first time that a colony of Europeans have asscociated themselves together for the establishment of a community on a business basis."* It was indeed a first—and a last—for Louisiana. And that does make Libuse and Kolin wholly different than any other towns in the state.

The article also says that at this point *"there are forty families on the tract trying it out, and about another 12 arrived last week, because of the excellent report of the other forty."* However, the first recorded land sale was on March, 14th, 1914. Albin Cecha was the first. Within a few short months more than 50 families did purchased property. However, all of these were before the actual incorporation of the towns and filing of the plat maps. If any of those who arrived in December 1913 and January 1914 stayed around it can not be said for sure and the community historians have no information on this.

It was also said that "a practical agriculturalist will live in the colony and instruct the farmers along the lines where they may need instruction." No such person is recorded as having been in the community, though some experts visited briefly. Conditions found were primitive and far more difficult than advertised. The cut over lands proved diffiuclt to work, first needing the clearing of thousands of stumps, which they did by hand. But they did start a community from scratch.

They built two hotels to house the men when they first get started. A few photos of the Kolin hotel survive. The only early photo of the Libuse hotel building shows a square one story structure with a wide gallery surrounding it on four sides. The black cooks and servants in the background of one of the photos indicates that Czechs were probably exposed to local cooking methods and foods. And that just possibly some African-Americans might have learned a Czech dish or two.

Because the Czechs arrived in raw wilderness there was a pressing need to build homes and other structures quickly. No detailed records or stories survive of these efforts and none of the earliest structures survive, though there are a few photos (see photo section.) What we know of these efforts come from the memories of settlers passed down to the descendants. But we can glean the basic process. The first thing they did was build a one or two room shack; usually windowless. Definitely any openings were covered just by wooden shutters. Glass windows, though, were added as soon as they could be bought.

Family patriarchs could rely on the labor of older sons; bachelors were on their own. So, as is typical of so many rural communities, there were communal building efforts as each family moved in. After the shack they built barns, cleared land, planted the first crops, fenced in pens and yards and only after that was done did they finally build a real house. The whole process took at least two to three years, if not more. They cut the lumber by hand if they could not afford to buy it precut.

The first stores were on Industrial Street and, again, they were built with the help of neighbors—who were at first really just strangers that they met. But they knew they were in this together so they helped each other. When the colonists realized that the town was not going to happen they dismantled their buildings on Industrial Street and moved them to the Holloway Prairie Road to take advantage of the "heavier" traffic. This traffic consisted of the few people who passed by on their way between Alexandria and Ferriday on the Mississippi River.

The colonists helped build the Holloway Prairie road into more than the dirt track it was when they first arrived. They worked on the Old Marksville Road, too. While with each passing year the roads were improved, it was not until the late 1920s that gravel was laid down. Neither was paved until the 1940s; they have, of course, been steadily upgraded as time marched on.

Five Companies Who Sold Land to Czechs

The Alexandria Lumber Company became active in selling the land that they seized from Louisiana Investment. This occurred mostly 1916 through 1926; only three sales are recorded after this, two in 1929 and one in 1930. From the Vendor index in the courthouse it appears that this company was selling almost entirely to Czechs. Of the approximately 120 land sales by this company 106 were to Czechs. They were selling "cut over lands" and reserving rights to strip the remaining timber and run their railroads and logging roads over the land they sold. They had several railroads through the area that was to become the Czech Colony. None were regular railroads, but rather were temporary, and purely for moving lumber from the forests to the mills. One was laid down in 1907. It was a standard guage line 6 miles long. In 1910 there was another standard line 8 miles long. An American Lumber 1912 report lists a standard guage line 15 miles and finally there was a line built in 1913 that was 5 miles long. All of these were on the 1913 Louisiana Rail Road Commission Map. None of these rail lines exist today; they were torn up when their use came to an end. This company was incorporated on April 25th, 1907; it was dissolved on June 2nd, 1928. No evidence was found that this company had more than the 7,188 acres it sold and reclaimed from Louisiana Investment.

Union Land and Timber sold 35 pieces of property to Czechs. The company was legally headquarted in South Dakota, yet legally domiciled in Mobile, Alabama, while claiming its principal place of business was Orleans Parish (New Orleans.) In neither of these three locations was I able to find any references to it. When it ceased business could not be determined.

Lee Lumber company sold 37 pieces of property to Czechs, including 4,000 acres to Albin Cecha. The rest of the sales were for much smaller parcels. It was domiciled in Alexandria and incorporated on May 20th, 1905. It is still an active company, now headquartered in Birmingham, Alabama, but with offices in Alexandria. At the time of the founding of the colony its president was Mr. S. R. Lee and its secretary was Mr. A. Albert. Their first names are not given in any documents. The president today is W. Pat Aertker, Jr. Whether he was related to the William Aertker who purchased land in the colony area at the beginning of the community could not be determined, though it seems likely.

The Guaranty Bank and City Savings Bank & Trust Company were less active in selling lands to Czechs in 1918 and 1919, mostly in the areas adjacent to the orginial colony or in Alexandria itself. There were 14 by Guaranty and 16 by City Savings bank. Guaranty eventually bought City Savings and that successor company was bought out sometime during the Depression by another bank.

No detailed records for any of these five companies could be found; it is likely that any corporate records were long ago discarded.

The Main Czech Real Estate Players

The facts and histories pertaining to the main founders and real estate players of Libuse and Kolin are the most confusing of all the stories to be told here. Around these men swirl most of the anecdotal and apocryphal stories repeated by the descendants of the colonists. How they got involved and what exact part they played is shrouded in mystery. The transactions they were involved with were convoluted, conflicting, strange and, at times, simply implausible. Little of what is said about them seems to be true. Less of what we know they themselves claimed to be their purpose and actions is true. The companies they started, or were connected to, did not do anything close to what they proposed to do. They were real men, but they are ultimately ciphers, even legends. The only thing we can know for certain is that without them there would be no Bohemian Colony and no Libuse or Kolin.

Albin Cecha

The first date that Albin Cecha is recorded buying land is on March 14, 1914. This is three months after the Hlavaty purchase. This makes him the second Czech person to buy land in Rapides Parish. It is also 11 days before Louisiana Investment's first resolution. He bought 120 acres from Stephan Sasser for $2,000, or $16.68 an acre. He put $300 down and agreed to pay the remaining $1,700 within one year. He owned this land for more than 30 years.

Cecha purchased "in aggregate" 4,000 acres from the Lee Lumber Company on June 1st, 1914, establishing what he called "Colony B." It was immediately adjacent to the Louisiana Investment/Alexandria Lumber lands, and straddled the Rapides—Avoyelles parish line. No plat map was filed. The purchase agreement is five pages long. It has an accompanying 2 page "resolution" by the board of directors of the Lee Lumber Company attached as an appendix to the actual purchase agreement. This resolution, "on motion of S. H. Fullerton, seconded by W. C. Beall," authorizes the company to sell the land described "for cash or upon terms of credit" to the purchaser. Twice the resolution says the price is "Five Dollars" an acre; both times the sum is capitalized. The first time it is written as "the purchase price for said property shall not be less than the sum of Five Dollars per acre" and the second time it is stated "that the purchase price of said land in *no event* shall be less than Five Dollars per acre." (emphasis added.)

The legal descriptions of each of the 13 parcels refered to in the document are riddled with "exceptions." These are set down in phrases like "fractional sections," "being the fifteen acres remaining in said forty acres after deducting the twenty-five acres owned by Riggby Thomas," "excepting however six acres therein, now being used for cemetery and lodge house," and "to be taken out of the whole width of the Southern part thereof." Only one of the 13 parcels is said to be an even amount—the 320 acres consisting of the south half of Section 12, a section being 640 acres. All the rest of the parcels are odd amounts, like "317.45," "245.08" and "148.71" acres.

Further exceptions were defined as "permanent right of way in favor of Tioga and Southeastern Railway Company...as now laid and constructed." There was also "a right of way for a period of three years, in favor of" of the railway to be "constructed at any time or times, running as a spur track" through several of the sections. Also excluded were "all pine timber on Sections Nineteen and Twenty in favor" of Lee Lumber, "with the accompanying right for said timber to remain and grow upon said land for a period of three years." Another provision allowed Lee Lumber "to enter upon said sections...with tram-road or railroad, and with teams, wagons, logging machinery, cutters, sawyers, teamsters" of Lee Lumber "to cut, fell and remove said pine timber." Yet another exception, set forth in a separate paragraph, says "also the improvements upon said land belonging to E. A. Slocum in Section Twenty-nine," and "excepting also the the railroad...its water works, pipe lines, and other accessories."

The total price was clear: $20,000. So, the price per acre would seem, as stated in the resolution, to be simply $5 an acre. However, there was really a complex downward sliding scale for the price per acre; the actual language of this agreement is difficult, if not impossible, to understand. Cecha paid $5,000 "cash in hand," and had 3 annual payments of $5,000, with this odd proviso: *"and as representing said deferred payments the vendee [Cecha] has this day signed and executed his three certain promisory notes, each for the sum of $5,000, bearing even date herewith, payable to the order of himself [Cecha] and by him endorsed in blank, bearing six per cent per annum interest from date until paid, interest payable annually."* Not exactly a mortgage as we understand it today and the only such language found in any record examined.

Even more confusing is that Cecha and Lee further "agreed" that Cecha could pay off portions of the note on a per acre basis before the notes were due. If the first note, "or any portion covering more than 40 acres," was paid before it was due, but "whilst all three of said notes given by" Cecha "are outstanding and unpaid," then the price would be $4.25 an acre. If the second note was paid before it was due, "whilst the two last maturing notes are outstanding and unpaid" then the price would be $3 an acre. If the third note was paid before its due date then the price would be just $1.75 an acre. Then there is this additional barage of legalese: *"and that the payments so made shall be credited upon the notes herein executed by the mortgagor" (i.e. Cecha,) "in the reverse order of their respective maturities, that is to say, by crediting all payments so made upon the note maturing four years after date, and after satisfaction, in case it is so satisfied, upon the note maturing three years after date, and in case of its satisfaction, in case it is so satisfied, then upon the note maturing two years after date."* It looks like English, certainly, but does it make any sense? I asked several of the abstractors and courthouse lawyers I encountered while researching in Alexandria what this meant—and none could make heads or tails or it. In any case, these terms, however understood by Lee and Cecha, do not comply with the resolution's "in no event shall be less than Five Dollars per acre."

Cecha managed to sell 1,363.43 acres of his Colony B between 1915 and 1918 for a total of $14,604.99. This he did in six sales: 4 for cash and two for payments. One sale, to John Trejbal in March, 1915, was for 639.98 acres (just 2/100s of an acre less than an entire 640 acre section) was for $6,911.79 in cash. This one sale represents a little under half the total acreage sold and nearly ½ the total he earned in this period. This is the period which his agreement with Lee Lumber gave him to pay off the purhcase. It is also slightly less than the $15,000 he needed. It seems clear that he paid off his notes to Lee for two reasons—one is that he was ultimately able to sell nearly all this land. The second is that there is no record of any foreclosure by Lee. However, no record of the dates he paid the notes or the amount of each payment or price per acre could be found. So exactly what he wound up paying per acre is impossible to determine, but was definitely never as low as fifty cents.

In total, between 1915 and 1936, Cecha sold 17 properties totaling approximately 3,290 acres. The total dollar value of all these sales was a little over $37,000. The selling price per acre ranged from a low of $10.51 to a high of $16.25; the average was right about $12. He also transferred a nearly 670 acre parcel in August of 1927 to his son Albin H. Cecha, though this document does not say whether it was a sale or gift, or something else.

There were several other transactions attributed to Cecha. In 1921 he sold his 1/3 interest in his lots in the Libuse Townsite to Joseph Ubl for $600 cash. He bought 5 other pieces of property totalling at least 170 acres, for one record the acreage is not stated. The last purchase was in 1930. There was one interesting set of transactions between Cecha and Alexandria Lumber. On February 24th, 1920, Cecha sold 82.04 acres to the company for $558.60 cash. This document states that he bought this exact land on May 12th, 1914 from the company, but we do not know the price. No record of this purchase could be found in either the Vendee or Vendor indices. Perhaps this was a clerical error? This is not known.

Finally, he definitely made a profit and had land left over. Strangely, even though he was buying and selling land, Cecha is not in the 1920 census; he is, though in the 1930 census. He lived alone; his son who bought land is not in the censuses. In fact, his son is listed as living in Douglas County, Nebraska. According to an obituary in Hospodar; Albin Cecha died November 15th, 1956, in Omaha Nebraska.

Joseph A. Ubl

There are 21 transactions related to purchases by Joseph A. Ubl between 1915 and 1930. 18 were for property. One was a timber lease, one was a correction of a deed and the final one was for a power of attorney he signed with George Kroupa. The purchases ranged from farm acreage (most of them) to multiple lots in the Libuse Townsite (including one on Cecha Street) to lots in the city of Alexandria. 14 of his purchases were for cash; several were joint purchases with other people. The first purchase he made was a parcel of 82 acres from Louisiana Investment in 1915; this was his only purchase from the company. He also bought 20 acres from Guaranty Bank. The rest of his purchases were from individual sellers, including a 3 acre parcel from the St. James Episcopal Church in the Cook and Alexander subdivision. In 1928 he bought one lot in the S.A. Guy subdivision. The rest were in Libuse or Kolin.

He made 24 sales. From the multiple lots he bought in Libuse Townsite he sold off 14 individual lots. Of all his sales, the first was recorded in 1918 and the last was in 1936. 9 were spread out through the 1920s; 8 were in the single year 1930. On June 13th, 1930 he sold five separate parcels of land to members of his family; they each paid him $600 in cash for their own 40 acres. This was not a subdivision of one large parcel, but rather various parcels that he purchased at different times. He had never purchased more than 80 acres at a time.

The Ubl family could not be found in the 1920 census, but Joseph is recorded in the 1930 census living alone. Yet they must have lived in the community for a while because in a written family history of the Anton Baroch family it is recounted that Anton's daughter, Marie, was "best friends" with Irma Ubl, Joseph's daughter. There are also stories that he was involved in running the first community meetings and helping found the schools. The end of his life has two stories. From a few sources in the community we hear that he hung himself in either 1936 or 1938. Yet, no obituary could be found in the Town Talk. On the other hand we have an obituary from Hospodar that seems to say he died of old age at Chicago, Illinois on the 15th of November, 1937.

John Hasik

John Hasik was one of the real estate brokers in the early community. He was in business with Edward Balej (and perhaps also Frank Balej.) They had two offices: one was in the New Jackson Hotel in downtown Alexandria, the other was in Abie, Nebraska. They placed ads in Hospodar to sell land. It seems they earned a commission, but the records are mostly silent or at best vague in the few references to this fact. How many real estate deals they facilitated can not be determined. Hasik himself never bought much land. He did, however, purchase a total of 397 acres in five separate purchases. 3 were from Louisiana Investment, two in 1914 and one in 1915, and two were from Alexandria Lumber, one in 1916 and one in 1917. In a circumstance that can not be reconciled with the records he sold 459 acres. The only conclusion I could come up with is that he purchased one (or more) parcels jointly with someone else. We do know that he bought the Kolin Townsite with Frank Balej on January 29th, 1915 for $720 cash. This land was the subject of a tortuous series of land sales as we will see in a moment.

Hasik was involved in another odd, convoluted and ultimately inexplicable situation. On April, 30th, 1917, he sold the 40 acres in lot 9 of section 30 to Alexandria Lumber—the price was $1 (one dollar.) He orginally had sold this 40 acres of land to Frank Bohata for $300 cash on June 26th, 1915; yet there is no record of Hasik buying this land from anyone nor getting it back from Bohata. On May 17th, 1917 Bohata bought back a small fraction, just 5 acres, of this same lot and section from the Alexandria Lumber for $60 cash. Further, on November 29th, 1927, Bohata bought this entire 40 acres of land again for $200 cash (the property description clearly includes, but does not mention specifically, the 5 acres he had already repurchased.) From whom he repurchased this land is not clear—it is one of the few documents that does not state a seller. However, in 1936 Bohata was able to sell this exact entire 40 acre parcel of land to his son, Rudolph, for $600. I discovered just these five separate documents that pertain to this situation; all were the standard transaction documents without any embellishments or explanations. This entire situation is a conundrum—I simply can not figure out the true nature of these transactions.

The Hasik family is not in either the 1920 or 1930 censuses. There is no record or anecdote that he ever lived in Louisiana; he stayed in Nebraska. He surely visted the colony, perhaps often, though that is not known for sure. John D. Hasik did, however, serve in the Nebraska legislature from 1911 through 1913 and again in 1918. He was a Republican from the town of Abie in Butler County, Nebraska (which just happens to be the site of the oldest established Czech church and parish in that state.) He also is listed in the 1926 "Blue Book," a registry of government officials in Nebraska. He died July 5th, 1948 at the age of 75 in David City, Nebraska.

The Balej (Baley; Bailey) family

The Balej family is the only one of the founding families to be found in both the 1920 and 1930 censuses. While the name was originally Balej, it was anglicized in the 1920 census to Baley, and then to Bailey in the 1930 census. In the Czech language ads it was still the Czech Balej. But the situation with this family is not completely explainable: their ages when they bought land and some of land descriptions simply do not make sense. Another confusing aspect is that Edward is usually considered the man who was involved in the founding of the colony, particularly Kolin, but it was his brother Frank who seems to have formed a partnership with John Hasik to sell lands. They apparently acted as commission real estate agents for both Louisiana Investment and Alexandria Lumber. The only land they ever bought together was the entire Kolin Townsite. They placed advertisements for their services in Hospodar. They even called themselves "Managers [of the] Kolin Colony." Frank must have been an extremely ambitious young man because he was not even out of his twenties when this all started.

It is not known if Edward was married. There are no records of a wife, but he was born in Bohemia. His father John and his wife, Anna, and their eldest son, Albert, were all born in Bohemia. Anna was 13 years younger than her husband. Once in America they had what could be considered a "second," and even "third," family of five more children: Betty, Frank, Lily, John Jr. and Emma. The first four were born in Pennsylvania, they ranged in age from 24 to 17 according to the 1920 census. The youngest, Emma, was born in Ohio; she was 10 in 1920. Albert was 15 years older than his next oldest sibling, Betty, and 17 years older than his brother Frank. Betty was 14 years older than Emma, making her 29 years younger than Albert. That is an enormous age range by any standard. Finally, one of Albert's children was a son named Charles, who was 5 years old in

1920. All of the ages are very clear in the censuses; the ages in 1920 conform to the ages listed in 1930.

Edward, John, Frank, Albert and Charles are all clearly identified in property records. The five of them, individually, purchased 17 pieces of property between 1914 and 1937; the majority were in the first five years of the colony. Frank is the first recorded buying land. He bought three parcels from Louisiana Investment totalling 240 acres. The first was in 1914. Two purchases were made in 1915. Following that he purchased two parcels from Alexandria Lumber. One was of 160 acres in 1916, the other was of 40 acres in 1922. The first odd thing is that in the 1920 census Frank was said to be 22 years old (and no older Frank is listed.) Again, his age is written very clearly in the census record. That means he was merely 16 in 1914 when his first purchase is recorded. It was not properly legal for a minor to buy land and yet, the document does not mention any adult. So how he accomplished this feat is not clear. And he was just 18 years old in 1916 at his second purchase; again, still a minor. In all, though, he bought 9 pieces of land, the last in 1937. 4 he purchased for cash, 4 he had mortgages on. The 1937 purchase was at a tax sale.

Edward also bought three pieces of land from Alexandria Lumber: a 160 acre parcel in 1916 for $750 cash; a 10 acre parcel in October, 1918 for $80 cash; and another 30 acres for $420 cash in December of 1918. His father John bought one piece of property: 30 acres for $420 cash in 1918. John's son, Albert, purchased two parcels. He bought a 40 acre parcel from Alexandria Lumber for $400 cash. And was involved with buying and selling the Kolin townsite, about which more in a minute. But first, in 1922, Albert's son, Charles, is clearly stated as the purchaser of 40 acres for $600 cash—the problem is that he would have been only 7 (seven) years old!

Now we get to strange situation with the planned townsite of Kolin. The Balej/Baley family is bound up in the land that was supposed to be the site of this town. Of this one parcel, the 40 acres in lot 16, section 30, also known as the Kolin townsite, there is a confusing chain of sales and purchases. The oddest thing with Edward Baley is that twice he bought the Kolin townsite.

But the land sales involved with Lot 16, Section 30, are strange to say the least. As previously noted, on January 29th, 1915, Frank Balej and John D. Hasik jointly purchased this land from Louisiana Investment for $720 cash. Frank, at 17, was still a minor. Edward's first land purchase was recorded on January 31st, 1916, when he bought a half interest in this lot, that is, the Kolin townsite, from Frank—for exactly one dollar. The land was not divided into 20 acre parcels, rather it was strictly an "undivided" half interest in the entire parcel.

There is no record that Hasik ever "sold" his half interest, not to either Frank or Edward nor to anyone else. It had to be extracted out of him by a lawsuit later.

There is a record that Hasik sold one small lot: 50 feet wide on the non-existent Beech Street and running back 116 feet to the proposed alley—this, too, was for exactly one dollar. The sale was made to one Joseph Koubik on March 6th, 1916. Neither Edward or Frank Balej are mentioned in this document, though presumably they should have been because one or both owned at least a ½ interest in the land. Koubik was from Suanders, Nebraska. This is the only document in which there is mention of him anywhere in the records. He is not in the censuses nor in the Vendors index—what became of him or the ownership of the lot he bought is unknown. But his lot was squarely in the middle of "town."

On July 2nd, 1917 Albert bought the lot from his brother Edward. The price was $100 paid in cash. This document does not mention Hasik, who presumably still owned a half interest in it. Nor is any mention made of the Koubik lot. About two weeks later, on July 18th, Albert sold this land to Joseph Stegner for $100 cash. Here Stegner is listed as a "single man." Which brings us to another interesting problem—there are two Joseph Stegners in the 1920 census, the 54 year old father and the 26 year old son. In the census, it is father Joseph and son Joseph A.—but in all the property records it is only Joseph, so it is hard to figure out which Joseph Stegner bought what. Since the Stegner in this property record is single, we can assume he was the son. Not only are Stegner and his family in both the 1920 and 1930 censuses, they lived out their lives in Kolin. In fact, the senior Stegner married a woman named Katherine Baley—probably Edward's sister. The marriage also probably took place in Pennsylvania where the younger Joseph was born—and where the Baley's resided previously. In the census report they are all listed as living next to each other.

Just barely a year later, on June 4th, 1918, Stegner sold this land back to Edward Baley, this time for $150 cash. This document does mention the Koubik lot, as well as a lot belonging to Francis J. Welcek. However, in a document filed on June 6th, 1918, Stegner (the younger, since it says he is single.) is the winner in a lawsuit awarding him sole ownership of the Kolin townsite, "less the public square and lots 5 & 6 of block 9, and lots 1 & 2 of block 14." The suit was against the "Bohemian Colonization Society," as it is written in the record. The officers of the society as listed in the papers are John Hasik, John Rosicky and Edward. J. Baley—but only Hasik is listed as the person transferring the property to comply with the judge's order. Since the adjudication date was in June the suit was certainly filed some months previously. It is in this document that we find "it is further understood that Baley will participate in the commissions due and collected from time to time." Which is one of the few references to a commission paid for selling real estate.

Finally resolving this whole confusing mess, on March 22nd, 1919, a widow named Marie Kment bought this same land from the succession of Edward Baley for $600 cash. According to the 1920 and 1930 censuses she lived with her three adult children on their farm (and they apparently inherited it from their mother)—the very land that was supposed to be Kolin.

Edward Baley was committed to the insane asylum at Pineville, Louisiana, where he died on October, 22nd, 1918, at the age of 40. Some people in the community say that Edward was Frank and/or Albert's father—but this is impossible. Albert was 39 in 1920 and thus 37 in 1918—and Edward could not have fathered him when he was just a 3 year old toddler. The census also is clear that Frank was John's son. According to most stories Edward went crazy from the pressures he faced with the reality that the colony was not going to be as successful as he hoped. This seems apocryphal at best, after all, other than buying the Kolin townsite he was not that involved in the creation of the community. Frank Baley died at the age of 80 in 1976 in Kolin; his obituary was in the Town Talk.

John Emmanuel Kroupa

John Emmanuel Kroupa is refered to as "J. Em. Kroupa" in some documents in which he is mentioned. Particularly as one of the original incorporators of both the Libuse Townsite Company and the First Bohemian Village. Yet, in two other property documents with his name he is either "J. Emmett," or just plain "John." In 1912 or 1913 or so he became assistant editor of Hospodar, a position kept at least until 1915 or 1916. Rose Rosicky, the daughter of John Rosicky, wrote a history of the Czechs in Nebraska which includes a glowing account of her father (understandably.) But she barely gave two paragraphs to Kroupa, noting only that he translated several English educational farming documents into Czech. He is not in either the 1920 or 1930 censuses in Louisiana. There is no evidence that he ever lived in Libuse or Kolin. There are just three property records related to him. He made just one purchase of land. On April 30th, 1914, he bought 80 acres for $1,196.23 from Louisiana Investment. The property description defines the land as the entire Libuse Townsite—less the property the hotel stood on.

He made just two sales. In 1921 Frank Hromadka bought a 1/3 undivided interest in lot 10, block 18 of the townsite for $25 cash. In 1922 he sold 3 lots for $80 cash to Frank Bejsovec. There are more than 40 sales involving lots in the townsite; none of the actual documents mention Kroupa. It was all sold by different individuals or the company. Indeed, it was Joseph Ubl who eventually sold most of the townsite to Ernest Jilek. Yet, there was no act of transfer found between Kroupa and Ubl. Kroupa died September 23rd, 1922 in Omaha, Nebraska.

Another Kroupa was named George, who in certain documents is said to be a shareholder in the Libuse Townsite Company or signed for the company. He is not mentioned in other documents when presumably he should have been. He may have been John's brother, but Rose Rosicky does not mention him, and there is no clear evidence for this. In 1922 he gave a power of attorney to Ubl, which may well point to the sibling relationship with J. Em. Kroupa.

Frank Dobrovolny

Frank Dobrovolny (whose last name means "good free") was also one of the original incorporators of the Libuse company and the First Bohemian Village. Yet, he is essentially absent from the community. He is not in the censuses. He is not listed in any of the advertisements for the community. He is not mentioned in anyone else's property record. I did not hear even one story about him from anyone in the communities. We have but one cryptic reference to him in the property records. On June 23rd, 1917 he supposedly bought a piece of property in a "tax sale," at least it is listed in the Vendees index in the courthouse. However, in the actual book of documents at that page number for this transaction there is no document remotely related to either Dobrovolny or anyone in the Czech Colony (though there is a document with this page number.) What he bought and from whom, if there even was a transaction, is buried deep in the tens of thousands of pages on file—and the index is perhaps incorrect—but it would be like finding the needle in the haystack. (I did look at the preceeding and succeeding five documents but found no Czechs in them either.) The only information I could ever find on him is he died on February 1st, 1947, in Pawnee City, Nebraska (not far from Omaha.) His obituary is in Hospodar.

The Jilek Family

Yet another family who was involved in many property sales in the area were the Jileks. They were from the Richmond, Virginia area. They are an interesting bunch and did things very differently from the other Czechs. This family consisted of the father, Vaclav, and his two sons, Frank and Ernest. Frank was married to Annie Chada; Ernest was a bachelor. Frank and Anna had two daughters, Bessie and Mary. Vaclav bought his 40.9 acre property from City Savings Bank on June 20th, 1916. He was one of the few who put down a $25 down payment and then had six years to pay the remainder of the $166.36. It was in the Czech community. There is no evidence, however, that he ever lived in Louisiana. In fact, neither Frank or Annie or Ernest are in either the 1920 or 1930 censuses. Frank died about 1926. The only evidence that seems to confirm this is that in 1925 Ernest got power of attorney from Frank and then in 1926 he was appointed executor for the estate. Ernest seems to have left Louisiana about the same time, but he remained involved from afar.

Frank and Annie bought their first land in 1919. The parcel consisted of a handful of lots. How many is not clear as they were all bought from John Lacombe in one package deal. They were in Alexandria and not in the Czech community. They were between 3rd Street and Front Street (also known as Main Street,) at the corner of Bellier Street. These were just 7 blocks south of downtown. While there is no mention of any specific buildings or improvements they did pay $10,700 cash for them. It is known that there were dwellings there just two years later. Oddly, Frank and Anna did not buy them together, as husband and wife, but they each bought an undivided half. That is, Anna used her own money and she owned her half as an independent woman, not a wife. This meant she did not need her husband's consent to sell the land.

In 1920 Frank and Annie also bought two parcels totaling 120 acres from Joseph Stremcha for $1,500 cash, and again, they bought it by combining separate funds. Annie was busy by herself, too. In 1919 she bought Frank Smutny's 80 acre parcel for $800 cash. In May of 1920 she bought a 3.47 acre lot on Country Club Road in Alexandria from Norbert Krenek for $1,800 cash. Presumably this lot had a house, too, considering the price.

Krenek is also interesting for several reasons. Not only was he married to Agnes Tuma, who was conceivably Emil Tuma's sister, (though this is not definite,) but he bought two pieces of property in 1917 in South Alexandria from C. M. Waters. One consisted of 30 acres and one consisted of several small lots. He paid $2,000 and $1,575, respectively. He did not buy in the colony area. But he did split up his land, selling one lot to Annie Jilek and divested himself of the rest in three other sales to non-Czechs in 1919. These three he sold for a total of $7,540, holding mortgages on the property. The whole time Krenek was living in Silver Hill, Alabama. This is a town populated by Czechs, then and now, (in fact, it is Alabama's version of Libuse and Kolin and is just across the bay from Mobile.)

Ernest was certainly a smart operator who moved fast. Ernest's first purchase was not for land, but for oil and gas rights. These he bought for $150 in November of 1920 from a man named W. D. Ball. His first property purchase was a house at 3rd and Bellier Streets which he bought from his brother Frank for

$10,000 cash in August of 1921. In 1926 he sold this house to a man named Cleveland Dear for $20,000. The sale was effected when Dear assumed two outstanding mortgages, one for $14,500 and one for $5,500. So, somehow Ernest extracted not only his original $10,000 purchase price, but an additional $10,000, leaving just mortgages. Property values in Alexandria did not double in 5 years, so this was a pretty mean feat.

On September, 1st, 1923 he bought nearly every lot in the Libuse Townsite that had not been previously sold. He bought it from the Libuse Company for $800 cash, which effectively put the Libuse Townsite Company out of business for it had nothing left to sell. Joseph Ubl acted for the company in selling this land. Seven weeks later, between the 22nd and the 29th of October, he made three sales from what he bought in September. First he sold a ½ interest in the Libuse lots to Joseph Ubl as an individual, for $500 cash, keeping half for himself. Another mean feat of real estate—buy it all for $800—and sell just a ½ for $500—to the very man who knew Jilek had just paid $800. This resulted in a quick $300 cash profit for Jilek plus keeping his half of the lots. Then just two days later he and Ubl sold two of these lots to Vaclav Bastyr (and in 1926 Bastyr bought another lot in Libuse from Ubl and Jilek.) Five days after that Jilek and Ubl sold 4 of the lots to Joseph Prochaska. Incredibly, in 1926 Jilek sold an additional 1/3 interest in his half of the Libuse townsite to Ubl for another $600 in cash. The last of the sales by the Ubl—Jilek team was in 1936. All told these two men account for at least 14 sales in Libuse.

Not only was Ernest involved in buying and selling real estate, and making quite a handsome profit, but he found the time to become a Louisiana Notary Public. In more than 30 property sales between various members of the community he is listed as the notary of record; he was a witness to a few dozen more. These were all between 1920 and 1926. He was a very busy man, indeed. After that he disappears from the record. Ubl became the man of record as the seller of the remainder of the land they held in common.

Yet, there was one sale that could be considered altruistic, or in keeping with the plan of helping the colonists make a go of it. Though even with this they made a small, but tidy, profit. In keeping with his and Ubl's real estate prowess, in January of 1925 they managed to buy 8 acres from Lee Lumber for precisely one dollar. Ubl owned 2/3rds and Ernest 1/3—giving us the rather strange situation of Ubl putting in 66 cents and Ernest putting in his 33 cents; who put up the extra penny is not recorded. In November, 1925 he and Ubl sold this 8 acre parcel to the Farmers Union of Libuse, "a community organization," for $40.

The Ends of the Founders

Of course, there are legends about these men, too, that circulate within the community. "They all came to a bad end" was George Tuma's quote. Many other people said something similar to me. One we know went mad: Edward Baley wound up in the Louisiana State Hospital in Pineville where he died. It is said that Joseph A Ubl hung himself in 1936 or 1938. I could find no obituary of him in the Town Talk and he is not buried in either Czech cemetery and there is that Chicago reference from 1937. He may well have gone to live with one of his children in the last year or so of his life. Frank Baley lived to the ripe old age of 80 and died peacefully in Libuse. Kroupa seems to have also passed away in old age in Omaha. The Jilek's seem to have sold their holdings and moved away, perhaps back to Virginia. Dobrovolny also died at advanced old age. John Hasik died in Nebraska where he had stayed the whole time. So from the unfortunate situation of one man involved in the founding of the colony sprung a multiple of stories about all of them.

The Property Transactions

There are 376 property records for the Czech Colony between 1914 and 1919. These first five years saw the most real estate activity of any period in the history of the community. Broken down by year we find that there were 61 sales in 1914, 69 in 1915, 76 in 1916, 59 in 1917, 61 in 1918 and 50 in 1919. There was one donation: from the Libuse Townsite Company to the Rapides Parish School Board. Also included in this are more than two dozen records related to the non-payment of property taxes in 1916 and 1917. No one lost their property and all the taxes were paid; the amounts were usually just a few dollars (literally $5.67 and such.) But the claim in the Czech corporate entities' charters that they would help the colonists with this tricky issue is shown perhaps to be more propaganda than action. So all told 362 properties were sold in this decade.

In my time in Libuse and Kolin I heard an oft repeated story of the founders buying land for 25 cents an acre and selling if for $5 an acre. I also heard repeatedly that the original colonists put down $25 and then had mortgages. This legend is in all the published sources. A careful analysis of the property records show that these stories are at best apocryphal. 201 of the purchases were paid for in cash with no mortgage whatsoever. Only 162 sales involved a mortgage of any sort. In nearly every case at least 1/3 of the purchase price was paid as a down payment and often more. Nearly all the mortgages were payable in three annual payments; the most was five years. Not one colonist lost his property for lack of payment or for any other reason for that matter. Furthermore, only 12 sales were for $25 down. One was for $11.67 down and the another was for just a $5 down payment. The lowest price per acre was $3.75, when Edward Baley bought 40 acres from Joseph Stegner for $150. The highest price per acre was the $33.

82 of the sales were by the Louisiana Investment & Securities Company to individual colonists in 1914 and 1915. The first was to Rudolph Stuchlik on April 10th, 1914. The last were to the Kalous brothers, Anton and Emmanual, on December 24th, 1915. The largest and most expensive piece of propety Louisiana Investment sold was 320 acres for $4,480. The lowest price they obtained was $160 for a 80 acre plot. The lowest price per acre they received was $3.57 in a sale to Joseph Ubl. The highest price per acre was $33 in a sale to John Hasik. But more than ¼ of the sales were for 40 acres for $720 and another ¼ were for 80 acres for $1,440. The majority were in the $11.50 to $18 per acre range. 71 sales were by the Alexandria Lumber Company (excluding that to Louisiana Investment.) These sales began on January 18th, 1915, when Fred Sedlasky bought his farm and continued until the end of the decade.

Clearly, both of these companies were for about a year selling at the same time; all the lands were contiguous. Other than the $1 sale of 1.5 acres to the Bohemian Cemetery the prices ranged from a low of $80 for 10 acres to a high of $4,980 for 400 acres. Interesting with these sales is that the prices were all over the place—it perhaps depended on any negotiations between buyer and seller. There is no other indication in the records for the price differentials; all the land was unimproved cut-over pine forests. For example: with 40 acre parcels the prices ranged from a low of $240 for a sale in 1922; in 1918 prices ranged from $320 for one sale to a high of $720. The most for 40 acres was $1,200 for a 1915 sale. For 80 acre parcels the price ranged from a low of $420 and climbed to $1,440, but again, was different for different people in the same year.

The Lee Lumber company made 27 sales during this period. The first and biggest was to Albin Cecha; the 4,000 acres of Colony B. To individual colonists the first was to Teresa Vondries on July 19th, 1914; she bought the land with her own separate funds. Just like with the Alexandria Lumber sales prices were different for different people. Two things stand out, however. One was that on the whole the price was less than ½ that charged by either Louisiana Investment or Alexandria Lumber. The other was that while the average (and most often charged) price per acre was $5 it ranged from a low of $4.67 to $15 per acre.

Other sales were made by City Savings Bank & Trust Company. They sold 19 pieces of land, ½ in 1916 and ½ in 1917. The Union Land & Timber Company sold 33 pieces of land beginning in 1914 and ending in 1919, but over ½ were in 1916. The odd thing about these sales were the prices—every one was for an odd amount; that is, prices such as $223.47, $311.47 and $558.42. No two properties sold by these two companies have the same price, though prices were never more than the $1,300 range. The big stand out is the exactly $7,000 paid to Union by Frank Datel for a 200 acre parcel. The Libuse Townsite Company made just 7 sales; they were for lots at $50 or $100 per lot. There were also 41 sales by non-Czechs to Czechs. These properties were about equally divided between farm land and city lots.

That leaves 83 sales from one Czech individual to another. The first sale of this type is tied up in a confusing situation. Louis Novotny paid just $55 for 40 acres (which is also the lowest price ever paid for land in the colony,) on September 5th, 1914. He sold this land to his wife, Emmilie, on January 4th, 1915 for $481.20. There is no clear reason for this odd transaction. The first "real" sale, that is, between unrelated parties, occurred on February 12th, 1915. This was when Albin Cecha sold a 47 acre farm in Colony B to John Hanak. The first sale (actually two sales) from one colonist to another was by Charles Kazda to Edward Locker. This was for two farm properties on August 9th, 1915. It is perhaps ironic that this same Charles (Karel) Kazda was one of those quoted in the original promotion materials singing the praises of the colony.

Property Taxes

Among the stated goals of the three original companies, Libuse Townsite, the First Bohemian Village of America and Louisiana Investment & Securities, was to assist the colonists in making sure the property taxes were paid. The annual taxes due by the Czechs ranged from a low of just $7 or $8 to a high of near $24, none are higher. Many of the colonists surely could afford these small amounts. Especially considering that more than half of them bought their land for cash in the amount of hundreds of dollars and some paid even more than a thousand dollars. Even those who had the three year mortgages of the era put down 1/3 or more of the purchase price. It seems improbable that a Czech could pay, say, $720 cash for land and then not have a mere $7.28 to pay the tax the very next year. Something, somehow, went wrong. First I will lay out the situation. I will then state some of the resolutions of the problems as found. Among them are many confusing situations that are simply unexplainable. Finally, I will draw some probable conclusions.

Between 1916 and 1919 at least 76 Czechs were said by the state of Louisiana to be delinquent in their taxes and in danger of losing their land in what is called a tax sale. This type of sale is conducted by auction on the courthouse steps by the parish sherriff. Its purpose is to sell the land to the highest bidder to effect the payment of the tax to the state. The highest bidder in each case paid the tax owed and some court and adverstising costs. Mostly this amounted to no more than $50 and usually less. These tax sales are recorded in the conveyance books in the courthouse. The bulk are in three large documents. The first group is dated May 27th, 1916, covering 34 people. The second is dated May 22nd, 1917, covering 20 people. The third is dated June 23rd, 1917 and covers 18 people. Four are found in singular documents in 1916, plus one in 1918 and two in 1919. Almost invariably the highest bidders were men known only as J. W. Martin and C. J. Martin, though there are a handful of others.

The solutions found are these: more than 1/3 of the sales were subsequently said to be based on an "erroneous tax." That is, the claim by the state that the tax was not paid was simply not true. Now, there are two explanations for this. One could be that the record keeping of the day, written by hand in big ledger books, simply was sloppy. Perhaps the entry for payment was not made in the correct place or not made at all. Or perhaps the record of payment at Alexandria was not forwarded to the state's main revenue office in Baton Rouge. Once the Czechs showed their receipts for the taxes paid the tax sale was rescinded.

Another explanation is also related to record keeping, but in this case it was spelling. Czech names are just so much different than the Anglo-French names that the record keepers were used to that the tax payments were entered into the books incorrectly. Looking through the alphabetized indices of Vendor and Vendees in the courthouse it was apparent that the writers of these records had constant trouble in putting Czech names in the right place alphabetically. The consonant clusters and seemingly missing vowels of Czech names simply confounded the record keepers. They had no experiece with Zmek, Zdarsky, Krska, Chvojka, Chruma and Dvorak and many others. In the indices the same Czech name was often put in several different places while non-Czech names were alphabatized correctly. Vowels were added where the record keeper thought they should be. Sometimes consonants like "n" were changed to "u," because that, after all, looked right. Different record keepers working at different times made up their own idiosyncratic new spellings. The variations were almost endless.

Even within one document a Czech name might be spelled differently every time it appears. These spelling errors were probably carried through each step of the process and thus taxes were not credited correctly because they were entered under different spellings. So, this led to some of the errors which were corrected once the receipts were produced. Joseph Kotera went so far as to file with the courthouse a document showing that there were multiple mispellings (Cotera, Costera, Koterka, Kosterna) of his name throughout the public record and thus his tax sale was erroneous; the problem is I can find no land purchase by a Joseph Kotera under any of these spellings. He was, however, recorded as correcting his tax situation.

All the other tax sales were resolved through "redemption." This is the process where the deliquent taxpayer pays the taxes owed thus rescinding the tax sale. The redemptions could have been necessary for several reasons. One may be the fault of the Czechs. They may not have known the proper method of ensuring that their taxes were paid and recorded. This may have came about through language difficulties. Or through the difference in the method used in the first American state they lived in and the Louisiana method. Or perhaps they mailed the tax payment to the incorrect office, say, to the parish tax office instead of the state tax office. Once this bureaucratic mess was straightened out the record shows a "redemption," there being no word in the law for a "correction," nor a legal term for "straightened out." I doubt seriously, however, that the Czechs did not have the money and nearly all the redemptions were within a year or two. That is, about the time it would have taken to straighten out the mess.

Another problem was that the tax was broken down into categories such as "Confederate Veterans Tax," "school tax," and "levee tax." The Czechs were not Confederate veterans, they operated their own schools and they had no levees, so perhaps they thought these were not taxes that they had to pay. Since they were new to the state this is possible. Once they figured out these were general taxes that everyone had to pay they quickly paid and set things right. No one who had one problem with the taxman ever had another problem. Indeed, other than these first few years, tax problems were few and far between. The next biggest group were during the Depression. In fact, I could not find one instance of any Czech actually losing his land because of nonpayment of taxes. Every tax sale was resolved.

Jacob Pletka's tax problem, however, was not solved until 1946. Stephen Fojtek's not until 1947 and Dohmil Twhala's not until 1956—all three were cancelled as "erroneous"—but 30 and 40 years after the problem arose. The confounding thing is that I could find no recorded purchase of land in Rapides Parish by any of these three men—or of any sale. They are not the only ones. The list is long of tax sales for land owned by people for whom I could find no land purchases or sales: Hnatek, Krepik, Soktak, Techy, Vyhanek, Zajicek, Zhrasky,

Hosek, Jirka, Martinek, Kosatka and on and on. All the land descriptions put them squarely in the heart of the Bohemian Colony and they are all clearly Czech names.

Nearly every entry in the tax sale documents has a handwritten notice that the land in question was "redeemed" or the tax was "erroneous" and there are many notations pointing to documents filed years later, by book and page number, with the correct name and property description. Someone went back and made these entries after the original filing—someone must have had documentation of some kind. But I have gone multiple times through the indices and they are not there under any spelling variant. They are a complete mystery. Nor could this be an instance of these Czechs losing their land—somewhere there would have had to be a purchase contract in order for the tax to have been levied in the first place.

Now, the explanations I have given so far are the innocent ones. But this being Louisiana there are two other possibilities for all these tax sales. One is that the Czech men gave their tax payments to Donald Despain, Clarence Smith or Lahroy Slusher, all of Louisiana Investment, expecting them to be paid and recorded—and these three men did not do it. Either they absconded with the money after the foreclosure of their company or played some sort of kiting or Ponzi scheme or engaged in outright theft. There are plenty of stories, all hearsay and memories to be sure, from the elders in the community to whom I spoke (though they were children at the time,) that these men were nothing short of crooks. Still, there is no doubt in my mind that the taxpaying Czechs would have kept some sort of receipt.

It is conconceivable also that the purchases not recorded in the indices were made by Czechs who were not in Louisiana. They were perhaps using these three men as proxy buyers for the property, handing over money at their alleged offices in Chicago and Omaha—and then the purchases were not actually made. Though each tax sale entry says the Czechs were residents of Rapides Parish no one in the community has ever mentioned them to me—they are no where to be found in any other record. Yet, who is to say that the three non-Czechs did not fabricate names and identities or hire posers when a live body was needed? We know, at least, that Despain and Smith filed plat maps for land they did not own. It is often said "where there's smoke there's fire," so I can not rule out these ruses—for there are few rational explanations of what is recorded in these three big tax sale documents.

The other explanation is just as sinister, of course, but is instead corruption on the part of people in the tax office, the courthouse, the sheriff's office and J. W. and C. J. Martin themselves. One or any of them could have failed to record the paid taxes or used any one of another imaginable and creative means to try and defraud the Czechs of the land they bought with hard earned cash. Here we have a small, tight knit group of powerful and well placed men in government and business in a still small city who find themselves with dozens of immigrants who speak English poorly, are new to the area, are unsure of their way and apparently have plenty of money (all those cash sales, after all.) It is a situation ripe for collusion, chicanery and corruption. Even more so in Louisiana, which has not been known for excessive civic probity. Indeed, tales of corruption are not only legion in this state, they are recounted as proud indicators of this special place. Remember this, Louisiana has had more governors and lesser politicians convicted of such shenanigans in its history than any other state in the nation. Whatever corruption occurred was nipped in the bud when the Czechs came up with receipts for taxes paid. No one lost their land.

How They Moved To Louisiana

The best description of the moving process in these times comes from James Dvorak, uncle of architect John Desmond, in his memoirs (though not members of the Czech Colony.) He was writing of moving from South Dakota to Minnesota but the process was the same, though the trip longer to get from northern and eastern states to Louisiana. It took nearly 3 weeks for the Dvorak family to travel the two hundred miles between their old and new places. For the colonists, the trip could have lasted upwards of six weeks. It was a complex and arduous trip. Amenities such as food and drink were either carried with them or purchased along the way. Lodging might have to be obtained while awaiting a connecting train; sleeping in their seats on a rattling train was nearly impossible. Bathing and basic hygiene were forsaken for the trip. Young children were an added burden. They all arrived tired, dirty and hungry. (And this method of moving was actually true for the many families and individuals we met in Part One of this book.)

Most of the Czechs traveled to Louisiana by rail. This often involved frequent changes of trains and railroad companies. For the few who arrived in their own automobiles the trip must have been grueling considering the lack of good roads. There are no reports that any traveled by steamer or other waterborn methods. Nor did anyone apparently make the journey using just horse-drawn wagons as the Dvorak family did in their much shorter move. Most of the colonists came from farms; those who came from cities most likely had a lot less to carry and ship.

While the people would ride in railroad passenger cars they shipped all their household goods and farm tools and implements in freight cars. This would include, obviously, furniture, beds and small kitchenwares, but could also include stoves, churners, washboards and tubs and other appliances of the time. The farm implements they brought were generally the smallest and most compact; shovels, hoes and the like. They often sold their largest equipment such as tractors (horse-drawn at that) and cultivators, because it was either impossible or cost prohibitive to move them. Many would have also sold all the mules, horses, cows and other animals that they had on farms up north. While it was possible to ship livestock by the train car load there are only a few reports that any Czechs did. Frances Hazmark says her father traveled with his cattle in the train car from Kansas. But in general this was not done since colonists had just a handful of cows and only one or two horses or mules and the railroads did not want to deal in small quantities of livestock. All that they left behind would be repurchased in Alexandria after they arrived. When they did purchase items it was reported by the Town Talk that "they buy only the best." Which is another indication of some prosperity and savings.

Dvorak relates that families would carry their belongings in horse-drawn wagons from their farms to the nearest railroad siding or depot. There, waiting pre-arranged, would be a freight car that was specifically for them to load up themselves. This initial part of the trip could be upwards of twenty and thirty miles from their farm. After that, they had to wait for a locomotive to come by and pick it up; they would literally camp at track-side to wait. In the farm country the railroads were spurs. The train would bring it to the main trunkline where it may have sat for a few days before hooking on to a train heading south to Alexandria. From there they either used the lumber railroad to get their belongings as close to their property as possible or it was off loaded at the depot in Alexandria.

In either case they then had to carry their belongings to their new farm, again using mostly horse-drawn wagons, though sometimes vehicles. The men and older boys of the family were enlisted in the first and last stages of the journey. At the beginning of the trip, if they did not have enough manpower (and few families had it) they obtained the help of neighbors they knew. Then they had to rely on strangers at the tail end to get this work done. They had to work in rain or shine, day and night, to get the job done within the time frame of passing locomotives. They had to make sure they met their goods for there was no one else to do the work; also there was some concern about theft. There were no moving companies.

Freight prices were usually figured for every 100 pounds of merchandise—you could ship using 1st Class to 4th Class. Prices ranged from a low of about 40 cents to $2 or more per hundred pounds per hundred miles. The tarriff cards, or rate sheets, for each railroad were different and often complex. There were dozens of variables in pricing. Some railroads did not go the entire distance and arrangements all had to be made in advance to enable each rail line to pass the freight car on to the connectiong rail line, thus to ensure the timely arrival of the goods. Fortunately, there were shipping agents who helped people in this process. Obviously, 1st class took precedence and was moved more quickly than 4th class. Being frugal people they would have tried to lighten their load as much as possible. While it does not seem like a lot of money today, it could easily cost $100 or more to ship the goods. This was not, however, an insignificant amount of money at the time; this could be a year's earnings. A family would have to make sometimes painful decisions to leave cherished items behind because the cost of shipping was higher than the replacement cost. Passenger tickets were yet another expense.

Many of the Czechs moved from six or seven hundred miles or more away from Louisiana. Some traveled from as far away as Washington State and Montana. For those arriving from due north the trip was easier as railroads were well established going north and south between Chicago and New Orleans and other points in Louisiana along the Mississippi River corridor. The rail spurs into the hinterlands of Kansas, Illinois, Nebraska and the Dakotas fed into these main lines. Those east of the Mississippi River usually crossed at St. Louis on the Eads Bridge (the first over the river.)

For those arriving from the Eastern states there were two main routes. Either the trip entailed heading west and passing through Chicago before heading south and crossing at St Louis or they went south to Atlanta and then westward through Birmingham, Alabama and Jackson, Mississippi, crossing the Mississippi River at Vicksburg by ferry. This is at least a 1,000 mile trip from Ohio; from Pennsylvania and New York it is nearly 1,500 miles. They were fortunate that Alexandria was a main railroad hub and along the main rail lines.

Since most of the colonists were moving onto undeveloped property when they arrived in Libuse and Kolin they had to stay at one of the two hotels there. Or they stayed at a more expensive one in Alexandria until they could build their sheds, barns and homes. How many of their belongings were ruined in rainy weather and the heat and humidity before they were able to get them into proper homes can only be guessed at. A fortunate few families sent the man of the family on a scouting trip to at least build a shed to store their belongings before he headed back north to pack up the farm, house and family. Added to all these travails was, of course, the language difficulty for those whose English was not that good. In this travel they were true pioneers.

Typical Farms

We can can get a general picture of what was on a typical farm from the inventories given in a handful of property records for developed farms that were sold. There may have been farms with more, but we have no record of their inventories. Presumably a house and a barn and a few out buildings were on the properties, though they are not usually clearly defined other than "improvements." The land made up about half the value of the farm, with the house and movable property making up the other half. There was no mechanized machinery; all the power came from horses and mules. There were implements of all kinds, many whose purpose is forgotten except in historical texts. All were from an increasingly bygone era. It does show, perhaps, the state of American farming at the cusp of mechanized modernization which had not yet come to the colony.

The crops themselves and seeds for next year's planting were considered an important part of the sale. It seems that these farms grew a multitude of crops. For self-sufficiency this would have been necessary, though, there was an excess for cash sale. There was not, however, the more typical large scale plantings that characterized farms in other parts of the state such as the hundreds and even thousands of acres planted in cotton, soybeans, sugar and corn. This would be in keeping with the Scientific farming methods to which the Czechs adhered. There were at most a dozen or so animals of various types; but apparently no goats or sheep. These are the examples:

Jerry Suchanek bought 80 acres and "improvements" and "together with all the growing crops theron consisting of corn, sweet potatoes and watermelons," from Floyd Holly. He paid $1,360 cash on July 6th, 1917. This may be one of the Holy family, who were colonists, though not Bohemians but Slovaks. Their surname was often miswritten as Holly. This is not clear that this is the case in this instance.

J. George Vonasek paid $6,000 cash to Gearhart Tanner for a farm of 8.23 acres in an irregular shaped lot 3 ½ miles south of Alexandria far from the Czech Colony. Since this was December 20th, 1917, he could be considered the first Czech colonist to move beyond the colony. The farm was along Bayou Roberts and the property description has such "landmarks" as a "large tree" and "an iron stake driven into the bank of the bayou." It was described as a "home and farm under fence" and the farm included "all farm implements [not further described,] 22 head of cattle, 2 horses, 2 wagons and harnesses." Basically, Vonasek was ready to step on to the farm and do its business.

On October 27th, 1919, the widow Frantiska Bejsovec and her bachelor son Frank purchased in "undivided ½ portions" a farm from Vaclav Vacovsky and his wife Antonie. They paid $1,725 for the land and pretty much every thing on it. They put $900 down and assumed a $350 mortgage to the Federal Land Bank. They were to make five annual payments, the first four for $125 and the last one for $100. The 40 acres was lot 16, section 3. The items in the sale were "one cow and one calf; 2 horses; a harness; hogs; peanuts; farm implements and household goods." No further description is given of the implements and goods.

J. F. Kadlek paid $1,700 cash to John Tipka for a 7 acre by 7 acre square at Barron's Spring. This was part of a larger parcel that Tipka had bought in mid-November of 1919 from a man named J. W. Lindsay; Tipka kept the remaining portion. Kadlek bought it on February 6th, 1920. Barron's Spring is at the east end of the colony; today several Czech families still live along Barron's Spring Road. The inventory is very detailed: *"3 sets of harnesses and 3 holders, 2 horses, 6 cattle, 1 sow, and 35 chickens; 1 farm wagon, 1 buggy, 1 disc, 3 plows, 1 lister, and 1 cultivator; also 1 rolling coulter, 1 wheel barrow; and one lot each of hog and barbed wire; 1 planter, 3 garden rakes, and 1 hole digger; 2 axes and 3 hoes; 2 cotton hoes and 2 wire stretchers—and one cooking stove."* There was also one lot of hay and one lot of seed peanuts which aren't further defined. In the document it is specified that $800 was for the real estate and $900 was for the inventory. Kadlek was a bachelor.

John Hlavaty paid $3,700 cash to Joseph Brozik for a farm of 60 acres on January 29th, 1918. Included in the sale were "all the mules, cattle, wagons, harnesses, farming implements, chickens and every thing belonging to the farm." These things are not further defined in the document. Oddly, Brozik, just 4 days later, on February 2nd, bought 40 acres from the Alexandria Lumber Company for $720 cash, presumably to start all over again.

Karl (Carl) Svebek and Stephen Marhefka bought the contents of a farm from Rudolph Stuchlik, but not the land, on November 20th, 1906. Stuchlik's name is wrong in the body of the document as Stublitz. His name is correct on the signature page. The price was $488 cash. The contents were: "1 black horse named Lib; 1 sorrell horse named Daisy; 5 cows; 2 yearling heifers; 4 calves; 4 hogs; 4 bales of cotton; 325 bushels of sweet potatoes; 50 bushels of corn; and 4 tons of hay." Farm implements including "grain binder, grain drill, disc cutter, cultivator, two middlebusters, 2 horse plows and a cream separater." There was also "one Studebaker two horse wagon;" which must have been more than a few years old because Studebaker had left the wagon business more than a decade earlier to concentrate on making automobiles.

Bessie Filipi and her two children John and Lizzie inherited 160 acres when Bessie's husband William Filipi passed away. On the farm was "one brown horsemule and one mare mule, one wagon, one harness, 2 cows and one plow." No mention is made of crops or seeds.

Big brother Charles Tucek acted as the legal tutor for his younger siblings Willie, Blanche and Eddie in the succession from their father Francis who had just passed away. There was $200 in one bank account and just $7.67 in a second account. $638.87 was "being held" by Francis Peroutka, though no further description of this is given. And the succession also included "10 head of cattle, 2 mules, various implement of farm machinery," "one second-hand Ford touring car [i.e. four door, open top]" and "one lot of household goods." There was also a $100 loan receiveble from Jacob Cizak. This Tucek family has the same surname as those first Tuceks nearly 200 years earlier who became the Touchet family. It is doubtful that they were related in any way. This Tucek family did not change its name either.

The four Frank children were minors when they inherited six pieces of property including 3 lots in the city of Alexandria, 2 lots in the Town of Libuse and one 40 acre farm. The estate also included $580.12 in a bank account, "one lot of shop equipment and tools located in the building of the decedent: Auto Sheet Metal Works." No tutor or other adult is mentioned in the document, but there must have been someone to run the affairs of the minor children.

As late as 1946 the farms were pretty much the same as evidenced by the sale on January 7th, of a 40 acre farm for $4,000. J. F. Chruma and his American wife, Katie Wright, sold it to L.D. Duncan. Mr. Duncan paid cash. The farm included "2 cows, 2 hogs, 15 chickens, I wagon and harness, 1 brown mule named Molly, 1 spotted mare named Nellie, 1 wood cook stove and 1 heater."

These are the only inventories I could find among the many property records I looked at, but they do show self-sufficiency at a level just above subsistance farming.

The Tuma Farm

George Tuma is a retired farmer and several of his sons still farm. One makes his living entirely by farming, the others are part-time. "Tuma's Taters" (sweet potatoes) are a well-known commodity in the area. When ripe they set up a farmstand on Highway 28 to sell them. George served as both president and board member of the Louisiana Farm Bureau; though more than 80 years old he tries to remain active in the organization.

Because they remained active farmers they did not preserve, or let lie fallow, the first buildings they built. They would dismantle older buildings when necessary to reuse the lumber in new structures or for lesser purposes. They upgraded as the years went by out of necessity. In fact, all the buildings on Tuma property are modern (except the post office used by Emil and Marie, about which more in the next section.) Yet, this farmstead is important for it is from George that I learned most about the farming methods of the early colonists; every family had the same work.

He tells a story from his childhood of seeing an "endless sea of waving tall grass that hid the pine stumps." As they walked their newly bought land they quickly realized that the task in front of them was far more daunting than they had imagined. Their first task was removing the stubborn stumps. These were often just a few feet from each other, their roots entangled. They used a variety of methods. After digging the dirt from around the main roots and exposing them they would hack them with axes and pickaxes. For the smaller stumps they used crowbars to try and pry the stump out of the ground. Using ropes and chains wrapped around the exposed roots of larger stumps they would attach horses and mules to try to yank it out of the ground. If that failed, as it usually did for larger stumps, they would hollow out a small bowl-like depression in the middle and then set a fire in the hole and let it burn for days. They kept it stoked with accelerants like kerosene and oil. Some of the stumps were three and four feet in diameter; this land was old growth virgin pine forest when the lumber companies arrived. Sometimes they would set dynamite at the bases and attmept to blow them out of the ground. The fields reverberated with explosions.

Often they had to tackle a stump with all these methods, using first one, then another. Sometimes a field would be ablaze with the many fires they set. After removing the stumps they dragged them into large piles and burned them. If it rained, as it often does in Louisiana, they had to wait until the stumps dried before starting the fires again. They lost the better part of a day's work if they set fires right before an unexpected rain storm sprung up. If it did not rain for a week or so the clay would become hard like concrete, yet they kept digging and hacking. The work was from sun-up to sundown, with just a break for lunch (dinner as they called it) and supper. Slowly, deliberately, yard by yard across the acres they removed one stump after another. The progress was slow going. It was dangerous and injury lurked at any moment. It was dirty, hard and exhausting—and necessary.

Though it may have taken months, once a field was cleared it was almost time for planting. But first they had to level the field. They filled in the natural ditches and depressions and removed the tops of the small hillcocks. They moved the dirt by hand using shovels and wheelbarrows. A field that was not level would flood in the depressions and cause too much runoff from the higher points washing away seeds and young plants. This was not the level ground that is found south of the Red River, this is the start of hill country.

Once a field was level enough to plow a whole new task was at hand. Their equipment to make furrows was horse and mule drawn iron plows and cultivators. The men and boys had to walk in front or behind to guide the animals and make the rows straight; often two men, one at each end, did this. Seeds were sown by hand by the women and girls as they walked along behind the plow. Potato seedlings were set in the ground by hand; they stooped to deposit each one in the earth. Too much rain and the fields turned to mud. Too little and the fields were as hard as rock. After planting the war on weeds began. Hoeing was a long, tedious and constant chore. Trash tree saplings would spring up that had to be removed.

That was just for crops. For chickens, hogs and cattle they had to build pens, fenced yards and fields. Fence posts were made by hand from the right size trees. These first had to be chopped down then stripped of branches before being cut into the proper lengths. Then the post holes were dug before setting the hand-hewn posts in the ground. For the smaller animals wire was stretched by hand and nailed into place on the posts. For the cattle split rail fences, not much different than those of Abe Lincoln lore, had to be built. Cattle was kept father from the house. Often, to get to those fields, they had to ford the small creeks and bayous. They built a few primitive bridges by felling trees and dragging them into place before laying hand planed planks across the two "beams" formed by the logs. They cut trees down using hand saws, one man to each handle.

Every day brought new tasks. There was no day of rest. There was even less time for leisure, especially in the first few years. They had no electricity until the 1920s. Water was drawn from a well; that was at least able to be drilled by the new machines then becoming available. But that entailed spending the few dollars they had. They slaughtered their own animals for a diet of meat and fowl. While they did not make their own clothes those they had were carefully and repeatedly patched and repaired as the rough farm work ripped and tore them. Throughout all this they were beset by flies and mosquitos, wasps and bees.

Snakes were present in the fields; a gun was kept nearby to take care of this problem.

Work was a constant. The division of labor was by age, sex and ability. The men did the hardest and roughest work. The older boys learned from their fathers. Younger boys took care of the hogs. The women and girls were busy inside the home cleaning, cooking and sewing. In the fields the men and older boys did the plowing. The women, girls and younger boys did the sowing and weeding. It was all back-breaking labor. Indeed, it was a pioneer life during the first few years of the colony. It was not until the early 1920s that more mechanization and store-bought goods were brought to the community.

The first two years for each family were definitely the most difficult. After that, things got progressively easier, better and "modern" once World War I had come and gone. By the 1920s the farms were established, the fields cleared and the hardest work behind them. I stood at the edge of a 40 acre field listening to Mr. Tuma tell these stories and saw a glint in his eye that seemed to suggest that he wouldn't have missed it for the world. There was a great sense of accomplishment about it all.

Building a community

Perhaps the most interesting thing about their efforts to build a community is that few of these people knew each other. At the most there were a few fathers and sons, and a brother-in-law or two who moved in at the same time. Perhaps someone they knew from their previous state (very rare,) had move into the colony, too. They had come from all over America and Europe (though, none directly so.) They were strangers to each other. And yet they were able to organize community meetings, start social organizations and build the structures they would need. Every one in Libuse and Kolin met the same conditions. The community was bound by shared hardships. No one stands out. Yet, there was a spirit of cooperation; they knew they were in this venture together. One person was quoted saying "no man had more authority than his neighbor, but it was not necessary when they trusted each other."

They trusted each other partly because they were all Czech, spoke the same language and were all from the same religious (or actually, non-religious) heritage. They also had to trust each other because they could not trust their American neighbors, as was shown repeatedly. They all faced the similar problems with getting property taxes properly credited. All the Czechs had to deal with local non-Czechs causing troubles at the Czech dance halls. There are reports of non-

Czechs stealing cattle and chickens. Also, non-Czechs burned newly built Czech bridges over the many streams and bayous as well as tearing up fences in a vain attmept to enforce a free range system of cattle foraging. The Czechs were buffeted from all sides by the "outside." Added to that was the vast language difference. Even if some of the Czechs spoke English it could not have been very good since they had spent all their time in Czech speaking communities before they arrived in Louisiana.

One can imagine new arrivals being met by the existing settlers and welcomed into the fold. The Bohemian Colonization Club was alerting those already there that newcomers were arriving on a given day. It was fairly well coordinated. The main Czech real estate players, like Ubl, Cecha and Baley aided in this effort. Usually it was the man and one or two sons who came to establish a farm and build a primitive house. They stayed in one of the two hotels. Many might have bought the land sight unseen and just showed up on a train one day. Only a little later did they arrange for their wives, daughters and younger children to join them. From this arose a tight knit community—one that is still somewhat leary of outsiders.

Work on the military's new nearby Camp Beauregard kept many of the first settlers solvent until their first crops came in. This work also gave them new skills or honed old ones as carpenters and painters which they put to later use in businesses in Alexandria. While there was work at Camp Beauregard it meant a five to eight mile walk through woods and across Bayou Flagon. There was need for carpenters, painters, roofers and metal workers. These were skills that some of the men possessed or learned quickly.

The colonists built their own road betwen the two towns; today, Louisiana Highway 3128 roughly follows its path. Proposals have been made to have this designated the "Louisiana Czech Highway." They built roads that straddled the edges of adjoining farms; many still bear Czech names. Among them are Varvarovsky, Nadrchal, Stuchlik, Kastanek, Hazmuka and Locker Roads. Indeed, one of the constantly recurring phrases in the property records is that "25 feet along section lines be reserved for a public road." They also immediately began building up the dirt tracks that were to become Highways 28 and 107.

Almost from day one community meetings were held. They were held usually every two weeks at the hotels and later the schools and halls. These meetings enabled people to appeal to their neighbors for collective action in getting a community started. Whether a school, or building barns, houses and fences, or digging a well, or creating a road to the farm, volunteers quickly came forward, each knowing that the rest would soon join them in solving their own problems. Proposals were made and debated, priorities established and decisions reached mainly through concesus. The hat was pased to raise money or labor was volunteered. These meetings were more than just business and usually dissolved into social events for entire families once the serious matters were dealt with by the men. As they had no church—nor had they plans to build one, for they did not believe in organized religion—these meetings also served for a little talk of God and Faith. Of course, all the meetings were conducted strictly in Czech.

Businesses and Post Offices

The stories of the post offices in both communities is an important part of the this history. Certainly they made it easier for those in Louisiana to keep in touch with their families around the nation and back in Europe. Plus, no one had to make the arduous trip into Alexandria to pick up the mail for the entire community. The establishment of post offices could also be said to have given the communities a sense of place—the towns were now recognized by an official government agency. It imparted a sense of realism and progress, even of hope, to the colony. In my time in Libuse and Kolin the stories of the post offices were mentioned frequently; members of the community have a strong emotional attachment to them. The post office at Libuse even today serves as a gathering place for sharing gossip and news of community members. In the beginning they also served as a lifeline to the colonists' cherished Czech newspapers.

In the first decades of the colony only Czech language newspapers were read by the residents. They came promptly to the post office to pick up their copies. This had the added effect of preserving Czech language and culture in the communities. They were reading Denni Hlastael (Daily Herald) published in Chicago; Slovan Amerikansky (Slavic American) from Racine, Wisconsin; Svornost (Unity) the oldest American-Czech daily, published at Chicago; and Spravedlnost (Justice) which was also published in Chicago. Of course, they were also still reading Hospodar (Farmer,) the newspaper that started it all. It was still being published in Omaha, Nebraska. Of all of these only Hospodar is still published.

Libuse Post Office

The first post office was established in Libuse in April of 1915. Bohous O. Vonasek is recorded as the first postmaster. He took office April 3rd. His first name is mispelled as "Bohns" in official post office records. The Daily Town Talk, in an article dated May 12th of that year, noted that "mail delivery began to Libuse yesterday;" the paper probably saw it as a major step towards the creation of a real town that they touted the year before. The first post office was in the store that Vonasek operated. It was on Industrial Street, across from the Komensky School. This is across the street from the current Czech Hall. Vonasek bought two lots in the Libuse townsite from the Libuse Townsite Company in August of 1915; he paid $125 cash for each of them. They were not adjacent, one was in block 18 and the other in block 19 of the proposed town. On at least one of them he built a small structure. This was next to the Melichar general store.

On March 8th, 1919, he exchanged his two lots and the building with Frank Hromadka for two lots and a building that Hromadka owned. The values for both were stated as $2,500 and it was considered an equal exchange. Why they did this can not be definitively determined. The transfer document is silent on this point. However, we know that by 1919 what was downtown Libuse was being disassembled and moved a short distance away to the Holloway Prairie Road. There were at least six other members of the Vonasek family in the community before 1920 and there are several sales and purchases by the Vonaseks after 1920. Yet, no Vonasek is in either census. He served until October 15th, 1919.

Martin Cizek took office as postmaster the same day that Vonasek stepped down. He operated the post office from his store, also on a lot bought from the Libuse company; that sale was in 1915. Cizek also owned two farms with a total of a little over 160 acres. His brother, Darwin, also owned farms in the colony. He served until December, 1921, when he moved to New Orleans. That is where he died the next year from an unfortunate accident leading to blood poisoning. (The Cizeks have the distinction of being two of the four people who moved into the colony from the farthest point in the United States: Yakima, Washington. Frank Kovar was also from Yakima. John Trejbal was from Odessa, Washington, which is just six miles from Yakima.)

Charles E. Voda (whose last name means "water,") was the third postmaster. He took office on December 19th, 1921. He served for seven years until September 15th, 1928. On his naturalization application he listed "postmaster" as his occupation, but according to family history he worked as a bookkeeper for Alexandria Steam Laundry in the city while his wife, Stephany, ran the post office. He and his wife also moved to New Orleans, leaving shortly after his term expired. But their son remains in the community even today. Neither the Cizek or Voda buildings survived.

On September 15th, 1928, Emil Tuma, Sr. became the fourth postmaster. First as acting postmaster and then after the 24th of that month as official postmaster. The position of postmaster has stayed in the family until today. There are probably not many other post offices in America that can make that claim. Emil served until January 1st, 1949, when he retired. The building he built to serve as the post office still survives on the Tuma farm in Libuse. Still intact are the cubbyholes for the mail, the counter and other fixtures; it is in fairly solid shape, (we can only hope that it will eventually be restored and preserved.) During some of his term he was paid $120 a year, paid in four quarterly payments; if he ever received a raise it is not known.

His daughter-in-law, Marie, (she married Emil's son George,) was born in Kolin, Louisiana, and moved to Libuse when she got married. She only completed school as far as the seventh grade, but she studied the post office regulations in preparation for taking over the job as postmaster. She did so when Emil retired. She served the longest of any postmaster in the town—35 years. George and Marie also operated a general store, and eventually built a newer structure in front of the old post office. The section inside this building that was dedictated to the post office also still has many of the fixtures necessary, such as cubbyholes and scales. At some point they even had a neon sign made to mark the location of the post office. She served until 1984 when she, too, retired. Marie died in 1997, but George is still living. George and Marie's daughter Caroline is now the postmaster.

Kolin Post Office

With the Kolin post office once again we come across Frank Balej. He served as the first postmaster here, gaining the position on April 4th, 1917. As I pointed out previously, if the census is to be believed, he was 22 in 1920, so he was just 19 years old when he assumed this position. That is a rather tender age for such an important position. He served until January 3rd, 1920.

The second postmaster was Joseph Tauber. He served from that day in 1920 until only March 13th, 1921. It was on this day that he was struck by lightning and killed while walking home from a neighbor's house. Despite her grief his wife, Margaret, stepped up to the position as acting postmaster on March 14th, becoming postmaster on May 31st, 1921. She served until March 6th, 1923. The Tauber's operated the post office out of their general store on the Old Marksville Highway, also known as the Centerpoint Road. In the 1920 census his occupation is listed as "merchant." Mail was delivered from Alexandria twice a week on Wednesdays and Saturdays. These days became the focal point of informal community gatherings as everyone came to pick up their mail. According to one story, all the youngsters of the community thought that the Tauber's daughter, Bessie, was the postmaster since it was she who gave out the mail.

On March 6th, 1923, Louis Filipi became postmaster. He was 23 years old. He served a little more than a year and a half until November, 18th, 1924. When he became postmaster he moved the office to his own grocery store down the road. This store was on land owned by his father, John, who had bought 80 acres in 1915. Louis bought a small lot carved out of the larger parcel in 1928 for one dollar. It had just 131 feet frontage on the highway in Kolin,

The next postmaster was Bessie L. Svebek. She took over from Filipi and served 11 years until September 9th, 1935. She moved the post office into a small shed-like building attached to her husband's automobile service station. That had grown out of the store that Carl Svebek (Bessie's husband) bought from Louis Filipi in August, 1925. There are two documents relating to this sale, one dated August 3rd and the other August 31st. They both relate the same basic information—a square lot that was 82 feet on each side; the price was $75 cash. Why the discrepancy between the 82 feet frontage of this lot and the 131 feet that Louis bought from his father is not clear. A 50 foot wide swath of land hardly seems useful to carve out of that small parcel.

Following Bessie Svebek another member of the Filipi family took over: Alvin Filipi. He was the younger brother of Louis Filipi. Alvin was 29 when he began serving in September, 1935, and he served until July 14th, 1937. Under his tutelage the post office moved another few yards down the road to his own combination grocery store and auto garage. None of these post offices were in anything like an official post office building. They were merely a small counter and rack of cubbyholes for the mail in the corner of a store, so moving them was quite easy.

On July 14th, 1937, Katherine Marhefka took over as the seventh postmaster. She and her husband, Stephen, moved the post office back to the store location that was Louis Filipi's and which they had purchased. However, there is no record of this purchase in the property records; it is possible, though, that they bought just the building and not the land. The Marhefkas bought the stock for the store from the Svebek's. Katherine was the postmaster for more than 20 years. Her job lasted until January 31, 1959. Betty Jo Hines was the the acting postmaster for a few months in 1959 until the Kolin post office was finally closed by the postal service. (She was the only non-Czech postmaster in the two towns.)

That the post office closed was not that surprising. The town, after all, had never grown to more than a few dozen families. However, for about the next 10 years, until 1968 or 1970, mail was still dropped off at Tauber's store for the convenience of the residents. Marie Tuma probably had a hand in this informal arrangement. The Tauber store finally closed in 1978. Mail delivery to local residents is now handled by the Libuse post office and the main post office in Pine-ville.

Early Businesses in Kolin and Libuse

In early Kolin there were at least five businesses. Their exact dates of establish-ment could not be determined. Even the Czech Heritage newsletter gives only approximate years. They were all started, however, in either the late 1910s or early 1920s. The surviving pictures are all from the early 1920s. We cannot even be sure if the buildings in the photos were the original structures or if they were built after the owners achieved some level of stability and prosperity. These five are Svebek's auto garage, Filipi's general store, Marhefka's general store, Tauber's grocery store and a dance hall. The Marhefka store succeded the Filipi business, so they probably occupied the same building. The photos do show, however, that the buildings were all very close to each other. The dance hall, according to the memory of at least one descendant, was across the street from the businesses. It was built by the Czechs for social events, but was torn down a little more than a year later. There is no surviving photo of it.

The reason for its short life according to the descendant with the clearest memory of it (and she was just a young girl at the time,) is that while it was a Czech hall it attracted a number of non-Czechs. These non-Czechs (probably all men,) regularly imbibed too much alcohol and became rowdy and disruptive. The Czechs found that the best way to control the situation was simply to remove the building—a little drastic perhaps, but certiainly effective.

The earliest known photo of downtown Libuse dates from July, 1918. It shows five buildings along one side of the road (most likely the Holloway Prairie Road,) with nothing but pine stumps on the opposite side. Four of the structures are clearly businesses, while the fifth structure looks like a house that is setback from the line of commerical establishments. While none of the buildings can be identified, it appears from a 1926 photo that at least one and maybe two of these buildings were still standing 8 years later. By comparing the 1918 photo with the 1926 photo we can tell that during this period the older buildings were removed and newer ones built. The buildings in the earlier photo are clearly spread farther apart.

Kolin and Libuse Hotels

There is not much surviving information about the first businesses in Libuse and Kolin. There are just a few surviving photographs, the census records and post office histories, and memories of descendants. Nearly all the early businesses were tied to the story of the post offices, recounted in the previous section. Sometime between the establishment of the businesses on Industrial Street and the early 1920s each of the buildings were dismantled and moved to the Holloway Prairie Road. By 1926 there was also a filling station and pie shop run by Anna Prochaska in a building that was built by her husband and Joseph Ubl. It is certainly an odd combination of businesses. There was also the Libuse Garage and Service Station owned by the Bejsovec family. A 1926 photo shows five of the businesses on one side of the road, with the Bejsovec business barely visible across the road.

We know that both Libuse and Kolin had "hotels," though they were more like boarding houses with just a few rooms. They are mentioned as early as 1914. Who built them is not known exactly, though we can guess that it was the colony's founders. The exact location of the Libuse hotel is not known, but we can guess it was on the existing Holloway Prairie Road. The Kolin hotel stood where the current Kolin WFLA lodge hall is located on B. Miller Road. Presumably these same men operated them, too; after all, no one else was around. The new colonists were busy building farms and there is no evidence that they were involved in running these hotels. There was at least one restaurant and it was apparently in the hotel in Libuse. If there was a restaurant in the Kolin hotel it is not mentioned anywhere. The one thing we know for sure about these two hotels is that they served multiple purposes besides being hotels. Early community meetings were held in them. They also served as the first school buildings. Social events were conducted in them. They were also the site of religious services. The Libuse hotel was torn down apparently by 1920, or perhaps just a little later; no one in the community remembers. The Kolin hotel building survived into the early 1930s at least, though the exact date it was removed is also unknown.

There are at several surviving pictures of the hotels. The ones we know that are definitely the Kolin hotel were long thought to be the only photos of either of the hotels. But it is obviously a different structure than the building in a picture that was recently sent to me by a man in Colorado. He happened across six photos of the "Bohemian Colony near Alexandria" in a stack of old photos he purchased (and which may be the only surviving photo of this building.) and made sure I got them. It must be of the Libuse hotel, though the handwritten notation on the obverse says only "Hotel on second colony." Both buildings are very similar, though the Kolin hotel seems a bit bigger than the Libuse hotel. Also, the Libuse hotel appears to be a more primitive structure than the one in Kolin. The Kolin hotel is roughly 60 feet across the front and appears to be rectangular (the pictures were taken almost dead on center.) The Libuse hotel is more of a square about 30 feet by 25 feet (the photo is a diagonal shot.) I am only guessing at the dimensions using the height of people in the photos as measuring guides.

Both had broad porches on all four sides; they were at least 8 feet wide. In later pictures the Kolin hotel has a the porch along just the front and on one side, in earlier photos it is clear that there was a porch on all four sides. This change came about in 1917 when two rooms were added; Walker reports their cost as $10.90. The Libuse hotel's porch clearly wraps around all four sides of the building. The Kolin hotel's porch has a railing (the two pictures of this hotel show different railings at different times.) The Libuse hotel's porch does not. The main door of the Kolin hotel is centered between four windows, and itself has a window in the top half, and there appears to be two other doors set between the windows (the photo is not clear.) The Libuse hotel's one door is all wood and on the left side of the building, with four windows towards the right side. Finally, the Kolin hotel clearly has a small bellfry on the roof, while there is none visible on the Libuse Hotel.

The picture of the Libuse hotel shows four African-American men standing on the porch, including one in a cook's outfit, complete with apron and toque hat. These were the men who probably worked in the restaurant. What sort of food was served was not recorded, yet we can assume that it was a combination of Czech favorites and local cooking. It must have been quite a learning experience from both sides of this cultural divide: the cooks learning Czech style cooking and the Czechs learning about Southern cooking.

The Czech Schools

A Czech proverb says "what a man has in his pockets his best friends may take away from him, but what he carries in his head the devil himself cannot shake out of him." In keeping with this sentiment, many histories of Czech communities around America show that among the first tasks of Czech immigrants was building their own Czech-run school for their children. This contrasts with many other ethnic groups who arrived during the great waves of immigrants beginning in the 1880s and continuing until World War I. They followed a pattern of sending their children to the nearest established American public school, not establishing their own—they sought rapid assimilation. Both Czech and non-Czech immigrants wanted to educate their children, after all, this was the promise of America. But Czechs had a different view of what was required—they wanted preservation of their culture—and they believed in the Komensky education system. So, they established their own schools which only later were absorbed by the American pulic school system. The Czechs in Libuse and Kolin were no different.

No history of modern education can be told without refering to Jan Amos Komensky (in Latin *Comenius.*) He was born in Moravia in 1592 and died in exile at Amsterdam, Holland, in 1670. In fact, he is often called the "Father of Modern Education." In his lifetime he published more than a 150 scholarly and philosophical books, textbooks, monographs, political treatises, and many other works, including the first illustrated book for children. He prepared the first dictionary of the Czech language. He is credited as the first to use pictures in a textbook. He was among the first to argue for the education of women as equals of men. He believed strongly that education was a lifelong affair, beginning in early childhood. He insisted that education be in the common language instead of Latin and that all languages were learned best through conversation. His Latin textbook, "Janua linguarum reserata" (The Doorway to Languages Is Open,) was one of the most widely read and used in Europe. He argued that education be centered on everyday life through contact with real objects in their actual environment. He advocated that religion and science could be reconciled at a time when Galileo was forced to recant his belief that the earth revolved around the sun because it contradicted Holy Scripture.

Komensky was also a teacher who eventually became the administrator of the Brethren Gymnasium, the college of the Moravian Brethren in Southern Poland. He is called the "last" bishop of the church, before its exile from Moravia at the hands of Catholic Austria after the Battle of the White Mountain in 1620. He taught briefly at Fulnek in England, another Moravian school, a few decades before Benjamin Latrobe studied there. He traveled widely in Europe establishing schools in many places. Among his educational treatises was the "Didaktika magna." In it he laid out a comprehensive system of education. After its publication the king of Sweden engaged him to reform the entire Swedish school system.

Komensky proposed systematizing all knowledge and Linneus, the Swedish-born "father of taxonomy," is believed to have been inspired by Komensky's ideas. His greatest proposed project was ambitious: the unification of all human knowledge. This "pansofia" was dedicated to nothing less than the reformation of the whole of human society. So great was his influence and reknown that, at least according to some historians, he was offered (and declined) the position of first president of Harvard University in Boston, Massachusetts.

It is therefore no surprise that the Czechs of Louisiana called their first school the Komensky School (as are many other schools established in Czech-America.) The hotel served as the first school, with classes beginning nearly immediately for the few children in the community in the first year. But a proper school building was clearly necessary as the number of children was growing rapidly as new colonists arrived.

It was built on Industrial Street on a lot in the Libuse townsite. Walker says it was ready for use in late 1914, though this date seems too early. Walker also says the Lee Lumber Company "dedicated a parcel" of land for this building—but there is no record of any such donation, gift or transfer. In fact, this land was not even owned by Lee Lumber; it was owned by Libuse Townsite Company. Hazmark says it was built "about" 1916, and this is probably correct, especially since it was the Libuse company that donated land for a school building in June, 1915. While the donation was made to the parish school board, as I noted previously, there is no evidence that the board accepted this donation. Johas Rosenthal signed for the donation as president of the school board, but it does not seem like they took the offer seriously. The board never took formal possession of this land. The conveyance document clearly puts the donated land right where the Komensky School was built and where the Libuse Czech hall now stands.

Perhaps the Czechs sensed, or figured out, that the school board had no intention of accepting the land or building a school. Clearly, members of the community took up the offer and built their own school. The new building served as both school and community hall. There are several surviving pictures of this two room building with windows on only three sides. It was about 60 feet long by 30 feet wide. It had a steeply pitched roof and from the full sized window under the gable it is obvious that there was at least some sort of useable space on a second floor.

During several meetings between July and September of 1914 colonists gathered at the home of John Vonesh to discuss the building of a school. Among the many present were Joseph Ubl, Louis Tlucek, Frank Stieninger, Anton Stransky and Peter Sostak. Tlucek was elected president and Stieninger was recording secretary. Stieninger, Stransky and Sostak proposed that all the colonists be asked for funds and other aid in building the school. Ubl suggested asking Louisiana Investment for funds. In a meeting with Donald Despain it was discovered that there were no funds available for a school. That was contrary to what the colonists had been promised in the glowing ads.

After that meeting Ubl suggested asking the Lee Lumber Company for a donation of lumber. The company apparently did not donate the wood. Instead, Walker reports that there was a bill for $433.21 for wood from Lee Lumber. Further, she quotes a letter sent to all the colonists saying that there "is an unpaid balance on our school building amounting to $113.49 which is due the Lee Lumber Company for materials furnished." She says this letter was learned of "according to information gathered from interviews;" if there is an extant copy of this letter it is unknown.

On July 26 a committee to manage the construction was appointed consisting of Adolf Rudolf, Joe Melicar and Anton Stransky. At this meeting it was agreed that $1,000 would be allocated for the school, but no money was to be spent until after meeting with Despain and officers of Lee Lumber. The colonists also agreed to provide either labor or funds to complete the project. 18 men from the community were listed as either donating labor or charging for it. Though of these 18 there are three for which no records of land purchases could be found. While there is a tally of the dollar amount of their work given in Walker's disseration it is not clear which was donation and which was paid labor. Windows and doors were bought from a company called Hayslip and Dear. Furniture was purchased from Hemenway Furniture. Both are in Alexandria.

On September 27th an audit committee was established consisting of Frank Hazmuka, Frank Novotny and John Rybar. The expenditures amounted to $1,242.85. Only $1,129.36 was collected. Hence that $113 deficit. The amount collected is reported by Walker to come from a $1,000 donation from the Bohemian Colonization Club in Omaha and $5 each from 24 of its members. These members were scattered across the country from Washington State to New York City and many points in between. Of these 24 only five are not recorded as buying land in the community. The rest did purchase land here. The deficit was made up by pledges from colonists in the amount of $92.10 and the remainder was to be raised by charging non-Czech students 50 cents per year. A woman named Effie Moseley was apparently the only one to take up this opportunity. Trustees to run the school were also appointed; they were Joseph Prochaska, Charles Pecinovsky and John Vonasek.

Other than the letter sent to the colonists in late 1915 there was apparently no further discussion of the school. In August, 1916 a new school committee was elected. Those serving were Martin Cizek, Joseph Stepan and Anton Kalous. Frank Kadlec offered to drill a well for 20 cents a foot if he got help to bring the necessary machinery to the site. Either old man John Malecek, or his son, also named John, donated the piping required, it is not clear which. Yet, it was to "neighbor Stepan" that $30.50 was paid for drilling the well. The Lee Lumber company was not paid their outstanding debt until December 30th, 1916.

In 1917 there were two decisions made concerning the school. One was that "the community decided that teachers were not allowed to loan out use of the building with the approval" of the the Czechs (Walker's words.) No mention is made of for what purposes teachers were lending out the school. The other decision made was "to act on the request by the Rapides Parish school board for the purchase of three more acres to be used for the school grounds." (again, Walker's words.) No document for any such purchase could be found.

In late 1919 and early 1920 John Skodacek tried to get modern toilets built for the school instead of the outhouses that were being used. He was elected treasurer of the school in 1920. Walker reports that there was no further recorded discussion of the school until 1923. It seems odd that a school could be operated for three years without any public discussion in a community were public meetings were the way that decisions were made. In that year John Skodacek and Charles Voda are reported to have asked the parish school board for money to make repairs "to the porch." The school board supposedly authorized $300 for this work. The problem is that none of the pictures show any porch at all. Walker reports no further discussion at community meetings relating to the school until 1928. Again, it seems odd to think that this school was run so smoothly that there was no need for additional discussion of any kind.

By 1928 the building was beginning to show its years. Made entirely of pine wood it was succumbing to the elements as well as wear and tear. Sometime during 1928 or early 1929 the parish school board floated the idea of issuing bonds to build a new school, or in the alternative, consolidating Libuse with the Pineville school district. This was a time of a major improvements in school buildings under the administration of Governor Huey P. Long. The community was apparently asked to decide for themselves what they wanted to do and surely this was a recognition by local and state authorities that the Czechs were a community unto themselves.

In 1929 this problem was "solved" by a "wind storm" that damaged the building to such an extent that it had to be torn down. Oddly, no one seems to recall exactly when this tragedy occurred, just that it was sometime in the "second term." It is remembered, though, that the students finished out the school year in the home of Joe and Annie Zmek just a few hundred yards away. This, however, occasioned several major developments in Libuse. It was decided that no new Czech school would be built; the community had lost its precious Komensky School. Czech children began to be bused (or walked) to existing parish schools in Pineville, just two or so miles away. There are plenty of stories about how they did not exactly fit in at first. Elders in the community speak of being teased mercilessly by their non-Czech schoolmates for their Czech-accented English, strange names and their appearance. It was on this Komensky school property that a new Czech hall was built the next year.

The second school in the community was called simply the "Kolin School." For the first five years it was held in the building it shared with the community hall that itself had previously served as the Kolin Hotel. During these years (and later) there was supposedly a second hotel in Kolin that replaced the one now being used as a school. I could find references to it only in Walker's dissertation. Various members of the community served on the school board, being elected anew each year. They included August Bernat, John Vonesh, Vaclav Dvorak, John Lehky, Frank Bohata, Joseph Wittera, Karel Steffek and John Vondracek, all of whom were property owners in Kolin. No non-Czechs served during this time. All the students were Czech and it was run by the community with little oversight by the parish school board.

In 1919 the Rapides Parish school board issued bonds to build a two-room school building using then current standards. It was built by the 1920–1921 school year. This was also the time of the creation of the Kolin Schood District #46 and it was definitely part of the parish system. This school was built in a style similar to other schools in the parish system. This building survived for 10 years. On October, 31st, 1930, it burned to the ground. For the next two years school was again held in the community hall. A new building was completed in 1932, but with only one room. Frank Baley (now anglicised to Bailey in the 1930 census,) mentioned so many times already, and now 37 years old, was the low bidder to construct it. His bid was $2,220. The actual cost was said to be just over $2,000. He bought the lumber from Bargain Lumber. This was a newly opened business operated by the Czech Carl Svebek in Alexandria.

Walker says Baley used the register of the Kolin Hotel to record the payments he made to the seven Czechs and a few other men he hired to help him build the school. But Baley's occupation is listed as "farmer" in the census of 1930 and not as either hotel keeper or in construction business. Plus, there is no hotel in any of the pictures of Kolin in this period. Nor is one mentioned in either Hazmark's book or the newsletter. Surely there would be a record of such a major business in a small settlement. The best I can figure is that it was an old register still existing—but why use a 10 or 15 year old book? In any event, in 1936 this school was closed because there were not enough students to warrant its continued operation. In 1937 the building was dismantled and the lumber reused for a building at Buckeye High School which was were the Czech students were being bused.

In the early 1920s there were a few other small one room school houses that existed at the fringes of the Czech communities. Among them were the Liberty and Philadelphia schools. They were all taken down as the schools were consolidated at the end of the 1920s. Not only was Huey Long on a school building spree, but buses and better roads and bridges made transporting students much easier. Only the Komensky and Kolin schools were exclusively Czech—the others had mixed enrollments. None of the schools had more than 30 to 40 students at a time and Komensky had the largest student body. While there were the usual grades in each school, sometimes they were combined (like second and third grades, or 7th & 8th) because there were not enough teachers to be matched up to the few students in some grades.

At least in the beginning the students were all speaking Czech as their first language and the teachers all English speaking. One elder I met said "On the first day of school the teachers spoke only English and the children only Czech." Many others recount the fun and games and posturing that ensued during the first year as the teachers began to get the kids to speak English. As the years rolled by all the students spoke English upon entering school, but many still spoke Czech at home. Kids being kids, one can imagine the havoc they caused and the fun they had at the teacher's expense while speaking Czech to each other. Another feature of the early Czech student body is that they are the ones who taught their non-English speaking parents the new language. Whether any of the teachers learned more than a few Czech words is not recorded or remembered.

Also, in the early years Czech students stayed in school until 14 or 15. This was a year or so later than their non-Czech counterparts. Czech enrollment was a higher percentage of the school aged children in the community than their non-Czech neighbors. It was only later that students, both Czech and not, were staying in school longer. All of the teachers' names are known, none were Czech, though one married a Czech. Interestingly, no mention is made by Walker about how much any teacher was paid. Finally, the one thing that stands out about both the Komensky and Kolin schools is that they were both started and operated by the Czech colonists before the parish school board became involved.

After being successful with ensuring that their children learned English the parents came on a new "problem"—the older children were losing their Czech language knowledge and the younger students were not gaining any. So, for a few brief years from 1925 to 1928 they organized Czech language summer school, held, of course, at the Komensky and Kolin schools. Joseph Subrt ran the one in

Libuse and Mary Rychter operated Kolin's. For a text book they used a monthly publication of the Bohemian Free Thinking School Society called "Svobodna Škola"—"Liberty School" in English. The Society had a motto: "Czech children belong in Czech schools." But perhaps at cross purposes to their intent the cover of their publication featured American patriotic themes replete with images of the American flag and eagles. Once the two original schools were gone so were the Czech language classes for the young.

First World War Soldiers

World War I came during the first years of the colony and President Woodrow Wilson's oratory about the rights of peoples immediately stirred up hopes of a free Czech nation in the hearts and minds of the Czechs of Rapides Parish. Among the 10 million or so men across America who were required to sign up for the draft were all the eligible men from the young community. 15 men registered for the draft in 1917, two others on the first call up in 1918, and 47 in the second call up in September of 1918. Of the latter group, it was probable that many wanted to join so that they could immediately become American citizens as a new law passed in May of 1918 allowed them to do. However, the army was just taking single men and most of these were married so could not take advantage of the law.

Out of the 66 Czechs from Libuse and Kolin known to have registered for the draft only 14 actually served in the military during the war. 11 stayed in Rapides Parish after the war, 2 moved out, and one did not move in until after the war. A fifthteenth man who served during the war was not from Louisiana, but married into a local family before moving away with his bride. Only one of those serving was married. The local boys were inducted into the service at Camp Beauregard which was just about 8 miles from Libuse. That is were most of them saw their service, too. Only two of them actually went to Europe itself for the war. Sadly, one died.

Albin Hajek served from September, 1917 until March of 1919, but he never traveled further than Camp Pike in Arkansas in his time in the Quartermaster Corps. Frank Hazmuka, Jr. served his entire war time service at Camp Beauregard just 8 miles from his house. His period of service lasted from September, 1918 to March, 1919; but he also served in World War II, seeing action in France. Rudolph Stuchlik enlisted at Camp Beauregard and served at a training center during the war. William Hrachovina served from May, 1918, to May, 1919, and he too stayed stateside. Edward Kastanek served his time stateside from July, 1918 to March, 1919; Anton Welcek served from May, 1918 to September, 1919. Joseph Stegner, Charles Zerbe and Fred Westerchil had similar experiences but their actual dates of service are unknown.

Charles Frank Nimberger was a member of the Motor Transport Corps, but did not see overseas service. He was discharged in January of 1919. He spent just enough time back in Louisiana to get married to a local Czech girl and then he and his new wife moved to Cleveland, Ohio, where he was born. Anton Holy Jr. enlisted at Camp Beauregard and was sent to France, but the war was already over. He served until 1921 and upon his discharge moved to Redding, California, though other members of his family stayed in Louisiana. (He also started the Ballpark hot dog company which is a rather large nationwide concern today.) Edward Walasek was a clerk in the army for just six months: July to December, 1918. He enlisted at Camp Dodge, Iowa. He was in Louisiana long enough to marry a local Czech girl, Anna Baroch, before returning to Omaha, Nebraska. Joseph Suba enlisted in July, 1918, in South Dakota where he was living after having immigrated from Bohemia. He was discharged just six months later in December, 1918, at a military camp in New Mexico. He made his way to Louisiana by the early 1920s and bought land in the Bohemian Colony.

It was Joseph Wittera, who joined the army in 1918, who died in Europe. In a sad irony he died the very last day of the war when the Germans unleashed one last furious and spiteful barage to use up the ammunition they knew they were going to lose under the terms of the armistace. Wittera was in the trenches and bled to death after having his legs blown off. He is buried at Arlington National Cemetery near Washington D. C.

What World War I did, though, was foster the creation of the Republic of Czechoslovakia. This resulted in a lower number of immigrants from the Czech and Slovak lands to America. That had a direct negative impact on the growth of Libuse and Kolin for the founders had been hoping that these expected immigrants would fill the towns—and now they were not coming.

Naturalization Papers

In the Rapides Parish Courthouse, in three slim volumes, are a rare collection of original applications for naturalization. This was the only collection of this kind that I was able to find in the many courthouses that I went to; what happened to other similar records could not be determined. A total of 31 men applied for citizenship. No woman are among the applicants, though wives are sometimes listed as dependants. The first application was dated 1917 and the last in 1924. The first thing to note is that all of the forms were filled out by the individuals themselves, showing them all to be literate. Furthermore, the handwriting is all practiced, neat and clear. Of these applicants, 27 stayed in Libuse or Kolin for the rest of their lives. This is the disposition of the remaining four:

George Madjarosh applied in May 1918, but he is not in the 1920 census of the community as are other members of his family. He does state on the application that he lived at 825 Jackson Street in Alexandria, but he is not in the 1920 Louisiana census anywhere. Anton Besta applied in May, 1918, a year after he bought 75 acres, but in 1920 he sold his land and moved. Peter Pinkava, who applied in 1919 and is in the 1920 census then disappears from the record. No sale of the farm he owned could be found. Two of them, Rudolph Lanicky and his wife, Mary, are mentioned no where else in any records in Rapides Parish. Why they applied here and then quickly left is unknowable.

The applications are rich in detail; some are interesting enough to be noted here. Among the details are age, height, weight, hair and eye color, and "distinguishing marks." The two who listed distinguishing marks were George Madjarosh, whose "2 middle fingers [were] cut off," and Anton Kostak, who said that he had "small pox scars on face." The rest left this line blank.

Other details include the town of their birth or last residence and the names and birthplaces of their wives if they had one. Only Carl Svebek had a non-Czech American wife, Bessie. She was born at Hattiesburg, Mississippi. Andres Brousek's wife was the daughter of Czech immigrants, but she was born at Mountain Lake, Minnesota. The forms also include the port they left Europe from and the name of the ship they traveled on and its date of arrival. One claimed he did "not remember" through which port he arrived.

The forms show that they almost all, 29 in fact, arrived by ship at various ports of entry: seventeen, or more than half, arrived at New York City, but also one each at Newark and Hoboken, New Jersey; four at Baltimore, Maryland; and four at Galveston, Texas. Of these last four, three were in one family: Joseph Prochaska, 47, was accompanied by his two sons, Joseph Jr., 20, and Charles, 18, in 1908. No wife is mentioned. Oddly, the two sons signed their forms on June 15th, 1923, while their father waited until April 9th, 1924 to sign his.

Two said they came through slightly different points in Illinois by way of different railroad companies from Canada—on the same day, March 15th, 1915. One was Frank David, who said he was born in Moravia and his last residence was Duffield, Alberta, Canada (a tiny settlement 40 miles to the west of Edmonton.) He said he traveled with his wife, Mary, (who was born, nee Doubner, in Bohemia,) on the Grand Trunk Railroad through Collinsville, Illinois. Meanwhile, the bachelor Anton J. David, almost certainly Frank's son, said he was born in Kladno, Bohemia, and came on the Canadian RailRoad Company from Alberta, Canada, to Glen Carbon, Illinois. Now, Illinois does not share a border with Canada. In fact, both Collinsville and Glen Carbon are suburbs of St. Louis, Missouri, deep in the Midwest. So exactly where they crossed is hard to say, though North Dakota is probable. One possibility for the difference in trains is that the parents came by passenger train while the son traveled with the family possessions on a freight train. That the Moravian father married a Bohemian mother surely accounts for the son's birthplace. The David family has the distinction of relocating from the farthest North American point; Edmonton is just under 127 miles farther away from Libuse than Yakima and Odessa, Washington, where four others came from: 2,497 miles versus 2,370.

In keeping with the general confusion of tracking down and identifying any immigrant from the Czech and Slovak lands they wrote the country of their birth in several different ways. 23 included the names of their town followed by a country. Of those who wrote the combination, nine wrote the hometown followed by "Bohemia" and five wrote it followed by "Austria." One used the combination "Bohemia, Austria." Another wrote "Bohemia, Austria-Hungary." One wrote "Bohemia, Czechoslovakia," and one wrote just "Czechoslovakia." One wrote "Mahran, Austria," but did not include a town at all. Mahran is the German word for the English "Moravia," which is what two others listed in English. Seven wrote just the name of town but not any country. One did not provide either town or country. Fianlly, one, Anton Holy, was from Ploesti, Roumania (he used the old spelling,) and one, Charles Voda, said he was born in Daruvar, Serbia. Both in fact are Czech as evidenced by their surnames. It appears that their parents were working in these other areas which was not that unusual within the Austro-Hungarian empire.

Most wrote that they renounced allegiance to "Charles, Emperor of Austria and Apostolic King of Hungary," which is quite a fancy title. Three seemed more disdainful by writing that they renounced allegiance to "the present Austro-Hungarian government." Charles Voda renounced allegiance to "Peter, King of the Serbs, Croats and Slovenes." Holy did not fill out the blank for renouncing allegiance. Joseph Koncinsky said simply that he was a "subject of Austria." Among the many Czechs in Libuse and Kolin most had obtained citizenship elsewhere in America. Surely this points to people wanting to become Americans as soon as was possible. Indeed, it seems the average number of years between arrival and attaining citizenship was just a year or two longer than the required waiting period of five years.

Initial Progress grinds to a halt.

The streets were never laid out as the land and weather conditions did not prove to be as attractive as billed by the promoters. Only vestiges of two streets survive—Industrial Street with the Czech Hall and Maine Street with a few houses. The land practices and the topography conspired against the neat square divisions that the founders envisioned. No craftsman and just a few store keepers moved to the colony. Farmers predominated. Some families moved away quickly, others stayed just a few years. When they first arrived by train and stayed at a hotel in downtown Alexandria they must have seemed to be the most exotic thing around. The Czech language, of course, was very different than any heard previously in these parts. The settlers who remained got to farming, having weekend socials and working at building structures. About a dozen of these structures still stand today. They overbuilt them, with a view towards lasting forever.

It took a lot of work to eke out a subsistance existence and grow wealth at the same time. The Czechs of Rapides Parish were doing fine. 15 years after the first settlers got into the business of town building the Great Depression hit the country. But the hard work and preparation and self-sufficiency of the Czechs made them immune to many of the problems which struck their fellow Rapides Parish citizens. But the Depression did kill any further dreams of building Libuse and Kolin into thriving metropolises. Then the war came and finally the post war economic boom and rush towards suburbanization—and that kept the two towns the small sleepy hamlets they are today.

9

Reality—The 1920s

The First Census in 1920

Overview

There were several large immigrant populations in Rapides Parish in 1920, mostly of Italians, Greeks, Syrians and Belgians. They were, though, scattered at addresses throughout the city and parish. They were not in specific communities or areas, though some did live close to each other. What makes the Czechs unique is their colonizing one area. The enumeration shows that the Czech families were all close neighbors. A few were in ward 4, the remainder in wards 9 and 10 (a ward is a geographic subdivision of a Louisiana parish; these three wards abut each other.) Nearly every family along the "Holloway [Prairie] Road" (ward 10) was Czech, only 5 were not. Yet, of all the families on Gravelpit and Donahue roads (both in ward 4,) none are Czech; these two were established roads before the Czechs arrived. The remainder of the Czech families are along unnamed roads in the three wards; these were so-called "unimproved dirt roads." There are 94 family names in the census of 96 households.

These dirt roads were built by Czechs. We know this because every property description for farm acreage purchased by a Czech has a provision that says "less 25 feet for a road along the edge" of the parcel—and there were no roads when they first arrived. Yet, as can be seen by this census report, sprinkled among the Bohemian families on these new roads were a handful of English speaking long-time Americans the vast majority of whom were born in Louisiana. There were also one French and one German immigrant families in this area. One can only imagine what these people perceived of their Czech neighbors with their odd language, odd names and insularity. Relations were cordial, but distant, according to many of the elders that I spoke with.

The Enumerators

The census reports were prepared by three different individuals over a 100 day period. An odd feature of the 14 sheets used to make the enumeration are the headings detailing the location of the enumeration. Even though all they had to do was fill in the blanks on the form for "township or other division," "name of incorporated place" and "name of institution" there was absolutely no consistency. One would assume that those filled out by the same enumerator would all be done the same, but on no two sheets are these headings the same. On one sheet the "institution" space was filled in with "Bohemian Colony," this space is blank on all the others. On several there are variations of "township or other division," ranging from the simple to the complex to the legal decription to nothing at all. On some it says "Pineville" and on others it says "Libuse" under either township or incorporated place. Quite amazing when you think about it.

O. M. Nally did his enumerating on the 13th, 14th, 15th and 28th of January. Thomas Daniel did his on four days in February; the 11th and then on the 26th, 27th and 28th. George Robertson did the most work. He took 8 days in March, the 1st, 4th and 5th and then 5 days at the end of the month between the 24th and 31st. The rest he did during the first seven days of April, missing only the 4th. As would be the only method at the time all the entries are handwritten. As also would be expected the three pensmenships are different, but all easy to read. Except Robertson and Nally apparently had their good days and bad days: some sheets are riddled with cross-outs and over-writes and blobs of spilled ink from their fountain pens—others are clear as a bell.

Of course, from this census we get the only detailed knowledge of who was in the communuties just six years after its founding. The 1920 census of Rapides Parish lists 408 individuals in 90 mostly Czech households. As would be expected there was a wide range of family configurations. Following is a statistical portrait of the colony as well as some of the more interesting situations.

Specific Numbers

There were eight bachelors. Two were boarders: Joe Dolezal lived with the Vondraceks and Joseph Subrt lived with the Zdarskys. They worked on the farm on which they lived. Five other bachelors owned their own farms: Frank Kawir, Wesley Klasek, Thomas Modrrech, Frank Pinkava and Rudolph Stuchlik. The 37 year old Frank Datel lived with his mother. The widowed Joseph Hrachovina lived with his 18 year old son, Frank.

There were 10 childless couples with their own farms or businesses. The youngest were the Ludwicks; they were in their early 20s, and the Kaderkas who were in their late 20s. Obviously they were just starting out. The Hromadkas, Lehkys and Zdarskys were in their mid 30s, we do not know why they had no children and there are any number of possibilties. The Broziks and the Janoliks were in their 40s, the Dvoraks in their 50s and both the Elicars and Nouseks were in their 60s. These last five may well have had children who did not move into the colony.

There were several families who were related by marriage or birth but who lived in their own household. Albert Baley, who had his own young family, was John Baley's oldest son. Anton Kastanek's son, Edward, just started his own family. George Petrasek, who was just married to a woman named Minnie, was Frank Petrasek's 24 year old son, but Frank also had a 6 year old son, Otto. Frank Suchy was a young man with a wife and two infant children; he was the son of Charlie Suchy. Frank Ludwick was married to May Krist, the 21 year old daughter of the recently widowed Mary Krist. The young couple lived with the Krist family. Frank Chruma's son Joseph was maried with young children.

As is so often found in the early years of the community, there is a confusing situation. On one census sheet, 36 year old Joe Melicar lived with his father-in-law, Anton Holy. He presumably was married to Anton's eldest daugher, Ellen, just 22. There is also a 1 ½ year old toddler "son" named Ameal—which is probably "Emil" since the name "Ameal" is not a name on any list of boy's names I could ever find. On another census sheet dated just 10 days later a 37 year old Joe Melicar, with his own farm, was married to a 23 year old woman named "Hellan" and they had a 1½ year old toddler whose name is indecipherable. Of course, *Ellen* and *Hellan* are very close and the thick accents of the respondants could account for this. Besides, both young ladies are listed as born in Roumania. Could Joe and his wife been visiting his father-in-law's at the first pass by Nally and then found again at their own home on the next pass? It is certainly possible.

There were four single female head of households. Mary Krist was obviously recently widowed as she had a daughter who was just 4 years and 4 months old. She also had six other children under the age of 12 living with her. She must have been widowed either right before or right after her arrival for the 4 year old was born in Louisiana, though her husband is not listed as buried in either one of the Czech cemeteries. She must have been very thankful that her son-in-law lived with her. Marie Kment was 51 and the mother of 3 adult chilren who lived with her, she was, of course, the woman who purchased the Kolin townsite as her farm. Mary Sedlecek was also not that long widowed; she had six children ranging in age from 25 to 6. Three were boys, including the two oldest, and 3 were girls. Mary Rychter is listed in her land purchase agreement as a "spinster." At the age of 32 she was operating an 80 acre poultry farm.

Other than Marie Kment, there were seven other families whose children were all in the workforce but all living at home. Of course, this was an era when children often left school at an age we would consider too young. The Fizacek, Frank and Welcek children were all over 18. Both of the daughters in the Vorisek family were working on the family farm and were not in school: 14 year old Zdenka and 16 year old Mary. The Teply family had two sons, 18 and 20, who worked on the family farm. The youngest child in the Wosterchil family was 16 year old Blanche; she worked as a domestic servant. The youngest in the Voda household was 15 year old Ludwiek. He was not in school and had no occupation listed, though he was probably a laborer on the family farm.

17 families had children both in school and in the workforce, yet who all lived at home. The number and ages of the children portray several different scenarios. One of these is that the mother of the family was bearing children with a frequency that modern times would find almost alarming, but that for the dawn of the 1900s was considered quite normal. For the largest families the children were just one or two years, at most three, apart. The Holy's had eight kids from 7 to 24. The Fabianeks' seven children ranged from 4 ½ to 17. The Kramel family consisted of eight children from 5 ½ to 19. The Legner family only had five children, but they were from 8 to 17.

Most of the families were in the middle age spread range. These families waited three to five years before having the next child. The John Baley's had five kids from 10 to 24 years old. The Filipi's four children ranged from 7 to 20. In the Kalous family were five kids from 5 to 19. The Kadlec's had four kids from 5 to 19. The Stegner's three children were 14 to 26. Still, the age differences are nearly 15 years in these families. The Wittera's only had two chidlren and they were 15 and 20.

But in some of the families there was an enormous age difference between the youngest and oldest. The Lamberger's four children were 9 to 23. The Prejcl's seven children ranged from just 6 months old to 19. Mary Sedlecek was the single mother of six children aged from 6 to 25 years. The Vlach's five children were a babe just 6 months old to 18. In the Vonesh family there were two children, one 6 and the other 18. The Hazmuka's had two sons who were 21 and 23, but then they had a late-in-life son who was 8.

And, in keeping with at least one confusing situation for every aspect of the Czechs there are the Maleceks. According to the census they were in their early

70s. They were actually the oldest people in the 1920 census. Their oldest child was a 36 year old son, but there was also a 12 "daughter" in the house. The census does not say if this young girl was the older Malecek's or if she was the daughter of the son. It seems highly improbable that this young girl was the daughter of 72 year old Mrs. Malecek, for she would have been 60 when the girl was born! But then we are left with the sad case of a mother dying in childbirth or soon thereafter. This seems the likely scenario here and thus we are confronted with the only mother among all the Czechs in the colony who died leaving a young child

The rest of the families, 33 in all, only had children of school age or younger. 86 of the school age children were in school, It was mostly older boys, 16 and older, and girls from 15 and over that were not in school.

Cohorts

There were 55 children 5 years and younger; none of these were in school. The youngest child, Charles Zerbe, was five weeks old. 89 children were between 6 and 12 and nearly all of these were in school. There were 40 teenagers between 13 and 15. 18 of these worked and did not go to school. There were 23 teenagers between 16 and 19, and only 4 of these were in school, the rest worked. 47 people were in their 20s. 61 were between 31 and 40. 52 were in the next age cohort of 41 to 50 Only 16 had lived into their 60s. Just 3 had attained the age of 70 or more, and not by much. They were the 71 year old Frank Chruma, and John and Josephine Malecek, both 72. No one was older. In a surprising finding there were only 190 females as compared to the 213 males; there are usually more females than males in any community.

Origins

Most of the parents where born in the old country and most of the kids (of any age for this analysis) were born in America. 24 of the children were born in Bohemia and it was always the oldest children in the family. The youngest child born in Bohemia was Sadie Smigura, who was just 8 at the time of the census, having arrived in 1914. Charlie Safarik and Fannie Holy were 11; the remainder were 14 or older. 3 "children" were born in Moravia: Josephine Fizacek was 22 by this time. 2 were born in Germany. All six of the oldest Holy children were born in Roumania.

By 1920 there were 25 children born in the communities of Libuse and Kolin. Bertha Goldstein was the first Czech child born in the colony; she was 6 at the time of the census. Agnes Krist, Eddie Tucek and Edward Zmek were all 4 years and a few months old. The remaining 20 children were less than 4.

The remaining 181 were born in 18 other states. Only 5 children were born in Southern states: two of the Westerchil boys were born in Arkansas and one child was born in each North Carolina, Tennessee and Texas. 2 were born in each Maryland and Oklahoma; one was born in New York and one in New Jersey. Among the Midwestern states, 13 were born in Wisconsin, 9 in Missouri; 9 in Iowa; 8 in Minnesota, 4 in North Dakota and 2 in Michigan. But five states were the birthplaces of the majority of children: 16 were born in Pennsylvania; 19 in Ohio; 21 in Illinois; 30 in Nebraska and the most, 32, were born in Kansas. These five states all have large Czech populations.

Of the wives (and thus the mothers) 12 were born in America. Five were born in Nebraska, 2 in Pennsylvania, and one each in Illinois, Iowa, Minnesota, Missouri, and Ohio. Of the wives born in Europe, 3 were from Austria (and at least two of these spoke German,) 2 were born in Moravia (thus they spoke Czech,) 2 were born in Roumania (but apparently of Bohemian parents.) One, Mrs. Skodacek, was born in "Hungary," but was really Slovak as evidenced by her "mother tongue." 57 were born in Bohemia. For only one wife we do not know the origin. Among the four single woman, three were born in Bohemia; Mary Rychter was born in Kansas.

Of the wives who arrived from Europe the earliest to arrive was Barbara Chruma. She came in 1867. 19 total arrived in the 1800s and 39 in the 1900s. The latest arrival was Josephine Smigura, who arrived in 1914. Among the three woman heads of household, 2 came in the 1800s, and Mary Krist came in 1904. However, the census is silent on the arrival dates of 17 of the wives, so some may have come earlier or later.

Of the adult men (including single male heads of households and also the fathers,) only 10 were born in the United States: three in Kansas, two each in Iowa and Nebraska, one each in Illinois, Minnesota and Pennsylvania. Of those born in Europe, 2 were born in Austria, and at least one of these, Mr. Locker, spoke Germany. One listed his birthplace as "Austro-Hungary," but spoke "Bohemian." The birthplace of Mr. Skodacek was listed as "Hungary," but he spoke Slovak. 70 listed their birthplace as Bohemia. Only one, Rudolph Stuchlik, listed "Czechoslovakia" as his birthplace; it was just a three year old country at the time. Of the men who arrived from Europe, the earliest to immigrate was Joseph Wittera, in 1865. The last to arrive was Joseph Zdarsky, in 1916. 30 of them arrived in the 1800s; 48 arrived after 1900.

There were two Moravian families: The Fizaceks and the Welceks. There is some confusion as to whether the Holy family was a Roumanian family or Slovaks. The Skodaceks were listed as coming from Hungary, but they were really Slovak, since that is the language they spoke. The Fabianeks were listed as coming from Germany, though they were Bohemian. The Lockers were from "Austria," along with two wives: Anna Steiber and Anna Kozorek.

75 of those born in Europe were citizens at the time of this census. 98 were not listed as being American citizens in the census. There were 45 of people who spoke only "Bohemian" as it is listed in the census of 1920. Almost all where the wives/mothers, but one was 10 year old Robert Smetak (though this is likely a mistaken entry.) These ladies no doubt spoke Czech to the kids, even though all the kids supposedly spoke English. Yet, there are reports that many children only spoke Czech when they first went to school, and then they were teaching their mothers the English when they got home from school.

Occupations

159 people were said to be employed. However, it is highly likely that everyone who was capable (and they all were, except the very youngest) was working in some way. On these self-sufficient farms there was always plenty to do. Nearly all those working were "farmers" or engaged in "farm work," (or some variation of this term,) on "general farms." Only 22 of those employed were not working on a farm, the remaining 137 were working in farming.

72 men who were heads of households were farmers who operated their own general farms. Wesley Klasek, John Nousek, Frank Chocholousek and Charles Zerbe were said to operate "garden farms." The difference between general and garden farms could not be determined from the census. Frank Ludvick was a "farmer," but he was the son-in-law of Mary Krist, so he really didn't have his own farm. Joseph Zmek, Anton Kostalek and Joseph Frank were said to be "farm managers," but it is not clear on whose farm they were working, though they all owned farms. Rudolph Sedlecek was the only person listed as "farm work out," which perhaps means he worked on someone else's farm. However, since his mother owned a farm this seems unlikely. About ½ owned their farms free from a mortgage and ½ had mortgages.

The three single mothers, Mary Krist, Marie Kment and Mary Sedlecek, were also among the farmers operating their own general farms. Mary Rychter was a "poultry farmer." This is the only farm listed as this specific type. Since she was living alone, perhaps one of the farm managers or Rudolph Sedlecek was working

there. Margaret Tauber was said to operate a "home farm," a term not more specifically defined, and this was the only time it was used.

It was the wives, sons and daughters who were listed as farm workers. They
were working on their family's farm. 21 of the wives and 5 daughters were listed
as farm workers. 19 sons were farm workers, as well as the two boarders, Dolezal
and Subrt. Albert Baley was the only head of household who was said to be a
farm worker, though he owned his own farm.

Age wise, the vast majority of the employed were 20 years old and older. Barbara Chruma, 68, and John Malecek, 72, were the oldest still working. Only seventeen were younger than 20. Of these, 15 were teenagers, including 13 year
Joseph Fabianek and 14 year old Zdenka Vorisek, who were farm workers on
their family's farm. 13 year old Bessie Tauber worked at her parent's grocery store
(and we know she assisted with the post office.) The two youngest listed as
employed were 7 year old Louie Krist and 9 year old Jerry Krist. Louie was actually listed as "working out." But they were probably doing something akin to
chores rather than real work on the family farm. Given that their mother was a
single woman, though, it is not surprising.

Of those not in farming, 8 were in retail of some kind, though all in the Czech
colony. Martin Cizek and his wife Franie ran their own general store (she is listed
as "retail clerk.") Frank Hromadka we know had a hardware store and was no
doubt helped by his wife, Jennie, though it is not stated on the census. Joseph
Tauber ran a grocery store. His young daughter, Bessie, was a "retail clerk" at the
store. (His wife Margaret definitely worked there, even though she is not listed
doing so. They had also just begun to run the post office, but that is not noted on
the census.) Frank Elicar was a shoemaker. Joe Melicar is listed twice in the census, once as a "merchant" and the second time as a "wholesale merchant." Anton
Welcek was a "machinest" at an "auto mechanic" business. This may have been
in his own garage along the Marksville Highway near his father's farm, but it is
not certain.

Just 12 people were working outside of the Czech colony. John Malecek, 36,
was working at a brassworks, presumably in Alexandria. Bohdan Kment, 27, was
said to be engaged in "other work," but this is not defined. Charlie Lamberger
was a 23 year old truck driver. 24 year old Fred Wosterchil was working in an oil
field and his 20 year old brother, Robert, is listed as a "salesman for a US company," which is not further defined. There were seven girls working as "domestic"
servants, ranging in age from 15 to 21. They were (from youngest to oldest,) Ella
Bohata, Victoria Fabianek, Blanche Wosterchil, Rose Sedlecek, Matilda Fabianek, Helen Vonesh and May Krist Ludwick (who was the only one out of her

teens.) 16 year old Jerry Kadlec was said to be a "servant," which was odd work for a young boy at the time.

The odd man out in the census was the 57 year old John Baley—his employment was listed as "coal miner." There are no coal mines in Louisiana. This was obviously a carry over from his time in Pennsylvania (where most of his children were born,) and perhaps even from Bohemia, where he was born. He did, however, own a farm, and thus farming was likely his true profession. One can imagine the enumerator chuckling a bit to himself as he wrote this down.

First Names

The first names present in the community show a rather limited selection of names. Several predominate. Among the adults born in Europe, 122 used English equivalents while 33 kept Czech versions. Adults born in the United States mostly had American names, more so among the men than the women. The majority of young children born in America were given typically American names: I will not list all here. But 22 who were born in the United States were given Czech names. Most of these were still children, but a few were young adults at the time of the census.

The most diverse group are the American born youths with Czech names. For females, we find a single instance each of Bozena, Albina, Jarmila, Zdenka, Libuse, Melada and Johanna. There were also 2 Olga's, 1 Veronika (but also one Veronica,) and 3 named Vlasta (it means "my country," and was often given to the youngest daughter in many Czech immigrant families across America.) Of the males, there was one each of Bohdan, Bohous, Bohumil, Brestislav, Ludwig and Otokar. There were also three Americanized versions of Ladislav: Laddie, Ladik, and Lad.

The break down among all females (other than the special cases above) show 20 Mary's—7 born here and 13 born in Bohemia (Marie is the Czech,) and 9 with the Czech Marie—6 from Bohemia and 2 from America; 18 Anna's—most born in Bohemia; 13 Helen's, of which 5 are Czech variants (Hillan or Hilan;) 12 Rosa's or Rosie's (Roza in Czech;) 9 Emma's—for which there is no Czech equivalent; 8 Bessies, one Lizzie and one Elizabeth—all born here; 8 Josephine's (Josefina in Czech;) 7 named Francis, but only one born in the United States (Františka,) and 2 Katerina's. So, Mary or Marie, along with Anna, comprise more than half of the female's names.

Nearly all the adult men were born in Bohemia, yet had English names, showing that they probably changed them shortly after their arrival in America. Many used the common Czech to English translations. For all adult (i.e. older than 18) males the breakdown is 30 Frank's (František in Czech;) 21 named Joseph, 5 Joe's and 1 Josef (the Czech form;) 24 variants on Charles, including one Karl and one Carl, who were father and son (Karel is the Czech form;) and 10 Anton's—of whom 3 were born in America (and for which there is no established difference between Czech and English;) and 19 John's (Jan in Czech.) These five comprise well over half of the men's names.

Of the rest, there are either no direct Czech to English equivalents (though for some there are common translations,) or the name is the same in both: 9 Edward's; 6 Emil's; 6 Jerry's; 5 Rudolph's (Rudolf in Czech,) 3 James's and 2 Jim's (most often from Vaclav, though this name in English is sometimes Walter and sometimes Wesley;) 5 variants on William; 4 Louis's; 4 Albert's, two from America and two from Bohemia; 4 George's (most often from Jiři, though this is sometimes translated as James,) 3 Henry's, 3 Fred's and just 1 Jacob.

Before any reader concludes that Czech culture has a paucity of first names, or that the majority of Czech men or woman, either here or in Europe have the same names, I will point out that many perfectly fine Czech names are missing from this list. In fact, in the Czech culture there is a tradition of "name days." Many people born on a certain day are given the name corresponding to that day. At the very least there is a male and female name for every day of the year. That there is not one Miloš, Miloslav, Zdenek, Petr or any of 100s of other male names is surprising. The same for females, the surprise is that there is not one Bohuslava, Miroslava, Ružena, Pavlina, Štepanka, or any of the 100s of other female names. Nor are there the English equivalents we could expect if these immigrants simply translated their names.

Now, among many of the property purchasers and their wives who are not in the census we do find other Czech names. The census itself shows many other names, also, as was seen in the previous section, but we are still left with this rather limited selection in the 1920 census. There are two possible reasons. One is that many of those who are called Frank, Charles or John, and Mary, Anna or Helen, in fact, had any one of the hundreds of possible Czech names and they simply chose the most popular American names of the era at the time that they began to adopt an American identity in Louisiana. Though, we do know from other records that Czech men used their Czech names in the community while apparently giving English versions to the census taker. The other possibility is, of course, that this is a statistical anomaly.

Property Transactions in the 1920s

The 1920s showed new residents as well as people departing. Yet, while land sales were brisk, there were nearly 100 less in these 10 years as there were in the preceeding five. There were a total of 258 transactions recorded during this decade. Broken down by year, we find 43 n 1920, 24 in 1921, 25 in 1922, 28 in 1923, 14 in 1924, 34 in 1925, 41 in 1926, only 9 in 1927, 16 in 1928 and 24 in 1929. 121 were to purchase farms and 26 were for lots in various subdivisions in the city. The most popular neighborhood was the Poplar Grove subdivision in the city of Alexandria, with six land sales there; but there were also lots in the West Alexandria, S. A. Guy, Barrett, Magnolia Park, North Alexandria and Hill Addition subdivisions, as well as four lots in the "old" city of Alexandria itself. One was for a property on Bayou Boeuf, and two were for properties along the Old Marksville Highway, that is, the present location of Kolin. 20 of the transactions were related to oil and gas rights and leases. 61 transactions were by non-Czech individuals selling to Czechs.

Nearly every Czech who sold property sold to another Czech. Though, there were several companies still selling to Czechs. The Alexandria Lumber Company sold 27 pieces of property, Lee Lumber Company sold 4, and Guranty Bank sold 12. There was the sale of the entire Libuse townsite to Ernest Jilek. Included in these were several successions: Joseph Trejbal, Vaclav Tucek, Barbara Chruma, Anna Jilek and Frank Hromadka, Sr.

The first land sale of the decade occurred just five days into it; on January 5th, 1920. Josef Stremcha sold 120 acres to Anna Jilek for $1,500 in cash. Stremcha had purchased this land as two lots from Alexandria Lumber. One was for 80 and one for 40 acres, in 1917 and 1918 respectively, for a total of $1,300 cash. There is no evidence that Stremcha ever moved to Libuse or that he made any improvements to the land; still he earned a profit. The last property transaction of the decade was on November 11th, 1929.

Governing the Community

No attempt was ever made to incorporate the towns. There was no mayor or town council. Instead, there were regular, but somewhat informal, community meetings all during the 1920s. If minutes were kept of the meetings, few if any survive. If they survive, they are still tucked into the attics and closets of those who have them; they have not surfaced at this writing. Because these meetings were conducted entirely in Czech they maintained a separation from the surrounding way of doing things. The common way of arriving at decisions was through consensus—majority voting was apparently not considered. But with this system, consensus was reached among the colonists to act in concert for schooling and a public hall and for holding any entertainments. The hat was passed and money was raised according to what people could afford, if they had no ready cash, labor was offered instead. There was a harmony within the early community that stands alone in Louisiana. There were few, if any, political squabbles, as the tasks before them were simple, completely understood by the people involved and they were not expensive. Consensus seems to have been reached on all issuses. These meetings were not much different than what occurred during the earliest years at the founding of the communities. In a 1933 New Orleans Times-Picayune article a resident is quoted, refering to the lack of government, "it is not necessary" he said, "when we trust each other. We can settle our affairs without having to have somebody to tell us what to do."

This is in contrast to other Louisiana towns of the period were politics, elections, budgets, political squabbles and machinations, and even corruption, are a primary source of historical information. There simply was none among the Czechs. In other towns there were leading families and powerful people to chronicle in history books. In Libuse and Kolin all were considered equal.

Czechs and the Law.

The Czechs had almost no occassion to use the law or law enforcement. They dealt with the roughians at the dance hall by simply removing the public hall and confining future events to the privacy of their National Halls. They set up their own anti-theft patrols. Mayor Vic Lamkin of Alexandria noted that "the residents have never given any trouble to law enforcement officers of Alexandria or surround towns." He said "they are what I would term most substantial citizens." So there is no story here. They were law abiding and avoided all temptation.

There were just two lawsuits between any Czechs filed during the early settlement and none between Czechs and non-Czechs. One was the Stegner—Hasik suit of 1918, already discussed. The other was also between family. On November 28th, 1922, Frank Elicar won a suit "after trial" against Mary and Louis Pokorny. The judgement declares "that the donation from Frank Elicar to Mary Pokorny, born Elicar, wife of Louis," was "null, void and of no effect and canceling and erasing said donation." It also states that the "pretended sale by Mary Pokorny to Frank Susek…and from Frank Susek to Louis Pokorny…be null and void." (Elipses for book and page numbers, and property descriptions.) The property in question was part of a parcel containing 40 acres. The situation involved Frank Sr., and his three children: Frank Jr., Mary and Agnes.

Frank senior bought this land on May 23, 1918, when he was 60 years old, paying $1,125 cash. He immediately made provision for half of this land to be donated, all in "indivision," to Frank junior, Agnes and Mary. He kept a half interest himself. In fact, this occurred within a day or two of the purchase. So, the father and mother owned half and the children owned half, all in indivision. The children were to have their undivided interest in this land as their own property, without dual ownership with their spouses. Three days after the donation, on May 25th, Mary, acted on her own (that is, without her husband,) and apparently without anyone telling the father and mother. She sold her interest in the land to her brother and sister together with her husband, Susek, for $1,550 cash. The Pokornys were living in New York City at the time and probably had more need for cash than land in Louisiana. Agnes and her husband Frank were also living in New York at the time. Where Frank junior was cannot be determined with surety, perhaps New York, perhaps Louisiana. Only the senior Elicar's are in the 1920 census.

On November 2nd, 1921, the three children split the remaining portions of land into three sections. The stated that "they no longer wanted to share." 20 acres were for Frank junior and 10 each for Mary and Agnes. (This split was also recorded on November 9th, no doubt due to the travel time between New York and Louisiana.) This, too, they apparently neglected to tell their father. This was barely two months after Frank senior's wife Mary had died in September, 1921. (Interestingly, she is Mary in the census, but Barbora, nee Zapotocka, in the property record; see first names in 1920 census above for a possible reason.) On May 1st, 1922, the Suseks sold the portion they had bought from Mary in 1918 back to Louis and Mary, this time acting together. The sale price was $1,000 cash. So now all three children owned the land again, but the two daughter's husbands were now also owners.

Meanwhile, back on November 28th, 1921, a few weeks after the children split their half of the property without the knowledge of their father, Frank senior donated his half interest to his son. So the father no longer owned an interest in the land and he believed that his three children owned it all together without their spouses. He did this because he was probably preparing to leave the community. It was at or near this date that Frank senior got wind of the situation and he was clearly not happy. He must have filed suit almost immediately given the judgment date exactly a year later from his donation of his half. After the rendering of the judgement he owned again his half of this land, together with only Frank Jr. and presumably Agnes alone again.

Though the judgment does not say anything specific about her, since the previous land sales were null and void, the situation would seem to have returned to the starting point. Except that Mary was no longer involved at all. We can also conclude this because the father not only gave Agnes a power of attorney on December 13th, 1922, he sold his re-acquired half interest in the disputed property to her for $360 cash the same day. Not only that, Agnes bought another 20 acres in 1924 from the widow Mary Cook, with her own paraphernal funds. Interestingly, Frank and Agnes Susek are in the 1930 census. Neither Frank, father or son, or the Pokornys are in the 1920 census. If Frank Susek Jr. ever sold his land he did so after my 1940 cut off date for historical research. The Suseks are buried in the Libuse cemetery. Frank apparently lived out his life on the farm owned solely by his wife.

Oddly, one of the most poignant examples of the feeling of community is the deal made between Agnes Susek and Frank Elicar. She was one of the woman who bought land with her own "paraphernal funds." Here's what they agreed to: "It is distinctly understood by and between the parties that should the within named consideration not be sufficient sum to pay the entrance fee of the vendor herein to the Chicago Bohemian Old Man's Home than in that event the Vendee will advance the amount needed on or before 10 years after date." Apparently all had been forgiven.

A Sense of Community

The 1920s saw a bustling community with stores and many improvements. Better houses and more prosperous farms were now occupied by larger families. Czechs lived next door to Czechs. The census forms indicated that families lived in bunches down "improved dirt roads." A map of the area with the families who bought land drawn in would see a 10 mile by 5 mile section of Louisiana that was owned by Czechs. There were a few neighbors of other nationalities, but in the Czech wards they were few and far between.

Despite the Czech-ness of the community there was the opposite tug of assimilation. Indeed, it is Hazmark who quotes elders in the community saying they were told by their parents that "they were to learn the American Ways." It is certainly a conflicting set of desires. On the one hand to preserve their Bohemian heritage and on the other to become American. Perhaps many felt there was some middle ground to be achieved through trial and error.

The two communities were not only self sufficient but socially active. Beside Czech cultural pursuits like organized brass bands that played polkas and Czech folk tunes, there were also American pursuits like baseball teams, complete with uniforms, and Fourth of July parades and picnics. From the Czech Heritage Newsletter we learn that "Libuse was to be the community for business and craftsmen and Kolin was to be the agricultural community" This seems not to be the case; there is definitely no clear evidence for this assumption. Indeed, given the formal layout of the "City of Kolin" there were plans to have to separate communities being basically the same thing—large and prosperous towns.

In the one Times-Picayune article that exists this is noted: "their native tongue is spoken in the homes and in dealings among the residents." It continues, "even the children, who have never been outside of Louisiana, have leraned the vernacular and use it fluently except when addressing strangers." This article goes further when it states that "a strong sense of loyalty to their community and a sense of pride in their ancestry prevails in the colony." These were people determined to be themselves, and not get involved in the surrounding culture.

Women in the Community

Woman during this era were of course expected to be working in the home. Though with such labor intensive small farms there is no doubt that they worked outside with the men, at least at the easier tasks like feeding chickens and hogs and managing the home garden. In many of the documents where woman did things it is a husband who "authorizes" his wife to act. But there were at least 10 women who bought land with "paraphernal" funds. Paraphernal is a legal term which means that it was her's alone and not part of the community property with her husband. More importantly, it meant she made the decision on her own, at least in theory. We just looked at how Agnes Susek came to own her land. And I already mentioned Annie Jilek, who was buying land on her own.

Veronika Tuma was married, but she bought three pieces of land, totalling a little more than 60 acres; she paid cash for two of the properties and paid off the third within 3 years. Josephine Ploc also bought three pieces of land: three lots of 40 acres each. Two she bought in 1920, the third in 1926. She paid cash for all of them. Josephine bought two of the pieces from Teresa Vondries, who herself had purchased the land with her paraphernal funds 6 years earlier. Vondries made an installment of $150 and then another of $250 to pay off the $400 total. For $700 Ploc bought the farm of Joseph Ubl, one of the founders, along with all the "stock and movable property," though that is not further defined. While the words "paraphernal funds" were usually sufficient, this purchase from Ubl has very specific wording: "She makes this purchase with her own seperate and paraphernal funds. The said property does not form any part of the commuity between her and her said husband."

Emilie Prochaska bought a lot in the Libuse Townsite for $60 cash. Anna Prochaska bought several lots in town for a total of $400; she too paid cash. Frances Skodacek purchased 40 acres in 1922 from Sherman Cook; the land was just outside of the original colony. She paid $500 cash. Anna Nadrchal paid $679.84 for slightly over 48½ acres. Elizabeth Elicar paid $600 cash to John Daniel for his 10 acres just outside of the colony area. Josie Stepan paid $640 cash for 40 acres directly to Louisiana Investment in 1914. Finally, there is Helen Hartman, whose maiden name was the Czech Kocorek, who bought from her brother Vaclav Kocorek. In 1937, in the depths of the depression, she paid $400 cash for the land and everything on it.

Two other independent woman were Anna Kubes and Barbara Bejsovec. Kubes was divorced from James Lande on May 18th, 1924, in Buchannon County, Missouri. Barbara Bejsovec was the widow of Jacob Steinmetzer, but it is noted that "her maiden name having been restored to her by judgement in the State of Wisconsin," bought her own land. She and her sister-in-law, Frantiska Jirak, widow of Joseph Bejsovec, each bought undivided half interests in the 40 acres of lot 16, section 3. They each paid $500 cash.

The Cemeteries

Almost immediately upon their arrival the colonists started a cemetery. It was built close to Libuse. The first burial here was poignant: an infant daughter of the Zmek family. She is perhaps the first death among the Czech colonists of Louisiana. The second burial was necessitated by a similarly tragic event, the death of a young daughter of Vaclav Tucek. Unfortunately, it was put in an area quickly flooded during a heavy rain. Indeed, on at least one occasion, they could not get into the cemetery for a burial because of standing water. There were just a few more burials here before it became apparent that this location was inappropriate. This problem was solved in 1921 when the original cemetery was moved to a new location. Before this, however, a second cemetery was started at Kolin in 1915. The colonists in this part of the colony, understandably, wanted to be closer to the graves of their loved ones.

During the first decades of the colony "decoration day" was an annual event. The community residents gathering for speeches and songs celebrating the lives

312   A Hidden Impact

of the departed. The first settlers were buried with eulogies delivered by speakers from the community. Indeed, many of the early obituaries record that various members of the community were called upon to say a few words at the funeral; no clergy are mentioned. Family members and others in the community are listed as pallbearers. Today, funerals and graveside services are held in the variety of faiths that were adopted by the second and third generations. These two cemeteries are non-denominational. While there is no requirement that the deceased be Czech or related to the families they are primarily used just for the Czech families.

There is little more surprising than finding a sign reading *Cesko Narodni Hrbytov*—"Czech National Cemetery"—in the middle of the piney woods of Central Louisiana. There is, however, no English translation provided on the sign. Fred Hajek made this sign by hand for a materials cost of $1,895, which was raised from members of the community. Among the many graves are nearly 70 of the original colonists. The Bohemian National Cemetery Association was formed in mid-1915 by residents of Kolin. Its first president, John Lehky, accepted 1½ acres from the Alexandria Lumber Company for a token one dollar payment on December 30th, 1915. It is commonly refered to as the Kolin Cemetery. The original one and a half acres is thickly planted with cedar trees and myrtles, giving it a sense of forested, shaded beauty. There is a circle in the center dedicated to the veterans of World War I. In 1978 a second acre was bought because so many people wanted to be buried there.

In 1921, Joseph Goldstein, one of the original colonists, donated an acre of his property to be used for the new Libuse Czech Cemetery. Today the cemetery covers 4 acres. It was expanded through more donations by the Goldstein family. In fact, a sign on the gatepost reads: "This cemetery land donated by Joseph Goldstein 1921." A unique characteristic of this cemetery is that the first graves are aligned in rows with burials next to each other in order of date of death. It is the only cemetary with this pattern in all of Louisiana. Only later were family plots established. There were five burials in the first year of this cemetery: Rozalie Koncinsky, in March, 1922, Vaclav (James) Tucek in May, Rosy Cizak, also in May, Joseph Kohout in October and the 1 year old Frank Kostalek in December. The cemetery has a scattering of shade trees, but is generally a large sunny space enclosed by a thick line of trees on three sides. Today, there are perhaps two hundred graves.

Each community still maintains its own burial ground. They are owned in common by members of each community. Descendants of the deceased hold meetings when necessary for the continued operation of the cemeteries. While never neglected, in 1982 the residents had to undertake a major repair project at both cemeteries to clear trees and vines, straighten headstones and repair the fences. This was a community project where most everyone, young and old, joined together to get the work done. For a number of years, Donald Tuma, grandson of Emil Tuma, has volunteered to mow the grass at both cemeteries on a regular basis.

Another unique feature of these two cemeteries is that nearly every one of the early headstones are inscribed only in the Czech language. This is certainly unique in Louisiana. I could find no other gravestone of a Czech buried anywhere in the state that has a Czech inscription. Perhaps even more amazingly, all the Czech is correct, except just one word. The only thing missing are the hačky and čarky. One can almost imagine family members standing over the engraver as he worked to ensure this; how many stones had to be redone can only be guessed at. For the monument engravers of Alexandria or Pineville this was surely a difficult job. This Czech-only tradition only began to change after World War II, though even some of these are in Czech.

There are examples of the prosaic: a number of stones say just "bratr" (brother,) "sestra" (sister,) "otec" (father,) or "maminko" (mother.) However, many of the inscriptions are poetic. They show a depth of feeling and understanding deeper than can be extracted by mere dates and "Rest in Peace." Unfortunately, there are a few stones that are unreadable, the inscriptions worn away by the elements. I present here a list of the inscriptions (protecting the privacy of the families I will not give the names of whose graves they are on.) These gravestones can be found in both of the cemeteries, I present them here together.

13 of the graves have the simple inscription "Zde Odpociva," which means "Here Rests," followed by the name of the deceased. 10 of the stones bear the inscription "Odpocivej V Pokoji," meaning "Rest in peace." Another 8 bear the legend "Spi Sladce," meaning "Sleep sweetly." One stone has both Spi Sladce & Zde Odpociva. These inscriptions are not very different from any number of English language inscriptions in graveyards across America. The remaining stones wax poetic:

Mily Manzel A Otec—"Dear husband and father"

Rozeny v Plzen, Vcechach/zemrela v Kolin, LA—"Born in Pilsner, Czech lands/ died in Kolin, LA"

Rozeny v Syra, Vcechach/zemrela v Kolin, LA—"Born in Syra, Czech lands/died in Kolin, LA"

Upokoji—"At peace"

Odpocivej V Pokoji Drahi Muj Manzeli—"Rest in peace my dear husband"

Drimej Vegny Sen—"Dreaming everlasting dreams"

Spanem Bohem Na Vecnost—"Sleeping with God forever"

Odpocivej po boji—"Rest after struggle"

Budic Ti Zem Lehka—"Let the earth be light"

Odpocivejte V Pokoji Po Boji—"Both rest in peace after struggle"

Mily Maminko, Odpocivej v Pokoji, Po Zivotnim Boji—"Dear Mother, rest in peace, after lifetime of struggle"

Osud Nas Daleko Od Vas V Zal Ale v Zpominkv Nase Jdou Stale Jen K Vam. Manzelka A Dilky—"Deliver us far from your sorrow, also our thoughts still remain just with you. Wife & Children"

Si Ra Peme Se Deli, Vysoke Obloha Na S Spojuje!—"The wide world is divided, the high sky unites us!" (This is actually the only stone with the English translation.)

Sli Tise Bilas Jsi Verna Zena A Uprimna Ke Vsem—"Sleep quietly, you were faithful wife and friend to all"

Zde Odpociva…Budis Ti Zeme Lehka—"Here Rests…Let the soil be light"

Odpocivej v Pokoji den Vzpominky Lrasme Zustavaji—"Rest in Peace, today remember…those living" (actually, there is no Czech word *Lrasme*, I can only conclude that it is a mispelling of a real word, but cannot discern what it may be.)

U Drahe maminky nasel krasny ser—"My Dear mother, found beautiful dreams"

Draha nase maminko slete sladce—"Our dear mother sleeps sweetly"

Mily Rodice Odpocivejte V Pokoji Po Zivotnim Boji—"Dear Parents, You all rest in peace, after lifetime struggle"

Byla verna zena, Hodna matka, A pratelska vsem—"She was a faithful wife, good mother, and friend to all"

62 Lete Spojeni Na Zemi Vecne Spojni Pod Zemi—"62 years together on earth, forever together under ground"

On a double stone: Zde Odpociva Ji Manzele "Here rest Husband & Wife"

Spi Sladce Nas Angelicha Anezka—"Sleep sweetly our angel Agnes"

Spi Sladce Nas Milacku—"Sleep sweetly our darling"

Spi Sladce Tatinku—"Sleep sweetly Auntie"

These gravestones and cemeteries show a people who kept to their cultural traditions for a long time after first coming to Louisiana and continue to do so. Very few original members of the colony were buried in other area cemeteries and not many of the second generation are either. Indeed, most members of the community I spoke with are determined that either the Libuse or Kolin cemeteries will be their final resting place, even those who are no where near their end. Interestingly, the Catholic Church in Kolin does not even have its own graveyard. Unlike many old family and community cemeteries around Louisiana, which are falling into disrepair and disuse, these two, now nearing 100 years of use, show every sign of continuing to serve the families that started them.

The WFLA—ZCBJ—and the Czech Halls

Prior to the mid-1800s there was no such thing as life insurance for the common man, though richer folks surely had such insurance. Czech and Slovak immigrants thought this was a problem, especially since some of the immigrant men died leaving wives and children. These unfortunates were then forced to fend for themselves. Seeking a remedy for this problem some twenty-five Czech and Slovak immigrant men met in a small tavern in St. Louis, Missouri to discuss what could be done. On March 4th, 1854, they formed the the Cecho-Slovansky Podporujici Spolek (Czecho-Slovak Protective Society—CSPS.) That the initials of the organization are the same in Czech and English is an oddity of language. This organization was the first fraternal life insurance organization in the United States. It went through several name changes, including being known as the Czechoslovak Society of America for many decades. It is now called CSA Fraternal Life. Headquartered today in Oak Brook, Illinois, it is America's oldest fraternal benefit society. It is also one of the most financially secure insurance companies in America. (On a personal note, I was a member of the CSA for nearly 30 years.) You do not need to be Czech or Slovak to become a member, though the membership is overwhelmingly so.

While its primary purpose was to provide financial security to the widows and their children, and money for the funeral of the deceased, it was more than a simple life insurance company. The membership was organized into lodges. The society set about building halls where the members could regularly fraternize. Meetings were held monthly. Social events were a big part of the organization. Members used the halls for parties, plays, musical performances, weddings, athletic programs and Czech and Slovak language classes, and many other social activities. These were all part of the benefits of membership. The lodge hall was the center of these events and community life and nearly all Czech-American communities soon had their own lodge hall.

In the waning years of the 19th century several members wanted to institute some changes in the operation of the society. Among the leaders of this group was John Rosicky, editor of Hospodar. They particularly wanted to include women as regular members and not just as social members. They also sought to change the insurance premium payments to a system based on the age of the member, employ a medical director to check on the health of applicants and create a reserve fund for the society. When the leaders of the CSPS balked at these changes the disaffected members split off and formed a new society. Meeting at Omaha, Nebraska, in February of 1897 they created the Zapadni Cesko Bratrske Jednoty (ZCBJ)—in English The Western Bohemian Fraternal Association. It was incorporated under Iowa law in June of that year and today it is headquarterd in Cedar Rapids, Iowa. It, too, is among the most financially secure life insurance companies in the country.

Almost immediately, this new organization formed 39 lodges having a total membership of nearly 1,000 people. Oddly, women were not admitted as full insured members until 1899 despite the claim to want to admit women as full memebers. Juveniles were admitted as full members beginning in 1919 and more than 600 immediately signed up. The lodges meetings were conducted only in Czech. It was not until 1922 that discussion began on forming English language lodges, which were instituted in 1923. By this year, membership had grown to slightly more than 21,000 in 261 lodges. Originally just in 11 Midwestern states with large Czech populations, Louisiana was the first state outside of the Midwest to have lodges. Over the years more were added in California, Washington, and Oregon, and Texas as well.

The CSPS had lodges in more states, including those in the Northeast, but was not in Louisiana. A proposed merger between the ZCBJ and CSPS was voted down by the membership of both organizations in 1923. They still operate separately and both now offer a wide range of insurance products. For many years the ZCBJ also went by the name "Western Bohemian Life Association," particularly after English language lodges were formed. However, it was not until 1971 that the word Bohemian was formally dropped, along with the rest of the Czech, and the name officially changed to Western Fraternal Life Association—now refered to as the WFLA. Even today the CSA (succesor to CSPS) is a larger organization than the WFLA (ZCBJ.)

In 1923 lodges were formed in Kolin and Libuse as lodge numbers 260 and 261. In the early months of that year Frank Harazim of Kolin and Joseph Ubl of Libuse arranged for Josef Drtina of the home office to visit Louisiana and assist in the formation of the lodges. The Kolin lodge was formed on April 17th. The Libuse lodge was formed on April 29th. At both meetings Drtina explained the benefits of membership, the life insurance product offered (and in the beginning it was just plain life insurance,) the proper way to conduct business of the lodges, as well as what was expected of the membership. Almost immediately everyone attending signed up: 29 at Kolin and 24 at Libuse. By the time of the ZCBJ annual conference, held towards the end of 1923, the membership in Kolin and Libuse had climbed to nearly 100.

In every lodge there were eleven posts that had to be filled. Members of the community assumed 10 of these positions in each lodge. Some of them are to be expected, the others are perhaps a bit surprising. Terms for most were for one year each. They, of course, used the Czech words for the offices: predseda for president, tajemnik for secretary, pokladnik for treasurer, and so on. You will notice here that the Czech forms of people's names are given, which of course shows how many were using the old names within the communities even after the 1920 census. Yet, when the census taker or other government official came along they used the English forms: Josef became Joseph, Karel became Charles—and these are direct translations. But Bohous was changed to Barney—and that's just pulling an American name out of the air.

In the records the women's last names were always the Czech forms, but I simplified it here. However, they were written, as an example, Pani Kostakova for Mrs. Kostak. This switching back and forth between Czech forms and English forms of names is common in the first few decades of the community (as in Czech communities throughout America.) This, no doubt, caused more than a little confusion among their English speaking neighbors and other English speakers with whom Czechs interacted, no matter where in America. It is also possible that this led to a certain level of distrust of the Czechs by the non-Czechs—after all, why would a man have two first names? Why would a family name be considerably different from one use to another? Why would a man's last name be "different" than his wife's? This pertained not just to spelling, but pronounciation as well.

Josef Brozik was the first president in Kolin, while Joseph Kadlec served in Libuse. Joseph Wittera was elected vice president in Kolin, with Anna Prochaska in Libuse. Bohous Smigura was secretary at Kolin, Charles Voda at Libuse. There were two finanical offices, the treasurer and the accountant, to collect and disburse funds and no doubt keep an eye on each other. For Kolin, Karel Steffek and Karel Svebek served, respectively. In Libuse it was Frantiska Voda and Josef Subrt. The parliamentarian made sure the meetings were run according to the rules, Marie Brozik took this task in Kolin and Josef Zdarsky in Libuse. There was an "inner guard" and an "outer guard," in English more commonly called the Sargeant-at-Arms, not that there was much disorder to contend with. Perhaps children running wild underfoot at most, as well as someone to monitor any teenagers who were hanging around outside while their parents were meeting. Glorified baby-sitters, if you will. Ed Vostrcil (Westerchil) and Josef Slezak took care of this at Kolin, with Josef Voda and Josef Zmek at Libuse.

There was a superindendent, or the person who ran the building; John Lehky at Kolin, Klara Kostak in Libuse. There was also a three member property committee, whose tasks overlapped that of the treasurer, accountant and superintendent. Members of this committee served for three years. The terms of the members of this committee were staggered so that after the first year there was at least one change in the membership of this committee each year. One member was the three year member, one for two years and one for one year. Vaclav Vostrcil, Frank Suchy and Josef Varvarovsky started the Kolin committee. Anton Kostak, Marie Kalous and Josef Vorisek were the first for Libuse.

After this first round of elections, each year saw different people serving in the different offices, and over the decades many people had occasion to fill the posts. These were always Czechs, however, and they were expected at each meeting. Since both lodges were meeting regularly well into the 1970s that list would be pages long.

The 11th position was that of Radovy Lekar—Medical Director. This position was almost always filled by a non-Czech in ZCBJ lodges across America. In Kolin it was Dr. Asbey and in Libuse it was Dr. Oglesby. They did not regularly attend meetings, but when they did they probably sat on the side wholly perplexed about what was going on until it was translated for them. If my experience in the CSA is any guide, not every thing was translated. Only what was considered important for them to know was. These doctors examined the Czechs when they first applied for insurance, though no evidence has ever been presented that anyone was turned down. These doctors also served the community for any medical situation that came up.

As for the lodge halls themselves, in Libuse the Komensky School served this purpose, too. And after it was destroyed, the new Czech hall was used for many years. In Kolin it was the hotel-turned school that was used until it, too, was torn down. While Libuse never built a dedicated lodge hall, the people of Kolin did construct a building, actually, two. Shortly after World War II the older building was severely damaged in a storm (which is something that happened more than once to Czech buildings in the colony.) The current WFLA lodge hall is the community hall for Kolin. It was built in the early 1950s.

The property was donated by Marie Wittera Brousek, who was the daughter of one of the early leaders of the Kolin community, (and sister of Josef Wittera who died in the First World War,) to the WFLA in 1949. Supposedly, this property was lost in a sheriff's sale when the Kolin Township did not materialize, but once again, this is a story told by residents. I could find no property record confirming this. Indeed, no entity with the name "Kolin" in it existed to have owned this property. It is likely that this was a section of a family farm that she acquired. In fact, it may have been part of either the Wittera or Brousek farms.

The main difference between the two halls is that Libuse's is older by about 20 years and is owned by the community in common, while the newer Kolin hall is owned by the WFLA for specific use as a community and lodge hall. Both are managed by Czech residents of the area. Both buildings, while different architecturally, as would be expected of building built 20 years apart, have several things in common. Both buildings are of wood frame construction, are one story and are painted grey. Though, the Libuse hall exterior has laterally placed wood planks and the Kolin hall has asbestos shingles, each using the common methods of their day. The interior of the Libuse hall is pine paneling, while the Kolin hall is painted white. Both have ample windows on two sides. Both have formal raised stages, about 25 feet wide, under 12 or 15 foot high prosceniums, with backstage areas, like any community theater. Both have a kitchen and pantries on the opposite side from the stages. Separating the stage from kitchen are large open spaces that can be used for any number of purposes.

While there is no longer a functioning Libuse lodge, the Kolin lodge is still going strong, even if the meetings are not as frequent. The two lodges were essentially merged, even if not officially. Ms. Wally Foral Sanson is the current insurance agent for the communities. One other similarity of the halls is that they are in near constant use. Indeed, they are busy enough that not everyone can get the date they want for their function when they try to reserve them.

Scientific Farming

Scientific Farming is more than a catch slogan—it is a well established method for securing the highest yields of crops year after year. The process is not modern. Indeed, for millenia farmers the world over knew of various techniques to improve the quality and quantity of their yields—but the term is just about 130 years old. In the early years of America farmers along the Eastern Seaboard used these techniques of crop rotation, plowing under the stubble after a harvest for fertilizer, letting fields lie fallow every few years and planting legumes to replenish nitrogen in the soil. Yet, for some reason, as settlement headed westward these practices fell by the wayside. Perhaps it was the influx of new immigrants, mainly from cities and villages, and without much farming experience. Perhaps it was the endless rich fertility that the prairie—and America in general—seemed to promise. In Louisiana, with its subtropical climate, it may not have seemed necessary: "anything will grow here" being a common claim. A good case can be made that the poverty and illiteracy of most Louisiana farmers left them unaware of the methods that would have helped them the most.

In any event, when the Czechs arrived in Libuse and Kolin to begin their farming ventures the lands north of the Red River where they settled were considered among the poorest in the state. William Roark, the county agent, is quoted saying that these were "the poorest land Central Louisiana affords." With most of the land still pine forest the small farms that did exist were strictly subsistence. The plantations of the southern reaches of the state, and actually beginning just on the other side of the Red River from the Czech colony, and along the Mississippi River, had for a long time been neglected. This neglect was brought on by the ravages of the Civil War and its aftermath. Only in the last two decades of the 1800s was there a change back to large scale productive farming. The plantation mentality still existed, though, and not just culturally, but in farming practices as well. Just as before the War the main crops of cotton, rice and sugar were planted across vast fields. Vegatables and other food stuffs were almost an afterthought, grown mainly in so-called kitchen gardens. Commerical production of these were virtually unheard of.

Because of the promotions used to lure the Czechs to Louisiana they probably expected to step right into productive farming. Furthermore, they were led to believe that there would be a ready market for their soon to be harvested crops in the "growing" city of Alexandria. It was not growing and there was no market. They were in for quite a shock as they discovered not only the thousands of pine stumps, but also the clay soil that they most likely immediately recognized as poor for farming. Added to this, existing farmers and Alexandrians saw the Czechs as a ready market for their own goods and produce—and the Czechs had little intention of buying anything from anyone. Both sides of this equation were disappointed to say the least. Yet, the Czechs, having bought their land, now were determined to make a go of it.

Remembering the organizations they belonged to in their previous states they formed Libuse Local Union 889 of the Farmers' Educational and Cooperative Union of America, a pre-existing organization. Informally called the National Farmers Union, it was founded in 1902 in Point, Texas, by a man named Newt Gresham. It still exists, but Louisiana and the other states of the Confederacy (except Texas and Arkansas) and all of the Mid-Atlantic and New England states (except Pennsylvania) are so-called non-member states (oddly, these were the states primarily involved in the Civil War; the Union's website does not say why these are "non-member states.")

This one outpost of the Union in Louisiana, however, was probably not well supported by the organization. But between 1915 and 1920 the Czechs relied on it for help in getting started. At one point as many as 55 Czech farmers belonged. In these first few years there were more members, but many of the Czechs left the colony, so membership rose and fell with each passing month. They also relied on Hospodar, which carried Czech translations of publications of the Kansas State Agricultural College. This college itself had begun to promote scientific farming in that state beginning as early as the 1880s. Other states also had farmer's organizations of various kinds and Hospodar carried articles on their findings as well as contacts for information. Of course, conditions were wholly different there than in Louisiana, so none could be of much help. Louisiana at the time had no similar organization so there was no help locally. Certainly no one on the local plantations or subsistance farms were of any help. Indeed, the locals probably thought that the Czechs were crazy for even trying.

Still undaunted, and working through their own experiments at making the most of their land, in 1921 the Czech colony formed "Farmářskeho Družstva"—The Farmer's Cooperative. The funniest thing about this name is that the first word is not really Czech—it is the English word "farmer" with the

322   A Hidden Impact

Czech grammatical case form for a possessive. Modern Czechs call this "Czenglish," and this is not the only example of such combinations among Czech-Americans who were losing their Czech skills (another is "drug-storičku,"—surely any reader can figure this one out!) Proper Czech would be "Zemĕdĕlske Družstva." No matter, they published bylaws and guides to productive farming containing the results of their experimentation and what they thought were the best procedures which were applicable from other areas. They opened membership in the Cooperative to non-Czechs as well. How they thought this would work when the guides were written in Czech and the educational meetings were conducted in Czech is anyone's guess.

They also joined fledgling organizations such as the Corn Club, Tomato Club and Potato Club. All were dedicated to increasing yields of these crops. It is hard to say which came first, the Czech clubs or the local clubs—it is sort of a chicken or egg situation. These clubs certainly existed on parallel levels—one wholly in Czech, the other in English. But they learned from each other and the level of cooperation between Czechs and non-Czechs grew.

In 1925 the Louisiana Farm Bureau was founded as part of a larger national effort to assist farmers across the country. The farm bureau system employed "county agents" to bring the best in current scientific farming methods, up-to-date information on preserving the harvest and other educational tools to farmers. Every parish in Louisiana, and every county in America, has a county agent, even cities like New Orleans and Manhattan. Soon the county agent was out at the Czech farms teaching the new knowledge, but just as likely to be learning from the Czechs. They, after all, had been at it a few years longer than the Farm Bureau. One thing for certain is that the way the Czechs farmed their lands had already led to increased yields and more prosperous circumstances. They far outstripped their non-Czech neighbors in productive use of the land in both the quantity and quality of their harvests. This also led to some level of jealousy on the part of non-Czechs.

Another first for the Czechs was growing crops that had never been grown in Louisiana before. George Tuma maintains that the Farm Bureau came to the Czech farmers to learn how to grow many crops that had never seen commerical production in Louisiana. The 1933 Times-Picayune article says "the residents are continually experimenting on their own initiative for methods to improve their condition. Several of the older inhabitants, who have retired from active farming, devote most of their time to experimental planting and cultivation. The results of these individual experiments have often led to introduction of new crops or procedures."

Many of these crops are particular to Czech culture. Like their countrymen in other states, they planted caraway, poppy, marjoram and other spices that were never grown or used in Louisiana. One thing they did not grow was hops. Given the historical importance of hops and beer to the Czech people this is somewhat surprising. This is perhaps the solitary example among Czech-American towns and halls across the country were beer is not allowed.

That the Czechs were able to get these temperate climate crops to grow in Louisiana at all shows a stubborn determination to keep familiar foods on their tables. Unfortunately, as the first generation passed away or moved towards working in the city, soon joined by the second generation, the skills and hard work needed to continue this atrophied. None of this remains. Indeed, only the Tuma family could be said to be engaged in active farming today and then almost exclusively in sweet potatoes.

What did remain, however, was this sweet potato farming, something far easier to do here. Typically, in 1923 a sweet potato curing association was formed, with Charles Suchy as president and Bohous (Barney) Smigura as secretary. Starting with a piece of leased property, for which they paid an annual one dollar rent, they expanded their efforts, eventually including twelve farmers in the project. In 1925 the Farmers Union of Libuse, "a community organization" as it is called in the property record, purchased an 8 acre plot from Joseph Ubl and Ernest Jilek. Earlier I recounted how these two bought the land for one dollar from Lee Lumber and resold it for $40 to the association. This land was between the Philadelphia Road and the never built Gum Street shown on the plat map of Libuse. At the time of the purchase Anton Baroch was president and Frank Hazmuka was secretary-treasurer. This sweet potato organization lasted until the late 1930s, with a new president and other officers every year. The land eventually passed into other hands. As near as I could figure, some of it may be among the land added to the Libuse cemetery.

This change in leadership was standard operating procedure for the Czechs—constant change in leadership made sure that no one person could accumulate too much authority or power. This is certainly in contrast with non-Czech Louisiana where once an official is elected or appointed it is almost impossible to get them out of office. Only moving up to a higher office, death or conviction for corruption seems to remove them. Consider this, Bob Odom has been the state's Commissioner of Agriculture for more than 30 years, (no one even runs against him in elections.) There are hundreds of other examples of unopposed longevity in office among statewide and local officials in this state. Yet, among all the Czech organizations in Libuse and Kolin there is a steady change in the roster of officials with everyone in the community seeming to get a chance to serve.

Another example of both cooperative efforts and scientific procedures is the cattle and dairy operations they created. On the farm of Jerry Drudik was a cow dipping vat that was available to all the Czechs. Drudik operated one of the largest dairies in the parish. Mayor Vic Lamkin of Alexandria is quoted saying "the cattlemen of Libuse are successful because they have kept their cows tick-free by private dipping, although located in the heart of tick-infested territory." This contrasted with their neighbors who simply suffered the ravages of ticks without trying to do anything about it.

There was at least one letter published in Hospodar about the tick problem in Louisiana. It was published in 1917 and refers to previous reports. A man named Frank Tupy wrote to the paper that Anton Baroch and an agricultural expert named Mr. Janak were wrong that the tick problem was non-existent. Tupy says that Frank Baley is right that ticks are a problem. The editor of the paper wrote a rather curt response to Tupy: "if you look at the article on this problem published in a previous issue of the paper at page 689 you will see how to solve it." The editor further flat out tells Tupy that he "complains too much" and that everyone knows "a farm takes hard work," and Tupy "should just get on with it."

There are two funnier things related to Tupy's letter. First, while the letter is datelined Libuse no one named Tupy is ever recorded in the community. Other than this letter his name appears no where. The second thing is that the Czech word "tupy" identifies a person who is slow, thickheaded, and a little dimwitted; while the editor did not tell Mr. Tupy that he was 'tupy,' his response alludes to this. My translator, Daniela Kratka, told me that letter was written in a very formal and elegant style, highly literate, using older verbs and nouns that have now been superceded by more modern Czech words.

One last example of cooperation in the area of farming among the Czechs was the formation of the "Chicken Anti-theft Organization" in 1927. Yes, an actual dues collecting organization, with officers and meetings and by-laws. Its purpose was to catch the chicken thieves coming out of the local non-Czech population who plagued the community once the farmers had added poultry production to their farms. The dues were dedicated to paying a reward to anyone who caught a chicken thief. Whether any theives were caught or rewards paid was apparently not recorded. Typically, as among the lodges, halls, cemeteries, cooperatives and other committees and organizations formed, the officers served without payment of any kind. Everyone who served simply volunteered for the task at hand, as they had for so many years in bringing Scientific Farming to the community.

Oil and Gas Leases

Oil and gas production has been one of Louisiana's biggest industries since oil was first found near the town of Jennings in the first years of the 1900s. Following the initial find, people all across the state went into an oil and gas frenzy. Some were actively searching and some were just buying and selling oil and gas rights and leases. Right and leases, slightly different transactions, did not convey the land, just the right to drill for oil at some unspecified point in the future. If oil or gas was found there would be three parties who earned money—the oil company certainly, but also the lease holder and the land owner who would be paid a royalty on the amount of oil and gas extracted. The amount of money paid for the lease was usually small, though this depended on the size of the tract leased. More than a few were actually for zero dollars, with only a promise to pay royalties later. But in general it ranged from a low of $1.00 to just over $500. The state was divided into "blocks," each with a descriptive name. The land the colony (and nearby non-Czech land) occupies is called the "Bohemian Block." Who named it is not known, but whoever did obviously had to know about the Bohemian colony sitting on top of it and thus it seems likely that it was named after 1914.

A 1914 promotion for the Czech Colony, you will recall, quotes John Krejzl talking about how "soon they will be pumping oil." Krejzl used the word "pumpovat" in the original Czech, which is one of those "Czenglish" words—the English "pump" combined with the Czech infinitive verb form "ovat." Czech has several perfectly good words for various types of pump, both noun and verb. Still, "pumpovat" actually made it into the Czech lexicon. It specifically pertains to pumping oil out of the ground; if you pump oil out of tank, or pump anything else, you have to use a different Czech verb. There is, though, not one oil well in all of the Czech or Slovak republics and perhaps that is why this word made its way from Czech-American into Czech.

Exactly when the first oil and gas lease was made on the Bohemian Block I did not try to determine because the block covers some lands never owned by Czechs, though it was certainly between 1914 and 1919, and probably involved a non-Czech. The first Czech I could find selling an oil lease on his property was Frank Hazmuka; actually two leases. A man named W. F. Swain was the buyer of both on December 10th, 1919. The next recorded oil lease that I could find is a sale from Ablin Hajek to a man named A. L. Johnson on January 9th, 1920. The next two recorded leases are interesting because one shows that Mary Rychter (in this record and the next she is listed as Minnie Richter, but it is definitely the same person,) sold a lease on her property to John Fairbanks on March 11th, 1920. She was paid $40. The same day, Rychter bought an oil and gas lease covering William Pospisil's land, but no cash was exchanged. So, she is the first Czech to buy an oil and gas lease. The next oil lease in the record shows that Ernest Jilek bought a lease from W.D. Ball on November 3rd, 1920, making him the second Czech to buy an oil lease. He paid $150.

No other oil and gas leases were made by Czechs in 1920. In fact, for the next four years apparently no oil and gas leases were made by Czechs on the Bohemian Block, though there appears to have been non-Czechs doing so, as we will see in a moment. In 1925 eleven Czechs entered into leases, all recorded in separate documents dating from July to December. Five of these were leases bought by five different Czechs from three non-Czechs. J. W. Wilbanks sold one to Frank Hromadka for $100. H. M. Wheeler sold leases on different properties he owned to Frank Pacholik, Frank Bejsovec and Alois Tlucek, collecting a total of $500. Annie Johnson, acting as "femme sole," sold to Anton Kostale; no cash was exchanged. Five showed that A. L. Johnson bought from five different Czechs with token $1 payments. One shows that Joseph Krska bought a lease from Frank Krska, making this the first family deal.

Now, Annie Johsnon was married to A. L. Johnson, and both were very active in oil and gas leases thoughout Rapides Parish, not just on the Bohemian Block. Sometimes they acted together, sometimes it was just 'A. L' (whose full name is never written out in any document,) and sometimes it was Annie acting as femme sole, that is, on her own with her own funds. Annie also sold leases in 1926 to both Peter Kotar and Cyril Foral, both Czechs. Sometimes either or both of the married Johnsons acted with W. F. Swain (full name also never given,) he of that first purchase from Hazmuka. Wilbanks and Wheeler were also active in buying and selling oil and gas leases throughout the parish as the indices clearly show. The Johnsons and Swain did not appear to do business with either Wilbanks or Wheeler, but these last two did business with each other. During this period from 1919 to 1925, with these few recorded leases, no oil company was involved. It was strictly individual to individual. It is doubtful that any of them had the means or the knowledge to actually drill for oil; certainly the Czechs did not have it.

Beginning in mid-1925 and through the end of 1926 there was a veritable explosion of leasing. Literally hundreds of leases were purchased by a few men from nearly every Czech in Libuse and Kolin. Except for a few individual records recording a lease for 40 acres here and 40 acres there the purchase agreements filed show long lists of leases all bought together. Each of the several documents refered to below go on for many pages. Since a lease was specific to a piece of property a Czech could sell multiple leases if he owned several parcels. That is, if he owned 80 acres, he could sell one lease for one 40 acre lot to one person and sell a second lease for the second 40 acres to a another, or he could sell one lease covering the whole 80 acres. In the few cases where less than 40 acres were owned by a Czech there would be only only one lease and 30 acres seems to be the smallest amount of land covered by a lease. Frank Kovar only owned 30 acres so he could only sell one lease. On the other hand, Cyril Foral owned slightly more than 160 acres and he sold one lease covering 65 acres and another containing 80 to two different buyers; it seems he did not sell a lease on the 15 acres that was closest to his house. Since many Czechs owned hundreds of acres they entered into one or more leases with various people. That is where the confusion begins.

One man buying leases was A. J. Johnson. Through late 1925 he not only bought nearly 30 leases from various Czechs, but on February, 2nd, 1926, he secured all their signatures on a document expressly "waiving annual payments" on those very leases. Signature after signature is witnessed by either Joseph Stepan, Frank Pacholik or Joseph Ubl (two witnesses per signature.) The two sales by A. J. Johnson to Kotar and Foral mentioned above were apparently because they refused to sign the waiver and bought back their leases for a dollar; the three documents all bear the same date. Three other documents executed by Johnson bear this date when he bought new leases from Stanley Smutny, Joseph Markovick and the estate of Charles Malecek. One can imagine them all meeting at the Libuse hall to effect this. It must have been a very busy day, with people coming and going. Poor A. J. Johnson likely sat uncomprehending as the Czechs all spoke among themselves in Czech. In August of 1926 Carl Svebek acting as an individual bought this whole package of leases covering nearly 2,000 acres from Johnson for $509 cash.

On May 24th, 1926, Carl Svebek and Frank Pacholik incorporated a company they called Bohemian Oil & Gas. Carl was the vice-president and Frank was president. This company bought dozens of leases on September 1st, 1926, from many of the Czechs in Libuse and Kolin. Carl acted for the corporation. It is not recorded buying leases from non-Czechs. All the leases are contained in one document. So it would seem that Carl, and maybe Frank, set himself up somewhere, probably the Libuse hall, and people came in to sign their lease sales. I use the words buy and sell loosely, though, for not one dollar was exchanged. The actual copies of the leases are long gone, thrown away as wasted paper, it is only the purchase agreement which survives. But we can assume that the lease specified royalty payments to the lease holder and the land owner.

The Libuse Oil and Gas Company is recorded by the state at the corporations office in Baton Rouge as being incorporated on November 8th, 1926, but it was already doing business in September in Alexandria. The delay is probably because it took a few days to get the paperwork to Baton Rouge where it became official. The owners of this corporation were Marshall T. Cappell, Joseph Pacholik and his father Frank Pacholik. The record does not state which, Marshall or Joseph, was president or vice-president, but it does state that Frank Pacholik was secretary-treasurer. Frank was authorized to act for the corporation in all matters pertaining to it. Both corporate domiciles were listed as Alexandria, though neither seems to have had an actual office in the city, at least no record for either entity could be found.

The transactions of the two Pacholiks and Cappell are a bit convoluted. Cappell assigned an interest in all the leases he owned to Joe Pacholik. Then on the same day Cappell and Pacholik, acting as individuals, sold these to Libuse Oil, which they owned. The odd thing is that the assignment is recorded a few hours earlier than the sale essentially meaning that Pacholik was selling what he did not officially own. All 118 leases in each document refer to the same properties. These two transactions were bound up with another man. From mid-1925 Jack H. Timms bought many leases from Czechs. He also bought from non-Czechs and from both the Alexandria and Lee Lumber companies. The Pacholiks and Cappell agreed to take over some but not all of the leases from Timms and also assuming $1,000 in debt that Timms owed. Timms agreed to retain certain leases. The two parties to the agreement agreed to swap still other leases. None of these leases were the same as the leases procured by Svebek. But between Libuse Oil, Bohemian Oil and Timms it seems that nearly every square inch of Czech owned lands was involved in an oil lease. The only Czech family which does not appear in connection with oil leases are the Tumas. About the only other odd thing about all this activity is that only one well was recorded as being drilled, and that was by Timms. No oil was ever discovered under the Bohemian Block. This was all wasted effort.

Birth, Death and Marriage between 1914 to 1930

In this section I will attempt to show the many familial relationships, family types and the joys of birth and tragedy of death among the Czechs of Libuse and Kolin. This section covers 1914 to 1930, or the first 15 years of the communty. As would be expected in any small town families in close proximity became related through marriage over the years. From the very beginning until at least the 1960s intermarriage among the Czech families was frequent. Indeed, there is evidence that even before some got here there were familial connections. However, it is impossible to track them all. It is certainly not within the scope of this book to build a genealogical database. That would require tracking down birth, marriage and other records from at least 30 states, possibly more, as well as in Europe. As anyone who has ever tried to build a family tree knows this is an enormously difficult task.

With Czechs it is seemingly harder. In America, Czech names, both first and last, were changed or altered in some way with an alarming frequency. Indeed, from record to record over the years, a Czech's name may be any one of several variations. Some were changed by Czechs attempting to join the American mainstream. Probably an equal number were changed by well-meaning but mistaken record keepers who could not cope with the consonant clusters and lack of vowels of Czech names. We have seen plenty of examples of this already. Moreover, in the Czech Republic you must know the exact church parish in which a person was born to elicit the facts. There was no national database, index or registry of births or marriages. Even knowing a town name is insufficient for there may be many parish churches in any given town. You would have to search through each one.

There are, though, tantalizing clues spread across the records examined. For instance, many property transactions record the maiden names of the wives of both the buyer and seller, but not every record. Many more property records give the town, or at least the county and state where the two parties resided at the time of the sale. Though many records give the residence as just Libuse, Kolin or Rapides Parish, even when there is no evidence that these people were actually residing here. Maddeningly, some records are totally silent on the residence of either one or both of the parties to the transactions. Obituaries are often a good source of information, but here we face the lack of Czech obituaries in the local paper before the mid-1930s. They saw no reason to publicly announce to the Alexandria community the death of a loved one. Not only that, some obituaries give maiden names and some do not. Also, the cemeteries give valuable, if sad, information on the deaths in the community. Suffice to say, this will be painted with a broad brush.

Births in the community

Bertha Goldstein was the first birth in the community. She was born in 1914. 23 other children were born in Louisiana between 1914 and the taking of the census in 1920. 11 were girls and 13 were boys. All were born to parents that purchased land during this time. 47 children were born in the 1920s; 18 were boys and 29 were girls. However, 3 said to be born in Louisiana in the 1920s, William, Philip and Mary Vinloske, are hard to explain. No Vinloske family is in the 1920 census anywhere in the state. While the family is listed in the 1930 census as owning property no property records for their parents could be found. Another anomaly is Joseph Varvarovsky who was 15 in 1930. He is listed as born in Louisiana. His family, however, is not in the 1920 census, though his family owned property by then. That property record says they resided in Creston, Louisiana, which is in Natchitoches Parish, when they bought their property, yet, they cannot be found there either.

Of course, these are the children that lived. These births must have brought great glee to the families and their fellow colonists; a sign that the community was going to grow.

Deathsin the community

The community had to contend with 33 deaths during the first 15 years of its existence. Tragically, 22 of them were under the age of 40. I essentially present these deaths in age cohorts, not the order of their death. However, the first death in the community was an infant in the Zmek family. The second was an infant in the Tucek family. For those superstitious this was perhaps not a good portent for the future of the community.

Sadly, 8 other infants or toddlers died: 3 of them were in their first day of life, including two in the Welcek family, and an infant in the Filipi family. Hattie Kaderka lived just 3 months. Two were just about 2 years old when they died, Frank Kostalek and Lily Smetak. Agnes Silhavy had just turned 3 years old. One was the 4 year old toddler boy, William Brousek. 3 more youths died before they turned 20: 10 year old Marie Francis Kramel, 17 year old Anna Vlach, and Frank Hrachovina, who died just a few months shy of his 20th birthday. Even more sadly for the family, his brother, George Hrachovina, died just a month later, barely over 21. Young Brousek and the Hrachovina sons died just when the Great Influenza epidemic was waning in America, though it is not clear that this is the cause of their death. No matter, for there is little sadder than for parents to lose such young children.

Two more young people to die were 21 year old Joseph Potmesil, and 23 year old William Filipi. Poor William died on his birthday; a day that was supposed to be joyful turned to sadness. 31 year old Mary Dvorak, 36 year old Frank Mad-jarosh, 38 year old Frank Suchy and 38 year old Josephine Potmesil complete the roster of those who were certainly too young to leave this life.

The next five could, for the times, be considered early middle age, though still young by any standard. They all died in their 40s: 41 year old Rozalie Koncinsky, 43 year old John Vondracek and 42 year old Edward Baley. Baley, you will recall, died in the state hospital in Pineville after being committed. The first family to truly experience the ravages of death were the Tuceks. 41 year old Vaclav Tucek died, and seven years later his widow Frances Tucek died at 47. They were the father and mother of the second infant in the community to die.

Those who passed away when they were over 50 included 56 year old Rosy Cizak, 55 year old Margaret Tauber and the 54 year old mother of the Hrachovina boys. She is identified on her gravestone only as "Pani" Hrachovina, which is Czech for "Mrs." and she is one of those people whose first name I could not find. She died 2 years before her sons, at the height of the flu epidemic, so she was at least spared a parent's nightmare. Another woman who is just "Pani" on her grave is the 52 year old Mary Krejci. Joseph Kohout died in his 73rd year and Thomas Marecek died in his 75th. With a small sense of irony, the last to die in this period was one of the oldest, the 70 year old Frank Voda, in 1929.

It is primarily these people for whom no obituaries could be found. This was the greatest period of insularity in the community, before they began to open up to the larger Anglo-French world that surrounded them. Once the 1930s rolled around obituaries started to appear in the Alexandria paper, though still not for every person who passed away.

Widows, Widowers & Spinsters

There were four widowers who came to the community between 1915 and 1918. Oddly, none came any later. John Trejbal was the first, in 1915. Thomas Marecek arrived in 1916 and died after just a few years in the community, as just noted above. Joseph Kohout was another who passed away not long after his arrival; he arrived in 1918. Charles Veverka arrived in 1918, having lived previously in Creston, Louisiana. That is were the Varvarovsky's had lived and he may have been the father-in-law. How else to explain two Czechs in such a small town? Yet, I have no proof of any relationship.

There were also four widows in the community. Marie Kment, who came to own the Kolin townsite, arrived in 1914 or 1915. Josefa Vonasek arrived in 1918. Frantiska Bejsovec arrived in 1919. One became a widow after moving to Louisiana, Mary Vondracek. There were two or three single and independent woman of marriageable age in the early years. Two are labeled with the old fashioned term "spinster" in their property purchase records. One was Tereza Kriz (later known as Theresa.) She was the sister of Annie Kriz, who was married to none other than Joseph Ubl. The other with the old label was Mary Rychter, who first bought land in 1914 and again in 1919. Though in the earlier document she is refered to as a widow the latter one uses spinster. Which it was I cannot determine. The fact that a younger woman named Minnie Rychter bought oil leases and land in the community seems to point to the widow designation. And it is Minnie Rychter who may be that third single woman. In one property record she is listed as "married, no children," and a year later she is said to be "divorced from Reichl." Unfortunately, her other two records say nothing on the matter so all we have is the contradiction. They were both certainly independent women though, for both bought using parapheranl funds. Minnie is one of only two people in the early years who was divorced. One problem with these women's identities is that sometimes both were referred to as Minnie or both as Marie.

Single women

Of course, there were other single woman of marriageable age in the early years. They were the 18 daughters of the families who were recorded in the 1920 census (though Anna Vlach did pass away.) They ranged in age from 17 to 24 (Bettie Baley was the oldest.) In the 1930 census there were only 8 daughters between 17 and 26 (Helen Kramel was the oldest.) I use 17 as the young age for possible marriage because there is evidence that a few of the married women were 17 when they got married. Thus, there were 25 eligible young ladies. None of these young ladies bought any land on their own. Of the 18 in 1920 all were married by 1930. Also, no single women of marrying age moved into the community looking for a husband.

Bachelors

Many men, however, moved to the commnity looking for a good Czech girl to marry. Determining the exact number of bachelors available for marriage at any one time is impossible. There was just too much coming and going, as well as men who definitely bought land but never seemed to spend any time in Louisiana at all. First off, I assume that a man must have been at least 20 years old to have considered marriage. Though one could argue for a 21 year old minimum age since for the most part a 20 year old would still be considered a minor during this era. Also, men in this era, in general, tended to wait a little longer to marry, so 23 and 24 would could be even more appropriate cut-off dates. Understandably, any man wanted to be somewhat established before taking on the responsibilities of family. The Czechs were no different. They also tended to seek brides that were two to three years, or more, younger than themselves. That would have almost forced them to wait until they were 22 or older before seeking a bride. There is evidence for this pattern in both the censuses of Kolin and Libuse and among the many Czechs and Slovaks looked at in Part One.

Between 1914 and 1930 there are at least 80 identifiable bachelors. This is deduced from a comparison of property purchases and the censuses, though there may have been other bachelors not recorded as such. However, there never seems to be more than 30 or 35 at a time. At any given point, at least half of these were sons in the community. There were 21 sons over 20 living with their parents in the 1920 census and 10 in the 1930 census. None carry over, those listed in 1920 either got married or moved away. Though four of these passed away. That leaves 76 eligible men at one time or another.

The 45 bachelors who bought land during this period bought a total of 67 properties. Robert Westerchil was the only son living with his parents who bought property. The remaining 31 were sons living at home who did not buy during this time. In their purchase agreements they are identified as such. Because these records do not give ages or reason for bachelorhood it is not possible to determine if they were truly marriageable prospects. Some may have been widowed or divorced, or so-called confirmed bachelors. One "bachelor" was listed as divorced, Charles Kaplan. He bought land in 1918, but though his property record says his residence was Kolin he does not seem to have spent much, if any, time here, for he is not in either the 1920 census or any stories. At least 11, though, were sons in the community, and they all went on to marry local girls.

The bachelors buying land were certainly good prospects. Among the purchases there were 34 cash sales versus 33 who had mortgages. 9 bought lots in either Libuse or Alexandria, the others bought acreage. Among the lot purchasers, Robert Westerchil and George Ubl bought in Alexandria, as did Ernest Jilek (he paid the most—$10,000 cash.) Interestingly, six of the lot purchases were in the Libuse townsite: Frank Vlach, William Vlach, Joseph Subrt and Joseph Pestal (the smallest of his 10 purchases.) bought individual lots. Frank Bejsovec bought with his widowed mother, Frantiska. Ernest Jilek, as previously discussed, bought every lot in town that had remained unsold. The acreage sales ranged between 4 acres (Albin Hajek) and 320 acres (Joseph Pestal,) though the vast majority were 40 acre farms. 31 bachelors bought land between 1914 and 1919 (only George Petrasek bought more than one piece of land; and he bought just two.) 21 bought between 1920 and 1930. Joseph Pestal (who bought twice after 1930) and Joseph Subrt were the most active purchasers. The first bachelor in the community was Albin Hajek, who bought 40 acres in 1914. Following him, there were a few new ones each year until 1930, except none in 1924.

11 bachelors never seemed to have lived in Libuse or Kolin at all. They are not in the censuses, descendant's stories or other early records. They bought and sold their land within just a few years. One of them, Joseph Pestal, apparently was just a real estate investor. He bought 10 properties between 1926 and 1936 totalling just under a 1,000 acres. He signed all of his agreements in his hometown of Winner, Tripp County, South Dakota, as indicated by the affidavits attached to the purhcase agreements. He eventually sold all his land, the last sometime after 1940. Joseph Hrdlicka owned land for just two years, 1918 to 1920, but never moved on to it. Karel Klima was in the community for just three years, buying in 1915 and selling in 1918. Joseph Hrubesh owned land from 1920 to 1945, but never lived in Louisiana, apparently remaing at his home in Waubun, Minnesota. Bedrich Vesely bought land in both 1915 and 1925, but apparently stayed in Cleveland, Ohio, though we have no sales record either. For Frank Nekuda, Frank Prokol, John Prokop, Sobeslav Cerny, Anton Jirka and Joseph Jurenka we only have a record of them purchasing land—not one other property transaction of any kind—so what happened with them is impossible to establish.

Marriages

20 Czech bachelors who got married are recorded in the Rapides Parish court-house between 1915 and 1931 (the last year of the indexed volume.) Two of the last names are spelled wrong in the record—both of the Zabavskys have their last name spelled as "Zabasky," and Charles Malecek's name was spelled as "Malesek," (interestingly, in the property records his name is the Czech for Charles: Karel.) The surname of Malecek's wife is "Javurek" in the marriage record but "Janurek" in their property record; because both are Czech names it can not be determined which is correct. 17 of these marriages are between Czechs, while three are a Czech guy marrying a non-Czech gal. They are easy to spot: the misses Barnes, Gilchrist and Corley. Two of the grooms are never recorded having lived or buying land in either Libuse or Kolin: Mevsek and Walasek. Four of the brides were not from local families: the misses Javurek, Mrazova, Janecek and Machek. Miss Mrazova is the only woman who uses the female form of her family name; the male form is Mraz. The remaining 31 people are from Libuse and Kolin.

Here is a chronological list of the happy couples and their wedding dates:

Charles Malesek (Malecek) to Tony Javurek 3/6/1915

Joseph D. Slezak to Elizabeth Baley 7/21/1917

John Kaderka to Katie Mrazova 4/15/1919

George Petrasek to Minnie Stegner 4/11/1919

Charles Nimberger to Mildred Pospisil 5/11/1920

Edward Kastanek to Martha Suchy 3/10/1920

Charles E Voda to Stephany Zabaskey (Zabavsky) 5/18/1921

Edward Walasek to Anna Baroch 11/19/1921

Francis Welcek to Mary M. Petrasek 12/20/1921

Josef Koncinsky to Anna Janecek 9/27/1923

Mathew Vlasek to Magda Machek 11/13/1923

Ed J Vonasek to Susie Gilchrist 6/11/1923

Edward Frank to Helen Vonesh 1/23/1924

Emil Drudik to Josephine Baroch 2/14/1924

Frank Daricek to Ella Barnes 9/7/1926

Frank E Baley to Bessie Krejci 9/22/1928

Jon Mevsek to Josephine Zacek 7/11/1928

Jerry Drudik to Mamie Krist 1/11/1930

John Zabasky (Zabavsky) to Corinne Corley 11/4/1930

Joe Kotar to Anna Bernat 6/18/1931

This is not an exhaustive list of bachelors who got married, for at least two others got married to local girls: William Filipi married Bessie Wittera and Louis Filipi married Annie Welcek. That all four lived in Kolin, which is on the highway to Marksville, the parish seat of neighboring Avoyelles Parish, points to this town as the likely location of the weddings. Frank Bejsovec married Mamie Vorisek sometime between his 1922 land purchase as a bachelor and his 1928 purchase with his new wife. It is not clear where the wedding was held or recorded.

The In-Laws

Because some (but not all) of the property records list the maiden names of the wives we can see that there were at least 16 families that were related by marriage. These were marriages that were performed elsewhere, so even prior to coming to Louisiana the families were related. All these wives were sisters or daughters of men in the colony. They are in all generations. Here is a list of the married couples; their last names confirm the in-law status between various families.

Frank Ludvik Jr. and Mammie Krist

Frank Ludvik Sr. and Lilly Stepan

Joseph Brozik and Marie Svebek

Vaclav Vlach and Anna Rybar

Frank Kramel and Mary Prochaska

Darwin Cizek and Mildred Fabianek

Norbert Krenek and Agnes Tuma

John Filip and Lizzie Helcl

Frank Dvorak and Mary Melichar

Jaroslav Sourek and Antonine Kostalek

Vincent Cervenka and Marie Malecek

Joseph Zdarsky and Emma Pavlik

Frank Harazim and Anna Varva

Emil Linek and Josefa Vlcek (Welcek)

Frank Chruma and Barbara Slezak

Victor Melicar and Mildred Kastanek

Finally, there is Mary Tuma. Her maiden name was Pospisil, but because she bought her land with parapheranal funds her husband is not listed in the record, so to which of the Tuma men she was married I could not determine.

First moves to the city

The slow trickle of Czech people moving into Alexandria and working there probably started virtually immediately. From the naturalization records we know that Josef Koncinsky and William Pospisil were cabinet makers and there was likely little opportunity to ply this trade in the rural areas so they most probably worked in Alexandria and Pineville. By 1924 Carl Svebek owned his own garage and there is every possibility that he started to learn this trade at an existing garage before he started his own. And, of course, there are the 12 Czechs, mostly domestic servants, that worked outside of the communities. There are, however, no extant city directories from the 1920s so we can not be certain for sure. But we know from the 1930s city directories that some Czechs owned businesses they must have started in the 1920s. Also there are a number of Czechs who owned houses in the city such as Norbert Krenek and the Jilek family.

10

Survival—The 1930s

1930 Census

If the census of 1930 merely showed the same people of the 1920 census 10 years older there would not be much point in examing it in detail. However, there was such enormous change in these 10 years that a detailed look at this census reveals almost a completely different community. There are 97 families in the 1930 census containing 351 people compared with the 408 people in only 90 families in the 1920 census. The decline of 57 people is alone surprising, especially since there were 7 more families. Moreover, only 58 of those listed as heads of families in 1930 were in both censuses. Of these, 11 were living in someone else's household in 1920. Nine of these were sons living at their parent's home in 1920, now they were on their own. Four of them were only teenagers and five were in their 20s. Plus, Frank Ludvik was living at his mother-in-law's house and Joseph Melichar was living in his father-in-law's house in 1920. Both headed their own houses in 1930. So only 47 who were heading their own family in 1920 still were in 1930. This means that 43 families moved out between the two censuses, or nearly 50%. At the same time 39 new families arrived. In addition, some of the original colonists were now living in Alexandria, while there were none in 1920. The census also shows a few other Czechs in the area who were unrelated to the colony, all except John Heidelberg arriving after 1920. First we will look at the Czech colony area, then the others.

This census taken was taken in April by two enumerators. Otto M. Nally, the enumerator in 1920 was also one of the enumerators in 1930. Nally only did the 19 Czech homes along the Holloway Prairie Road. A person identified only as W. H. Humble did the other 78 Czech households in the colony. There are some major differences in the way they filled out the forms. This impacts on what we can learn. Czechoslovakia was the approved word for the 1930 census and it is used throughout the state wherever Czechs were found (sometimes as one word,

338

other times hypenated.) Humble consistently used the words Czechoslovakia and Czech for birthplace and original language of the European born Czechs. Except for Emmett Vinloske, for which he used Bohemian, and John Zacek who is listed as a Moravian. There are also a few non-Czechs. Nally is the only enumerator in the state who consistently used Bohemian for nationality and not Czechoslovakia. Except in the language column he crossed out Bohemian in every entry and wrote Czech above it. Not only were there these problems, but for certain people, their ages, birthplaces and other information recorded about them do not square with other more established facts. So it appears that both Nally and Humble made mistakes. While I will analyze this information as set down in the census, it probably means that there are a few numbers off by one or two. We cannot even determine if, and how many, people were not counted, like the Vlachs who died in Libuse after 1930 but are not in the census.

The 1930 census also sought to list both the value of each home and if there was a radio set present, categories not considered in 1920. However, Humble only fills in the home values for about half of his entries in the colony area and most of those are the Americans living among the Czechs. He only filled in this column for 12 of the foreign born Czechs and 7 of the American-born Czechs he surveyed, or just 19 out of 78. Nally lists the values for 14 of the 16 homes he listed as being owned by their residents. For Frank Pacholik's home he wrote "2" and "un" for ownership status and value, repectively, with no clear indication of what these notes mean. The value written for Joseph F. Kadlec is unreadable. The three others were renting. So only 33 of 97 Czech colony properties had values listed. 12 were worth less than $1,000, one of which was rented; 11 were between $1,000 and $2,000 of which only two were over $1,300; two were $2,000 and two $2,500; four were $3,000 and 2 were $4,000. Only eight Czechs were said to be renting their homes while more than half their American neighbors were renting.

Francis Welcek Jr., Charles Prochaska, Emil Tuma, Frank Bejsovec and Joseph Stephens were the only Czechs said to have radios. Though less than 10 of their Anglo neighbors did too. However, since this column is mostly not filled out it is impossible to know if anybody else had a radio. Nally makes one entry for 66 year old Joseph F. Kadlic, whose farm was worth $1,500—and one entry for Joe Kadlec, 54, with a home worth $3,000. They are on different sheets of the census with different neighbors. There was a Frank Kadlec who bought land with Joseph Kadlec in 1916, though, "Joe" Kadlec is in the 1920 census, and Frank is not. Joe's oldest son in 1920 is 16 year old Jerry. There is nobody named Kadlic recorded buying property. Interestingly, when you do an Internet search for

Kadlic the first question Yahoo! asks is "did you mean Kadlec;" in red letters. Kadlic turns up 1,160 websites, Kadlec has nearly 250,000. So something does not quite add up here. One man or two? If two, where does the mistake lie?

The handwriting of Humble is very crisp and clear. Nally's is very poor, even faint, so some information is unreadable. Nally's handwriting is so poor, in fact, that the computer database built from the microfilm of the originals misspells every single surname he wrote except for Tuma and Pospisil. Veronika Tuma's first name is "Varnarck" in the database. Ironically, Humble took the census of the Nally household; he lived one house away from the adjoining farms of the Frank's. Nice and clearly it was noted that his house was worth $1,000. Even more amazing, who ever recently entered the data into the dateabase on the Internet identified more than a few as Bolivian rather than Bohemian! With these sorts of mistakes it is perhaps not a wonder that Louisiana historians did not pay much attention to Czechs in the state.

The 19 Czechs on Holloway had only 5 American neighbors. Three of them rented their homes, probably from Czechs. The Holy family lived on Donahue Ferry Road, while the Kraneks and Kostaks lived on "Flagon Falls Road." This name is kind of funny because there is no waterfall in this area (in fact, Louisiana's only waterfall is 60 miles away in St. Francisville.) It is most probably Flagon Road. The remaining homes are all unnumbered farms on nameless "improved dirt road(s)." There are a lot more Anglo neighbors in 1930 than in 1920. In the latter census only one road is completely Czech. The vast majority of the neighbors were native born Louisianians whose parents were native born Louisianians.

Of the 351 people in this census John Nousek was the oldest person in the comunity at 74. The youngest was one month old John Stuchlik. There were four others less than 6 months old. There were eight others who were over 70. There were twenty-seven people in their 60s. 39 people were recorded in their 50s. Only three of those over 50 were born in America. 53 year old Joseph Chruma was born in Kansas, Vencel Bastyr was born in Minnesota and 60 year old Edward Kramel was born in Pennsylvania. Of the 44 in their 40s only five were born in America. Four were men who were all 42. One was 41 year old Mary Brousek; she was married to the Czech born Andrew Brousek. Of those thirty-four in their 30s half were Czech born and half were American born. Of the fifty-seven in their 20s only 14 were born in Europe. 135 were twenty or younger. 61 were between eleven and 19. Of these, 22 were born in Louisiana. There were seventy-one kids born since the last census. 60 of them were born in Louisiana. The vast majority of Czech homes consisted of parents and their children. 16 couples were childless; the youngest of these were in their 20s and just starting out. 24 year old Charles Prochaska and his 19 year old wife were the youngest without children. His 27 year old brother Joseph Jr., and his wife, 24 year old Annie, also had no children.

However, there were several who had a different relationship. There was of course, Blanche and Eddie Tucek, young Charlie's sister and brother. 21 year old Louis Voda, born in Nebraska, was living with his brother, 29 year old Czech born Josef. 71 year old Mike Steigel was the father-in-law living at Charlie Nickel's house. Charlie had a newly married daughter, Annie Varsa, living with him, too, but there is no mention of Annie's husband. Frank Baley had his 52 year old mother-in-law, Mary Krejci, living with him. 26 year old John Repta was married to Joe Goldstein's daughter Vlasta. The Repta's had a two month old son, Arthur. They lived in Goldstein's house. Joseph Hrachovina, who had lost his sons and his wife, had his sister, 73 year old Elizabeth Haubenschild, living with him. Depending on which enumerator you want to believe, Jennie Holy was either a 19 year old living with her brother Charlie, or was a 21 year old living with her father Anton; she is the same person listed twice. Rebecca Johnson, not a Czech, was a border at the home of Ed and Ollie Wosterchil. She was a teacher at the Kolin school.

Among the households, 3 were headed by women; Anna Suchy, 35, and Jennie Hromadka, 45, were recently widowed. Mary Kment, 63, moved into the community as a widow. Among the 94 male heads of house 75 were born in Europe. 55 were labeled Czech and 15 Bohemian, meaning 70 were Czech. John Zacek was listed as Moravian. 60 year old Frank Kewir was Austrian, 46 year old Jack Cizak was from Poland, and Peter Kotar, 48, was Yugoslavian. Charles Holy, 25, was born in Roumania, but his father Anton was Bohemian according to both the 1930 and 1920 censuses. Charles' mother was born in Roumania and most of her children were also born there. The four who were teenagers in 1920 and had their own households in 1930 are Charles Holy, along with twenty-four year old Alvin Filipi, Frank Kramel, 27, and Charlie Tucek.

Tucek had it the roughest. In 1930 he was just 22 years old and employed as a painter. He was responsible for his 16 year old sister, Blanche, and his 14 year old brother, Eddie. Their father died in 1921 and their mother died in 1928. Charlie and Blanch were born in Illinois, while Eddie was born in Louisiana. Their parents bought 80 acres from Union Lumber in 1916; the farm was paid off by 1920. At least Charlie was left a car, making it much easier to get to work. But it must have been a tough way to start the Depression years.

Of the wives, 63 were born in Europe. 44 were labeled Czechoslovakian and 12 labeled Bohemian. Anna Pokorny was from Poland and Anna Kocourek from Austria. Matilda Fabianek Cizek was born in Germany to Czech parents. Helen Melichar, born in Roumania, was Anton Holy's daughter. Ursula Kotar was from Yugoslavia and Frances Zacek from Moravia. Elvira Holy is listed as Bohemian in 1930, but Roumanian in 1920. 10 were from northern states, one each from Illinois, Minnesota, New York, New Jersey, Ohio, Pennsylvania, Oklahoma and Wisconsin, 2 from Iowa, 3 born in Nebraska and four native to Kansas. These were all daughters of colonists. Only Ollie Westerchil was born in Louisiana; she was a teacher at the Komensky school. Bessie Svebek was born in Mississippi. Of all the wives only Lillian Ludvick had an occupation listed; she worked at her husband's garage. Only three of the daughters were employed. Mildred Tuma, 17, and Anna Bernard, 19, were servants in private homes. Jennie Holy was a saleslady at a "retail store" in one listing and at a "coffee shop" in the other.

The occupations listed for the male heads of households shows a few less farmers and a few more people working in city jobs. Frank Ludvick was the proprietor of an auto garage in Tioga, an adjacent area. Carl Svebek was an "auto manager" on the Old Marksville Highway. Charles Holy, Charles Safarik, Charles Prochaska, Rudolph Bohata and Frank Bejsovec were auto mechanics. Louis Filipi and Albert Helcl were carpenters. Frank Pacholik and both father and son Joseph Prochaska Sr., and Joseph Prochaska, Jr., were in construction work. Darwin Cizek was a delivery man for a steam laundry. Frank Harazim was reported to be a farm laborer. Frank Pokorny earned a living as a peddler of farm poduce. Joe Suba was a roofer. Charlie Tucek was a painter, as were James Koncinsky, Joseph Nickel and Frank Kramer. Joe Melichar and Steve Marhefka owned their own grocery stores. Vencel Bastyr's and Joe Kadlec's occupation cannot be deciphered. Joseph Frank and Ed Wosterchil had poultry operations. Three had no occupations listed (written in as "none.") 70 year old Albert Richter and 67 year old John Filipi were probably retired. Why the allegedly 26 year old Matt Vlasek was unemployed is not clear, but he is the only male head of household who was not employed. However, four years later he was dead and his gravestone says he was born in 1860, meaning he was really 70 in 1930, not 26. To add to the confusion, his wife is listed as 24 in the census, which would seem to agree with his stated age of 26, but no wife of Mathew is buried locally. 66 were general farmers. At least 61 owned their farms. Only Frank Harazim, Ed Wosterchil, Josef Voda and Frank Pokorny were recorded as renting farms. Six of the men were living alone: Jack Cizak, Frank Kewir, Vencel Bastyr, Joe Suba, Albin Cecha and Joseph Ubl. These last two were, of course, founders of the community.

There were 86 sons living at homes in the community. 38 were born in Louisiana. 46 were from other states—five were from Pennsylvania, one each from Maryland and New York, and the remaining 38 were from midwestern states. Of these 46, only 10 were younger than the colony itself, meaning they were recent arrivals. One son's age was unreadable. Carl Safarik, 21, was the only one Czechborn. Joseph Kotar, 22, was born in Germany. Thirty-one of the older sons had jobs. Villie (Willie) Vonesh was the youngest male working; he was a 16 year old helper at a blacksmith shop. Joseph Kotar was a laborer at a glazier. Eddie Locker was a logger. Carl Safarik, Gus Bernard, Frank Hromadka, Rudolph Bohata, and the brothers Emil Jr., and Harry Tuma were mechanics. William Pospisil was a carpenter. Herman Stephens (Stepan,) Elmer Kramel, and John Zabavsky were painters, as was Louis Voda (though listed as brother, not son.) Anton Goldstein worked as a roofing laborer. 23 year old Joseph Steffek was a salesman at a furniture store, probably in Alexandria, and 21 year old Carl Steffek was a salesman at a wholesale store, probably the Melichar's. Paul Chruma was an oil field laborer. Joseph Zmek was a part time office boy, but was also attending school. Twelve were working on the family farm. Of the sons of working age only Frank Chruma, 22 and Louis Smigura, 18, were not employed. Of 46 school age boys, 43 were in school, only Zmek had a part time job. 6 year old Marvin Filipi, 5 year old Joseph Koncinsky Jr., and 12 year old John Koncinsky were not in school. 9 sons were under 5. In this cenus 81 sons had English names. There were 8 Josephs, the remainder showed a wide variance. Only Cestimir Kubis, Anton Goldstein, Emil Tuma, Emil Holy and Villie Vonesh did not have typically American names.

There were 71 young daughters living at home. Mary Richter (Rychter) was a 44 year old daughter living with her father, Albert, and she was born in Europe. There were just five over 20, with the 26 year old Helen Kramel and Lillie Stephen being the oldest, and only Jennie Holy, 21, was born in Europe. They were too old for school, but only Holy worked. 2 birth places were unreadable. None of the younger daughters were born in Europe. Two were infants, 3 month old Emily Holy and 5 month old Margaret Nickel, though Jarmila Tuma was probably an infant also, her age, though, is unreadable. 31 were born in other states, five in Pennsylvania and one in Maryland. The remainder were born in various Midwest states. 39 were born in Louisiana. 64 daughters had American names, with a wide variance, though 7 were named Mary and 9 were named Helen. Only seven had Czech names. There were 3 girls named Jarmila, who were the youngest or only daughter in the Kubis, Stuchlik and Tuma familes. All were born in Louisiana. There were three Vlastas—Safarik and Smigura from

Louisiana and Harazim from North Dakota. There was also one year old Olga Kotar, also born in Louisiana. 33 of the girls were in school, 12 of school age were not in school and 21 were too young. Only three daughters worked: Holy, as mentioned, but also Anna Bernard, 19, and Mildred Tuma, 17, both of whom were servants.

One major change was in the number of people who were said not to speak English. Just 14 of the wives were said to speak no English, of whom one was 26, the remainder over 40. Among men, only five were said not to speak English, the youngest was 45. Of adult woman, only two could be said to have Czech names, Vlasta Repta, 26, and Veronika Tuma, 42. Mary, Anna and Helen were still the most popular, but only about 1/5th had these names, the remainder were various names with no pattern. Among the adult men only 9 had what could be considered Czech names. Four of them were Kasper Gernett, Karel Suchy, Vaclav Kocourek and Vencel Bastyr, who was not only the youngest, at 59, but also the only one of these four born in America. There were also five named Anton, three born in Europe. The remainder had American names, and though Frank, Joseph and Charles were the most prevalent, all together these 3 were less than ¼ of the men's names. All the rest varied over a wide range.

So in 1930 there were far fewer residents who did not speak English (but most elders stll spoke Czech among themselves.) There was also a much wider range of American first names, no longer were children being given Czech names. Far fewer woman were said to be working, though this could be the way they were listed, for there is little doubt that women were still working in some way on the farms. But there were less farms, too, and more people were employed in non-farm occupations. There were also fewer teenagers working and more of them still in school. This certainly conformed to wider trends among both immigrants and Americans in the decade between 1920 and 1930.

Child labor laws and standards had changed. More children were being educated into their high school years. The flow of immigrants had declined. Less people were working on farms. The Czech colony was merely mirroring the mainsteam of America. The biggest change was in the make up of different families present in the colony. The nearly 50% turnover rate surely presented some difficulties for both long time colonists and new neighbors. This occurred on a number of levels. For old timers, they saw friends move away. Adjustments also had to be made in the social order to accommodate the newcomers. Still, it remained a very cohesive Czech community.

The other big change involved just four families. August Bernat Americanized his family name to Bernard, Joseph Stepan translated his to the very American

Stephens, the Melicars of the 1920s became the Melichars of the 1930s (but still pronounced it the same,) and the Balejs of pre-1920, which had been changed to Baley by 1920, were now the Bailey family. No other Czechs further Americanized their surnames since the previous census. The only other further Americanization of names occurred later, and then just two did so. Wosterchil was changed to Westerchil and a few of the Hazmukas became Hazmark. Which brings us to those Czechs who had moved into the city by 1930. Among them was the only other Czech who apparently changed his name. He is listed as Alois Stybr prior to 1920, then became Stieber, and finally Louis Staber. But he moved to Alexandria and no longer lived in the colony area.

Louis Staber, 43, and Anna Staber, 41, both born in Czechoslovakia, lived at 702 Foisy Street in downtown Alexandria. They owned a restaurant. He is listed as proprietor while she is listed as the cook. The census says she still did not speak English, but since she arrived in 1905 this is unlikely. Stybr and Staber were the same person, given that their ages correspond, their wive's names were the same and both were from Bohemia. Whether this was a misspelling or not cannot be determined. However, in the Libuse cemetery their names on the gravestone are Alois and Anna Styber. There is though, no mention of their two children, Stanley and Mamie, who would have been 19 and 17 respectively.

Anton Welcek, 42, was born in Czechoslovakia. He was an auto mechanic. His wife, Marie, 33, was born in Nebraska to Bohemian parents. They owned a home worth $6,000. Anton is recording living at home in Kolin in 1920. Tereza Vondries is listed in 1930 as "Theresa Von Dreis" She rented a house at 830 9th Street in downtown. Living with her were her daughter Rose, 23, who was born in Oklahoma, and Mary Rougeau (Cajun French,) 58 years old, was their "roomer." Theresa was a "seamstress" and Mary was a "dressmaker," both working from home. Rose was a saleslady at a dry goods store.

At least one, Mildred Tuma, 17, was counted twice. Once at her father's home in Libuse, and then again listed as a servant living in the home of Herman White and his wife and young son on Tensas Avenue. Sadie Smigura, 19, was a boarder living in the home of William O'Pry, and working as a cashier at a furniture store in the city. Mary Pospisil, 18, was a live-in servant at the home of Louis Levy on Jackson Street. Their families still lived out in the colony. Emil Meydrich, 60, who was born in Czechoslovakia, lived at 1835 "Yale-Harvard Street." These are really two different streets and later city directories say it was 1835 Yale. Along with him was his wife, Mary, 43, born in Illinois. Their house and grocery store were at the same address and combined had a value of $3,500. Their son, Anton, 20, born in Illinois, was a "radio operator." All were in the 1920 Libuse census.

Finally, there was poor Antoinette Varvarovsky, 27, born in Bohemia, who was a patient at Central Louisiana State Hospital when the cenus was taken. For what we do not know.

Also in Alexandria were several other Czechs not related to the colony. If Nally and Humble had difficulty recording Czechs, among whom they lived, whoever took the census in Alexandria was really having problems. Among the Czechs were Morris Weiss, 55, and his wife and son, Hannah, 55, and Samuel, 29. Weiss was a retail clothing merchant, all were born in Czechoslovakia, but Weiss is listed as speaking Hungarian. He was most likely Jewish and the census taker had no real idea what his mother tongue was. Elmer Barta was born in Iowa to Bohemian parents. Barta is a Czech name, but no one by this name is in the property records. He was 26 and lived at 1833 "Yale-Harvard" Street. His wife's name is unreadable, though it could be something like "Vega." She, too, was 26 and born in Iowa. Her father was listed as being born in "Prague, Bohemia"—this is only the second time a city was named in any census report that I have seen. Barta was a traveling salesman for margarine products, which were new at the time. That the Bartas lived nextdoor to the Meydricks is an interesting coincidence. Though, there was no daughter listed in the Meydrich family in the 1920 census, so "Vega" was probably not related to them. Plus, Meydrich's wife and children were born in Illinois, not Iowa. It seems improbable, however, that they did not know of each other's Czech origins.

Then there was the very international John Valentine, 49, who was born in Moravia. His father was listed as English and his mother German, but his mother language was listed as Bohemian. His wife, Grace, 43, and son Joseph, 7, were both born in Louisiana. The English father explains the name Valentine. Since Joseph was born in Louisiana it seems they were in the state as early as 1923. They lived at what looks to be 2220 Marage Street—though that is almost certainly wrong; the writing is hard to read. There is a Murray Street in Alexandria and it is the alternative offered when searching the Internet for Marage Street. There is no Marage Street. John was a "bridge building foreman," for a "steam railway," possibly meaning that he helped operate the railroad bridge over the Red River. Also working with the railway, but as a clerk, was Sanford Chambers. His age is written as 21, but his wife, Rose, was listed as 26. She is listed as speaking Slovak as her original language, and she supposedly arrived in 1904. Her parents were listed as Austrian, but this is explainable because Austria ruled the Slovaks. However, buried in the Libuse cemetery is Rose Baroch Chambers—the daughter of Anton, who was born in Bohemia and was 22 in 1920. So this is yet another unexplainable error. They had a daughter Mary L., who was just 2 ½ years old. They were living as roomers at the home of Robert Ebert at 1205 Magnolia Street.

Three Czechs were living in the rural precinct of ward 8, while the Czech colony was in the adjoining wards 9 and 10 (though it appears that either the ward boundries were changed slightly between censuses or ward 8 is incorrect for two of them.) Frank Dudacek, 74, was living alone. He was born in Czechoslovakia and worked as a farmer. It was recorded that he owned his farm, but no property record could be found for him. He did not live near any other Czechs, the census pages before and after the one where he is recorded are filled with a sea of native Louisianans. He is not named by any source from Libuse or Kolin. So who exactly he was and why he came to be in Rapides Parish is a mystery. His name can be translated to English as a "little piper," from "dudak," piper and "cek," the diminutive suffix. He definitely lived in ward 8.

Another Czech who was supposedly in ward 8 was Anton Baroch, 55. He lived with his wife, Mary, 54, and their 11 year old daughter Francis. The parents were born in Bohemia and the child in Louisiana. They are in the 1920 census in ward 10, and Anton did buy land here in 1916. It was in section 45, township 5, and only Baroch, Frank Varva and Vaclav Vlach bought land in this section. Varva is not in either census. While the Vlach family was in the 1920 census they were not 1930, however, the Vlachs are buried at Libuse (and did not die until more than 25 years later.) The Vlachs and Barochs lived on the same road in 1920, along with the Potmesils and Hromadkas (who bought in section 41 as did many Czechs.) It is highly improbable that Anton sold his land to move to another farm and no such record could be found. So either the ward border ran between these two sections or the ward number is listed wrong. The Barochs' had 8 children; only one was a son. Other than Francis, six other Baroch children were old enough to have gotten married or moved away, so it is not surprising that only their youngest daughter was still living with them. In fact, we have just seen how their daughter Rose was living in Alexandria. The four oldest were born in Bohemia, two were born in Ohio, and in keeping with confusing situations, a daughter Annie is said to be six months old in 1920, while Francis is 3 months old. They were probably twins, though, and both were born in Louisiana. Why Annie is not listed with the parents is not apparent. She is not one of those said to have died at a young age.

But then we come to the strange listing of the "Charles Blaisdell" family. They lived just down the road from the Barochs on a "narrow guage road." Both are on the same census sheet with just five farms separating the listings. He was born in Illinois and his parents were listed as born there, too. At the age of 50 he was working as a delivery man for an ice company. His wife, Olga, 41, was born in Nebraska to Bohemian parents, though she is listed as speaking Czech as her mother tongue. They had six children. Fred, 18, was born in Nebraska and worked as a welder at an "auto shop," which was a common occupation among the young Czech men. His 16 year old sister, also named Olga, was also born in Nebraska. That seems to point to the marriage taking place in Nebraska. 13 year old Veronica was born in Missouri. But Charles, who was 9, is listed as being born in Moravia! (Both Missouri and Moravia are so clearly written that it is impossible to confuse them.) The two youngest children, Fanny, 3, and Nellie, just six months old, were both born in Louisiana.

So it seems at first glance to be just another confusing situation of a peripatetic family—until we look back at the 1920 census. There we find 46 year old Charles Blazel, born in Illinois to Bohemian parents, with a 31 year old wife named Olga born in Nebraska, an 8 year old son named Fredric and a 5 year old daughter Olga, both born in Nebraska, a 3 year old daughter named Veronica, born in Missouri, and six month old Charles—born in Missouri—not Moravia—and all living in ward 10. The Blaisdell family was not some world traveling anomaly, showing up only later—they were the Blazels living in the same place for more than 10 years—now wholly transformed from census to census. The father Charles' age is wrong in one or the other censuses, for sure. The other ages all correspond, as do the birth places—except for young Charles. Ward 10 or ward 8 I cannot explain. Blazel to Blaisdell is a bit of leap.

It is interesting to note that the last name Blazel is derived from one of two Czech words. Blazen (no hacek) means "crazy" and Blažen (with hacek) means "blissfully happy." (Not that far apart in concept when you think about it.) We do not know from which word comes the family name since the diacritical was not used in America; in the Czech Republic there are both. But without the hacek was Charles unhappy with being known as Mr. Crazy? That would be a fairly good incentive to change his surname, though only the Czechs would have known the translation and they surely were not fooled by the new Blaisdell. Or did the census taker simply take it upon himself? That is an unsolvable mystery.

One problem arises, then, with analyzing the census of 1930 of the colony. When we include the Barochs and the Blaisdells there are really 99 families, not 97. There are really 362 people and not 351. But the overall conclusions remain unaffected. After 1930 the move in rate declined drastically, as did the number of those who moved out. Though this still was occuring as late as the early 1940s. The 16 childless couples and the single men eventually passed away or moved away. The majority (but not all) of families with children in 1930 form the basis of the community which exists today. The children of 1930 are now the elders, more than a few of whom I met; many still have a command of the Czech language.

It is also this generation of children who are entangled in a complicated web of in-law relationships among the Czech families. I can only estimate, but it appears that some 80% of the Czechs married other Czechs between the founding of the community and about 1950. This was not small town inbreeding, as might be supposed, of various degrees of cousins marrying cousins. None of this generation were related by blood. All of these families arrived from different points in America, in turn arising from a plethora of towns and cities in the Czech Republic. Probably 95% arrived without knowing each other until they met up in Libuse and Kolin. The children of these children are wholly integrated into the surrounding communities and I would estimate that 90% of them did not marry Czechs at all.

Property Transactions in the 1930s

There were just 80 property records from the 1930s. 32 were in 1930, and five of these sales were from Joseph A. Ubl to members of his family. One was a correction of a sale made a few months previously by Ubl to Joseph Pestal, so this accounts for two of the transactions. There were just 17 transactions between 1931 and 1935, reflecting the depths of the Depression. Two were by Czech individuals to non-Czechs, and one was by a non-Czech to a Czech. One was the succession of Matthew Vlasek. Not only did he have land to transfer, but he had $3,210 in the bank and his mechanic's tools. There were eight transactions in 1936, thirteen in 1937, just 5 in 1938 and 6 in 1939. There was only one tax sale, that is, one person "bought" the land for the unpaid taxes by paying this amount to the state of Louisiana. This does not, however, necessarily mean that the deed was transferred. The people who did not pay the taxes had three years to redeem the property by paying the taxes, with interest, to the one who "purchased" the land. Good old Frank Baley made this purchase. It was Joseph Chruma and Joseph Slezak, who owned the property together, who did not make the tax payments. There were two redemptions, one by Frank Krobat for $27.74 in 1930, and one by a man we know only as Mr. Pulkrasek, for $27.14. Three of the transactions in 1939 were by non-Czechs buying oil leases, or the right to look for oil, one from Joseph Chruma and one from Katie Chruma, but they are separate transactions on different land, and one from the Chocholousek family.

Seven sales in the decade were from non-Czech individuals to Czechs and eight were from Czechs to non-Czechs. There were five sales by corporations to Czechs, all in 1930. One sale was by Rapides Bank & Loan Association to Darwin Cizek. Two purchases were made by James Koncinsky from the Home Bank & Loan Company. The last recorded sale by Alexandria Lumber was made to Anna Suchy in 1930. Carl Svebek bought a small "irregular" lot from Louisiana Oil Refining on the Marksville Highway. This was one of the few purchases by Czechs among all the hundreds made that involved what could be called a traditional mortgage: 51 monthly payments of $30 each and one last one for the odd balance left. The document does not say if the gas station he came to operate was included in the sales price of $1,564.58, but given the price I assume it was. In February of 1937 Jennie Pacholik sold a portion of her land fronting the Red River in downtown Alexandria for a levee that was being constructed. She was paid $6,000 cash. Only other three sales in the 1930s involved lots in Alexandria, the rest were in the colony.

15 sales in the 1930s still used "Libuse Townsite" as part of their legal description. In fact, there a total of 46 total sales during the 25 years since the colony was founded using this description. Of these 46 sales only one ever involved a non-Czech. James DeFuentes sold a lot he purchased from Ubl and Ernest Jilek to Frank Kramel—that is, he sold it back to a Czech. Considering that the price was $1,600 it probably involved the house that the Kramel family owns today on Highway 28. Seven of these sales were by Joseph Ubl and seven of them were by members of the Tuma family. Of these 14, two were from Ubl to Emil Tuma. Frank Kramel was married to Emil's daughter Helen.

Throughout this decade, when America was in the throes of the Great Depression and thousands of people across Louisiana lost their land and homes to foreclosure for nonpayment of mortgages or taxes, or both, there is not one recorded instance of a Czech family losing their land. The vast majority owned theirs outright, free and clear of any encumbrances. For the few who were still making payments their hard work and frugality enabled them to continue to do so. In fact, of the 60-some odd purchases in the 1930s 55 were for cash. Svebek's gas station purchase was one exception. James Koncinsky was another of those rare individuals who took out a conventional mortgage; one property he bought from Home Bank was for $700, payable in 60 payments of $11.65 each. Just three months previously he purchased a parcel from Frank Varsa for $451, on which he put down $251 and agreed to pay the remaining $200 in one year.

Among the other exceptions was one by Method Hruban, who purchased from Ubl and was somehow related to him. He put down $1,500 and agreed to pay $2,200 within one year. Joseph Pestal bought from Ablin Cecha in April, 1930, putting $2,700 down and agreeing to pay $250 every six months until the mortgage was satisfied. Frank Nikuda bought from a non-Czech, putting down $200 towards a $500 price and taking on 3 annual payments of $100.

Two of the sales were between family members. Wesley Drudik bought his father's farm for $4,000, paying $1,000 cash at the time of sale and agreeing to pay the remaining $3,000 within 10 years, but no specific time table is given. Also, the father, James, was to retain a usufruct, or the right to live on the farm, for the next 10 years. Frank Bohata sold two parcels for a price "payable on demand," with nothing down, but he apparently thought the buyers were well enough off to make the payment when requested. One was of 20 acres to his son Rudolph for $600 and the other of 10 acres for $300 to his daughter Ella and her husband Joseph Turek. Frank and Rudolph were living in Bossier City, Louisiana at the time and the Tureks were living in Chicago.

Out of all the Czech-related records during the Depression there was just one seizure of land for nonpayment of a mortgage and it was actually on November, 30th, 1929, five weeks after the stock market crash of October, 1929. Joe Melicar was forced to foreclose on John Gunter, a non-Czech, for non-payment of $225. Literally later that afternoon on the same day he sold this land to Frank Pacholik for $231.65 cash.

The Depression and WPA Reports

I heard many proud recountings of the self-sufficiency of the Czech Communities during the depths of the Depression and the fact that no Czech families needed government assistance. There are three known sources corroborating these claims. Here we will look at two Works Progress Administration reports, one for each community, but first a ½ page article that appeared in the New Orleans Times-Picayune of December, 3rd, 1933. I have already relied on this article earlier for other reasons, but the true focus of the article is the self-sufficiency of the Czechs. The article is actually the only one that I could find on the colony in any state newspaper between the first Town Talk articles in 1913 and 1914 and Town Talk articles that started to appear in the late 1970s. It is the only article that the Times-Picayune ever seems to have run on the colony. It ran under a banner headline: "Louisiana Colony of Bohemian Planters Seeks No Relief." Mortimer Kreeger is the reporter who wrote the article. Like in any newspaper article there is wheat and chaff and I will try to separate the two.

It warrants extensive quoting, and not just because it is our only published source during these times, as we shall see. Its opening sentence is: "There is at least one community in Louisiana which asks no help from the ERA, CWA, PWA, AAA or any other of the recovery agencies set up by the president [Roosevelt] and which has not a single resident and has never had a single resident on a welfare or relief roll." This was during a time when tens of thousands of Louisiana residents were being hired by these agencies because they could find no other work and tens of thousands more were on the welfare rolls. A look through the paper from 1931 to 1936 shows barely a day without one or two articles about the desperate plight of people throughout the state. Farm relief, mortgage relief, tax relief, welfare assistance, food assistance, charity drives, church appeals, tax sales, foreclosures, bank closures, unemployment, mass hiring programs, jobs programs, make-work programs, government programs, and a myriad of requests by state-level politicians, mayors and city councils for relief of all kinds—all are a constant refrain. Not one corner of the state was unaffected. This being Louisiana, there are even more than a few articles about favortism, nepotism and corruption pertaining to this great relief effort. I did not take a statistical count, but it seems that there were no less than 1,500 articles on the subject of the Great Depression's affect on Louisiana. I took the survey of other similar articles because, one, this article stands out in an amazing way, and two, I wanted to see if any previous or further reporting on the colony could be found. Unfortunately, no one wrote before Kreeger and no one followed up.

The article continues: "Not only are these people remarkably free from the necessity of federal aid in these difficult times, but the record of their National Farm Loan Association is unsurpassed by none other in the New Orleans district." This district included not only Louisiana, but Mississippi and Alabama, too. "Their secret?" the article asks before supplying the answer: "The people are hardworking, industrious and thrifty." It also notes "this explanation does not come from any sentimental moralist. It is in the official records of the emergency relief adminstration and the farm credit administration and in a statement issued by Mayor Vic Lamkin of Alexandria." The article says that in 1917 the colonists organized their own farm loan association, "known in the records as the 'Bohemia N. F. L. A.' It was one of the first associations in the district." Further, "in every periodic report issued since that date by government directors of farm loan bodies in the area, the Bohemia N. F. L. A. has been classified in the highest group according to their solvency and integrity."

In 1916 Congress passed the Federal Farm Loan Act which established 12 Federal Land Banks. This was the umbrella system overseeing smaller cooperative

associations that loaned money to farmers throughout the nation. While the start up capital came from the federal government the various associations relied on their members for future operating capital. The Bohemians clearly established their own cooperative, essentially pooling their money and loaning it back to themselves. Unfortunately, while the Land Banks still exist, there seems to be no extant or readily avi
 able records from the early years. It was not a corporation so it is not in the Louisiana Corporations database. All Internet searches for this organization were fruitless, turning up only modern entities. In fact, according to one source, American cooperatives had a total revenue in 2003 of over $125 billion. The Federal Land Bank in this state is known as the Louisiana Land Bank and it is a fully functioning organization with its own website—but no historical information. However, considering the way the Bohemians did business their meetings were conducted in Czech only among themselves thereby ensuring that they kept control and thus did not have to worry about the solvency or "integrity" of any outsiders.

In the article, an official of the Federal Land Bank in New Orleans is quoted saying, "the record of this community has always been among the best we have had. Since their organization they have not been out of the first rank in our classification." As part of a greater federal action to solve the banking crisis of 1933, over a period of several months all such associations were declared "ineligible to do further business because of temporary insolvency." However, the Bohemian group was "in the last group to be disqualified." The group was not insolvent at all. It was just caught up in the broad sweep of federal action: "they have paid up most of their loans, and we believe they will be on a credit basis before long." The article notes that "they might be the first to regain solvency" in the state. Quoting this official further, "there has never been a foreclosure in Libuse through federal farm agencies. Our field agents report that payments are made promptly and willingly, and have never been willfully defaulted. The people are hardworking and thrifty." And presumably "promptly" means on time and for the full amount due. My search of the property records surely bears this out, for not one foreclosure document could be found. Indeed, by this time, most of the original Czech farms were paid off. Any business Czechs had with the Federal Land Bank was in buying more land and to buy more modern equipment.

The article says there is but one "curt paragraph" in the files of the emergency relief administration office in Alexandria mentioning the colony: "The Bohemian colony of Libuse asked for no aid. These farmers are thrifty and industrious, and on their farms they raise sufficient vegatables and staples to supply their families through the winter, besides marketing their products." So, not only were they able to feed themselves, they were growing enough to sell to others. The reporter writes "Quite contrary to receiving aid, the colonists have usually contributed an annual sum to the Red Cross and similar organizations." It was only because of lower prices that "a donation could not be raised" this year. It appears that they were acting more as a relief agency than a people in need of relief. This was in stark contrast to their neighbors.

Kreeger writes "the very suggestion of receiving help from a federal relief agency arouses the indignation of a resident." He quotes one of the "most successful farmers and dairymen," saying "We don't need any aid, and we don't want it. We can take care of ourselves. Of course, we borrowed money from farm loans to help us get started and to improve our farms; but we're paying back every cent of it. And no Bohemian is going to be on any welfare roll." Since there are pictures of both Albin Cecha and the Drudik family accompanying the article, and James Drudik is quoted by name elsewhere, it was probably one of these that Kreeger was quoting for this comment. No other Czechs are quoted.

For the conditions Kreeger reported in Libuse in 1933 he relyed on non-Czechs and thus are more objective; such as Vic Lamkin really was Alexandria's mayor at the time. But when Kreeger gives a little history of the colony he had to rely on either Cecha, Drudik or other Czechs unnamed. That is were two old subjective stories surface. He writes "many of the early settlers were inexperienced farmers, tradesman or townspeople, who had never tried to make their living from the soil. They gave up in dispair and left for Northern factories and shops." However, we know from the censuses and the property records that the vast majority of Czechs came from the Midwest farm states, which are not known today for their urban centers, and definitely not in 1914 to 1930. Furthermore, when we look at the counties and towns within those states they came from (which are stated in many property records) we can see that almost all came from rural farm communities. And not only were they farm communities, many were previously established Czech farm communities.

James Drudik himself had come from Crawford County, Wisconsin, which is a rural county (with only 17,000 people today and 16,000 in 1930) on the Iowa border far from any city. Even more evidence of some level of farm experience can be found in the obituaries of European born Czechs in the Town Talk—every one listing a hometown indicates a small farming town in the Czech Republic—and not one from any of the larger cities of that country. This also leaves the question of why any "tradesman and townspeople" would give up their trade and life they knew to start out afresh in a strange place where farming was going to be the main occupation—and anyone buying forty to eighty to 160 and more acres surely knew that farming was going to be his job. Plus, other than the few store owners already recounted, no Czech ever seemed to have tried to start a store or trade shop of any kind. This is one story that would not die.

Of course, there is the other story that Kreeger relates: "But the saddest blow of all was when the officers of an investment company, through which the Bohemians purchased the land from the lumber company, suddenly disappeared with the receipts. Many of the settlers had paid in full for their land, in cash." The last statement is definitely true—and is one reason they lost no land to foreclosure during the Depression. The company refered to is no doubt Louisiana Investment, but it did not act as a middleman between the lumber company and the Czechs. The land the company sold it had bought—and the lumber companies were not involved in those sales. Not once does a lumber company name or one of their executive's names appear in those records. The land that the Czechs bought directly from the lumber companies show not one piece of evidence that any member of Louisiana Investment was involved at any time. Not once does the name of an officer of Louisiana Investment or the company itself appear in those records. Indeed, conveyances from the lumber companies mostly started after Alexandria Lumber foreclosed on Louisiana Investment.

Moreover, even if we assume that there were some sales that were affected by the chicanery of Louisiana Investment there should be some evidence. Whether of restated sales, corrections, refunds, lawsuits, greivances, applications for lost deeds and titles—something, anything—but there is nothing. Other than the purchase by Cecha of 4,000 acres from Lee Lumber, all his purchases were individual to individual. Drudik himself bought his land from the bachelor Frank Datel and not from or through any company at all. In fact, the only mistakes that could be found in Drudik's property records is that his wife's maiden name is given as "Sedlecek" in one, "Ledlecek" in a second and "Sedlack" in a third. Perhaps the last irony is that her first name was Libuse.

That these two stories, among others based in fiction, keep reappearing is, frankly, amazing. Since there are so few published sources on the communities they have fed on each other. Some would say that where there is smoke there is fire, yet all I could find is a cold, wet blanket. So Kreeger relies on unanmed sources to present them in the only article ever published by his paper on Libuse, giving the impression that they are true. Anyone relying on this article years later, as Walker does in her dissertation, would simply relay these two stories as based in fact. (That Walker misstates both the date and page number of the article in her bibliography does not help.) Why they were told in the first place I cannot figure out. Who made them up is not known. Perhaps the stories of one or two individuals snowballed, as gossip does. There were perhaps one or two tradesmen who came because of the promise of a new town. But hardly great numbers of them.

That these two stories originated from Czechs is perhaps born out by the other story Kreeger relates about the founding of the colony, which he also had to learn from Czechs in Libuse he spoke with. He says that the effort to found a colony was started in 1913 by J. E. Kroupa, "the editor of Hospodar." As we know, John Rosicky started the effort in 1905 and he was the owner and editor of the paper. Rose Rosicky, John's daughter, became editor after he died in 1910. Kroupa was assistant editor in 1913 and 1914. Kreeger says the three man committee to look for land was made up of Joseph Ubl, "a member of the Hospodar staff," Frank Bailey, "who had settled in South Dakota," and "J. Jira, of Kansas." He says that the committee looked at Tennessee, Virginia, South Carolina, Missouri and Arkansas, besides Louisiana. Maybe they did look in these states, but the known settlement efforts by Hospodar all occurred far west of the Mississippi River and these states mentioned are all in the opposite direction.

There is no evidence that Ubl ever worked for the paper, not even in Rose Rosicky's "History of Czechs (Bohemians) in Nebraska." Frank Baley was born in Pennsylvania and was only 22 in the 1920 census, so he was just a 15 year old teenager in 1913 (17 if his obituary is right.) Which ever age is right, it was hardly the age to be making such decisions, never mind settling in South Dakota. In fact, there is no evidence that Baley ever set foot in that state; his youngest sister was born in Ohio and his brother was married in Iowa. In fact, the one property record which records Baley's residence outside of Louisiana says it was Council Bluffs, Iowa. Who "J. Jira" was I have no clue—this is the only time his name ever appears in the history of Libuse. Plus, the historical marker in Libuse says the three men were Wosterchil, Posvar and Sobatka. If that was not enough, Kreeger says Ubl was the town's first settler. Many bought land in 1914 before Ubl's first recorded purchase in 1915.

So, all the objective facts that Kreeger reports based on non-Czech sources we can either corroborate or have enough circumstantial evidence to conclude he was correct. The lack of any other published contemporary source is limiting, but not enough to discount the primary facts of the article. For the subjective facts he had to have learned from some Czechs he was way off the mark and no one ever came along to correct him. Which leaves one last question: were no Czechs ever on the welfare rolls? We can never know for sure. Perhaps not in 1930 through 1933, but what about later years of the Depression? Which brings us to the WPA reports.

The Works Progress Administration (WPA) was one of a handful of agencies set up by Franklin Roosevelt to provide employment to the many unemployed people in the country. They included the Civilian Conservation Corps, Emergency Relief Agency, Agricultural Adjustment Agency, Civil Works Administration, Public Works Administration, among others (the "alphabet agencies" listed by Kreeger.) The WPA is best known for sending its workers out across America to catalog what existed. Through photography, creating card catalogues in libraries, recording oral histories, recording folk musicians, updating archives, preparing indices of all sorts of records, and writing reports on every community and city neighborhood in the country, its vast and comprehensive output was probably the largest project of its kind ever undertaken.

Libuse and Kolin were swept up in this effort. The Kolin report was prepared by Velma Juneau on June 5, 1936. Juneau says Kolin is a "Czecho-Slovakian farming community" for the most part "made up of self-sufficient farms." The report continues, "It has a good, modern school, two stores, two filling stations and a Presbytarian church with Sunday School and services every Sunday." There was no Czech church, though there may well have been a Presbytarian church in the vicinty. I quote here the body of the report:

"The residents came to the community from the midwestern agricultural states. The leading crops of this vicinity are cotton, corn, oats and peanuts. Larger acreage is also planted and harvested of such crops as sweet and Irish potatoes, chicken grain crops, sugar cane, clovers and legumes, truck crops and fruit. This community is noted for its thrift and industry. It went through the so-called depression absolutely free of any governmental aid of any kind, having at all times producded sufficient feed, food and cash crops to take care of itself. Dairying, hogs and poultry raising are on extensive scale are also practiced.

Fishing and hunting is unexcelled.

Good drinking water is obtained from wells at depth of forty to sixty feet.

Pine and hardwood timber at present are the main natural resources.

The topography of the countryside is gently rolling and well drained."

Juneau lists Francis Welcek as her "bibliography." Based on his age in the 1930 census Welcek was a 51 year old successful famer when he made this report. The underlined passage here is underlined in the report. The last four sentences stand alone in the report.

We get a similarly glowing report about the "Bohemian Colony" at Libuse. The report notes that it was made on a "side trip to Catahoula Lake out Highway No. 123," (now Highway 28.) I quote the report nearly in its entirety:

"Libuse, population approximately 300, is located nine miles northeast of Alean-dria on State Highway No. 123. The inhabitants are of Austro-Bohemian extraction. The community has been settled during the past thirty years by families from the North Central States, and from Wisconsin in particular, having migrated there from Europe. Assuming the customs of their adopted homeland, they are proud today of their American citizenship. While their native tongue is spoken by the older persons rather generally within the community, the younger persons cannot be distinguished by their language. The accent is not retained as with some other social groups

Noted for their thrift and industry, the Libuse community is one of the small group whose residents at no time during the depression applied for governmental relief. Although located on cut-over pine hills in contrast to the alluvial lands of the bayous and river bottoms, these colonists have prospered. Their well-built houses and barns are in striking contrast to many of the shacks used by native settlers whose livlihood is attained more easily. The settlers in this community devote their efforts to general farming but give considerable attention to dairying, poultry raising and truck farm-ing.

The younger children attend grade school at Libuse. High school students attend Bolton High School, Alexandria. The community is unique in that it has no church. The reason for this as given by members of the community is that "as a whole, we are not religiously inclined. We were attracted to America because of the freedom which prevails here, and especially were we attracted by the freedom to worship or not to worship as we choose."

Wesley Drudik is listed as the bibiography, after a "resident interview" on January 12, 1937. He was 35 years old when he gave his report.

Several things bear closer study. Exactly who Velma Juneau was is unknown, but given her French surname she may well have been a local woman. How Juneau came to pick just these two people to question and no one else is not known, though she does refer to "members of the community," so perhaps she did speak to more people. Welcek lived on the main highway, but Drudik lived on one of those dirt roads off the main highway. Juneau does write the word "cooperative" in her bibliography, so it is possible that she went to the sweet potato cooperative to talk to someone and Drudik was there. The population given in the Libuse report is about what we find in the census data. Though, no popuation is given for Kolin. Kolin was much more rural than Libuse and did contain less people, so maybe she could not come up with a number. In 1936 and 1937 the communites were about 20 years old, not thirty, as Juneau states. Also, in these years America was still in the grips of the Depression, though Juneau refers to this period in the past tense. That the Czechs were thrifty, industrious and frugal was perhaps well known in the area, but that would not have been known by just any government worker coming in from outside, again pointing to Juneau being a local woman. Her comparison of Czech homes to native Louisianian homes also seems to point to her local origins.

The two communities were very similar, indeed, almost identical, so why she does not mention the stores and businesses in Libuse and only those in Kolin is a mystery. She calls Kolin a community of "Czechoslovakians," yet refers to those in Libuse as "Autro-Bohemian." The first is fairly correct, the latter would grate on any Czech's sensibilities. They are wholly unrelated people and the German speaking Austrians rode hard on the Czechs. About the only thing "Austro" about Bohemia is that Austria dominated Bohemia for 300 years as an imperial power. No Czech would have ever said they were "Austro-" anything. Also, by this time Czechoslovakia was an independent country for twenty years. Plus, Czechs would have refered to themselves as Bohemian or Czech, and not Czechoslovakian—for they were not Slovaks. So why Juneau used this term is not clear, nor why she used two different terms for the same people.

Both reports point out that the Czechs did not require government assistance, though in only one did she underline this fact and the reason for that underlining is not clear. Maybe Welcek really stressed this, while Drudik merely mentioned it. As to whether this claim is true for every Czech, perhaps we can never know. It was certainly true for most of them. However, from more than one elder comes the same story: in the first years of the Depression a government aid worker came among the colonists to offer help. He, or they, were said to have visited farms and the halls (merely variations on the same story told by different people.) After finding a translator, he asked his questions about the need for assistance, which so many native Louisianians required. The Czechs had their own question: "what's a Depression?" They were still reading mostly Czech language papers and were blissfully unaware, apparently, of what was going on around them. They simply continued doing what they had been doing for nearly 20 years. That at least a dozen elders told me this story, at different times, on their own volition, and more than 50 years after the fact, shows how powerful this story has remained in the community. I heard these stories well before I ever came upon the two reports and it is the reports which corroborate the stories. I never thought to ask about the Depression, nor had reason to do so.

From these same stories it seems that government workers would periodically visit Libuse and Kolin, yet, no matter how deep the Depression was the Czechs said they required no assistance. George Tuma told me that his father, who owned a store, would extend credit to non-Czechs who seemed to be in dire straits with no ready concern for ever getting paid. George also says that his father sent him and his brothers with baskets of food to some elderly non-Czech neighbors, leaving them annonymously on their back steps. So not only did the Czechs not need assistance, at least one acted as a social service agency himself. This, of course, parallels John Horecky's efforts in Church Point.

As for the American origins of the colonists where Juneau got "mostly from Wisconsin," is hard to fathom. Drudik was born in Missouri, though had farmed in Wisconsin, and Welcek was born in Europe. Only eight families appeared to have spent any time in Wisconsin as can be determined by the birth places of their children. By 1930 only 4 of those remained. In fact, the colonists came from nearly twenty states, though most of those were "north central," which we would refer to as the Midwest. If any states stand out, it is Nebraska and Kansas. It is interesting to note that Juneau points out that many elders still were speaking Czech. That seems to indicate that they did not "assume the customs of their adopted homeland," as completely as other immigrants. As for the children's supposedly unaccented English, the elders of the community tell stories of being teased for having accented English when they entered the American schools in 1930. Maybe six and seven years later, when these reports were written, that had changed. However, many of those who were children at the time of the reports even today do not speak English with the typical Southern accent that is prevalent in Central Louisiana; only the second and third generations do. (One funny thing, when my mother and George Tuma spoke Czech with each other in 1998, it was obvious that she spoke it with a New York accent while he spoke it with a slightly Southern accent; strange how their American accents came through in their Czech.)

So, we are still left with the question of whether any Czechs received assistance during this difficult time. We still cannot answer it.

Religion in the Community

Louisiana is divided into two main religious traditions, separated by the so-called Bunkie line. This small town south of Alexandria is often refered to as the point were South Louisiana meets North Louisiana. To the north are the Scots-Irish who were, and are, primarily Baptists, Episcopalians and other Protestant denominations. In the southern part of the state Catholics predominate, coming as they did from French, Spanish, Irish or Italian heritage. The Germans were split between Lutherans and Catholics. At least prior to World War II there was a greater uniformity of religion among these ethnic groups within the two regions.

It was rare to find a non-Catholic French, Spanish, Irish or Italian person. As is was rare to find a Catholic among the Anglo settlers in North Louisiana. Even today, while certainly there are Christian churches of all denominations in both regions (and Jews and other religions as well,) Protestants are the majority north of Bunkie and Catholics to the south. A cursory look at, say, Shreveport and Monroe in the north and Lafayette and Houma in the south shows that especially among older church buildings (found in or near their downtowns,) Baptist churchers are larger and older than Catholic churches in the north and just the opposite in the south.

The Czechs in Rapides Parish defied this easy classification, for they belonged to neither tradition. Like many Czechs in America, they were "Freethinkers," also known as Hussites, even if they did not call themselves this. The lack of a church in Libuse speaks volumes about the religious proclivities of the Czechs here. Juneau makes note of this in her Libuse report. Uniquely among ethnic groups in Louisiana the Czechs did not build their own churches. There was definitely a sufficient number of them in Libuse and Kolin to build their own if they were inclined to do so. It was not until after World War II that Sts. Frances and Ann Catholic Church was built in Kolin. Prior to this, the people of Kolin were just as nonreligious as those in Libuse, or rather, they did not adhere to formal, established religious traditions. They surely had a faith in God, they just did not believe in organized religion. These are not the only Czech communities in America that did not build churches.

We can learn a lot about religious beliefs by looking at obituaries. The first thing to note, though, is that in the first 15 years or so of the community there were no obituaries of Czechs published in the Alexandria Town Talk. Only after 1930 do Czechs appear in these columns. Several of these early obituaries mention only a member of the community "officiating," or at most giving "a Christian service." They were just common people who knew the deceased. Anton Baroch and Emil Tuma seemed to be the two who were called upon most for this duty, but others also spoke. More than a few obituaries do not list anybody officiating, saying only that there would be graveside services at one of the two Czech cemeteries. While we cannot know for sure, it is impossible to believe that a resident of the community did not officiate at these, too. Certainly no clergy member of any denomination was mentioned.

This stands in stark contrast to the obituaries of non-Czechs which were published alongside the Czechs'. In nearly every one of these the deceased was said to "belong to" or was a "member of" a particular church. A reverend or priest was nearly always listed as officiating. It is only beginning in the very late 1930s that a slow, but steady, increase in the mention of clergy occurs in Czech obituaries. However, this was never in a majority of obituaries. Many still simply said "graveside services." When clergy was mentioned there is a wide variety among the names listed. Yet, no particular religious denomination or institution were mentioned.

It is only after World War II that any Czechs were said to belong to a church. This, however, ranged across a wide number of denominations and none stand out. None of these denominations were Czech based. Instead, it appears that Czechs joined existing churches in Alexandria and Pineville. In this they were becoming more Americanized, or more like their fellow Louisianians. The first and only church in the colony area centered in Libuse seems to be Philadelphia Baptist Church. It is almost directly across the road from the Libuse cemetery, but has its own graveyard. The two nearby cemeteries is often a point of confusion in obituaries. Sometimes the Libuse cemetery is refered to as "the Philadelphia Czech Cemetery or just the "Philadelpia Cemetery," but the vast majority of Czechs buried in Libuse are at the Czech Cemetery, which does not have "Philadelphia" in its name. It is only with the establishment of Sts. Francis and Ann Catholic Church in Kolin in 1949 that any Czechs were buried according to Catholic rites. Though this church does not have its own cemetery and Czechs who attended were buried down the road at the Kolin Cemetery.

The exact reason, or instigation, for the establishment of this parish seems to be lost to history, but it was not a specifically Czech church. Rather, it seems to be a response by the Alexandria Diocese to serve the growing suburban community that was spreading out of the inner city. Certainly a number of Czechs were part of the request to the Diocese to establish a church. It was Marie Brousek who donated the land to the diocese for the site. There were, however, numerous other Catholic churches also established at the fringes of Alexandria and Pineville at the same time. It was the Czechs who built the original wood building, though. In 1949, Albert Helcl and Frank Baley essentially took an unused barrack at Camp Claiborne and dismantled it, moved it and remodeled it into a church. It was only in 1989 that funds could be raised for a brick structure. By 1949, the majority Czech population in the original colony lands had morphed into only about half of the people in the area. This was not a decline in the Czech population, but an increase in the number of non-Czechs who were able and willing to buy land among the Czechs in the post-war suburban exodous from cities. And many of them were Catholic.

In at least one concession to the Czechs who filled the pews of the church the Diocese did appoint two Czech priests to Sts. Francis and Ann. Fathers Mark

Horacek and Ernest Zizka were assigned to the ministry there. While they apparently spoke Czech, there is no evidence that services were ever conducted in anything but English. Father Horacek in particular is listed frequently in obituaries for about 10 years for those who were professing Catholicism. This joining of the church by Czechs seems more a response to the Catholicism prevalent in the area rather than any long standing unmet Catholic faith held by Czechs. And still, Catholic funeral services never seemed to amount to more than ¼ of all funeral services. Nor did other Christian denominations gain hold of more than a ¼ of the residents. Even many recent Czech obituaries do not state any clergy or church.

As Juneau mentions, some Czechs in Kolin belonged to a Presbyterian church when she did her report. But this, too, was a pre-existing church and not Czech built. In the post-war years more than a few of the later obituaries mention Protestant and Catholic churches in Alexandria and Pineville as the locale for services since there was no local church to hold services from. It is an odd coincidence that of two churches that stand on Czech colony land the Catholic one is in the southern portion and the Baptist one in the northern portion—exactly mirroring the division in Louisiana as a whole.

In another odd coincidence, while Father Horacek's surname can be translated as "the little mountain," there is a certain bit of irony that Father Zizka bears the surname of one of the leading generals of the Hussite armies against the Catholics centuries ago. Religion being what it is, I never queried current residents on their beliefs or practices, or those of their parents. The only thing I will note is that never in my times in the community was I ever invited to join anyone at a church, which has happened frequently in my other travels and business around Louisiana. In my time with the Tuma family, with whom I am most familiar, none ever went to church on Sunday. The Freethinking spirit still lives here.

The Community Matures

Despite the insularity of the community, with Czechs trying to keep separate from the surrounding population, there were interactions between the two groups. There was always current commentary, as there is today, about "those people," the people with the strange language and strange ways who kept to themselves out in their neck of the piney woods. We can grasp a clear picture of Czechs in the 1930's moving into the city continuing. Whether just jobs, or residences and businesses, too, the 1938 City Directory for Alexandria is a wealth of information. The city had approximately 35,000 people and the greater metro area had 45,000. Pineville across the Red River had about 5,000 people. Libuse and Kolin had approximately 600 people combined, with nearly 400 of them Czech. By 1938 nineteen Czechs were earning a livelihood or living in the city.

In alphabetical order we find Joseph Filasek working at Harry's Body Shop, yet keeping his residence out in Libuse. Joe Kotar was a glasier at H. H. Fuast. His residence was listed as "rural district, Pineville," which essentially meant Libuse. He was maried to Anna. Steven Marhefka and his wife, Kate, lived in Kolin, while he worked as a "shipping clerk" at City Lumber Company. Otto Prochaska was a painter at Pearce Chevrolet Inc., who lived in Libuse with his wife Bertha. Carl Safarik and his wife Zdenka were neighbors of the Prochaskas, but Carl worked in the city as a mechanic at Dunnam Motor Company. His son Charles was a "2nd mechanic" at the same company as his father. He was starting a new family with his wife, Mary, out in Libuse.

Edward Westerchil of Kolin was a truck driver for City Lumber Company. Charles, Edward and Elmer Tuma all worked at Harry's body shop, but only Elmer lived in the city, at 2009 Rapides Ave. Emil Tuma Jr. lived at 402 1st Street in Pineville. Harry Tuma owned this body shop, which was at 915–917 Washington Street in Alexandria. Harry lived in Libuse. Helen Tuma was the operator of Modern Beuaty Salon, but resided in Libuse. Carl Svebek was the manager of City Lumber Co., and he lived at 2003 Hill Street. Albena Zabavsky lived at 1415 Levin Street and was retired. Helen Zmek was an employee at Cotton Bros. Bakery, a bread maker. Joseph Zmek was a mechanic at Dunnman Motor Car Compay. He lived at 22 Ball Powell Street.

Anton Welcek and his wife Marie lived at 2330 Hill Avenue in Alexandria. He was a mechanic at City auto machine works. Finally, there was William H. Vonesh who was an employee at Mayeaux body works, but lived in Kolin. These were the only Czech names that are present in the directory. It shows that the Czechs still preferred to live out on their farms. The few who had city jobs lived out in the rural areas and commuted.

Two other Czechs were found in 1938, but not subsequent records. They were Herman Karasek and his wife Ezell. He was the service superindentent at the Hotel Bentley. They lived at 306 4th Street in downtown Alexandria. They were not members of the Libuse and Kolin communities.

Entertainments

Especially during the first decade or so of the community people worked sunrise to sundown six and even seven days a week. It was necessary labor to get the farms underway. But just as soon as there were people in Libuse and Kolin they sought to lighten their load with Czech music and other entertainments. Francis Welcek wrote that "soon after coming to Kolin a brass band was organized. They held concerts for the community at the Czech hall twice a month on Sunday afternoons." This was apparently at first an informal group. Walker reports that in 1921 the Kolin Band was formed. Typically, a committee was set up, officers elected and dues collected. The dues were used to buy sheet music, though any Czech sheet music would have to have been purchased through mail order. Not one store in Alexandria would have carried these items. Fortunately, there were companies advertising in Hospodar and other Czech newspapers that provided this service.

"Libuse, too, had several bands and such accomplished musicians that they were able to provide instructions" to others, Walker wrote. She notes that Emil Meydrich gave string and brass lessons to the youth of the community. Walker continues, "it was unusual if there was a family in which at least one member could not play a musical instrument or sing." Several other bands were organized over the years. Two were the Libuse Czech Band and the Polka Dot Band. Emile Tuma, Jr., was involved in these two organizations. While Czech music was a major part of the fare offered, it is also probable that as the years went by American standards (or actually, at the time, new music) were added. Thomas Nadrchal is mentioned as one of the accordian players in the community.

Mortimer Kreeger, in his article on Libuse and Kolin in 1933, devotes a few paragraphs to the social aspects of the communities. He writes "they do manage occasionally to have social affairs, at which sometimes older residents, who remember the Old Country, participate in traditional Bohemian dances." This would be polkas and waltzes and what is called the Beseda, or round dance. The Beseda is perhaps best likened to what Louisianians would call square dancing, though, of course, it is not American square dancing. Kreeger continued, "music for dances and festive occasions is furnished by a community band composed of the younger men of the settlement, and directed by William Pospisil, Sr." He also labels the celebration of the 15th anniversary of the founding of Czechoslovakia as "extremetly important." His article is accompanied by a picture of a Czech band. There are twelve men in the picture, each dressed in white pants and shirt, with a black tie, along with a navy-style hat. Some are holding instruments, such as a trombone, trumpet, a large tuba and a small tuba, and a French horn. A set of drums sits squarely in the middle of the ensemble. The band or its members are not identified. Yet, this obviously was a very organized and formal group.

Over the years there were various bands and membership changed as people either left the community or grew older and no longer engaged in such frivolity. No one in the communities seems to have kept track of exactly who members were or when they performed. It is reported, however, that many members of the community knew how to play various musical instruments. We know that the Safarik family was very involved over the years. Carl played the trumpet and the accordian, his brother Jerry also played the accordian, and their sister, Vlasta, played the saxophone. Albert Filasek was the drummer. Carl organized a band called "Carl's Little Bohemian Band." This was during the 1930s. According to the Czech Heritage Newsletter, "in 1938 they broadcast on KALB radio station in Alexandria." This was almost certainly the first time Czech polkas and waltzes were ever presented to a wide audience of Louisianians. What listeners thought of this was unrecorded, but it must have turned a few heads.

Other entertainments were "literary debates, plays, talks and recitations," according to Welcek. Exactly what was debated and recited was not recorded, though we can assume that it was Czech literature, poetry and legends. It is per-haps appropriate here to note that among European nations it is the Czechs and Slovaks who have erected more monuments to poets, writers and artists than the generals and war heroes so common elsewhere. Moreover, of all the political fig-ures ever to have reigned or held national office anywhere in Europe over the cen-turies only the Poles and the Czechs have ever elected artists to national office. Ignace Paderewski was a concert pianist and composer who served as Prime Min-ister of Poland during 1918 and 1919. Vaclav Havel is a playwright, poet and author who served as president of the Czechs for 13 years, first of the combined Czechoslovakia (1989–1992) and then of the new Czech Republic (1993–2002.)

What plays were presented was also not recorded, but there are plenty of plays in the Czech national idiom that community groups could perform. All of these events were conducted entirely in Czech during the first 15 years or so, with English added only as the children were coming of age. Walker reports that Joseph Subrt formed a "divadlo," or theater, to perform on a regular basis. Both of the current Libuse and Kolin halls, as previously mentioned, have stages on which such productions took place. In the beginning the hotels, which already doubled as schools for both Libuse and Kolin, were the scene of these entertain-ment and social gatherings. After the Komensky School was built in Libuse it served as locale for the fun times. In 1930 the Libuse hall itself was built and has served as the entertainment center of the community ever since. In Kolin the hotel lasted longer and since the school building there was state property it was probably not used as much for entertainment. The WFLA hall was used after it was built in 1950. But again, no one ever kept records and there are precious few stories about these events. There was also the dance hall that existed for about a year in Kolin before it was torn down.

Welcek, and others, record that baseball games were held on Czech built ballfields near the two halls. Others report that the teams had uniforms and were sponsored by local Czech stores. If they engaged in anything like league play with non-Czech teams it is not recorded. He also notes that the community observed "all the national holidays," and presumably this meant both American and Czech holidays. "About twice a year a communtiy fish-fry was held on Big Lake attended by two hundred or more adults and children," he wrote. He also notes that "the reasons for the slowing up of all such admirable customs lies not with the Czechs but with the troubling influences and fights caused by native outsiders in attendance."

Relations with Non-Czechs

It cannot be said with any degree of certainty what was the relationship between the newly arrived Czechs and the locals who had long lived in the area. All we have are anecdotes and faded memories. Yet, we can also make some informed suppositions. That there was a glaring difference between the two groups cannot be disputed. Never before had a large number of foreign people been summarily plunked down in the middle of the long established community of rural Rapides Parish. There is simply no other similar example or comparison with any group. That the Czechs were concentrated contrasts with the handful of other immigrants who moved into the area. Nearly all of those had moved into Alexandria as a family here and a family there. Surely they may have seemed exotic, but it was at least, say, a manageable situation. And while Alexandria was not a big city, it was definitely more "cosmopolitan" (to use the word loosely) than the rural area to its east. All of sudden, within five years or so, there were hundreds of very strange people in an area that had not changed in over a hundred fifty years. It was an alien invasion the likes of which had never been experienced in Central Louisiana. This was bound to be a tense situation.

It has already been noted that non-Czechs disrupted Czech dances and caused various types of trouble at the halls. Whether this was a regular occurance or just that some people remember the most outrageous examples cannot be determined. Helen Locker Henderson, in her article in the Czech Heritage Newsletter, wrote "my first experience with violence" occurred at the Kolin dance hall. But she was a young girl at the time and perhaps it was more frightening than life threatening. There are no recorded or oral stories of any physical damage inflicted on Czechs. It is also probable that since Czechs outnumbered any intruders it was the latter who received the worst of whatever did occur. Plus, when you think about it, when quick moves and coordination against intruders were required the Czechs had the upper hand since they could relay their plans to each other in Czech, which the intruders could not have understood. Mayor Vic Lamkin did report to Kreeger that law enforcement was never called out to the communities. So what ever did happen apparently was not of too serious a nature. Surely a little bit of bouncing had to be performed, and perhaps a fist fight or two, but no gunfire or stabbings and such were ever recorded.

On the other hand, I did hear from more than a few elders that at least for the first two decades or so there was some tension with the surrounding non-Czechs. The chief cause of complaint seems to be that Czechs worked on Sundays and the locals thought this inappropriate. That the communities did not have churches surely led to suspicion about the workings of the Czech communities. After all, the locals were very religious and now there was this group of foreigners in their midst who eschewed church. But again, the stories are told by people who were children at the time so it is impossible to ascertain the extent of any real animosity or confrontation.

Another source of possible friction was the fact that the Czechs spoke Czech and not English. One can imagine that if a few Czech men and family members went into Alexandria or Pineville to buy supplies or pick up items shipped to them, or meet newly arriving Czechs during the first years, they spoke Czech amongst themselves before conducting and concluding any business. This must have perplexed the locals. No such language had ever been heard here before. Addison Sheldon, a teacher in Nebraska also reported that this language barrier was a cause of friction there so it was likely to be the same in Louisiana. It is also to this day true that Americans are not entirely happy when people speak a foreign language in front of them. There are suspicions that something is being said that is inappropriate or the foreigners are hiding something. This attitude was just as prevalent then as now.

Yet another source of tension was the near continuous work that Czechs did. Kreeger points out that the Czechs worked during every daylight hour. They grew crops that had never grown before on land that was considered unsuitable for farming. They definitely cleared hundreds of acres of pine stumps by hand.

They are repeatedly refered to as "thrifty and industrious." Their barns were bigger and more strongly built. Their barns even had windows. A sense of jealousy would surely have been aroused in natives when considering their own situation with the apparent prosperity quickly achieved by Czechs. In the WPA reports Juneau alludes to this with her comment about the "striking contrast" between Czech farms and homes and the locals' "shacks." And jealousy leads to friction. Small town gossip being what it is, it is also likely that word of Czechs buying land for cash leaked out of the courthouse. This when the native Louisianians were either sharecroppers, renters or mortgaged. Economic disparity leads to tensions also.

Still another source of friction that Czechs reported to me came from fence building. These lands had been owned in huge unobstructed tracts by the lumber companies. These companies simply ignored the free range cattle that walked over their lands since they could cause no harm to their timber operations. Now that the Czechs bought the land and were putting up fences and building roads the long standing local tradition of letting cattle wander about was in jeopardy. That anyone even bought this land surely perplexed the natives. Local habits die hard and it is not hard to believe that they did not like them end. In a place that had been wilderness for generations, and then cut-over pine forest, all of a sudden there were houses and farms, families and children, and men working—none of whom were very good with English at first. The Czechs would no doubt have first chased away the free range cattle that was not theirs and then prevented their return. They were also probably adverse to any trespassing by strangers on their newly developed farms. There had to have been interactions between Czechs and non-Czechs as this was sorted out. This was bound to be a source of trouble.

While no robberies of homes were ever recorded, there was chicken theft at least and probably a few natives who helped themselves to Czech crops. Walker reports that "farmers had to remain on their property day and night to protect them." She also relays the story of Louis Krist, who "spent the nights in the field with his gun so he could be on hand to frighten away unwelcomed intruders." She writes that "he contracted malaria and died." Whatever he did die of in the 1920 census his widow was the head of a family with seven children the oldest of whom was only 14. This must have been a devastating blow to the family.

A further source of tension surely occurred as the locals watched the Czech children go to schools built by Czechs while many of their own children remained unschooled. The level of literacy among poor Louisianians was far lower than that of the Czechs. This, too, was probably apparent to the locals. Gossip about the Czechs' high school enrollment was probably spread by the native teachers employed in the Czech schools. When the Czech children joined local children after 1929 it is reported that the former were often at the head of the class. We all know that no one likes the smart kids. Plus, it is possible that Czech children spoke Czech to each other if they wanted to share secrets, as children do.

So a group of literate foreigners engaged in hard work, with no church or apparent religious beliefs, speaking a strange language, displaying an obvious difference in economic fortunes and bringing about the end of free range cattle and untrammeled passage across the land all combined to create a palpable sense of separation. This was bound to cause a level of concern, apprehension, jealousy and even disdain among native Louisianians against the Czechs. That the Czechs wanted to remain separate and did not join the larger culture did not help allieviate this situation. It could also be surmised that the Czechs looked down at their neighbors as being lazy and ill-informed, even if they never broached the subject. But the perception by locals that Czechs thought this is not hard to imagine. And yet, whatever the tensions and frictions were it never broke out into any Hatfield and McCoy type feuds. Again, no shootings or murders, house or barn burnings, violence or anything major was ever recorded. Indeed, after the initial shock, both groups engaged in a steadily growing acceptance and respect towards each other.

Murder, Death, Mayhem and Quashed Dreams

Between the 1930 census and the 1938 city directory, when we last had specific information about where some of the Czechs lived and their occupations, the people of Libuse and Kolin were faced with the reality that the dreams of a large Czech colony were not going to come to fruition. In 1933 they had celebrated the 15th anniversary of the founding of the Czechoslovak Republic. Kreeger makes brief mention of the joy in the community at this milestone. He reports that there was "patriotic singing and speeches." The article itself is accompanied by a picture of the local Czech brass band. But this celebration was tempered by the fact that few new immigrants were coming to America. As Kreeger wrote "their cousins at home enjoy political liberties and privileges which they themselves had had to cross the ocean to seek." Added to this were the immigration restrictions put in place by Congress. Reports of the difficulties encountered in Louisiana had no doubt spread to Czechs nationwide. Whether through the comments of those who had briefly lived here but left, reports to the Hospodar or letters among families it was clear that Louisiana was not the inviting place that was first promoted. With the Depression itself not many people were going to be starting anew during such tough economic times.

By 1938 the world seemed to be coming apart. Momentous changes affected America, Europe and Asia. The worldwide Depression had been weakening, but still had a grip on America. The Dust Bowl of the early 1930s caused tens of thousands of people to leave the lower Midwest, most heading for California. Senator (and former governor) Huey P. Long was assassinated in Baton Rouge in 1935. Louisiana as a whole remained desperately poor. Internationally, the Spanish Civil War had raged and General Franco seized power by 1936. The king of England had abdicated. The Japanese were ravaging China and other Asian countries. Stalin was purging the Russian people of those he said were enemies of the people. Mussolini had invaded several countries in Africa with dreams of reestablishing a Roman Empire. And Hitler rose to power in Germany.

For the Czechs it was particularly an anxious time for almost immediately after his election as Chancellor Hitler was claiming parts of the territory of Czechoslovakia as rightfully German. This was called Sudetenland by the Germans, or "South Germany." It was a thin border area along the German-Czechoslovak frontier. The Czechs called it North Bohemia and it had been part of the Bohemian homeland for a millenium. While Germans had lived here for centuries they were never more than a 1/3 of the population. Many of the Czechs in Rapides Parish had relatives in Czechoslovakia. People with whom they had been in contact with over the years, not forgotten cousins. Many, in fact, were parents and brothers and sisters of the elders of the community. There can be no doubt that the Czechs of Rapides Parish watched these domestic and international developments with great unease. The Czech language newspapers they were reading were filled with tense news from the old country. They perhaps knew better than their fellow Louisianians that trouble was brewing.

By mid-1938 Hitler was threatening European-wide war unless Czechoslovakia gave up the Sudetenland. At the infamous meeting in Munich on September 29–30, 1938 the leaders of Britain, France, Italy and Germany agreed that Czechoslovakia would give up the territory that Hitler demanded. The Czechoslovak government was not invited to the dismemberment of their republic. Just days later they were powerless to stop the incoming German army. The Czechoslovak government at least had the sense to know that they would lose a fighting war. All they could hope for was a better future in a smaller country. Prime Minister Neville Chamberlain got off the plane in London with a piece of paper in his hand proclaiming "Peace in our time." Few man had ever been so wrong.

Hitler did not just seize North Bohemia—he annexed Austria at the same time. On November 9th, 1938 Hitler began his pogrom against the Jews of Germany. This was the infamous Kristallknacht—the Night of Broken Glass. Thousands of Jewish businesses, synagogues and homes were destroyed, looted and burned and tens of thousands of Germans Jews were rounded up and sent of to concentration camps. In March 1939 Hitler's armies marched through the rest of Czechoslovakia. Hitler told Chamberlain that his quest for so-called Liebensraum—living room for the Germans—had been satisfied. Chamberlain bought this hook, line and sinker and declared once again that peace was at hand. No one lifted a hand or said a word to help the Czechs and Slovaks preserve their independence in one of the most democratic countries in Europe at the time. In September 1939 Hitler and Stalin invaded Poland in the "Blitzkrieg," the Lightning War. World War II In Europe had started in earnest. It took until December 7th, 1941, and the bombing of Pearl Harbor before the United States became involved in the war.

Given the history of the 1930s there is perhaps no better place in this book to look at some of the most tragic deaths and occurances to befall Libuse and Kolin. They did not all take place in the 1930s. Of course, there were the deaths of infants, children and young people during the 1920s, tragic in themselves, but perhaps explainable as the vagaries of life. Another young child to die was Emilie Vit, just 8 years old, who died in 1945. In 1964 the community lost another young man in the prime of his life, 27 year old Thomas Tuma. He owned the B & A Autoparts store on Monroe Street in Alexandria. Young Bob Louis Pospisil passed away at the age of 22, a little more than 10 years later than Tuma.

Joseph Tauber was the first to die from what could be called unnatural death in that he was struck by lightning in 1921. The next unnatural death was that of Frances Tucek. She died from burns sustained in an explosion in her kitchen stove. The article relaying the sad story says she "was attempting to build a fire hurriedly and poured some oil in the stove to accelerate the blaze, but the explosion resulted." Her clothes caught on fire and she was badly burned. The article ends in a hopeful note "however, she was not burned in the face and will eventually recover." Alas, this was not borne out and she passed away on August 28th, 1928. She was already a widow and she left three young children, with the oldest, Charles, having to take charge of his brother and sister, both minors.

On January 13th, 1929, Frank Hromadka was murdered by a hunting companion, C. C. Conrad. The murder was reported on the front page of the next day's Town Talk. Apparently, the two men had set off on a weekend duck hunting excursion in the wee hours of Saturday night, arriving in the area of Hamburg, a small settlement just south of Marksville, at about dawn. They met up with a local youth identified as Mr. Gauthier to lead them to the duck blind. Gauthier is reported as riding on the "running board" of the car while they traveled. While doing so the youth told the police that the two men began to argue. Then, on the middle of a bridge over one of the many bayous in the area the car stalled. The arguing men sent Gauthier to his father's house nearby to try to obtain help in getting the car off the bridge, the better to work on it. The article reports that the father said "Let them get off the bridge the best they can." While at the house, the Gauthiers heard two gunshots. Other neighbors were reported to have heard four or five shots. Hromadka was shot in the chest and "died instantaneously" according to the coroner's report. Conrad told the sheriffs called to the scene that the gun discharged accidentally. The sheriffs did not believe that story (since you do not need a gun to push a car off a bridge,) and arrested Conrad immediately on murder charges. Conrad was taken to the Marksville jail. Hromadka was 47. He was the owner of "the very successful" Auto Sheet Metal Works in Alexandria and "was well known throughout all of Central Louisiana," according to the article. The sheriffs told the paper that the two men had been drinking heavily. The moral here is that guns and liquor do not mix.

Another death by gun shot was not murder, but just as tragic. The Town Talk reported that early in the afternoon on March 2nd, 1950, Edward Frank was "making sauerkraut" with his wife, Helen, when he heard a disturbance among his chickens. Spotting a chicken hawk he picked up his shotgun and "went out to investigate." While "walking behind the barn he stepped on a barrel hoop which entangled his legs." As he fell his gun went off. The shot hit him in the head and the coronor's inquest ruled that death was instantaneous. Mrs. Frank went out to investigate when he did not immediately return and discovered his body with "the hoop…still entangled around his legs." Frank was a 57 year old farmer who left his wife and three children.

Still another death by gunshot is perhaps the most tragic of all. On August 11th, 1951, Peter Kotar died of "self-inflicted gunshot wounds." He was 69 years old. He was survived by his wife, a son and five unmarried daughters. All deaths are sad, many tragic, but suicide is the least understandable or explainable.

We saw earlier that in 1929 the Komensky school was destroyed by a storm, though fortunately no one was injured in that disaster. The community not so lucky in October, 1957. On the 23rd of that month another powerful storm hit Kolin. This storm destroyed all the work buildings on the Varvarovsky farm (spelled Barbarovsky in the news account.) The report does not say if the family house was one of those "buildings." Several other houses and barns in the area were also destroyed. Including the home of Mrs. Frank Bailey (that Frank Balej/ Baley) The home was across the street from Kolin's Catholic church. The article says that the storm hit at 8:15 AM and "struck a direct blow to the Bailey home." Two neighbors, Chester O'Kuinn and Mrs. Mattie Lee, were the first to reach the scene. They found Mrs. Bailey "hysterically trying to free her mother from the wreckage." O'Kuinn was quoted saying "she might have been alive at that time." By the time they were able to flag down a passing utility truck which then radioed for an ambulance Mrs. Marie Krejci had perished. Francis J. Welcek was a witness, reporting "it didn't look like any tornado. I heard this awful noise and here came this cloud that looked more like a fog. Then I heard the crash of trees and I guess it was the Bailey house going." Another witness, B. M. Johnson, a local storekeeper, also said there was no funnel cloud typical of tornadoes. Mrs. Krejci was 85. Perhaps if she was younger she would have survived the carnage. Her daughter, Mrs. Bailey, was rushed to the hospital with multiple lacerations and bruises, but recovered. Many areas of Alexandria and Pineville were reported to have suffered from extremely heavy rain, flooded streets and wind damage that day.

11

Americanization—The 1940 to 1965

The twenty-five years from 1940 to 1965 saw the most momentous changes in the community since its inception. In this, Libuse and Kolin were perhaps no different than America at large. Several things stand out, however. No new Czechs arrived to join the colonists. The oldest generation began dying, or at least retiring. No more children being born to Czech mothers and fathers received Czech names. Virtually all the adults had anglicized their first names. Community meetings were no longer conducted exclusively in Czech since the newest generation did not learn the language. Those youngsters of the 1920s and 1930s, though they had learned it, no longer felt comfortable speaking it. The elders around them were becoming more comfortable with English themselves. Contact with the relatives in the old country stopped completed during the World War. The rise of the Communists and Russian domination after the war further inhibited contact. Plus, the language skills necessary to maintain contact were lost.

The Libuse and Kolin business districts had reached their apex and were now slipping into somnolence. The war put a stop to all further development as resources were needed for the war effort and no longer put towards local development. Immediately following the war the suburban spread of Alexandria began in earnest. Many of the sons and daughters of the original colonists had gotten married, or were soon to do so. They either moved into Alexandria, moved to other cities in Louisiana or they left the state entirely. Obituaries now included the names of faraway towns and cities, and the married names of daughters. When they inherited their parent's land they sold it to non-Czechs, for there were few Czechs in the community buying any more land. Retired Czech farmers, knowing that their children would not continue working on the farm began to sell portions to non-Czechs for houses. By the 1960s several families were actively carving up their farmsteads to create subdivisions. The Koncinsky family led this effort. Many farms lapsed into untended fields and even back into the pine forests which their parents had cleared.

Many of those who got married during this time, and following the trend that had begun in the late 1930s, were chosing non-Czech husbands and brides. Their children had little interest in Czech culture. They were fully part of America. What these kids learned was at their grandparents' knee. As with all children, stories were probably listened to with half an ear and a quick desire to get away from what must have seemed foreign to them. The grandparents memories were based on their own inaccurate understanding they picked up as children new to Louisiana. Indeed, this combination of faulty memory and half listening spawned and spread the many misconceptions held in the community about its founding. The young went to American schools and pursued American sports, music and movies. Elvis Presley and the Beatles were far more exciting than Czech polkas and waltzes sung in the old language.

Czech newspapers were no longer being read in the homes. They themselves had been declining in number from a high of about 50 in 1920 to less than 20 by 1950. Hospodar, now published in the town of West, Texas, and not Omaha, had been ignoring the community for more than two decades. While I have not been able to determine the date of the last reference it appears to be about 1937 when Anton Baroch wrote a small obituary-like article about Joseph Ubl for its pages. It was written in Czech and it was doubtful that any of those born after 1930 could even read it.

The WFLA still held its meetings at the Kolin Hall, but instead of every other week it was often less than once a month. This organization itself ceased publishing its newsletter in Czech, adopting English for its communications with its members; indeed, its very name was made American. There were still regular social functions at the halls and weddings and parties and such, but they were increasingly dominated by the newly married and their children. They cavorted in English while the grandparents sat off to the sides and watched, as old people do. The Cold War and the Red Scare also served to limit expressions of the local Czech culture as no one wanted to be perceived as or accused of harboring Communist sympathies. Central Louisiana was a conservative, religious, patriotic and fiercely American place. While the brouhaha over the Czechoslovak trade mission in New Orleans in 1949 probably did not get mentioned in the local paper the same sentiment prevailed. There was no room for foreign sentiments. The last vestiges of a strong Czech culture was slipping away into the past.

By 1965 the Czech presence on the old colony lands had dwindled to less than 50%, perhaps less. There were those who could not escape it, especially the elders of the community, but even they were just children when the colony was founded. These people, now in middle age, had at most limited contact with any relatives in the Czech centers of the Midwest. Many had simply lost contact as the previous generation went to their reward. The dream of a Czech Colony had all but disappeared. Even the use of the Czech language on headstones had ceased. There was no escaping their heritage, but they were all Americans now. This was not a quick process, nor intentional. It was just that the larger forces surrounding them had conspired against them. That any Czech culture survived at all was more a miracle than a concerted effort. So isolated were the Czechs of Rapides Parish that what could be called mainstream Czech-American culture around the nation simply forgot about them. Indeed, the common response I encountered from Czech organizations nationwide as I researched Libuse and Kolin was one of utter amazement that these two communities existed.

Since the details of censuses of 1940 and 1950 have not yet been released we can only get a fuzzy snapshot of the coummunity. By looking at the 1945, 1951 and 1957 dictories we can follow the major changes in the lives of the Czechs at least as regards to the city. The directories did not cover rural areas. I chose these dates somewhat arbitrarily, though they do encompass the greatest changes from one half-decade to the next. The interceding years only show incremental changes. Some information can be gleaned from obituaries that were published later.

Veterans of World War II

At least fourteen men from the community served in World War II. This we know from their obitiuaries or gravestones. It is possible that others served, but it is not recorded. These were the sons of the original colonists. Charles Tuma and Oldrich Tauber were veterans of the war, but of which branch I could not find out. We know, though, that Charles Tucek was a private in the Army, but again, not where he served. Joe Kaderka and Emil Holy were also veterans of the army. Marvin Helcl was a veteran of the army in both World War II and the Korean conflict. Jerry Safarik was also a veteran of the army in both these wars. Joseph Varvarovsky had served in the navy and was still in the service in 1945. Aldrich Pospisil also served in the Navy during the war. Frank Hazmuka had reentered the service at some point in the war and saw action in Europe. The extent of their service, such as whether it was in a combat theater or stateside has not been divulged to me by their families. Nor whether they were drafted or enlisted.

Two non-Czech men who had married Czech women served in the armed forces, too. Emmett Lee Baker was married to Blanche Smigura. He was staff sergeant in the air force during World War II and also served in Korea. The airforce was just coming into its own as a separate service branch at the time of the big war. John William Weatherford was married to Lillian Krejzl. His headstone says the he served in the Louisiana Technical 4201st Ordinance Depot Company during the war. He probably did not see overseas service.

The story of Elmer Kramel, Sr., is better known, since it takes up the majority of his obituary. He was a combat veteran in the European theater against the Germans. To quote his obituary does more justice to his level of service than I could give: *"In connection with service in Germany in 1945, he received the bronze star and presidential citation for meritorious acheivement. A sergeant then, he led his squad in carrying vital supplies through icy streams and across a river, making 10 crossings. He then led his men in making repeated trips across 800 yards of open, fire-swept terrain under arduous conditions."* Fire-swept, of course, meant gun fire from the Germans. He was a sergeant in the 104th "Timber Wolf" infantry division.

Robert Cespiva of Pineville was on a Navy flagship at Saipan and went ashore with a 10-man team to establish communications between ship and shore. "It was a tough landing. There were bodies out there. The water wasn't all that bad. The reefs were bad," he said.

Finally, we have Sergeant Frank Chruma, who probably served in the army. We know that he died in January 1945, five months before the war ended in Europe and eight months before victory over Japan. I could not find an obituary on him in the Town Talk and thus I could gather no further details. But from the date of his death it would seem that he was a casualty of the war. And that would make him the only Czech from Libuse or Kolin who met that fate.

Property Transactions

While I stopped my index search of property records in 1939 I still looked at 45 property transactions in the 1940s. The reason for this is that earlier documents made reference to these later transactions. All the references were handwritten in the margins, presumably by the clerk of court office to point the way to clarifying information. Some widows had remarried. For instance, Betty Filipi, the widow of William Filipi, had married a man named Joe Hluchanek and was living in Texas in 1944 when she sold her Louisiana property. Since Mr. Hluchanek had never lived in Louisiana and Mrs. Hluchanek had never conveyed property in

Louisiana under that name a reference to the succession and prior purchases by the Filipi's was entered on both the earlier and later documents.

More than a few were "sweetheart" sales within families. Barney Smigura sold 40 acres to his daughter Sadie and her husband J. F. Richard for $500 in August, 1945. Barney himself had purchased this land in March of the same year from Frank Zak, also for $500. Barney also sold 10 acres to his son Louis and his wife Willie Lee Sayes for $150 in August, 1945. The father had bought it from Magda Vlasek, widow of Matthew, in November, 1940. She in turn had acquired sole possession of it after buying out the interests of her children in the late 1930s. This land was in Section 30. In a turn about, Louis had bought 80 acres adjoining his father's farm in Section 37 in 1940. He sold it to his father in June, 1943, for $1,500 cash. Barney sold this property to Mrs. Beverly Parker in October, 1943. She paid agreed to pay him $4,000 with her parapheranl funds for the entire 80 acre farmstead. She put $1,500 down and had five annual notes of $500. Included in the sale was "the kitchen stove, rocking chair, all the household goods and farm items, except china and china closet, victrola and divan."

In March, 1941 the two sons of James and Mamie Krist Drudik agreed to give their parents a usufruct and $15 a month and also build them a $1,000 house on a portion of the family farm. The sons had already bought the entire farm from them several years earlier. January, 1945, saw another sale that was for both house and possessions. Frank Hromadka, the son of the murdered man, sold the house he and his wife, Melba Cook, lived in. Hromadka owned it as paraphernal property (one of the few men with this separation of property,) to Joe Pacholik and his wife Jennie Krulis, the widow of Frank's father, and thus his mother. The price was $9,000 cash. $7,000 was for the house and the remainder was for "all furniture, furnishings and effects in the dwelling erected."

In one of those serendipitous finds beloved by historians I found perhaps the most interesting document of this period. While searching for one document I had turned to the wrong book. At the exact page number I was seeking, but in that wrong book, was this: In March, 1944, Wesley Hromadka sold a half interest in his "hire cab" business to Victor Melicar for $2,500 cash. The sale included three cars: a "1941 4 door Mercury with hire license 381-089," a "1941 Ford Sedan," and a second "Ford Sedan commericial hire cab." Only the one license number was given, and the second Ford's year was not given, and it was the only one with its particular description: three cars; three different descriptive accounts. Also mentioned as part of the sale was the "Office of Defense fleet unit certificate war necessity, operating as taxi fleet." Another car sale that made it into the conveyance records was the sale of "Ford pick-up truck" from Louis Smigura to "Bang Smigura" for $600," in June of 1943.

That 20 of them were from Czechs to non-Czechs reflects the continuing dilution of the Czechs in the colony lands. That 27 were for cash shows that even during the war, and shortly after, people had money saved. The other commonality among the property records from the 1940s is that they were related to successions. The children who inherited land were selling amongst themselves or to others. Mostly they did not live in the community or even Louisiana.

Working in the City

By the 1940s the number of active farmers had declined by about half. Those who were retired kept experimenting or putting their experience to good use with local 4-H clubs and other farmer educational organizations and programs. A much larger number were working in the city than in the 1930s. The continuing assimilation and more moves into the city, yet retaining ties to the land, can be seem through the 1945 City Directory for Alexandria. While nearly 30 Czechs were working in Alexandria the majority kept their residences in Libuse or Kolin. These were the first inklings of the suburban sprawl and commuting into the commercial heart of the city. A few Czechs owned their own businesses and made it a habit of hiring their own family members or other Czechs to work for them. The remaining settlers out in Libuse and Kolin did their best to keep traditions, folklore and their way of life.

Fred Westerchil was a store keeper at Camp Livingston. Milton Voda was an enginer with Alexandria Broadcasting Company. William Vlach (misspelled Vlech in the directory,) was a body man at Andress & Abbott Company, a car repair firm. All three lived in Libuse. Joseph Varvarovsky and his wife, Rita, owned their house at 2712 Southwood Boulevard in Alexandria. He was still in the United States Navy. Harry Tuma and his wife, May, resided in Libuse and he still owned Harry's Body Shop at 917 Washington Street in Alexandria. He employed his two brothers. Jerry Tuma was a mechanic at the shop and he too lived in Libuse. Emil Tuma and his wife, Willamae, lived in the nearby rural area of Tioga. His exact job at Harry's shop was not recorded. With no civilian cars being built during the war business was probably pretty good as people endeavored to keep their pre-war cars in running order.

Raymond. E. Smetak was a "chef" at Lott's Cafeteria. He and his wife, Virginia, lived at 120 Live Oak Street in the city. John Skodacek had an office at 2903–05 Lee Street, Alexandria, but it is not recorded what he did at this office.

He and his wife, Frances, had a home on the Holloway Prairie Road in Libuse. Stanley Stieber is listed in the city directory, but neither his occupation or residence was. But he must have been doing something in the city to get listed. His family name was variously spelled Stybr, Styber and Staber as well as Stieber. It was his father, Louis, who owned the restaurant in the city in 1930. Louis died in July of 1945, just as the directory was being published.

Frank Pacholik was a painter and decorator working at 13 Prospect Street in Alexandria. The directory lists his business phone number "3261," making him one of the few Czechs to have one. His wife Josie worked at Alexandria Termite Control in the city. They continued to live in Libuse. Their son Frank J. Pacholik Jr., worked with his mother; he was a painter for the firm. He was married to Estelle. Their address was not listed. Emil and Mary Meydrich were still living and working at the grocery store at 1845 Yale Street as they had been in 1930. Their son, Anton, worked as a clerk for them as well as lived with them. Helen Melichar was a bookkeeper at Neilson Breithpat Underwriters in the city but her residence was in Libuse.

Victor Melichar was married to Mildred. He was a body man at Stanley's Body Shop. They lived in Libuse. Stanley Hromadka, the murdered Frank's son, owned and operated Stanley's Body Shop at 500-02 3rd Street. You could phone him at "3947." Stanley and his wife, Rita, lived at 395 20th Street in the city. Louis Krist, who was married to Amelia, was a bodyman at Stanley's. They, too, resided in Libuse. Mildred Kotar lived with her sister, Rosie, at 1424B 6th Street, just outside of downtown. Rosie worked at Cahe Personal Finance Company. George Koncinsky was an "appr," at E. Levy & Son in the city. Oddly, the directory does not say what the abbreviation "appr." means, though it could be apprentice. Mattie Hrachovina was a cashier at Franklin's, 701½ Monroe Street downtown. Her last name was misspelled "Hrachorrina" in the directory. Finally, there was Wesley Hromadka, who owned and operated Auto Sheet Metal Works. He and his wife, Ruth, lived in Libuse. That the brothers Hromadka and Harry Tuma were all in competition with each other is interesting. They did not corner the market for this industry, they just had 3 of the 7 firms doing such business at the time.

We find three other Czechs that were all in the army living in Alexandria at the end of the war. They were not members of the Libuse and Kolin communities. William Krasik and his wife, Hannah, lived at 507 Beauregard Street. Major William W. Koskela and his wife were living at 1839 Yale Street. Which was just a house or two away from the Meydrich's. Edward I. Novak and his wife, Essie, had their residence at 106 2nd Street in the Enterprise Addition. Mrs. Sophia

Strzempa was an office clerk at French Unique Chair Company at 615 DeSoto Street. We know they are Czech only because their last names are Czech. All were gone from Alexandria with a few years.

The Communities as Growing Suburb

The nearest estimate I can come up with is that the growing Czech families numbered slightly less than 500 people living in the Alexandria metro area in 1951. This included grandparents, parents, children and grandchildren. While the older generation was entirely Czech, each succeding generation had more mixed marriages. None of the grandchildren were out of school yet. The metro area population was about 45,000 at the time. So Czechs comprised just about one percent of the total. However, in the Libuse and Kolin area they still were about 50% of the population. The vast majority of the metropolitan area was divided roughly in thirds ethnically. Cajun French, Anglo-Scots and African-Americans were the three primary groups. The Belgians who had settled along the westside of Alexandria had long been assimilated, and could not be considered a distinct ethnic community. But they did leave behind some street names like Sterkx Avenue, which is a major thoroughfare. A look through the pages of the city directory for this year shows very few families of other ethnic groups. At most a few Italians, Poles, Russians and Middle Easterners lived in the city. The Czech names, however, bounce off the pages.

The city directory did not cover Libuse and Kolin so we cannot get a clear picture of this area. In the city we find just over 30 Czechs working or living there, or both. Some were the same as six years previously, but there were some additions and subtractions. Also by this year, the Marksville Highway was completely paved from Alexandria to Marksville, about 30 miles distant. The name Holloway Prairie Road had also moved into the past. Now it was state highway 123. It, too, was a modern highway. The developed areas of Pineville were fast encroaching on Libuse and Kolin.

In the 1951 City Directory for Alexandria we find these Czechs:

Charles. R. Westerchil and his wife, Marjorie, lived at 3505 Presscott Road in the city. He was a junior civil engineer for the city of Alexandria. Anton L. Welcek and his wife, Marie F. Mehan, lived at 2330 Hill Ave. Carl Svebek was president and owner of City Lumber Company, living with his wife Bessie on the prestigious Horseshoe Drive. Their daughter Nell Svebek was the company's bookkeeper, but she lived alone at 352 Rosewood Street. Stanley Hromadka was still operating Stanley's Body Shop at 500-02 3rd Street. In a sign of the economic growth of the city his phone number had an additional digit, it was now "2-3947" Stanley and Rita also still lived at 395 20th Street. Charlotte A. Smetak lived at 1208 Maryland Avenue. Next door at 1206 Maryland Avenue lived Raymond E. Smetak and his wife, Velma. Raymond probably owned both residences, or perhaps it was double house, since he lived in an owned home and Charlotte was renting. He was employed as a butcher at the Hotel Bentley, which was the most prestigious hotel in the city, with nearly 300 rooms.

The situation of the Meydrichs had changed. While Anton still worked the grocery at 1845 Yale Street, and made his residence there, too, his name was listed as Art Meydrick. Whether he changed it or the city dictory misspelled it cannot be determined. He was married to Mariam. That is probably why his mother Mary Meydrick, now listed as the widow of Emil, was living at 1716 Dartmouth Street. One major change was that Edward and Mae Locker were living in the settlement of Dry Prong. This is technically outside of the metropolitan area, but his job as "checker" at Colfax Timber and Creosote Company apparently warranted his inclusion. Yet another change was the addition of Joe Kotar's Glass Shop at 715 6th Street downtown. He made his home on Masonic Drive. Frank Hromadka was now a "watch engineer" for the city, living at 112 Roberts Street.

A major addition to the commercial scene in the city was the opening of the Pospisil Furniture Company. Robert and Lorena Pospisil owned this company which was at 1505 Rapides Avenue. They sold "furniture, appliances, linoleums, International refrigerators and Apex washers" according to the ¼ page display ad the company had in the directory. Their phone number was "2-0850." The directory lists their house at the same address as the store, but this is probably a mistake given the strictly commercial nature of this street. Plus, their address in the 1957 directory gives their home address as Libuse. Robert's brother, Charles W. Pospisil and his wife, Ethel, lived at 3304 Prescott Road. His work was listed as "Floor Covering Sales and Serivce," so he may well have worked for Robert. The third brother, Aldrich, was a mechanic at Harry's (Tuma) Body Shop. He and his wife Maxine lived at 2403 Albert Street.

There were four Tuma brothers working together at Harry's Body Shop and they all lived near each other in Libuse. The four and their wives were: Harry and Mary, Charles and Helen, Edward and Edna, and Emile Jr, and Emily. That the last two had wives whose names were the female form of their male names is at least a charming coincidence. Another brother, George, and his wife Marie were working out in Libuse. She was the postmaster for the town, but the city directory did not think this important enough to list. George was still a farmer who also helped run the family retail grocery store.

Another family that had moved off the farm were the Vodas. Carl E. Voda was a radio repairman at Sears & Roebuck. No wife was listed for him. He lived at 1315 Rand Street. Charles E. Voda and his wife, Stephanie, were living at the same address. Stephanie worked at Southern Newsstand. No occupation was listed for Charles. Milton Voda was still a "radio man" at Andress & Abbott. That Milton and Carl had similar occupations is intriguing. His wife earned her own entry as Mrs. Marion Voda. She was a clerk at Guranty Bank and Trust Company, which was the same bank that had sold land to Czechs in the years before 1920. The lived at 49 Carlton Street in the city.

So 32 Czechs and there spouses were now living and working in Alexandria. That left about 40 more still living on farms in Libuse and Kolin. The Smigura's had moved to Marksville, in neighboring Avoyelles Parish. It is also likely that other Czechs were working in non-farm jobs outside of Alexandria, but since there is no city directory for rural areas it can not be said for sure. The Tuma, Voda, Pospisil, and Hromadka families in particular stand out as assimilating by moving off the farm. Though, many still lived outside of the city forming the first cadre of commuters in the metropolitian area. Finally, we find just one Czech who was not part of the Colony. Henry Shataska, and his wife, Virginia, lived at 1821 Stanford Street in the city. He was a "dirt contractor."

Further Assimilation

The six years between 1951 and 1957 show another remarkable change in the life of the communities. In the earlier year there were some 30 working in the city. In 1957 there are nearly 60. Many were the grandchildren of the original colonists. All were born in Louisiana. Because the city directory did not cover Libuse and Kolin we cannot get a clear picture of what was happening there, but we can see that many working in Alexandria continued to commute. We can also see that some Czechs who owned businesses were not only successful but very stable since year in and year out they had the same addresses, phone numbers and staff. At most they added family members to their staff. Many of those listed in 1951 had the same jobs in 1957. Maddeningly, the Town Talk was not indexed until 1975, so it was not possible to determine if any articles were published about the community during this period. Obituaries for those who died after 1951 show only that with rare exception people were dying naturally of old age, there were no young deaths.

The only article I was able to find about a Czech business was a puff-piece on Stanley Hromadka's body shop, published on January 9th, 1954. Even this I ran across through happenstance. The occasion was the installation of new "Fostoria gold plated patented Evenray reflectors" to ensure that "the fresh paint [is applied] exactly the same way the automobile manufacturers do when the car is new." The installation was "in keeping with Stanley Hromadka's policy of giving motorists in Central Louisiana the finest in auto body, fender and radiator work by using the very best equipment available—in the hands of highly skilled technicians." His shop was noted for doing "the job quickly, satisfactorily and economically." A nice piece of free advertising, certainly.

1957 R. L. Polk City Directory lists these Czechs:

John Zabavsky and his wife Louise were living at 2811 Sandra Street. Though the directory lists the occupation as "Nurse, Baptist Hospital," it does not clarify who in the couple was the nurse. Given the year, however, it was likely Louise. Gertrude G. Zehrung was an office secretary at a major law firm in the city, Provosty, Sadler, & Scott. Her husband Warren K. Zehrung was a painter with the city street department. No address was given for the couple. It was Gertrude who was Czech, while her husband was of German extraction. They are both buried in one of the Czech cemeteries, however. Bill Zerbe was an attendant at MacArthur Conoco Service Station. He was a grandchild and apparently lived at his parent's house in Libuse. MacArthur in the station's name refers to the main ring boulevard surrounding Alexandria and not the owner's name.

Charles R. Westerchil was now an engineer at Gravier & Harper. He and his wife, Marjorie, still lived at 3505 Presscott Road. Edward Westerchil was an administrator at Nehi Bottling Company, a soda manufacturer now long gone. His wife Ollie was a "checker" at City Cleaners. They lived in Libuse. Anton Welcek was retired, living with his wife at 2330 Hill Street. Carl E. Voda had moved up to to the position of supervisor at Sears. He was apparently recently married to Melba and the young couple made their home at 63 North Drive in the city. Charles and Stephanie Z. Voda still lived at 1315 Rand Street. One or the other was the time keeper at the Hotel Bentley. Since he was in radio repair six years earlier it was probably her job and he was retired. Another son, Louis, was now over 18 (the cutoff age for the city directory.) He was a painter at Kramel Brothers Paint Shop. Kramel Brothers was owned by Frank W. and Elmer E. Kramel. The business was identified as "Contractors" with an office at 813 10th Street, near downtown. Elmer and his wife, Josie, and Frank and his wife, Mary, still lived out in Libuse. William Vonesh was married to Patricia, and he was employed as a mechanic at Service Truck & Body Shop. They resided in Kolin.

The Tumas were all still working together at Harry's Body Shop. Harry and Mary, Emil and Emily, and Edward and Edna were all still living in Libuse. Two new addtions to the Tuma staff were Charles and Harry F. (Harry's son, but not strictly a junior.) Charles lived with his wife, Helen K. Tuma in Libuse. Harry F. and his wife Barbara lived at 2404 Orange Avenue. Both men were mechanics at the Tuma shop.

Not much had changed for Carl Svebek and his wife Bessie. They still lived on Horsehoe Drive, but they added a phone to their house with the number "2-7381." His business, City Lumber, was still at 602 Monroe Street, but its phone number was still the four digit "9716." It ran multiple ads in the 1957 directory as it had in the 1951 edtion. There is a full page ad in both years that were plain and simple: the name of the company, his name followed by the word "owner" beneath that, then the legend "All Kinds Building Materials." Underneath that was a clipart like picture of a suburban home under a tall tree. Finally, there were the words "New Homes," all in capitals, with "Subdivision Developments," "Sales" and "Rentals" finishing out the ad. The other ads were strip banners running vertically along the edges of many pages throughout the directory. Apparently he had a significant advertising budget. Joining him at work was his son Donald, who was listed as "sales manager." Donald and his wife Ruth lived at 1424 Horsehoe Drive, down the street from his parents. Their phone number was "3-5836." In the listing for Carl and his wife's residence, the last name is misspelled as "Seubek."

Raymond Smetak was still a butcher at the Hotel Bentley and he and his wife still lived at 1208 Maryland. Otto Prochaska was a "bodyman" at Andress & Abbott, which was were Milton Voda had been working in 1951. Otto and his wife Bertha were living in Libuse. Josephine Ploc was listed as the "widow of Alex" and lived in a rented house at "Rear 4111 3rd Street." Joseph and Anna Kotar still lived on Masonic Drive and he still owned the Kotar Glass Shop at 715 6th Street.

The Koncinskys had some major changes in their lives. James Koncinsky now owned Koncinsky Builders & Supply at 621 N 3rd Street, they were purveyors of "building materials." James and Mary Z. lived out in Libuse. George Koncinsky was the manager at Koncinsky Builders. His wife, Helen, worked at Koncinsky Reality. They lived at 1727 Shirley Park Place in Alexandria. This was just a few years before he filed the plat map showing the suburban subdivsion. George had a separate listing under Koncinky Reality, which was identified as "real estate sales and building contractors." Only George and Helen's residence phone number is listed: "4-3522."

Frank Hromadka was the assistant engineer and "pbx operator" (an old style switchboard system) at the City Electric Department. His wife Corrine was the office secretary to Walter La Croix. They lived at 2147 Boyce Street. Stanley Hromadka still owned Stanley's Body Shop, which now had two locations, the old one at 500 3rd Street, and a new one at 711 2nd Street, which is just a few blocks away. They still lived at 395 20th Street. Living with them was a son Joseph S., who was a student, but he must have been over 18.

Anton Goldstein was a driver for Koncinsky Builders whose residence was listed as "DeVille." "Edna" Goldstein was a seamstress at La Cashet and she too lived in DeVille, but it is not clear in the directory how her and Anton were related, however, "Elma" and Anton are buried with each other as husband wife, so the directory probably got her wrong name. Deville, as it is now spelled, is really Kolin, but was a new name applied as the area was developing. Irving and Lillie Goldstein were living at 1760 Albert Street; he worked at B. Gisenbergs, which was a clothing store. Edwin Frank was a glazier working at Joe Kotar's glass shop; he lived in Kolin.

Kathleen Krist was a clerk at the local office of GMAC (General Motors' new car finance division.) Her husband Louis worked as a "repairer" at Stanley's Body Shop. They lived at 1406 4th Street. Cestmir Kubes worked at Alexandria Body Shop and lived at 3326 Hobey Street. Albert C. Filasek was married to Mary. He worked at Better Body Shop. They rented a house at 502 Wheelock. Jerry Filasek was married to Helen, and he was a repairman at Southern Chevrolet. They owned their home at 6 Martha Lea Street. Joseph Filasek was also a repairman at Southern Chevrolet, but he resided in Libuse.

Emily Filipi was an office secretary at the Louisiana Baptist Training Union, and lived in Kolin. Mrs. Ermine D. Filipi was a clerk at Cammack's Rexall Drug Store, and resided in Kolin. Eugene Filipi was married to Yvonne P., and was a mechanic at Harry's Body Shop, their residence was in Libuse. What looks like "Jim" Filasek was a carpenter with Henry J. Rockhold. His name is unfortunately blotted in the directory and only the letter J is clear, while the M is only half visible. But he lived in Libuse. He also probably got his job through Marvin Filipi, who was the foreman at the Rockhold firm. Roy Filipi was a helper at the Central Garage, and lived in Kolin.

Finally, the Pospisil Furniture Company was still going strong, only now its offerings were listed as "home furnishers, electric appliances, floor coverings, mattress, and bedding." Robert and Lorena still owned and operated this business at 1505 Rapides Avenue and still lived in Libuse. Robert's brother, Charles W. and his wife, Ethel, had moved to 716 Dale Street, and he had opened his own flooring company. This company was at 1150 Rapides Avenue, which is down the block from Pospisil's Furniture. Not bad for a family: buy the flooring and furniture from one and go to the other to get it installed. Meanwhile, Clyde V., Charles' and Ethel's son, lived with them and was listed as a "mechanic" at his father's store. Another son, Charles Jr., was a bookkeeper at Rapides Bank & Trust; he too lived at his parent's house. Robert's other brother, Aldrich Pospisil now owned his own body shop, called, unsurprisingly, Pospisil's. He and his wife Maxine still lived at 2403 Albert Street. The business was at 1403 Melrose Street.

There were also four Czechs living in Alexandria but who were not part of the community. Edward G. Novak was a bookkeeper at L. I. Huffman Merchants. He lived with his wife, Essie, at 1815 Simmons Street. Andres and Elizabeth Nemcik lived at 1828 Rennsalear Street, but no occupation is listed for either. Mrs Laquitta Michalek was a nurse at St. Francis Cabrini Hospital who lived at 129 Edwards Avenue. Robert Mihalik and his wife, Anna, lived at 2438 Jackson Street, Apartment 4. He was a field representative for Link Aviation.

So 64 Czechs were working in Alexandria and 23 were still commuting from Libuse and Kolin. That so many were employed in the auto body, repair and service businesses is certainly interesting. They did not corner the market, but it was nearly impossible to avoid them if you owned a car in Alexandria in the 1950s. Two of the city's five building supply companies were owned by Czechs. So if you were so inclined in 1957, you could buy the materials from Svebek or Koncinsky to build a home or buy or rent an existing home from either. Then furnish it at Pospisil's Furniture and have the flooring installed by another Pospisil while having your cabinets and shelving built by a Czech. You could get the glass installed by the Kotar firm and the new place painted by the Kramel's. You could do all while driving to your various appointments in a car maintained or repaired by the Hromadkas or Tumas and have a young Czech service station attendant gas it up and check the oil. Considering some of the other occupations, it was almost possible to do all your business with a Czech if you planned it right. One wonders if anyone, Czech or not, noticed this confluence. It certainly showed a community that had assimilated into America and moved off the farm.

12

Awakening—1965 to Today

By 1965 very few of the Czechs were involved in farming. What was Alexandria like in the 1960s? Lumber was still king and the oil boom of northwest and south Louisiana never took hold in an area with just a few wells. Fort Polk and England Air Force base exerted their influences and we know that a few serviceman passed through who were of Czech heritage. Whether they ever noted the Czechs among them is not known. We can take one last look at the city directory because all this information is 40 years old and far enough in the past that none of it reveals current personal information. The 1967 R. L. Polk Directory included both Alexandria and Pineville. It shows there were 76 Czechs living and or working in Alexandria.

Donald Zerbe and his wife Myrtis were living in Deville; he was employed as a stock counter at Standard Printing. John Zabavsky was the foreman at T & P Rail Road. His wife Corine was a clerk typist at Central Louisiana State Hospital. They lived at 920 Warren Street. Charles Westerchil was still an engineer at Gravier and Harpy. No wife was listed. Anne Vonesh was a cashier at Baptist Hospital and lived at 145 Nalley Road, Pineville. William Vonesh was a bodyman at Service Truck Body Shop and his wife, Patricia, was the assistant coffee shop manager at the Baptist Hospital. Marie Welcek was the widow of Anton, but still lived at 2330 Hill Street. Jospehine Ploc, the widow of Alex, was still living at 4111 3rd Street.

Carl Voda worked at Lafayette Radio Electronics and his wife, Melba, was an office assistant for the Louisiana Baptist Convention Executive Board. They now lived at 5712 Circle Drive. Joseph F. and Sylvia D. Voda were retired, living at 2310 England Drive. With them was a son, Kenneth, who was a student. Louis and Helen still lived in Libuse and he still worked as a painter at Kramel Brothers. Milton was a service man at Pospisil Furniture. He and Marion lived at 23 Baywood Drive, Pineville. Stephanie Voda was now listed as the widow of

Charles, but she was also now working as a dressmaker out of her home at 1315 Rand Street.

The Tumas had not changed much at all. Emil and Emily still lived in Libuse, he still worked at Harry's Body Shop. Harry, the owner's son, was a bodyman at his father's business, and still lived in Libuse. John J. Tuma and his wife Raye lived at 1416 Hickory; he was still a bodyman at Harry's. As was Stanley, but he lived in Libuse. Harry's was now nearing 50 years in the same location at 917 Washington Street. The one brother who had not gone into the auto business was George and he had never appeared in the city directory before. But in 1967 he was president of the Rapides Parish Farm Bureau so he now warranted mention. He lived in Libuse with his family.

The Pacholiks were now living and working in the city. Frank Pacholik Jr., and his wife Estelle owned Pacholik Furniture Works. While they lived at 11 Prospect Street the company was at 1814 Rapides Avenue, just about three blocks from the Pospisil furniture store. One can suppose that they sent business back and forth to each other depending on the condition of the furniture encountered. Frank's son, also named Frank, was married to Judy and they lived down the block from his father at 61 Prospect Street. He was listed as the "manager" of Alexandria Termite & Pest Control, but his half page advertisement says he was the owner. The ad says the company was "serving Central Louisiana since 1923," but he probably bought this existing firm. It, too, was located at 1814 Rapides Avenue. Jeanie Pacholik, martiarch of the family, was the widow of Joseph and retired, living at 2143 Boyce Street

The Kramel brothers Frank and Elmer still owned the company that bore their name and it was still at 90 16th Street. Elmer and Josie lived at 1115 Berry Street, while Frank and Mary still lived in Libuse. Frank Hromadka was a watch engineer at the City Light & Power Department. He lived at 2147 Boyce Street, which was a just a few houses from his mother, Jeanie Pacholik. Stanley and Rita still lived at 395 20th Street and he still ran Stanley's Body Shop which was still at 500 3rd Street. Now their children were over 18 so they were listed. John was a student and Susan was a clerk at St. Francis Cabrini Hospital.

Eva Helcl had moved off the farm into the city. She was the widow of Albert. She was still working, though. She was a seamstress at Blackman Laundry & Cleaners. She lived at 3345 Prescott Road. Irving and Lillie Goldstein were retired and living at 1768 Albert Street. George and Helen Koncinsky were still running Koncinsky Realty. While they still lived at 1727 Shirley Park the office was now at 621 North Third Street. Koncinsky Building Supply had closed. Joseph and Anna Kotar lived at 6140 Masonic Drive and he was a driver for the

Parish School Board. Mildred Kotar was an office secretary for the Rapides Parish Police Jury (the Louisiana term for "county legislature.") She lived at 1113 Berry Street, which was next door to Elmer and Josie Kramel. This was the same house her mother Ursula had lived in, and her obituary points out that she died while gardening, "apparently she suffered a heart attack."

Albert Filasek was still working at Better Body Shop. He and Mary still lived at 410 Wheelock. Their sons Jerry and Joseph were still bodymen at Southern Chevrolet. Jerry lived at 1303 Martha while Joseph lived in Libuse. Andrew Brousek had retired from farming and now lived at 2016 Madeline Street in Alexandria. Doris Drudik was the assistant credit manager at Clark Dunbar, a home furnishings store. She lived in Deville, or Kolin really.

There was changes in the Filipi family as well. Mrs. Annie G. Filipi was an attendant at Central Louisiana State Hospital. Her address is give as a rural route in Pineville, but this is really Libuse. Today, many people in Libuse have a similar address. Eugene was still married to Yvonne and he was still a bodyman at Harry's Body Shop, and they still lived in Libuse. Clarence A. Filipi was said to be employed at "Mobil Service," but it is not further identified. He lived at 5215 Sallie Street. There was also a store called Filipi Park & Shop Grocery on Masonic Drive across from the Masonic Hall. Among its offerings were "groceries, fresh meats, fresh and frozen vegatables, and magazine department." But no specific owner is given. Since this was, however, at the beginning of what we would refer to today as convenience stores it is quite possible that Clarence owned this as part of the Mobil gas station. It being a fairly new concept at the time the city directory perhaps did not have a way to list it under their procedures.

Aldrich Pospisil was now in his tenth or eleventh year at Pospisil's Body Shop. No home address was listed for him and his wife Maxine. But the shop was still at 1403 Melrose. Clyde V. and Jo Ann Pospisil were still running C. V. Pospisil Floor Covering Company at 1156 Rapides Avenue. They advertised "Armstorng Vinyl Corlon. For every floor in the House." They lived at 1611 Fulton Drive, a rather fashionable address in the city. Charles W. and Ethel were retired and living at 4207 Earl Street. Charles Jr., was a student who lived with them. The Pospisil Funiture Company was still going strong at 1505 Rapides Avenue. Lorena and Robert, its owners, still lived in Libuse. Mrs. Pam Pospisil was an instructor at World Wide Health Studio. Her address was also listed as a rural route in Pineville, meaning Libuse.

There were a number of Czechs not related to the communities. Joseph A. Konecni and his wife, Claudia, were living in retirement at 2105 Madison Street.

They had two sons living with them. Joseph A. Jr., was in the United States Air-force, probably stationed at England Airforce Base. Ronald was a student. Edward Novak was still at Huffman Mercantile and his wife Essie was a waitress at Burger Chef. Living with them at 1915 Simmons was their daughter Janice, who was a student. Two other airforce men of Czech heritage were living in Alexandria. George Vrska and his wife Rita lived at 1811 Tipperary. And Donald and Alice Praska lived at 40 Ida Street.

So many things stayed the same over the ten years from 1957 to 1967, though there were some significant changes, too. But this all means that assimilation was going strong and fewer and fewer Czechs were involved in farming. By this time Libuse had just the store and post office run by George and Marie Tuma. Kolin's lone grocery was in its waning days and its post office was to close completely in 1974. In one of the few instances of Czechs being in the public eye, in 1971 George Koncinsky was named Builder of the Year by the Home Builders Association of Central Louisiana.

Preserving What Remains

There has been a consistency of observing Czech traditions in the community. This has been through weddings, funerals, parties, WFLA lodge meetings, music, even some theater. This preservation has been more than just an occasional festival or get together with mere vestiges of the heritage. This has been a steady, if quiet, drumbeat of Czech life. While the period from the late 1960s to 1975 perhaps saw the lowest point of preserving Czech heritage it never vanished. Elders in the community did what they always did—speak Czech among themselves. The Libuse post office is still a rallying point as people come and go getting their mail. Various families continue to cook Czech favorites. Different families explored their roots in other Czech-American communities and in the Czech Republic. Some have kept in touch with relatives in the old country or worked at re-establishing contact. After the fall of Communism, some visited their ancestral towns. Some families have been better at handing down traditions, all wish they were better at it. Throughout all this time there was an undercurrent of thoughts, ideas and conversations about preserving the heritage and even reawakening the community to its Czech roots.

The Czech Halls still functioned for weddings, parties, community meetings and Czech festivals. The cemeteries were still lovingly maintained. Donald Tuma, grandson of one of the founding members of the community, has for a long time mowed the lawns and cleared the weeds. The cemeteries have been in continued use with funerals occuring as older members of the community pass away. These are not forgotten places that are in need of restoration as with so many other old cemeteries around the state.

While the Libuse Czech Hall was built in 1930 on the site of the original Komensky School this building was always used. It is one of the longest lasting buildings of its type in the state. The Kolin hall is still owned by the WFLA membership. It too has functioned without interruption since it was built. Now going on 56 years of operation it is one of the longest surviving community halls in the state. It, too, is operated and maintained strictly for the benefit of the local Czech community. Both halls are in no danger of disappearing. They are not in disrepair. They are active and vibrant. Now they are both eligible for inclusion on the National Historic Register. That is a project that hopefully will be gotten underway soon. It would open up an avenue of funding to truly ensure the survival of these historic structures.

The residents of the two communities do not perhaps see eye to eye on some matters, but they are well aware of their commonality. They are together in spirit if not completely so. As might be expected for such long lasting places with many families and personalities there are people within the community who have petty feuds with this or that person, but when the time comes they get together to get what needs doing done. When it comes to dealing with the outside world they are all Czechs first and residents of the separate communities second.

Louisiana Czech Heritage Association

The Louisiana Czech Heritage Association was first contemplated at early as 1975. It was conceived with the purpose of preserving what was left of the Czech heritage in the area as well as exploring the history of the two communities. Among the creative forces behind this organizaton were Marie Tuma, Francis Hazmark, George and Helen Koncinsky, Robert and Lorena Pospisil, and Rosie Walker. Many others, too numerous to mention, have been involved over the years. The Heritage Association was incorporated in October, 1984. Walker wrote her dissertation in 1986 on the creation of the Czech schools, which was the first effort at a written history of the colony. The newsletter was started at about the same time and Frances Hazmark has been its long time editor. Marie Tuma, Rosie Walker, George Koncinsky, Lorena Pospisil and Carolyn Tuma have all served as president. It is a 501(c)3 non-profit educational corporation. It gives scholarships to descendants of the original colonists to go to college. It meets regularly, usually at the Libuse hall, but also at people's homes or in the

Kolin hall. It is an active and hardworking group of a few hundred members. Knowledge of it has been slowly, but inexorably spreading. Besides the newsletter, Frances Hazmark has also compiled a brief history of the communities, focusing on the men who served in World War I.

The Czech Colony Historical Markers

In 1992 or 1993 Dr. David Holcombe, who is not Czech but knew members of the community, made the suggestion that a historical marker be erected in Libuse. Members of the Czech Heritage Society were intrigued with the idea, but alarmed at the cost. A marker would cost over a $1,000. Once the idea of one marker was considered it was decided that there should be one at Kolin also. So now they needed to raise $2,000 minimally. To frugal Czechs this is an enormous sum. Markers such as these are fabricated by the state and erected at hundreds of locations around Louisiana. So long as a group or community is willing to bear the cost the state is willing to place the marker. Fundraising began and within less than two years the necessary money was in hand. Virtually everyone in the community donated something, which is just as it had always been whenever a community project was required. That the money was raised so quickly perhaps surprised some people. But there is enormous pride in having created this outpost of Czech culture. Many non-Czechs also contributed, since they knew that these two towns are unique in Rapides Parish. Most people, Czech and not Czech, of course, do not realize how unique they are in the whole state and even the entire country.

In November of 1995 the marker was unveiled in Libuse. Some 75 people attended the dedication, according to the article announcing their installation. There were probably more. A short while after the Kolin marker was set in place. Both markers essentially say the same thing, except one is titled Libuse Czech Colony and the other Kolin Czech Colony. The Libuse marker is unfortunately on the little used Industrial Street, in front of the Czech Hall so it is unlikely to ever be seen by anyone driving through the area. The Kolin marker is in front of the Welcek homestead on Highway 107. It is seen by hundreds of people every day who travel this busy highway. How many stop to read it is anyone's guess. While these are well intentioned efforts, and points of pride in the community, they bear the same legends about the founding of Libuse and Kolin that I have discovered are not true. They both mention the fabled 20,000 acres. They both mention gentlemen named Posvar and Sobatka about whom nothing else could be found in any record located to date. Perhaps they were involved. But it cannot be proven yet. For the short term they will stand where they are, commorating one of the most unusal exercises in town building that Louisiana has ever seen.

The Louisiana Czech Festival

The annual Louisiana Czech Festival, held in March, is more like one big family reunion for the colonizing families than a public festival. But all are welcome, and there are some parish-wide promotional efforts. They bring in Czech bands or individual musicians for the event every year. It was started in 1984. Each year it alternates between the Libuse hall grounds and those of the Kolin hall.

From an article in the Town Talk on March 10, 2002, by staff reporter Eugene Sutherland, we get a good picture of the festival. It was entitled "Czech Community Celebrates Heritage." I can do no better justice than simply quoting the entire piece:

LIBUSE—The Czech community here and those from abroad got together Saturday to "nech ty dobré časy plynout." For the uninitiated, that's "let the good times roll," and it applied to about 400 people who crowded into the historic Libuse Czech Community Hall for the 18th Annual Czech Heritage Day. Children adorned in kroj, or native costumes, waltzed to accordion and piano rhythms and authentic dishes such as the danish-like kolache were served. "That's what this is all about, for Czechs from here and other places to get to know each other and have a good time," said Lorena Pospisil, president of the Louisiana Czech Heritage Association. "Keeping our heritage and history alive is so important. My parents helped keep it alive for us as children. We're doing the same here."

Visitors from New York, Texas and Mississippi took part in what some called a family reunion. Making the trip from Rochester, N.Y. were Helene Cincebeaux and her mother, 84-year-old Helen Zemek. Cincebeaux and Zemek visit the Czech Republic each summer. There, the two hold tours for Americans of Czech heritage. "I am so impressed with the people here. Seeing the young and the old together," Cincebaux said. "Especially the young people. That's what we need to keep our culture going. It's touching."

Helen Zemek, whose parents moved to the United States in 1912, also said she was impressed. "I never knew there were Czechs here who knew so much about our culture. Now, I know better…It was so pleasing to see the kids be a part of this."

The Czech Heritage Dancers, an authentic dance group composed of locals and formed 14 years ago by Dr. David Holcombe of Alexandria, left a lasting impression on the crowd. Dressed in vests embroidered in sequins and beads and white shirts beneath, the group waltzed and polkaed like they were in Prague, not Libuse.

"My great-grandmother (Jennie) is from Romania, which is near the Czech border," said 17-year-old dancer Jennifer Drago, of Libuse. "She shows me some dance moves, and I use them. It brings us closer together...I'm proud to be Czech."

The kinship was generated throughout the day; adults proudly viewed the children's dress parade, which featured kids strutting around in classic Czech wear. And it was as easily smelled as it was seen. The large spread of foods included "nic", a deep-fried, dough-like piecrust, hoska, a sweet bread with nuts and fruits, and poppy seed cakes.

"This is a celebration, a homecoming," said Czech Heritage Association Treasurer Frances Hazmark, the event's organizer. "The food, the dancing, the reunions. It's tremendous."

This festival gets a bit bigger each year and is in no danger of shutting down.

Louisiana Czech Dancers

The Louisiana Czech Dancers were formed in 1988. They dress in traditional Czech costumes called "kroje." All of them were handmade by members of the community. This group has performed across the state. It was not a Czech person who started this group, but Dr. David Holcombe and his wife Nicole. They learned of the Czech communities shortly after their moving to Alexandria. They were both interested in folk dancing, folk music and ethnic cultures. Both of them are also accomplished artists whose works have been exhibited in Alexandria's art museum and local galleries. From what I gathered from my talking with both of them they felt there were enough efforts to preserve Cajun culture in the state, but there was little to preserve the less well known ethnic cultures. So they sought out the Czechs and became friendly. They taught themselves the Czech dances and music and traditions and brought in those with some expertise at developing a dance troup. From the first suggestion to residents about a Czech dance group they received enthusiastic support. Almost immediately they had enough people, both women and men, to create a dance troup. They were off to a running start. Both are still actively engaged in the activities today. The group regularly meets to practice old dances and learn new ones. They are a regular feature at all Czech events in Libuse and Kolin, as well as any folk festival in the area.

The Ceske Domuv

Set back a few hundred feet from Highway 28, where Pineville meets Libuse, is a non-descript metal warehouse. Almost invisible to those driving by, it looks like any one of thousands of such buildings across Louisiana. Its purpose is indecipherable; inside is another story. On one of my early trips to Libuse I was ushered inside and beheld a sight for sore eyes. On open shelves and spread across the floor are literally hundreds of items from the early years of the Czech Colony. Toys, kitchen tools and utensils, photographs and stacks of papers, glass objects, farm tools and implements, a desk from the first school and many other items are hidden here. It is the private museum of George and Helen Koncinsky. He established it in the early 1990s; though he had been collecting things for years. It was not conceived as a musuem, but rather just one man's collection of stuff. It is not open to the general public; but during the Czech Festival and on rare special occassions, select members of the community and invited outsiders gather here to view the objects and recollect old stories. This, too, is probably unique in all Louisiana.

By 2002, Koncinsky and the Czech Heritage Association arranged for a tiny portable building to be put closer to the highway; in reality one of those ubiquitous boxes with just a door and two windows that are at the edges of construction sites. Now, mostly by appointment only, though sometimes open with "regular" hours to the general public who know about it, people who want to learn more about the Czech Colony can see some of the more special items collected by the Association. They call it The Ceske Dum—the Czech House. Continuing the long tradition of insularity it is still really a private museum—it is not promoted or advertised.

The Louisiana Czech & Slovak Museum

The impetus for this book was my involvement in what was originally named the Louisiana Czech Museum. Now that so much more has been learned about Czech and Slovak heritage in the state it should rightfully, I think, be called the Louisiana Czech & Slovak Museum. This is already a 501(c)3 non-profit corporation and there are a number of people working and thinking on this project. What is in this book is what will be in this museum. It will be in Libuse since this is the center of Czech culture in Louisiana. More than a local project, it will chronicle nearly 300 years of Czech and Slovak heritage in Louisiana—a heritage that has had a remarkable though hidden impact.

Bibliography & Sources

Methods

This bibliography is only a summary of the sources for this book and an explanation of how I found it. I looked at more than 3,000 sources. No one place had any more than one or a few facts. Since there had never been anything written on this subject every fact I found could be said to be from a primary source. I have built several data bases for all this information. I made a copy of nearly every bit of information, and definitely every obituary, article or document. These are posted to the internet at www.creativeintellectual.com/czechbookbib. And that is because listing every citation for what I found would be hundreds of pages long. I am certainly happy to share any of this information or copies—which is rich in details—with anyone who asks.

I do, however, feel that an explanation of how this information was found is necessary. Chief among them is that as a starting point for my research in the many repositories where this information is found I asked the person in charge "what information do you have on Czechs and Slovaks in Louisiana?" Incredibly to me, to a person they not only said "we have nothing," but many *insisted* they had nothing. This was true even in the courthouse barely 10 miles from the largest Czech community in the state. In fact, more than a few told me that there were no Czechs and Slovaks in Louisiana at all.

For those who may desire to eventually write histories of the other admittedly small ethnic populations in the state (Yugoslavs, Hungarians, Lebanese, Belgians, Syrians, Poles, Russians, etc.)—this method will work for you, too. I constantly ran across references to these other immigrants (those naturalization papers in the Rapides Courthouse contain dozens of other immigrants)—this information is out there. Do not be daunted or discouraged by those who say this information does not exist. There is far more to Louisiana than just Cajuns, French, Italians, Germans and the American-English. Seek, and you shall find.

Property Records:

I examined over 800 property records (and a few other documents) in the Rapides Parish courthouse, from 1913 until the 1940s. The process I used was not much different than what a professional real estate abstractor uses; and this is standard in every courthouse in Louisiana (early New Orleans is a special case.) There are two indices—each arranged roughly alphabetically in a large book about 3 inches thick. One index lists transactions by "Vendors," or the people and companies that sold land; the other index lists "Vendees," or those that bought. Essentially, this results in a cross-referenced index system. Each index has four basic pieces of information: the names of both the buyer and seller, the date of the transaction, and most importantly—the number of the book and page for the the actual document. The eight vendee and eight vendor indices that cover the 35 year period that I looked at contain thousands of entries—so one may wonder how I found the Czechs among them: I already had names from the local histories published, names from the cemeteries and names from the censuses—but because Czech names are mostly "unusual" as compared to the other entries, the names just jumped off the pages at me. When you see a name like Hlobil, Skodacek or Zdarsky you know they're Czech.

An example of a book and page number is "78–145," and armed with this you can proceed to the 4" thick "conveyance" books which are stacked (conviently in their own cubby hole) about 15 high along several aisles. Pull out book 78 and turn to page 145, which is hand stamped in the upper right hand corner of the page—and you will find what are really typed transcriptions of the original signed document—there is no handwriting in them. They are all on paper of uniform size and weight; the originals are stored in a secured archival area.

For people in Part One of the book I looked up specific individuals; I knew there were no larger number of Czechs and Slovaks to search for. I followed the same procedure as in Rapides Parish. Early New Orleans presents a special case because there is no index to speak of; though they are working on this problem. Each notary kept his own records; unfortunately some were lost to fires or floods, or were simply thrown out after a number of years. What survived is in the New Orleans Notarial Archives; there are millions of documents. Only a small percentage have been indexed in a searchable database, and fortunately the records of the notary who the Kohn's used was indexed; I made copies of all these documents. For others it is impossible to find documents at this point in time. Beginning in 1900 or so the records of New Orleans were indexed using a system similar to the other parishes; after 1985 it is all computerized.

For the Czechs on the German Coast in the 1700s I went to the State Archives in Baton Rouge, where all the originals of the earliest notarial and property records are being gathered and then microfilmed. If they are not microfilmed yet, they are not available to the public. However, there is an index of sorts that enabled me to look up the Touchet's and Novak's; once I found the microfilm page number I simply located that on the reel. I did make copies of these documents, and these, too, are available for those who wish to examine them.

Obituaries

The Alexandria Town Talk, and most other Louisiana newspapers, are unfortunately not indexed. The newspapers of only the biggest cities in Louisiana have been mircofilmed. However, since I knew the dates of death I simply searched the (microfilmed) paper for the next day or so until I found the obituary; after all, they always appear a day or so after a person's passing. There is an old fashioned card catague index of obituaries for New Orleans in the Loyola Avenue branch of the New Orleans Public Library; it is being put online now. There are several newspapers that are referenced: Times-Picayune, States-Item, Bee, etc. I looked up the name of every immigrant who settled in New Orleans and found the citation, and then looked at the microfilm of the newspaper for the obituaries of those who died in the city and for which an obituary was published. I made a copy of every obituary and article—and these are available to those who wish to see them.

Censuses

With censuses there was also a difference between the way I looked up people in Part One and in Part Two. For those in the first part I used HeritageQwest—a website available through most of the state's public libraries; I used the State Library in Baton Rouge. This website is searchable by serveral criteria: name, parish, city, and others: but most importantly it can be searched by ethnicity. For these Czechs and Slovaks I used these search terms: Czech, Slovak, Czechoslovakia, Bohemia/Bohemian, Moravia/Moravian and Slovak/Slovakian, and also Slovakland (after I discovered a few entries with this made up name.) However, because the census records sometimes listed a Czech or Slovak as coming from Austria, Austro-Hungary, Hungary, and more rarely, Germany, I searched all these entries too—the Czechs and Slovaks were found by looking under the "language" column. Those who spoke "Czech" "Bohemian" "Moravian" or "Slovakian" were the ones I sought. This website allows you to see not only a computerized list of the entries, but also an image of the original document. There was no one search term that brought up everyone I sought.

For Rapides Parish, I turned to the microfilm reels of the census records in the State Library in Baton Rouge. This was in the days when a census enumerator went door to door—and thus you can find everyone on a street or road listed one right after the other. Because all the Czechs settled near each other once I found one I found them all—they are in the reels marked "Rapides Parish—Ward 9 & 10." Page after page are filled with the entries for the Czech families; about 20 pages each for both the 1920 and 1930 censuses. There were no Czechs prior to 1914, so I used HeritageQwest for earlier years; the 1940 census has not been released yet. But all of these are also in the HeritagQwest website.

City Directories

City Directories list addresses and occupations for everyone living in a city at a given date. There were three main repositories of City Directories that I accessed. The Historic New Orleans Collection has those from the 1800s on microfilm, though only New Orleans had city directories during this century. I looked at every directory available there for Czech and Slovak names. It is only after 1900 that there were regularly published city directories; some cities started later than others. The main branch of the New Orleans public library has the directories for that city. The State Library in Baton Rouge has those for all the major cities of the state (New Orleans included.) I was, of course, able then to simply look up the names I sought in the alphabetical listing within the directory. For the 1900s the system I used was to start with the earliest existing directory and then look at the succeeding directories in five year increments. The intervening years are almost all identical in the information they present; where necessary I turned to these directories.

The Internet

The Internet was a wonderful tool for finding information—but other than the website I eventually set up myself as an overview of this subject
(www.geocities.com/louisianaczech)
there is no one place where this information is available. Over a five year period I spent hundreds of hours pouring over literally hundreds of websites—they are not all listed here, just the main sites. One thing I did do was search on both Yahoo! and Google for every name in this book. References to individuals and families might have been on 5, 10 or 20 or more websites; literally just a sentence here and a fact there (such was the case with the Touchets, among many others)—very little of it was ever categorized or identified as being Czech or Slovak.

I also used the internet for much background and historical information, such as the history of Czechs and Slovaks in both Europe and America, the history of Louisiana, and the section on language and names. As anyone who has ever used the Internet for research has discovered, you must use many variations of a search term to find what you are looking for: Louisiana Czech, Louisiana Czechs, Czech Louisiana, Czechoslovakians in Louisiana; the slightest alteration in a search term often turned up a completely different set of results. Some Internet searches resulted in nothing; looking up "Bohemian Louisiana" brings you only to sites that are related to the modern English use of the word "bohemian," (except the Louisiana Czech Museum website and my own site.)

Descendants of the Immigrants

I came into contact with the descendants of Czech and Slovak immigrants in several ways. In Rapides Parish I met these people as I was involved in organizing the Louisiana Czech Museum. For the Czechs and Slovaks around the state they contacted me, wanting to share their family history. Many of the daily and weekly newspapers around the state published the query letter I sent them or a blurb about this book project: Damon Veach put my query in his Louisiana Ancestors column in the New Orleans and Baton Rouge papers. Smiley Anders mentioned my quest in his column in the Baton Rouge Advocate. The Blake Pontchartrain column in New Orleans Gambit publicized my website and this project. The Cameron Pilot placed a small article on my efforts to find Slovaks in that parish. The Times of Acadiana (Lafayette) published my query as a letter to the editor. The Houma Courier posted a brief blurb about my quest. Some found me by doing their own search on their family histories—they found my website and contacted me. These were mostly descendants who no longer live in Louisiana. In addition, several Czech and Slovak websites, like bohemica.com; the National Czech and Slovak Museum and Library in Cedar Rapids, Iowa; and the Czech Center in New York (operated by the Czech government) put overview articles I wrote or a link on their sites. In addition, two Czech language newspapers published in America, Americke Listy (published in Glen Cove, New York) and Ceskoslovenske Noviny (Brooklyn, New York) carried articles on this subject. Even the Prague Post, an English language newspaper in the Czech Republic, published something about this project. Each mention resulted in e-mails from either descendants or others with information.

Books

Rapides Public Library, Alexandria
History of Slovakia
History of the Czechs
Hill Memorial Library at LSU, Baton Rouge

CONRAD, Glenn R.—LAND RECORDS OF THE ATTAKAPAS DIS-
TRICT, Volume 1, the Attakapas Domesday Book: Land Grants, Claims
and Confirmations in the Attakapas District, 1764–1826

CONRAD, Glenn R.—LAND RECORDS OF THE ATTAKAPAS DIS-
TRICT, Volume 2, Part 1 Conveyance Records of Attakapas County,
1804–1818

CONRAD, Glenn R.—LAND RECORDS OF THE ATTAKAPAS DIS-
TRICT—Volume 2, Part 2 Attakapas St. Martin Estates, 1804–1818

CONRAD, Glenn R.—ST. JEAN-BAPTISTE DES ALLEMANDS: Abstracts
of Civil Records of St. John the Baptist Parish to 1803

CONRAD, Glenn R.—ST. CHARLES PARISH: Abstracts of the Civil Records
of St. Charles Parish, 1770–1803

CONRAD, Glenn R.—THE GERMAN COAST: Abstracts of the Civil
Records of St. Charles and St. John the Baptist Parishes, 1804–1812

FONTENOT, Mary Alice—ACADIA PARISH, LOUISIANA, Volume 2—A
History—1900 to 1920

SOUTHWEST LOUISIANA FAMILIES IN 1785: The Spanish Census of the
Posts of Attakapas and Opelousas. *Winston De Ville.*

SOUTHWEST LOUISIANA FAMILIES IN 1777: Census Records of Attakapas and Opelousas Posts

Special Collections, Hill Memorial Library Items Material Location

Nichols (Irby C. and Family) Papers—Frankenbush references

Louisiana State Library, Baton Rouge

Southwest Louisiana Sacramental Records

v.1. 1756–1810. —v.2. Church and Civil Records 1811–1830. —v.3. 1831–
1840. —v.4. 1841–1847. —v.5. 1848–1854. —v.6. 1855–1860. —v.7. 1861–
1865. —v.8. 1866–1868. —v.9. 1869–1870. —v.10. 1871–1872. —v.11.
1873–1874. —v.12. 1875–1876. —v.13. 1877–1878. —v.14. 1879–1880.
—v.15. 1881–1882. —v.16. 1883–1884. —v.17. 1885–1886. —v.18. 1887.
—v.19. 1888. —v.20. 1889. —v.21. 1890. —v.22. 1891. —v.23. 1892. —v.24.
1893. —v.25. 1894. —v.26. 1895. —v.27. 2896. —v.28. 1897. —v.29. 1898.
—v.30. 1899. —v.31. 1900 —v.32. (1901–1902) —v.33. Supplement. Mixed
records (1903–1953). Slave/Black records (1765–1886). Corrections & additions (1756–1904). —v.34. Supplement (1833–1900). —v.35. Church and civil
records 1903. —v.36. 1904. —v.37. 1905. —v.38. 1906. —v.39. 1907. —v.40.
1908. —v.41. 1909.

New Orleans Public Library

Leo Baca, Czech Passenger Ship Lists

History of New Orleans
History of the New Orleans Street Cars
Phone books for Louisiana Cities
Radomir Luza, The Hitler Kiss
Louisiana State Library
Bertram Korn, Early Jews of New Orleans
Leo Baca passenger lists
Sugar Reports for Bohemia and Blahut Plantations
James E Boyle, Cotton and the New Orelans Cotton Exchange, The Country Life Press, garden city NY 1934
My Personal library
The work of John Desmond & Associates
Memoirs of James (Vaclav) Dvorak (Uncle of John Desmond)
Those Who Served; the Czechs of Rapides Parish in World War 1; Frances Hazmark
Chcete Mluvit Ceske? Do you want to speak Czech?
Velky Anglicko-Cesky Slovnik
Fronek—Cesko-Anglicke Slovnik

WPA Reports

Louisiana State Library

Journals

Lousiana State Library, Baton Rouge
Medical History of Orleans Parish
Terrebonne Life Lines
Catholic Register of Sacramental Records
Louisiana Historical Quarterly
The River Road
Houma Public Library
I Dup up Houma, Terrebonne
Lafayette Public Library
History of Vermilliion Parish, publishd by Vermillion Historical Society, 1983
Alexandria Genealogical Library
Czech Heritage Newsletter
Louisiana State University, Middleton Library, Baton Rouge

Rural Sociology Journal
Journal of the Czech Genealogical Society QE 351.C415 V.38, 1993

Newspapers

Alexandria Town Talk
    Hill Memorial Library 1913 to 1975
    Louisiana State Library 1975–2000
Post Offices
Louisiana Czech Festival
Louisiana Czech Dancers
Louisiana Czech Heritage Association
Obituaries
New Orleans Times Picayune, Louisiana State Library
Trade Show Fracas
Czech Jewish Rabbis
Uprising of 1874
New Orleans Bee
New Orleans States-Item
Lake Charles American Press
Lafayette Advertiser
Church Point Times
Horecky Family

Websites

Name Articles
Czech and Slovak surnames and first names
Motichek Family website
Pastorek Family website
Czech and Slovak History
Boney Diaries
Diaries related to Blahut
Czechoslovakian-Made Mardi Gras Beads
Rosalie Beer: Breweriana websites
New Orleans Gambit—Charles Zimpel
Louisiana Czech Museum website
Czech Cemeteries in Rapides Parish

Czechoslovak Society of Arts and Sciences
Moravian Church
Czech Jewish History
Charles University
UNO Prague Studies Program
Louisiana Secretary of State Corporate Database
Iarelative
John Rosicky & Hospodar
Idaho and Oregon Czech Communities

Archives:

Historic New Orleans Collection
Paxton City Directory
Soards City Directory
Letters of Carl Kohn
Papers of Francis Soyka
Tulane Archives New Orleans and Carrollton Railroad Records;1834–1896. Collection no. 27 Itinclude reports, contracts, finacial records, and only very little correspondence. Includes a letter from Judah P. Benjamin, 1836.
New Orleans Cotton Brokers Correspondence; 1831–1850.
Collection no. 132 (0.1 cubic feet).
Letters from various firms including Cohen (aka Cohn) and Bullock, concerning market and agricultural conditions of cotton as well as tobacco and sugar.
Pokorny Family Papers; 1851–1957 (bulk dates 1915–1945).
Collection no. 74 (0.4 cubic feet).
Materials document the estate of Michael Pokorny and emigration from Germany to the United States, his shoe store and real estate businesses in New Orleans
New Orleans Public Library, Loyola Ave
Samuel Kohn Suits
New Orleans Notarial Archives
The Kohn Family
Louisiana State Archives
Touchet Family
Laska Family
Novak Family

Property & Other Records

New Orleans Recorder of Mortgages.
Immigrants in New Orleans.
Rapides Parish Clerk of Court office
Property Records
Corporate Records
Marriage Records
Naturalization Records
Terrebonne Parish Clerk of Court office
Blahut and Zelenka families

Census Records

Louisiana State Library
HeritageQwest website for each decade 1860 to 1930 (except 1890, records burned in fire)
Microfilm of Rapides Parish for 1920 and 1930
New Orleans Public Library
Partial Census for 1890

City Directories

Louisiana State Library Polk Directories for Alexandria, Lake Charles, Lafayette, Shreveport, Monroe.
Directory for Houma, 1897,
Directories for New Orleans,
New Orleans Public Library
Polk Directories for New Orleans

Family Histories

Email and regular mail correspondance with descendants of familes:
Pohorelsky, Horecky, Touchet, Dubovy-Silkep, Frankenbush, Pokorny, Motichek, Pastorek, Sterba, Sedlak, Baroch

Personal Interviews

Nick Kalivoda & John Desmond, Baton Rouge
Residents of the Libuse and Kolin Communities
Czech workers at Wal-Marts
Frances Hazmark—community historian of Libuse and Kolin

978-0-595-40372-1
0-595-40372-7

Printed in the United States
64183LVS00003B/16-24